Reading *for* Academic Success

READINGS AND STRATEGIES

Jill Lewis, Ed.D.

NEW JERSEY CITY UNIVERSITY

Houghton Mifflin Company

Boston · New York

Editor in Chief: Patricia A. Coryell
Senior Sponsoring Editor: Mary Jo Southern
Associate Editor: Kellie Cardone
Editorial Associate: Danielle Richardson
Senior Project Editor: Kathryn Dinovo
Senior Manufacturing Coordinator: Priscilla J. Bailey
Marketing Manager: Annamarie Rice
Marketing Assistant: Sandra Krumholz

Cover image: Civic Center Park © 1995 by Malcolm Farley

Printed in the U.S.A.

Library of Congress Control Number: 00-133842

ISBN: 0-395-96709-0

123456789-DOC-05 04 03 02 01

One writes only half the book;

the other half is with the readers.

—Joseph Conrad, letter to Cunninghame Graham, 1897,
cited in *The Oxford Dictionary of Quotations*,
5th ed., ed. Elizabeth Knowles
(New York: Oxford University Press), p. 234

CONTENTS

Chapter 2 ✍ *Understanding the Vocabulary in Academic Texts* 41

Chapter 4 ✌ Understanding Details

Chapter 5 ✎ *Patterns of Organization in Academic Texts* 149

Chapter 6 ✎ *Strategies for Critical Reading and Thinking* 201

Chapter 8 ✍ Strategies for Active Listening and Note Taking   313

Chapter 11 ✍ *Readings in Business and Business Technology*   417

Chapter 12 ✍ Readings in Health Science and the Helping Professions 447

TO THE INSTRUCTOR

Reading for Academic Success has evolved as the result of my twenty-five-plus years of experience teaching students enrolled in developmental reading courses at two- and four-year colleges and assisting high school teachers who are concerned about their students' academic readiness at the start of their college careers. During this time, our knowledge about the reading process and how students learn has grown considerably; the population we teach has changed; and the academic goals for and expectations of students have been reshaped to include a greater concern for critical thinking and personal response. Many of the readings, strategies, and activities in this text are based on these considerations. Those instructional strategies that have continued to serve students well over the years are also included. Many features of this text make it unique and give students ample opportunity to develop the reading and study strategies they need for academic success.

You will find that this text:

- **Includes high-interest and challenging reading material.** Models, practice material, and longer selections are drawn from sources that are commonly assigned to college students. Some selections have a multi-cultural theme; some are on other topics that are relevant for today's students. Each adds to the knowledge base students will bring to other academic situations. High expectations encourage students and give them a reality-based context in which to practice reading strategies.

- **Provides an introduction to many areas of concentration studied at college.** Part 2 of the text is arranged purposefully so that students learn *about* typical areas of study, such as the sciences, the social sciences, the helping professions, and business, while they apply strategies to readings in these areas. Specific strategies for reading each are introduced; readings in each section familiarize students with some topics studied in those areas.

- **Uses a process-oriented approach to instruction.** Part 1 takes students through the *thinking processes* used to achieve such reading/study goals as recognizing and creating main ideas, making inferences, determining meanings of words from context clues, drawing conclusions, note taking, and reading visual aids. Students have opportunities to apply these strategies to other coursework and in other contexts throughout the text.

- **Develops metacognitive habits.** In each chapter, students reflect on approaches they use for comprehension and self-monitoring. This ongoing practice encourages students to develop the habit of thinking about *how* they are reading *while* they are reading. They develop reading flexibility, adapting their reading style to accommodate the demands of the reading tasks and the student's own purposes. Self-assessment is continuous.

- **Promotes critical and creative thinking.** Students are frequently asked to justify selected answers or written responses, to evaluate and modify their reponses after discussion and review, and to critique the responses of others. Part 1 contains a chapter on critical thinking. Each reading in Part 2 contains a "Critical Thinking: Reaction and Discussion," section by which students extend knowledge gained from that reading to other contexts.

- **Facilitates prediction and use of prior knowledge for comprehension.** Chapter and reading previews prepare students for the contents that follow. In Part 2, each reading is preceded by an activity designed to help students recall what they already know about the selection topic. The activities are varied, and students learn multiple ways to tap into prior knowledge before reading, a habit necessary to academic success.

- **Integrates reading and writing.** The processes of reading and writing are mutually supportive. This is demonstrated repeatedly in models throughout this text, and the activities included in each part often engage students in both processes. Students learn to use writing as a complement to their reading and to clarify meaning for themselves.

- **Integrates using technology as an instructional tool for developing academic literacy.** Part 2 provides students with opportunities to develop critical and creative thinking by integrating activities that use technology, including the Internet, in unconventional ways. "Using Technology for Further Understanding" appears at the end of each reading in Part 2. The Instructor's Resource Manual for this text also offers suggestions for integrating technology with activities in Part 1.

- **Provides for partner and collaborative activities.** Every chapter of Part 1 has several stopping points at which students compare their responses to questions with those of a peer or a group. This offers additional opportunities to think about reading processes and to understand personal responses to what students have read, as well as to understand different perspectives. Such "Working Together" activities are identified by 🖼. Many activities in Part 2, including those in each "Critical Thinking: Reaction and Discussion" section, are designed for collaboration.

- **Supports a variety of learning styles.** Questions and activities throughout the text are varied. Part 1 contains many visual models to accompany explanations of concepts. Built-in opportunities to discuss strategies, concepts, and interpretations with peers provide another avenue for learning. As students use the language of the text, they gain confidence in the use of new discourse patterns, concepts, sentence structures, and vocabulary that are common in academic settings.

- **Gives students responsibility for their own learning.** This text puts students in control of their reading. Rather than reading author-determined chapter summaries in Part 1, students create their own, based on ideas that will be useful to them. This process encourages students to take ownership of the ideas and to think about their wider application.

- **Provides alternative assessment opportunities for the instructor.** The "Extended Application" section at the end of each chapter in Part 1 invites students to apply developing strategies to whole texts. Every activity in Part 2 can be used for ongoing assessment. These options give instructors a fuller view of student progress than do traditional multiple-choice and standardized tests.

- **Lends itself to a variety of curriculum formats and teaching styles.** You may prefer to use this text in a straightforward way, starting with Part 1 and proceeding chapter by chapter to Part 2; on the other hand, you may prefer to alternate between both parts of the text: students can apply the strategies from Part 1 to chapters in Part 2, as needed, or you might prefer to give more direction to the coordination between the two parts. You can also assign different chapters to different students, based on their learning styles, self-assessments, and areas of interest. Classroom activity can be largely independent, or you may want to convert independent assignments in each part into group and peer activities in order to increase the number of these already available.

However you decide to use this text, I hope it will meet your needs and serve your students well.

Acknowledgments

I wish to thank the many reviewers whose advice at different stages of the development of this text assisted me: Mary A. Eastland, Hill College; Dennis Keen, Spokane Community College; Nora Davenport Lawson, Alabama State University; Susan Messina, Solano Community College; Kevin Nebergall, Kirkwood Community College; and Sheila R. Swanson, Wright State University.

Many individuals contributed to the efforts and encouragement necessary for completion of this book. In particular, my thanks to Mary Jo Southern at Houghton Mifflin, who played a key role in helping to define the final shape of the second edition text, and to Kellie Cardone, associate editor, whose guidance through development was greatly valued. I am also indebted to project manager, Merrill Peterson of Matrix Productions, for his ongoing support, assistance, and attention to detail. At New Jersey City University, I owe much appreciation to the Separately Budgeted Research Committee and to Vice President Larry Carter and President Carlos Hernandez for periodically granting me release time. A special thank-you goes to the Board of Directors at the Center for Public Policy and Urban Research, New Jersey City University, and my friends at the New Jersey Reading Association for helping me through the rough spots. I would also like to express my continuing gratitude to my e-mail companions and my love to my friends Freda Wasserstein Robbins and Enid Friedman and to my family, my husband Gray, and my children, Miles and Allison, for listening and—most especially—for waiting.

Jill Lewis

To the Student

Imagine that you are driving your car in an unfamiliar town, perhaps trying to get to a doctor's new office. You don't recognize street names. You don't know where to turn. You don't have any idea of the distance from one point to the next. And, even more distressing, since you are a stranger in this town, landmarks known to local residents are totally unfamiliar to you and you cannot use them as reference points. A map with clearly labeled street names and understood landmarks would certainly help you find your way around this unknown territory.

Reading unfamiliar text is similar, in a number of respects, to driving in such a situation. If you don't know the subject matter you need to read, if you are uncertain about which comprehension strategies will help you with interpreting the material, or if you are unfamiliar with the writing style commonly used in a certain field, you are at a disadvantage compared to students who do. Students who have a variety of strategies to use in different reading situations and who are already familiar with basic concepts and technical language of fields studied at college will find the reading assignments and related classroom lectures easier to understand.

This book can serve as your *road map* to college reading. In this book you will learn and apply reading and study strategies necessary to comprehend and retain academic material. The following pages also will introduce you to areas of study. You may need to take courses in these areas before you begin more specialized study in your major field. Further, you will be shown the special reading requirements of each area, and you will participate in a number of activities that will serve as checkpoints for you in your travels through each of these.

The "Table of Contents" of this textbook identifies the "points of interest" on this map that you will encounter on your journey through this text. It also gives you the general picture of where you are. If you take a quick look at it now, you will notice that this text is divided into two parts, each of which has a different purpose.

Scan the entries for "Part 1: Handbook for Reading and Study Strategies" to see what topics will be discussed. No doubt you are already familiar with much of the language in the chapter headings of this section, such as *topic, main idea, details, inference.* These are critical elements of text that form the basis for reading comprehension. Your ability to take notes and listen to lectures are also important for success in college.

Numerous activities in the "Handbook" let you apply the reading and study strategies that are discussed in this section of the text. Although short reading passages are used within the "Handbook" for most of this practice, the "Extended Application" section at the end of each chapter asks you to apply the strategies to the complete articles found in Part 2. You will find many opportunities in the "Handbook" to work with your classmates to share and refine your understanding of the strategies, and to evaluate your success with applying them. Such "Working Together" activities are identified by .

This "Handbook" is different from traditional skills development materials. It is based on the idea that it is more important for you to know *how* to do something than it is for you to get the right answer to every activity question. You are frequently asked to think about the processes you are using to answer questions and to consider whether you need to make refinements in the strategies you use. This kind of practice will help you to transfer strategies you learn in the "Handbook" to your college reading assignments.

Another difference you will note is that in this book you are often asked to assess your ideas while you read and to write about what you notice about your reading process. In this way your reading and writing abilities are used to support each other. In many activities in the "Handbook," you are also asked to justify, or to prove, your answers. To do this, you must think about *why* your answer is adequate or correct. You will need to look for evidence in the material. Making this self-analysis when you read is similar to what you do when you drive. When you are driving, you have a goal—a destination. You must ask yourself where you are going. Then you understand why you are making a left turn or a right one, or why you have chosen to turn at the third traffic light, not the first one. You also have goals when you are reading and interpreting text. As you work with the activities in the "Handbook," it will not be sufficient just to select an answer. You will need reasons for your choices, and you will need to be able to explain them.

Many routes to learning these comprehension strategies are possible. Two people who are using the same map may start their journey from different places. If two people wanted to get to New York City, for instance, their routes could be different, even if they are using the same map of the United States; one person might be starting from California, another from Michigan. In the same way, your instructor may have different students start from different points in the "Handbook." It is also possible that everyone in your class will make a similar journey, starting from the same place. Your instructor may choose to use only portions of the "Handbook," and to do so as a supplement to "Part 2: Integrated Practice for Reading and Learning," or it may be the core of your course, with the readings in Part 2 as the supplement. On the other hand, both sections of the text may be given equal instructional time.

Return to the "Table of Contents" and note the organization of "Part 2: Integrated Practice for Reading and Learning." This part is organized by fields or areas of study. They have been selected because of the frequency with which they are required as part of the general requirements for all college students and/or because of their popularity as majors. Every chapter in Part 2 has a similar organization. Each area of study begins with a section titled "Guidelines for Reading" and several essays within the chapter. Here you are informed about the writing style or organization that is typically used in that field, the perspective from which authors generally write, or the reading pitfalls common to the discipline that you, as a reader, will want to avoid. These guidelines differ from strategies presented in Part 1, because they are specific to a field of study. The essays in each chapter of this text provide a sampling of issues, events, or concerns related to that area.

For each essay there is a "Preview." In this part of the chapter, there is a brief introduction to the essay, and you will be asked to consider a question, complete a diagram, or work with a partner on some activity related to the forthcoming reading. The major purpose for most of these prereading experiences is to help you recall what you *already* know about the topic of the essay to be read. Students who can *activate prior knowledge* have more information to use when reading to help them understand the new material.

A section titled "Postreading Comprehension Development" follows each essay. Within this section, you will have an opportunity to evaluate your own understanding of the essay. In the case of the introductory essay, you will verify your .... discipline itself. The questions following the oth ....nding of the content of the particular ess ....estions focus on aspects of textual ....ndbook." Each "Postreading C ....egins with an activity that ask ....e and identify the reading stra .... Then you will rewrite some in .... ng your own words, but keepi ....ere are many possible answers. ....nal "Postreading Comprehensi ....n opportunity to go beyond the essay .. .. related to it. Often it is suggested that you w. .... small group on these. Opportunities to use techno.. ....rovided.

The essays in this text may be longer and more difficult than those you have read up until now. Many are taken from college-level textbooks and other sources that are typically used in college courses. Your ultimate aim is to read with comprehension and to remember what you have read. You will be working toward this objective. Thus, you should not expect that you will immediately understand everything you read in this text. Consider this text as a starting point. It is the map, or plan, to help you reach academic literacy. But you are the driver. Ultimately, you will choose the path to take and will need to figure out how to handle the curves and bumps along the way.

It is my sincere hope that once you have worked with this text, you will feel better prepared for academic reading assignments because you can better comprehend academic text and because you know more about several areas of study. You should then be able to experience success and enjoyment as you continue on your journey toward your college degree.

Jill Lewis
New Jersey City University

Reading
for
Academic
Success

Handbook for Reading and Study Strategies

CHAPTER ONE

Preparing for Academic Success

WHAT DOES IT TAKE TO BECOME a sports superstar? Some people might say that superstars are born, not made. But just ask a football or track star, and you'll learn about the many hours of practice, concentration, and dedication it took them to get where they are. Most likely, you'll hear the same answer if you ask businesspeople, chefs, or nurses how they got to be good at what they do. Even if a person seems to have a "natural" talent for something, refining that talent through practice and learning new methods or strategies is critical. It can make the difference between being only a good player and being a superstar.

The same principles apply to developing reading comprehension for academic subjects. Even if you learned to read naturally, enjoyed reading, and never struggled through reading material, as reading assignments become more complex, new approaches to learning and remembering what you read will become necessary.

The purpose of this chapter is to help analyze your talents as a student. It also provides some pointers about reading textbooks that will help you achieve superstar status on the academic playing field.

Assessing Your Academic Self-Esteem

How do you feel about your reading strengths right now? How confident are you about your ability to participate in an academic environment?

How high is your academic self-esteem? It is useful to assess how you feel now about these issues. Then you can set your goals for improving those areas where you have the least confidence. Through this self-assessment process, you will be able to identify your learning strengths and use them while you work on improving other areas.

The survey that follows asks a series of questions that should be answered based on your experiences and your knowledge of yourself. Think for a few minutes about each question before you rate yourself. Be as truthful as possible. The results can be used for your own benefit. This is not a test!

Survey of Academic Self-Esteem

Directions: For each item, circle the number that you feel best describes you as you are now. (1 = not true of me at all; 4 = very true of me)

1.	I can successfully prepare to take exams.	1	2	3	4
2.	I can determine what will be asked on tests.	1	2	3	4
3.	I have successful strategies for taking notes on lectures and reading assignments.	1	2	3	4
4.	I know how to preview my textbooks.	1	2	3	4
5.	I know how to come prepared for class.	1	2	3	4
6.	I know how to mark and underline reading material for review purposes.	1	2	3	4
7.	I know how to make predictions when I read.	1	2	3	4
8.	I can answer questions in a college classroom.	1	2	3	4
9.	I am able to read a college textbook with understanding.	1	2	3	4
10.	I know when to slow down my reading rate for better comprehension.	1	2	3	4
11.	I know how to use context to get the meaning of unknown words in college-level material.	1	2	3	4
12.	I have good strategies for thinking critically about things I have read.	1	2	3	4
13.	I can figure out the main ideas of college-type reading materials (for example, sociology, business, psychology, science).	1	2	3	4
14.	I can set purposes for my reading.	1	2	3	4
15.	I can read and interpret maps, graphs, and charts.	1	2	3	4
16.	I know how to create summaries and visual aids to help me remember what I have read.	1	2	3	4

17.	I know how to distinguish between important and unimportant details when I read.	1	2	3	4
18.	I can participate successfully in a college classroom.	1	2	3	4
19.	I can ask a professor for help when I have a question.	1	2	3	4
20.	I believe that I will be admitted to the major of my choice.	1	2	3	4
21.	I believe that I have a lot of knowledge to share with others.	1	2	3	4
22.	I believe that I will graduate from college.	1	2	3	4
23.	I believe that I will have a successful future.	1	2	3	4

Let's analyze the results of your survey. The following chart shows the category into which different items fall. Place your ratings on the chart. Then respond to the question in Activity A.

SURVEY ANALYSIS

Category	Question Nos.								
Study Skills		1	2	3	4	6	14	16	
	Your ratings:	___	___	___	___	___	___	___	
Reading Skills		7	9	10	11	12	13	15	17
	Your ratings:	___	___	___	___	___	___	___	___
Participating in College Classrooms		5	8	18	19	21			
	Your ratings:	___	___	___	___	___			
Expecting a Successful Future		20	22	23					
	Your ratings:	___	___	___					

Source: Questionnaire adapted from Jill Lewis, "The Effects of a Precollege Reading Course on the Academic Self-Esteem of Underprepared College Students," *Inquiries in Literacy Learning and Instruction,* College Reading Association Yearbook (fall 1993): 47–55.

ACTIVITY A: Identifying Your Learning Strengths and Goals

1. Based on the information you've obtained from this survey, what are your area(s) of greatest confidence? _____

_____

2. In a few sentences, describe the academic self-esteem goals you would like to achieve this term. _____

_____

Taking Control of Your Learning

Doing this self-analysis is the first step in taking control of your learning. But taking control also involves knowing and using strategies that will allow you to learn to your fullest potential. These strategies include the following:

* Creating the best environment for your learning
* Performing in class so that you can learn the most from that experience
* Using your textbooks to your best advantage
* Reading in ways that maximize your comprehension

Take Control of Your Learning Environment

One type of self-help tool enables you to examine and then, as far as possible, create your optimal learning environment so that you can complete your reading and other class assignments on time and come to class ready to participate in discussions. You will learn how to do this in this section.

Plan Your Time

Your college no doubt offers you many opportunities to get involved, such as clubs, special events on campus, athletics, and new friends. These activities will all compete for your time and attention. Many college students also have obligations to fulfill, such as full- or part-time jobs, family, religion, and other personal commitments. You may feel overwhelmed, but a planned approach will help you gain control of your time and accomplish more of what you want to do, along with all of what must be done.

Activity B: Creating a Schedule

The first thing you can do to control your learning environment is to plan a schedule. This should let you accomplish all of your obligations—things you have to do no matter what. You will want to decide what your "must" activities are and how much time you need to spend on each. Some examples of daily activities might include

Personal hygiene

Child care

Houskeeping

Time at a job

Transportation to a job

Transportation to college

Class attendance

Sleeping

Eating

In the space below, make a list of your daily or weekly "must" activities. Then, for each activity, decide how much time you think you will need to spend reading and otherwise preparing for class. You may, for instance, need time for writing papers or doing lab work.

Activity	Daily Time Needed
_____	_____
_____	_____
_____	_____
_____	_____
_____	_____
_____	_____

_____   _____

_____   _____

_____   _____

_____   _____

_____   _____

_____   _____

_____   _____

_____   _____

Next, make a list of the courses you are taking this semester. Then, although it may be too early to tell and assignments do vary, estimate how much time you think you will need to spend on outside assignments for each class. A rule of thumb: You need two hours of outside time for every hour in class.

CLASS	TIME NEEDED FOR OUTSIDE ASSIGNMENTS
_____	_____
_____	_____
_____	_____
_____	_____
_____	_____

———————————————   ———————————————

———————————————   ———————————————

———————————————   ———————————————

———————————————   ———————————————

———————————————   ———————————————

Finally comes your wish list of activities you would like to do. A few examples are

> Dating
>
> Volunteer work
>
> Clubs
>
> Visiting friends

WISH LIST

———————————————

———————————————

———————————————

———————————————

———————————————

———————————————

———————————————

WORKING TOGETHER

With a partner, review the lists you have made. Determine if you need to add or remove any items or to shift any items from one category to another.

PRELIMINARY SCHEDULE

	SUNDAY	MONDAY	TUESDAY	WEDNESDAY	THURSDAY	FRIDAY	SATURDAY
6:00 A.M.							
7:00 A.M.							
8:00 A.M.							
9:00 A.M.							
10:00 A.M.							
11:00 A.M.							
NOON							
1:00 P.M.							
2:00 P.M.							
3:00 P.M.							
4:00 P.M.							
5:00 P.M.							
6:00 P.M.							
7:00 P.M.							
8:00 P.M.							
9:00 P.M.							
10:00 P.M.							
11:00 P.M.							

You are now ready to use this information as a self-management tool. By realizing early on how you need to budget your time, you will be able to manage your day-to-day commitments better and reduce your tension. You will also feel more in control of your learning environment because you have made an effort to manage it.

Use the full-page grid on page 10 to draft a schedule that you will attempt to use for the next two weeks or so. You will revisit it to see how it has worked out for you and will be able to chance it based on your experience. All the days and hours of the week have been indicated, and hours range from 6:00 A.M. until midnight. You may add additional hours if you start your day earlier or end it later.

Use pencil to record your tentative schedule. As you live with it, you may find that changes are necessary, and you can easily make revisions.

Learn about Your Instructor

One of the first things beginning college students often notice about their college classes is that, unlike their teachers in high school, the instructors don't always "follow the book." In high school, your teachers may have gone through each textbook chapter, page by page. Homework was assigned on a particular chapter, and class time was spent reviewing the homework. High school teachers are usually bound by a set curriculum that must be followed by all teachers in that school system (sometimes in that state) who teach a certain subject to a particular grade. But college instructors have more leeway with what and how they teach.

The result may be that your college instructor seldom discusses the reading you have done outside of class, even assigned reading. Class lectures may seem to have little relationship to the assigned reading, but this is usually not so. You need to look for points of overlap. Perhaps the reading and lecture carried the same theme, were about the same time period, or were examples of the same principle. You need to make such connections on your own. However, many instructors do use class time to review and clarify outside readings. They may ask students to identify points of uncertainty from the reading or question students directly about what they have read.

Your job is to find the relationship between the lectures, the text, and the assignments. This knowledge will help you prepare for class and know how to use the information from each.

Another difference you may find between high school and college is that college instructors may have much higher expectations of their students. You are given much more independence in college—you make many decisions on your own about your personal life—and your instructors expect you to make decisions about your academic life as well. No one will check to see whether you have completed your assignments. You don't get a "detention" for coming to class unprepared. Instructors expect that you will do assignments, and do them *well*. But it may not be until you take the final exam that you have an opportunity to show that you have been keeping up with the assignments and that you understood them.

It is critical, then, that you have some strategies for using your textbooks that will help you manage your academic reading on your own.

Taking Control of Your Comprehension

To be a successful reader, you also need to be in charge of what you read, how you read, and what to do when you do not understand something you are required to read. This means that you know strategies that can enable you to comprehend what you read, strategies that you can call on when you have difficulty reading something. When you are in charge, you know whether or not you understand the text while you are reading. In addition, you know what to do whenever you read a passage you don't understand. In the remainder of this chapter, you will learn some of these self-help tools for comprehending texts. Because you are in charge, however, it is your decision whether or not to use them. You are in command of your reading development from this point on.

Learning about Your Text

For practically every course you take at college, you will have at least one assigned text. You should spend time becoming familiar with each. Most texts have the following features that can assist you with your reading.

INTRODUCTION TO THE STUDENT.   This part of a textbook is often ignored, but it is very important. It explains the text's purpose and probably tells you the author's point of view, or perspective. By knowing the author's purpose and biases from the start, you are better able to evaluate that author's interpretation of events or situations. For example, a liberal-minded person who is writing a critique of the Clinton presidency will most likely offer an assessment very different from that of a conservative author.

In the introduction or preface, you may also find the author's suggestions for using the book. The preface may identify different sections of the text that can assist you, and it may give an overview of the text's contents and an explanation of how each part contributes to the whole text.

TABLE OF CONTENTS. The table of contents provides a map of the entire book. Consider each chapter title as a point of interest along the way. By scanning the table of contents, you can determine the major areas that are covered in the text and the typical length of each chapter. By looking at chapter headings, you can learn the direction the text will take. For instance, information may be arranged by topic or in time sequence. In the table of contents for some books, you may also find a listing of the subsections within the chapters, which give you an even better picture of the overall contents.

CHAPTER INTRODUCTIONS. An introduction to a chapter prepares you for what you will find in the pages ahead. The introduction may be separated from the rest of the contents. It may even appear in a different type style, or it may be integrated with the rest of the contents at the beginning of the chapter. You can often tell that a section is the introduction because it doesn't begin with a subheading. Information provided in introductions varies. Some introductions give you the major thesis or main points you will be learning in the chapter. Use each main point like a peg on which to place the details as you proceed through the chapter. Other introductions may be anecdotes or questions intended to spark your interest before you read the chapter. Assess the purpose served by the chapter introductions in each of your texts and use them accordingly.

CHAPTER SUMMARIES. The chapter summary is a review of the main points of the chapter. You will be making good use of the summary if you try to recall the details from the chapter that are related to each main point. The summary may be separated from the rest of the text and may even appear in a different type style. Or it may just be at the end of the chapter, integrated with the rest of the text. Read the chapter introduction and summary before you proceed with more detailed reading. By doing so, you will see the total framework for the chapter. You will understand where the author is headed and will be more able to follow the route, through the details, along the way.

CHAPTER TITLES AND SUBTITLES.   These two features of textbooks are *organizing aids* that keep you focused while you read. Scan these quickly before you read, and you will know the scope of the topic within the chapter and how the author has organized the information. You will also be able to estimate how familiar you are with the subject. This information will guide the amount of time you should allow for your reading assignment.

GRAPHIC AIDS.   Many books use graphs, charts, diagrams, and photographs to clarify information or to serve as examples for material in the text. To use a graphic aid effectively, analyze how the information on it is organized. Usually, a title tells you what is depicted. *Graphs* usually contain quantitative data, such as percentages. They often show comparisons of the data and, frequently, comparisons over time. *Charts* may be used to organize information and to show relationships among people, events, and ideas that might otherwise be difficult to explain. For instance, a chart may show the variety of play activities of children in different countries from birth to age twelve or forms of environmental pollution and the most common causes of them, as well as strategies for eliminating each. Clearly labeled *diagrams* can help you visualize information that is otherwise descriptive, such as a diagram showing cell division or one depicting how a television camera works. *Photographs* are subject to different interpretations. However, your textbook author may clarify for you, within the body of the text, what interpretation is preferred. Try to see it from the author's perspective, but don't be afraid to make interpretations of your own. In fact, with any graphic aid, try to draw your own conclusions in addition to those that are mentioned in the text.

CHAPTER QUESTIONS.   These are extremely useful for studying textbook material. Chapter questions let you know what information the author believes you should have gained from your reading and what interpretations and conclusions could have resulted. It is a good idea to read these even before you begin the chapter. As with the titles and subtitles, prereading chapter questions helps keep you focused during your reading.

GLOSSARY.   The glossary is your dictionary for the book. Technical terms, which may or may not have been defined in the chapter where they first occurred, are listed here. Refer to it as you come across terms you do not remember that are important to the subject you are reading.

INDEX.   The index appears at the end of a text and alphabetically lists topics discussed in the text or references particular people or events, along with their page numbers. It assists you in finding material quickly.

ACTIVITY C: Assessing Your Textbooks

Complete this checklist for a textbook you are using this term. If your text does not have one of the features listed, note this.

Text: _____

_____

Course: _____

_____

How useful do you think each feature will be? Give reasons for your answer.

Introduction to the student _____

_____

Table of contents _____

_____

Chapter introductions _____

_____

Chapter summaries _____

_____

Chapter titles and subtitles _____

_____

Graphic aids _____

_____

Chapter questions_____

_____

Glossary_____

_____

Index_____

_____

Other features of this text_____

_____

Preparing Yourself to Read

Each time you begin a new text chapter, it is critical that you mentally prepare yourself to read. By doing so, you are again taking charge of your reading—putting yourself in control. Several strategies will help you do this.

ACTIVELY PREVIEW THE CHAPTER. You will want to know what the chapter contents are before you begin reading the chapter. Does that sound odd? How can you know what it's about before you have read it? Actively previewing the chapter is the key. To preview, read chapter introductions, summaries, chapter titles and subtitles, questions at the end of the chapter, and graphic aids. Whenever you have to read a new chapter or plan to review one you have already read, begin by skimming these essential parts. As you skim, think about how the chapter is organized, what the main topics are, what kinds of questions you are being asked, what the author's purpose for writing seems to be. Become as familiar as you can with what lies ahead in the chapter.

DETERMINE YOUR PRIOR KNOWLEDGE OF THE SUBJECT. Ask yourself such questions as: How much do I already know about this subject? What have I read or heard about it? What about it is of interest to me? How can I apply this information to my life? If you recognize your prior knowledge of a subject before you begin reading, your memory will provide information to help you comprehend new material in the text. Your memory will assist you in recalling related concepts, similar situations or characters, and your emotional responses to the subject. You will be able to make connections between the new information and what you already know, and these connections will make the new material easier to learn and more meaningful for you.

SET PURPOSES FOR YOUR READING.   This is another way to prepare for in-depth reading. Before you begin to read, you want to know *why* you are reading. Your reasons for reading can affect your speed and concentration as well as your ability to recall the material at a later time. Six common purposes for academic reading are to:

1. Preview a chapter to determine its contents.
2. Review major points from the previous night's reading before going to class.
3. Read with the intent to share the information with someone else in a study group.
4. Respond personally to what you are reading.
5. Learn everything in a chapter, including the minor details, in preparation for a test.
6. Assess the logic of an argument presented by an author.

Whatever your purpose, identify it at the outset.

SET AN APPROPRIATE READING SPEED.   Your reading speeds should vary, and they should be determined by your purpose for reading. Even if you are reading the same material several times, you may need to read it at a different rate each time.

Once you set your purpose, you can begin to assess whether you should skim the material quickly, as you would for purposes 1 and 2, or whether you need to read at a moderate speed, as you would for purposes 3 and 4. For purposes 5 and 6, you would need to use an even slower rate.

An additional factor that influences the speed at which you can read the text with comprehension is the *difficulty level of the material.* After you preread, assess your prior knowledge, and establish your purpose, you will be able to identify any difficulties the material may pose for you. Thus, the level at which the text is written, your background and interest in the material, and your purpose for reading all influence your reading rate. To achieve an appropriate pace, try the following:

❋ Make an initial estimate of how quickly you can read a certain number of pages in the text (for instance, ten pages in one-half hour).

❋ Read at your intended pace, but make sure you are comprehending the material.

❋ See whether you reached your target. (Did you read ten pages in one-half hour with comprehension? Did it take more or less time?)

❋ Adjust your target accordingly so that you stay at a comfortable speed, maintaining comprehension while accomplishing your purpose.

ELIMINATE DISTRACTIONS.   Finally, before you start your in-depth reading, identify those distractions that cause you to take your mind off your reading once you begin. This is sometimes the hardest step to take because it may require big changes in a few of your well-established study habits. Your determination to succeed, though, will get you past this hurdle. To eliminate distractions, you will first need to identify them. Distractions may include phones ringing, people talking, concerns about family or friends, poor lighting, music or television in the background, and other obligations. The list is practically endless. Once you've identified the negative influences on your studying, *develop a plan of attack*. For instance, if you are concerned about noise, music, people talking, or phones ringing, you obviously need to find a more suitable place to study. Sometimes even libraries are noisy. If this is the case in your library and noise disturbs you, look around campus or your neighborhood for a quieter place. (If you can't find one, try using foam ear plugs.) You can take the phone off the hook during your study time to eliminate calls. Make a to-do list *before* you begin studying so that you will remember to call family or friends or to take care of other obligations afterward. By making the list before you open the text, you have eliminated the need to remember these things and thus will be more able to remember the text information.

THINKING ABOUT YOUR READING AND WRITING

ACTIVITY D: Strategies for Preparing Yourself to Read

Think about the strategies you have learned here for preparing yourself to read. List the strategies you think will be most useful to you. Explain how you will apply each one.

_____

_____

_____

_____

Staying Mentally Active While You Read

At the end of a reading assignment, have you ever felt that you had no idea about what you had read? It's as though you hadn't spent the time reading the material at all! Many students have such experiences. Often it happens because you weren't aware that you weren't comprehending the material while you were reading. Your mind wandered and you didn't notice this. There are strategies to use to help you avoid this experience, or at least to catch yourself before you have read many pages. These strategies keep you from having to reread all the material again, save you time, and improve your comprehension. What you do during your in-depth reading is at least as important as your prereading activities.

SELF-MONITOR. When you *self-monitor,* ask yourself questions about the text while you are reading it. Self-monitoring makes you more aware of how well you are comprehending the material. As you read and self-monitor, identify those parts of the text that you do or do not understand, note the ideas that seem particularly important to you, and determine whether you can see connections between ideas. Ask yourself: Does this make sense? What does information on a new page have to do with what I have read on previous pages? What can I predict or hypothesize based on this information? What conclusions can I draw? Your responses to these questions suggest to you whether you have comprehended the material. The monitoring also keeps you very focused on what you are reading.

CREATE QUESTIONS AND TRY TO ANSWER THEM.   Self-monitoring also involves using the subtitles of the chapters to ask questions *before* you read and then checking whether you can answer your questions *while* you read. For instance, you may read a chapter that includes the subheading, "Successful Television Advertising." The questions you create before you read this portion of the text might include: What are some characteristics of successful television advertising? What are some examples of successful television advertising? After reading the section, you can immediately verify your understanding of it by attempting to answer your questions.

RESTATE THE AUTHOR'S IDEAS IN YOUR OWN WORDS.   This strategy is critically important to your self-monitoring process. When you restate the ideas, use your own language. If you can answer the questions you've created by restating the author's ideas in your own words, you will know that you have comprehended the material. If you cannot, there are two possible explanations: (1) You may have had an unsuitable question, or (2) you may not have comprehended. You will need to either revise your question so that you can include the important information in your answer or reread the material. The benefit of doing this is that you will have realized your difficulty comprehending the material well before getting to the end of the chapter. Now you can give yourself another chance to understand the section you did not understand before going further with your reading. Some practice in paraphrasing and identifying ideas in sentences is provided later in this chapter.

Taking Ownership of Ideas in Texts

You know now that you can improve your comprehension of academic material by practicing paraphrasing, or restating the author's ideas in your own language. Your goal is to restate the author's ideas well enough so that you can create a sentence that conveys them but expresses them comfortably for you. Authors sometimes use very formal language. By restating the author's ideas in your own language, you verify that you have understood the main points. If you do not comprehend the material, you will not be able to do this. Furthermore, by restating the ideas, you take ownership of those ideas. You will remember them longer. Paraphrasing the key points also gives you an opportunity to rehearse those ideas for a later performance, such as a class discussion or an exam. When you restate ideas, you need to:

1. Identify the essential ideas in each sentence.
2. Look for important *embedded* ideas within long sentences.
3. Rewrite the ideas so that the main points are clear.

The process to use for these three steps is described next.

Identify Essential Ideas in Sentences

You are no doubt aware that most textbook authors write sentences that are quite different from everyday conversation. Text language is more formal, and ideas are sometimes complicated. A key to understanding academic texts is to apply some of the same language knowledge to reading text that you use when you are having a conversation.

When you listen to someone speak, you are trying to get to the essential meaning of what is being said. The same goal is true for reading. There are things you already know about sentence structure, and you use this knowledge automatically when you listen to someone speak. When you read academic texts, you may need to deliberately apply this knowledge. A brief review of some elements of grammar will help you recall how sentences are structured. Knowing about sentence structure is critical for comprehending text.

To find the essential meaning of a sentence, you need to determine (1) who or what is being discussed and (2) what is being said about the *who* or *what*.

These two parts of the sentence are sometimes referred to as the *subject* and *predicate* of the sentence. They provide the fundamental meaning, the basic thought, of the sentence. You may now start to recall some grammatical features of sentences that you have learned in English classes. You should remember that:

1. Some sentences may have more than one subject or more than one verb. The two subjects or verbs are usually joined by *coordinating conjunctions* such as *or, but, and, for,* and *yet.* Both subjects or both verbs are important.

Example:

John Dewey *and* Jean-Jacques Rousseau had some worthwhile ideas about how children learn.

2. Some sentences have two or more important complete thoughts in them. Each thought has its own subject and verb. Each thought is critical to the meaning of the entire sentence. These two thoughts are also often joined by coordinating conjunctions, and they are separated by a comma. They may also be joined by a semicolon and no coordinating conjunction.

Example:

We do not know exactly how many regular gamblers are unable to control their gambling, *but* some experienced gamblers estimate that it is as high as 50 percent.

or

We do not know exactly how many regular gamblers are unable to control their gambling; some experienced gamblers estimate that it is as high as 50 percent.

3. Sometimes a sentence will contain two ideas, but one idea is more important than the other. In these cases, one part of the sentence, the most important part, is called the *independent clause.* It makes sense by itself and does not depend on the rest of the sentence for its meaning. The part of the sentence that also has a subject and verb, but which cannot stand alone as a sentence, is called the *dependent clause.* It depends on the rest of the sentence for its meaning. The two clauses are usually separated by a comma. Dependent clauses are often introduced by clause markers such as *because, when, as, since, that, so, although, where, if, unless, who, after, while, even though, which.*

Example:

If the union officials could not agree with management on a settlement, there would undoubtedly be a strike by the railroad workers.

ACTIVITY E: Identifying Essential Ideas in Sentences

Decide whether each sentence is an example of sentence structure 1, 2, or 3. Write your answer in the space provided.

1. Energy can exist in several forms and can be converted from one form to another. ____
2. A sound studio needs some essential equipment; for instance, it cannot be set up without a high-quality mixer. ____
3. General Electric and other large companies have found robots to be more effective in some work than human workers. ____
4. Jury panels are selected from voter registration or tax lists, and such panels are supposed to be generally representative of the community. ____
5. Meteorologists forecasting and reporting the weather have critical roles to play during weather crises. ____
6. No one was quite certain if the spread of the disease would be halted, although every precaution had been taken. ____
7. It was Muller who helped convince biologists that it was possible to think of the gene as a molecule. ____
8. In 1900, House representatives had no personal staff, and senators averaged fewer than one staff member each. ____

WORKING TOGETHER

With a partner, create one example of each of the three types of sentences described earlier. Identify each type.

MORE ABOUT CLAUSE MARKERS   You now know that clause markers often introduce a dependent clause. They can show the type of relationship that exists between the dependent clause and the independent clause in a sentence. This relationship can often be determined by figuring out the question the dependent clause answers about the independent clause. The marker introduces the answer. Here are some common questions clause markers introduce. In the example, the dependent clause is underlined, but the clause marker is italicized.

1. Which one (ones)?

Examples:

The businesses *whose* offices were in the building next to the playground closed for the month of August.

The plants *that* had not been treated with the chemical showed greater leaf loss over a shorter period of time.

2. When?

Examples:

The interest rates on home mortgages were expected to rise *after* the Federal Reserve Bank raised the prime rate.

When the twentieth century began, America was already an industrialized nation.

3. Who?

Examples:

The candidates *who* had presented their views at the open meeting had a good chance of being elected.

The runner *who* came in last was cheered into the home stretch by the crowd.

4. How?

Examples:

The new recruits looked *as if* they were ready to furnish the needed strength.

The social workers spoke *as though* the family would soon be reunited.

5. Why?

Examples:

You will need to take a course in keyboarding *so that* you can type more easily and more accurately.

It was nearly impossible to identify the origin of the skeleton *because* it was so badly deteriorated.

6. Under what conditions or circumstances?

Examples:

If she touched the clay models, the blind girl was able to describe the clothes worn by the Victorians.

> The community resolved to establish its own nightwatch *unless* the police could do a better job keeping the gangs and drug dealers away.

Note that several questions may be answered by several clauses within a single sentence, as in the examples that follow. The clause markers have been italicized.

Examples:

a. Children usually make greater progress in their schoolwork *if* the number of hours of TV they watch is reduced *so that* they have more time for their homework.

b. The scientists *who* investigated global warming found *that* temperatures of the earth's surface had risen only slightly during the past ten years.

c. The countries *that* were near the North Korean border were feeling more threatened recently *because* the United Nations' investigators had not been able to determine North Korea's nuclear power.

d. *After* she had investigated for two months, the anthropologist concluded *that* the shaman was well respected in the village.

WORKING TOGETHER

With a partner, decide which questions are answered by each underlined clause in Examples (a) through (d) above.

Find Embedded Ideas in Text

Textbook sentences are often lengthy. This can present a major problem when students try to restate main points because several ideas are often stated within, or embedded in, one long sentence. In such sentences, the author is using multiple clauses and phrases. Readers must be able to unravel the sentence in order to identify the several ideas it contains.

It will help if you remember that even very long sentences have at least one independent clause with a main subject and verb, even though the subject and verb may be separated by dependent clauses and modifying phrases. The following two example sentences illustrate this point. In each sentence the independent clause, consisting of the subject and predicate, has been underlined, the clause markers have been circled, and those phrases that modify only the main clause or a dependent clause have been italicized.

Examples:

   a. A number of small businesses, (which) are businesses (that) are usually started *by people* (who) have developed a product or service (that) can be produced and sold only *in a new business* (which) is set up *for that purpose,* often evolve into large corporations.

   b. Executives at the 308-bed hospital in Pittsburgh, (who) wanted to address problems *of inefficiency* (that) caused patients to repeatedly answer the same questions and (that) would improve the flow *of information among caregivers,* decided to implement a clinical document system (that) would integrate data *from the various departments.*

Dependent clauses and modifying phrases may also appear at the beginning of the sentence. In such cases, you need to look further on in the sentence to find the main clause. The main clause is underlined.

Example:

   (When) the darkroom and his camera equipment were ready to go, the photographer, who had been asked to submit an entry to a national contest, realized he needed a different type of lens to achieve the effect he desired.

In other long sentences, the subject and a verb are very close to each other, but the sentence length prompts us to look toward the end of the sentence for the main verb. If you do this, you may feel as though you have lost your place in the sentence. This type of sentence is illustrated next. The main clause is underlined.

Example:

   The sugars and other organic materials formed by green plants constitute the basic fuels for all of us, for when we walk, pound on a keyboard, or sing a lullaby, we are using the energy released by the combustion of sugars in our body.

Once you have identified the main subject and verb, you can separate out all the key ideas that are embedded in the rest of the sentence, as in the two examples that follow.

Example 1:

Parents who remain separated without divorcing, or who attempt periodic but unsuccessful reconciliations, cloud the issue for their children, increasing the uncertainty they already feel.

In this sentence, the main idea is that <u>parents cloud the issue for the children</u>. The following ideas give important information about this and are embedded in the remainder of the sentence.

Some Embedded Ideas

1. Parents sometimes separate but do not divorce.
2. Separated parents sometimes try to reconcile.
3. Some reconciliations are not successful.
4. Children of divorcing parents are uncertain.
5. When parens stay separated but don't divorce, children are even more uncertain.

In the next example, the main subject and verb are near the beginning of the sentence, and they are followed by a series of descriptors that would be important to know if you were studying this material.

Example 2:

After developing and evaluating objectives, <u>the manager selects the overall policies</u> that will fulfill the company objective and still satisfy market, industry, and company criteria.

Some Embedded Ideas

1. Managers develop objectives.
2. Managers evaluate objectives.
3. Managers select policies that are designed to meet the company objective.
4. Managers also have to consider the market when they set policy.
5. Managers also have to consider the industry when they set policy.

Determining which embedded ideas are important is usually a matter of finding those ideas that answer questions about the main subject and verb of the sentence. In Example 1, the question "How do parents cloud the issue for their children?" is answered by the embedded ideas. In Example 2, the main subject and verb phrases generate the question "How does the manager select the policies?" The embedded ideas listed provide answers to these.

ACTIVITY F: Finding Embedded Ideas in Text

For each sentence, list as many important embedded ideas as you can.

1. From the reign of meat and potatoes to the sushi-and-salsa 2000s, America has undergone many revolutions in taste—and few people have done more to liberate the nation's palate than Julia Child.

Embedded ideas:

a. _____

b. _____

c. _____

d. _____

2. Companies make use of general-purpose software such as word processors and database systems, as well as more specialized software to manage records, prepare payroll, produce accounting reports, and analyze business finances.

Embedded ideas:

a. _____

b. _____

c. _____

d. _____

Rewrite Sentences

Once you have identified the embedded ideas in a sentence and have restated them in your own words, you are ready to create a new, less complicated sentence that restates the author's idea. You need to determine which of the embedded ideas are more important. You already know that important ideas answer questions about the main subject and verb. In addition, consider the major focus of the paragraph, chapter, or article. This process is outlined in the following example, in which a key sentence has been italicized and then restated.

Example:

> When Nelson Mandela speaks to black audiences, he often reminds them that democracy and majority rule in South Africa will not change the material circumstances of their lives overnight. *He rarely practices the modern politician's art of telling his listeners what he thinks they want to hear.* His message to white audiences is also sometimes not typical of an elected official who would like to be reelected. He tells the white citizens of South Africa that they must take responsibility for the past and that they will have to accept that their nation will now have majority rule.

> **Restatement** (based on focus of paragraph and important information preceding and following sentence):

> Nelson Mandela is not like most politicians because he does not speak to his audiences in ways that will especially please his listeners.

ACTIVITY G: Rewriting Key Sentences from Text

Each of the following paragraphs contains an underlined key sentence. Rewrite this sentence, keeping its main idea but simplifying the language. Refer to the rest of the information in the paragraph to be sure that your sentence still fits the ideas in the paragraph.

1. Some people looking for their first job simply seize upon the most promising local opporunity and proceed to make the most of it. <u>In choosing the company for which to work, however, you should look toward the future, both your future in the company</u>

and its future in business. You should consider management excellence, reputation, financial soundness, growth record, innovation in new product development, location, and people. Information concerning these criteria can be obtained from local customers of the company, bankers, the company's annual report, and Dun and Bradstreet reports.

L. Con Megginson, et al., *Business* (Lexington, Mass: D.C. Heath, 1984), 651.

Your restatement: _____

_____

_____

2. Rhythms that are complex and uneven mark contemporary music, particularly jazz. Dave Brubeck's recording of "Take Five," played in 5/4 time, or his "Unsquare Dance," in 7/4 time are short jazz pieces with uneven rhythmic patterns. Similarly, rhythmic patterns can shift, and when these changes occur suddenly or frequently, the effect is one of tension and excitement. Shifting meters are now frequently found in all types of music, but when Igor Stravinsky's *Le Sacre du Printemps* (The Rite of Spring) was first performed in 1913, its shifting rhythms together with its unusual, discordant harmonies caused a small riot among shocked members of the audience.

Judy Nagle, "Rhythm," *The Responsive Arts* (Sherman Oaks, Calif.: Alfred, 1980), 256.

Your restatement: _____

_____

_____

3. Most of the materials which we can see around us can be distinguished either with the naked eye or the microscope as consisting of two or more materials which are distinct from each other. Such non-uniform materials are said to be *heterogeneous*. Wood, granite, concrete, and milk are examples. It is usually possible with the naked eye to see that granite is composed of at least three minerals: quartz, biotite, and feldspar. If granite is crushed so that the particles are the size of fine sand, it is possible to pick out the quartz and separate it mechanically from the biotite and

feldspar. Milk normally appears to be homogeneous, but under the microscope, particles of various kinds can be seen suspended in water. Milk is not a solution; it is a heterogeneous mixture. One type of particle (in this instance, globules of fat) can be separated from the other particles of milk by a device called a centrifuge or cream separator.

R. Smoot et al., *Chemistry, A Modern Course. Teacher's Annotated Edition and Solutions Manual.* (Columbus, Ohio: C. Merrill, 1971), 44.

Your restatement: _____

_____

_____

WORKING TOGETHER

Compare your restatements from Activity G with those of a partner. Did your sentences for each paragraph convey the same idea? What were some differences? Make any revisions to your sentences that you now think would improve them. Make sure that you are comfortable with the language and that the restatements keep the original idea.

When you compare your answers with a partner, you have an opportunity to share your knowledge with someone else. This is another effective strategy for taking ownership of ideas in texts. People sometimes say they like to "talk through" their ideas because it helps them clarify their thinking. You might recall doing this with your friends. By talking with classmates about the ideas you have read, you can (1) think through the ideas and restate them in a way that someone else will understand them and (2) clarify them for yourself. If you cannot discuss the ideas with someone else, them you most likely don't understand them. This should be a signal to you that you need to reread the material.

Writing out what you know, making a permanent record of your text summaries and restatements, is also a good comprehension strategy. Again, you are working with the text language and trying to reconstruct its meaning so that you will understand and remember it. If you copy the information from your text word for word, you have not learned it; you are merely copying. Rewriting, restating, and rewording are critical to remembering what you read.

THINKING ABOUT YOUR READING AND WRITING

ACTIVITY H: Strategies for Taking Ownership of Ideas in Texts

Think about the strategies you have learned in this section. List those that you think will be most useful to you. Explain how you will apply each one.

_____

_____

_____

_____

Assessing Your Learning

The practice of checking your comprehension applies not only during reading but also *after* you have completed the entire reading assignment. In the postreading assessment process, concentrate on tying together the main points of the material and connecting them to other knowledge you have. There are several steps to take in order to assess what you have learned. Although these steps take time and effort, they can be rewarding and will help you realize how much you have learned from your reading.

SPEND A FEW MINUTES MENTALLY SUMMARIZING THE ENTIRE CHAPTER.   What were the key points? What details for each key point can you recall? How does each main idea contribute to the whole of the information? Look again at headings, subheadings, and technical terms. Be sure you see the chapter as a whole, not just as bits and pieces of facts. The author has chosen to put all the details into a particular chapter because they have a relationship to one another. Focus on that relationship for a while.

If you still don't understand some part, it is critical that you reread that section for clarification. Again, try to connect the details and main points to see whether there are any remaining areas of uncertainty.

THINK ABOUT HOW THE NEW INFORMATION YOU HAVE LEARNED COMPARES TO WHAT YOU KNEW AT THE START OF YOUR READING. To do this, you must recall the prior knowledge you had during the prereading phase. Ask yourself: What did I know then? What do I know

now? You might also ask: What more would I like to know about this subject? These comparisons will show you how much you have gained from the reading; they also will enable you to connect your prior knowledge to new ideas and to adjust your thinking so that any misconceptions you had before reading will be modified.

CONSIDER THE OPINIONS AND ATTITUDES OF THE AUTHOR AND COMPARE THEM TO YOUR OWN.   This step is especially important if your reading is about a controversial subject. It requires you to make distinctions between facts and the author's opinions, to assess the logic of the author's ideas, to reconsider your opinions, and to identify support for either the author's ideas or your own.

THINK ABOUT HOW YOUR NEW KNOWLEDGE AFFECTS YOU PERSONALLY.   Once you have assessed your knowledge and are clear about the information, you can ask yourself: How can I apply this knowledge to my life? You may be reading about social issues, environmental issues, the economy, philosophical issues and points of view, or business matters. This process will make what you have learned more meaningful for you and will help you remember the material.

THINKING ABOUT YOUR READING AND WRITING

ACTIVITY I: Postreading Assessment Strategies

Think about the strategies you have learned for postreading assessment. List those that you think will be most useful to you. Explain how you will apply each one.

_____

_____

_____

Using Outside Sources to Gain Background Knowledge

Textbook authors have often spent many years learning about a subject before they write their books. You do not have that privilege. You need to learn the information today, this week, or this term. Since the authors are so familiar with their subject, they often assume students have enough background knowledge to help them read the text. This is not always so. When you are confused or feel you can't understand some portion of your assigned reading, you can do many things to get outside assistance. The most obvious is to find a tutor on campus. Your college probably has many students majoring in the subject that gives you difficulty. Some of these students are likely connected to a tutoring service. The only drawback to using the college tutoring service may be that student tutors often lack teaching experience.

Another source of assistance is other books on the subject that may make fewer assumptions about what you already know. Such books may be available at your college library. You may find them at the public library, where the adult section as well as the young adults section may have books about your subject. In the past decade, there has been an explosion in informational books for young readers, some of which are quite remarkable in their depth and quality. (If you feel embarrassed checking these out, you can always claim it is for a younger relative.) A third source for additional material is the federal government, which publishes many informational brochures. You can obtain a listing of them from the Government Printing Office in Washington, D.C.

Also consider people you know who could be sources for information and assistance on particular subjects. A relative who works in an auto factory may have considerable knowledge about auto technology. A friend working at a local restaurant or pharmacy can possibly explain, in simplified terms, some business principles to you. A teacher you know may be able to shed some light on issues raised in sociology or psychology texts. Try to explore every possible avenue for sources.

Once you have gathered all the outside information you need to help you understand the text material, sort through it and decide which ideas are more important or worthwhile. Reread the text material, which should now have more meaning for you. Then synthesize your new information with the knowledge you already have from outside sources. You are now ready to record the vital information, in your own language, for later use.

The following list gives you an opportunity to reflect on the outside sources that are available to you for courses you are taking this term.

Outside Source Action List

Course: _____

Outside Sources Available to You: _____

_____

_____

Preparing for Tests

Students who have taken charge of their reading also know that tests are a fact of academic life. Examinations are the primary way in which many instructors can assess whether you have learned course content. Different instructors may give tests once or twice a term, weekly, or every few weeks. If you have used the strategies described in this chapter, you are well on your way to success with tests. You will have used all available resources to check and expand your understanding, and you will have recorded what you know in language that is your own so that you have a usable set of study notes. There are, however, still a few remaining tasks to do as you prepare to take tests. You should use some of these strategies several weeks before the exam. Others you will want to do shortly before the exam, and some are strategies to use during the exam.

Several Weeks before the Exam

1. Practice distributed review. This means to review your notes at regular intervals throughout the term. Don't wait until just before the exam to begin studying.
2. Find a study partner. Study partners can help each other tremendously if they really focus on their task. They can prepare questions for each other to answer, and they can listen to responses to see whether the information is adequate. They can keep each other focused and provide encouragement.

Shortly before the Exam

1. Make a final review of your notes the evening before the exam. Don't do anything afterward that will interfere with what you have reviewed, such as going to a party.
2. Get up a little earlier than usual the next morning to review your notes once more.
3. Take all materials you will need during the exam. These include a watch as well as any paper and pencils or pens you might need.
4. Be on time for the exam. If you arrive late, you are setting yourself up to do poorly. If you arrive too early, others may distract you.

During the Exam

1. Sit in a quiet spot away from talkative and noisy people.
2. Read over *all* the directions on the exam before you begin. Spend a few minutes thinking about what is required before you begin.
3. If you come to a question you can't answer, remind yourself that you don't need to get *every* answer right in order to pass.
4. Work from your strengths. If there are questions you definitely know, answer these first so that you can feel self-assured before tackling the more difficult questions.
5. Budget your time. Don't spend too much time on any one question.
6. Use all the time allowed to you. There is no need to be the first one finished. If you finish early, use the remaining time to review your answers and to spot and correct careless errors.

THINKING ABOUT YOUR READING AND WRITING

ACTIVITY J: Test-Taking Tips

1. Which of the tips about taking tests will benefit you? _____

_____

_____

_____

_____

2. What else do you think you can do to improve your test-taking
   strategies? _____

_____

_____

_____

Congratulations! If you have been working with the strategies mentioned
in this chapter, you have taken control of your reading. You now understand what is necessary for successfully reading academic texts, and you
have accepted responsibility for monitoring your own comprehension.
You can congratulate yourself on a job well done!

▶ Chapter Summary

Based on your reading of this chapter, list at least five ideas it contains that you
believe will help you with future reading assignments. Write in complete
sentences.

1. _____

_____

_____

_____

2. _____

_____

_____

_____

3. _____

_____

_____

_____

4. _____

_____

_____

_____

5. _____

_____

_____

_____

▶ Extended Application

Now that you have worked with the strategies necessary for taking control of your reading, you can practice applying them to full-length reading selections. Choose (or your instructor may choose) a reading selection from Part 2 of this book that is typical of what you will be expected to read for your other college courses, such as an essay or a textbook chapter. Use this selection to practice:

 ❋ Preparing yourself to read
 ❋ Staying mentally active while you read
 ❋ Taking ownership of ideas in the text

Decide on the practice strategies you will use. Apply them to your selection. Then write, in a few paragraphs, a description of what you did and how the strategies you used worked for you.

Name of material used: _____

Page numbers: _____

Your description: _____

CHAPTER TWO

Understanding the Vocabulary in Academic Texts

WERE YOU EVER SURPRISED BY AN ad for a movie? Perhaps you'd already seen the film that was being advertised and thought it was awful, but the reviewers say the film is wonderful. They are quoted as reporting that the movie is "very appealing" and "for one and all." How could this be? You do a little investigating and learn that the film reviews had not been flattering at all. In fact, one reviewer had actually said, "This movie is not very appealing." Another wrote in her review that "An evening at home, rather than a night out to see this film, would be best for one and all." Obviously, the words quoted in the ad for the film had been taken *out of context*. The advertisers used only parts of sentences from the reviews. The context, all the words originally surrounding the quoted portion, conveyed critical information that moviegoers reading the ads did not receive.

Context is important. It supplies needed information. Words in academic texts, such as book chapters or journal articles, take on particular meanings depending on the context in which they are used. The context helps the reader define words. In this chapter, you will learn how to analyze the context to help you comprehend the meaning of unfamiliar words. You will also learn additional strategies for building vocabulary, a critical skill for reading academic materials.

How Will Context Help You Read Academic Text?

What's the first thing you should do when you're reading and you come to a word you don't know? Did you say, "Look in a dictionary for the meaning"? If so, you might be surprised to learn that this may not be the best course of action. You don't always need the dictionary to define unfamiliar words. In fact, you can often figure out the meaning of such words by using the word's *context.* That is, you can guess at the meaning of one word by thinking about the ideas that are suggested by the other words and sentences near it. This approach to vocabulary, called *using context clues,* lets you continue your reading. You don't interrupt your comprehension, something you would do if you took the time to use a dictionary. In fact, when you use context clues, you are doing some extra thinking about the meaning of what you have read, and you are therefore simultaneously developing vocabulary and comprehension skills.

You probably already use context clues even without being aware of it. In this part of the chapter, you will increase your ability to use them. To see how you can determine the meaning of unfamiliar words by using the context, complete both parts of Activity A.

ACTIVITY A: Learning What Context Clues Can Do for You
Fill in your responses to Parts 1 and 2 in this chart.

PART 1	PART 2	PART 1	PART 2
1._____	_____	6._____	_____
2._____	_____	7._____	_____
3._____	_____	8._____	_____
4._____	_____	9._____	_____
5._____	_____	10._____	_____
		Your Score: _____ %	_____ %

Part I. Here are some words you may not know. For each **boldfaced** word, select what you believe to be the best definition. Place your answers in the chart under Part 1.

1. **myriad** (a) miracle (b) great number (c) skilled person (d) painting
2. **permeated** (a) appointed (b) allowed (c) spread through (d) harmed
3. **castigate** (a) punish (b) support (c) confuse (d) search
4. **indigence** (a) poverty (b) culture (c) innocence (d) knowledge
5. **dogmatic** (a) courageous (b) cruel to animals (c) weak (d) dictatorial
6. **feign** (a) destroy (b) pretend (c) graceful (d) emotional
7. **renounced** (a) refused to follow (b) announced with force (c) expected (d) encouraged
8. **shun** (a) frighten (b) a Danish coin (c) voice an opinion (d) avoid
9. **replete** (a) full (b) imaginative (c) brightly colored insect (d) cautious
10. **purge** (a) disease (b) remove (c) oppose (d) publicize

Part 2. Select the meaning for each **boldfaced** word from the choices that appear beneath each sentence. Place your answers alongside your answers for Part 1.

1. Because the sky was so clear, we were able to see a **myriad** of stars.
   (a) miracle (b) great number (c) skilled person (d) painting
2. When the smoke from the cigar **permeated** the lounge, the visitors apologized.
   (a) appointed (b) allowed (c) spread through (d) harmed
3. The dictator said he would **castigate** anyone who opposed him.
   (a) punish (b) support (c) confuse (d) search
4. The family's **indigence** meant they could not afford to buy a house or to send their children to college.
   (a) poverty (b) culture (c) innocence (d) knowledge
5. The **dogmatic** leadership style of the chairperson practically guaranteed that she would not be reelected for a second term.
   (a) courageous (b) cruel to animals (c) weak (d) dictatorial

6. If she could **feign** sleep, the child thought that she would not have to take her medicine.

   (a) destroy (b) pretend (c) graceful (d) emotional

7. The newest fraternity pledges **renounced** what they were asked to do, and later they protested in front of the frat house.

   (a) refused to follow (b) announced with force (c) expected (d) encouraged

8. In order to protect himself, the new boy in school had to **shun** the class bully.

   (a) frighten (b) a Danish coin (c) voice an opinion (d) avoid

9. The Christmas tree was **replete** with ornaments that had been collected over a fifty-year period.

   (a) full (b) imaginative (c) brightly colored insect (d) cautious

10. The prisoner was found wrongfully charged, and as a result the courts had to **purge** his prison record.

    (a) disease (b) remove (c) oppose (d) publicize

The answers to Parts 1 and 2 are b, c, a, a, d, b, a, d, a, b. Check your work. How did you do? Did your context clues help you? In a few sentences, describe the results you found.

_____

_____

_____

_____

What is the Process for Using Context Clues?

You can best understand the answer to this question if you try to observe yourself and what you do when you read material containing an unfamiliar word. Read the following paragraphs and try to figure out the meaning of the word that is italicized. As you do this, ask yourself, "What am I doing to get the meaning of this word?"

Paragraph 1

During this second half of our century, while we are at the height of urbanization, mass production, mass communica-

tion, and computerization, there is a *resurgence* of the arts.
During the past few years, in the United States alone more
people have attended concerts and art exhibits than baseball
games, while theatergoers have outnumbered boaters, skiers,
and golfers combined. This is not to imply that baseball fans
are not art fans or vice versa; to the contrary, it shows that
both sports and the arts are very much in the mainstream.
Judy Nagle, "The Arts: What Are They?" in *The Responsive Arts*
(Sherman Oaks, CA.: Alfred, 1980), 1.

What do you guess is the meaning of *resurgence?*

_____

_____

In a few sentences, explain how you formed this definition.

_____

_____

_____

Paragraph 2

Often the federal government by law requires state and local
governments to perform functions or undertake tasks that
Congress deems in the public interest. Many of these federal
mandates are "unfunded"—that is, Congress does not provide
any money to carry out these functions or tasks even though
they impose costs on states and communities. For example,
environmental protection laws passed by Congress require local governments to provide specified levels of sewage treatment; the Americans with Disabilities Act requires state and
local governments to build ramps and alter curbs in public
streets and buildings.
T. R. Dye, *Power and Society,* 7th ed. (Belmont, CA: Wadsworth,
1996), 168.

What do you guess is the meaning of *mandates?*

_____

You may find that you have used a combination of strategies to figure out the meanings of unfamiliar words. Some commonly used strategies are listed next. Check all that you used.

- ✳ I used my prior knowledge of the word. _____
- ✳ I tried to pronounce the word. _____
- ✳ I looked for roots or prefixes in the word. _____
- ✳ I looked for definitions in the sentence. _____
- ✳ I looked for words in the sentence that had the opposite meaning. _____
- ✳ I looked at the other sentences in the paragraph for relationships to the sentence with the unknown word. _____

WORKING TOGETHER

Compare your responses to this checklist with a partner's. Did you use the same strategies? Why do you think your strategies were similar or different?

If you are skilled at using context clues, you will be able to figure out an approximate meaning of the unknown word. There are several different types of context clues. The next section introduces those that are most useful for reading academic text.

What Are the Most Useful Types of Context Clues?

Several kinds of context clues appear in academic texts. Five that we review here are

Contrast, or antonym, clues

Restatement, or synonym, clues

Definition clues

Illustration, or example, clues

Experience, or commonsense, clues

Each type has certain signal words that are associated with it. *Signal words* alert readers to the type of clue being used. Here are illustrations of these five common types of context clues and the signal words often present with each type.

Contrast, or Antonym, Clues

One type of context clue is the *contrast clue,* or *antonym clue.* With this type of clue, the author provides you with a word or phrase that is the opposite, or antonym, of the word you may not know. If you know the meaning of the contrasting word, you will be able to figure out the definition of the unknown word. The antonym usually appears in the same sentence as the unknown word, or very close by. Signal words within the sentence containing the antonym may be used to alert you to it. These contrast signal words include *although, on the other hand, however, but, nevertheless, on the contrary, instead, yet, unlike, conversely, in contrast, than* _____. These are often used to indicate contrasts between individual words or concepts. There can also be a contrast between individual words or concepts without the presence of a signal word. In this case, you will rely solely on the context, without the signal word, to help you determine the meaning of the unknown word.

Example:

> The mood of the music on the radio was *somber,* unlike the cheerful tunes the child had been singing before she got into the car.
>
> ***Antonym or contrast clue:*** cheerful
> ***Meaning of unknown word:*** sad
> ***Explanation:*** The word *unlike* is a clue to the contrast between *somber* and *cheerful.* Since we know what *cheerful* means, we can guess at the meaning of *somber.*

Example (without signal word):

> The mood of the music on the radio had become *somber.* The cheerful tunes the child had been singing before she got into the car were gone.
>
> ***Explanation:*** The contrast is still here but without the signal word. However, the verb phrase *were gone* indicates the contrast between *somber* and *cheerful.* Since we know what *cheerful* means, we can guess at the meaning of *somber.*

ACTIVITY B: Contrast, or Antonym, Clues

For each word in italics, indicate the opposite or contrast clue available to you in the sentence(s). Then write the meaning of the unknown word.

1. He was *undaunted* when he had to speak in front of his class but was very fearful about giving a talk before the entire group of freshmen.

   Antonym, or contrast, clue:_____

   Meaning of unknown word:_____

2. The honor *bestowed* on the athlete was taken away once it was learned he had been on steroids.

   Antonym, or contrast, clue:_____

   Meaning of unknown word:_____

3. I would have *squandered* my whole week's earnings; however, my best friend encouraged me to save some of the money for next week's dance.

   Antonym, or contrast, clue:_____

   Meaning of unknown word:_____

4. To many, the old man seemed *eccentric,* but to those who really knew him, he was perfectly normal.

   Antonym, or contrast, clue:_____

   Meaning of unknown word:_____

5. Her story was *incongruous.* No one found it appropriate.

   Antonym, or contrast, clue:_____

   Meaning of unknown word:_____

Restatement, or Synonym, Clues

A second type of context clue is the *restatement clue,* or *synonym clue.* A word or phrase that has a meaning similar to a word you don't know placed in or near the sentence with the unknown word gives this type of clue. If you recognize the similar word or understand the meaning of the phrase, you will be able to approximate the definition of the word you do not know.

Example:

> She made a *resolution* she would quit smoking, the fourth time she had made such a promise, so we were not convinced she would really stop.
>
> ***Restatement or synonym clue:*** promise
> ***Meaning of unknown word:*** promise
> ***Explanation:*** The phrase *such a promise* contains a synonym for *resolution*. The meaning of this phrase refers you to what has just been said. This makes it easy to figure out that *resolution* means *promise*.

ACTIVITY C: Restatement, or Synonym, Clues

For each word in italics, indicate the clue available to you in the sentence(s). Then write the meaning of the unknown word.

1. Jose's *gratitude* was immeasurable. He couldn't thank his girl-friend enough for helping him find a part-time job.

   Restatement, or synonym, clue: _____
   Meaning of unknown word: _____

2. After the injury to his leg, the tennis star quickly regained *mobility*, and he could move easily on the court.

   Restatement, or synonym, clue: _____
   Meaning of unknown word: _____

3. She was so *incensed* at the animal trainer's cruelty that she could not watch any more of the animal acts without being angry.

   Restatement, or synonym, clue: _____
   Meaning of unknown word: _____

4. There was such a *preponderance* of mail for one member of the rock band that the others began to be jealous of her huge pile.

   Restatement, or synonym, clue: _____
   Meaning of unknown word: _____

5. During the highly negative campaign, each candidate sought to *discredit* the other.

   Restatement, or synonym, clue: _____
   Meaning of unknown word: _____

Definition Clues

The *definition clue* is much like the restatement, or synonym, clue, except that the author *deliberately* provides the meaning of the unknown word. This is often done through the use of punctuation: commas, parentheses, brackets, or dashes that set off the definition. Helping words such as *that is, such as,* or *which means* are also sometimes used to signal the definition.

Example 1: Definition with commas

> The doctor's income was *commensurate* with, or equal to, his ability as a surgeon.

> **Clue indicator:** commas that set off the definition
> **Explanation:** The unknown word *commensurate* is defined by the words between the commas.

Example 2: Definition with parentheses

> *EEGs* (tracings of the brain's brain wave activity) were first systematically used in the 1930s when researchers began to study eye movement.

> **Explanation:** The words in parentheses provide a definition of EEGs.

ACTIVITY D: Definition Clues

For each word in italics, indicate how the author signals that a definition is being provided.

1. The *Anasazi,* a group of American Indians living in the Southwest from 1000 to 1300 C.E., lived in cliff dwellings.
   Author's signal: _____

2. It is a *universal* truth—one that all people accept—that success is usually the result of a combination of hard work and good luck.
   Author's signal: _____

3. Our *forbearance,* or patience, made it possible for us to complete the entire experiment properly and to get satisfactory results.
   Author's signal: _____

4. The *petiole* (the stemlike part of the leaf) joins the blade to the stem.

   Author's signal: _____

5. *Photocopying* is the practice of making copies of parts of books, magazines, newspapers, or pamphlets.

   Author's signal: _____

Illustration, or Example, Clues

An author may provide *illustration clues,* or *example clues,* to define a complex concept or clarify very important ideas. The reader is able to use these illustrations or examples to create a definition for that concept or unknown word. Words that signal an illustration or example include *for example, for instance, such as, to illustrate.* These phrases are very common in academic text.

Example 1:

> Our college is very *accommodating* to dorm students. For instance, the college furnishes each student with a bed, mattress, desk, chair, dresser, and bookcase. Students can also have air conditioners and refrigerators for a small fee. Each spring, students can participate in the room selection process, and they have a wide number of room choices, ranging from singles to quads. If a dorm student wants to have a friend stay over, arrangements can be made for a room in the campus "guest hotel," and this costs only $10 per night. Sometimes I think it is preferable to be a dorm student than to live in an apartment.

> ***Explanation:*** The unknown word, *accommodating,* is explained through the examples that are given about the treatment of dorm students. These examples describe things that would make dorm students' lives better. The word *accommodating,* then, must refer to something that is positive.

Example 2:

> Some people believe that morality in our culture has *retrograded.* For instance, young people are no longer waiting until marriage to have sex. News articles regularly report increases in all kinds

of crime. Everywhere one can see growing evidence of crooked politicians. Perhaps the critics are correct.

Explanation: The unknown word, *retrograded,* is clarified through the use of examples. A close look at the examples shows they each refer to changes—change in attitudes toward premarital sex, growth in crime, and increase in crooked politicians. None of these changes are positive. Note also that the first example is introduced by the signal words *For instance.* Using all this information, we can determine that *retrograded* must mean going backward in a society or degenerating.

ACTIVITY E: Illustration, or Example, Clues

Use the information in each paragraph to define the italicized word. Write your definition in the space provided.

1. The legend you may know as Lawrence of Arabia is actually T. E. Lawrence (1888–1935). He achieved fame as the result of his many *exploits* in Egypt. For instance, he helped organize the Arab revolt against the Turkish Ottoman Empire. Another example is his devotion to the Arab cause and his military genius that led to the defeat of the Turks and the entry of the Arabs into Damascus, the capital of Syria. It was in keeping with his character that Lawrence was later killed in a motorcycle accident in England.

   Your definition: _____

2. A popular way to use imagery is through *mnemonic* devices. The basic process of a mnemonic system consists in taking something that has known imagery content and then associating to it images of things to be learned. Stage magicians use this process, for instance, to learn the names of people sitting in the audience. A person good at this procedure can learn the names of 100 people after hearing them only once.

   Adapted from Anthony E. Grasha, *Practical Applications of Psychology,* 2d ed. (Boston: Little, Brown, 1983), 112.

   Your definition: _____

3. B. F. Skinner, a psychologist, constructed a special cage with a food-release mechanism to study *operant conditioning.* He found

that a rat placed in the cage eventually learns that pressing a bar releases a pellet of food. At first, the rat explores its cage. This leads to a period of trial and error before the rat accidentally performs the correct act—pressing the bar. Food is the reward for pressing the bar. By rewarding the rat for pressing the bar, the rat is more likely to repeat the act. The rat learns to associate the action of pressing the bar with the reward of food.

Adapted from W. D. Schraer and H. J. Stoltze, *Biology: The Study of Life,* 4th ed. (Needham, MA: Prentice Hall, 1991), 798.

Your definition: _____

4. Managers can improve their efficiency by *delegating* work. Delegating is important for several reasons. First, it frees a manager from some time-consuming duties that can be performed by subordinates. Second, decisions made by lower-level managers usually are more timely than those that go through several layers of management. Third, subordinate managers can reach their potential only if given the chance to make decisions and to assume responsibility for them.

Adapted from Jerry Kinard, *Management* (Lexington, MA: Heath, 1988), 191.

Your definition: _____

5. My eighth-grade math teacher had few friends among the student population. We considered him a highly *captious* individual. For example, he often put poor-quality homework papers on display and never told the unfortunate souls who wrote them how they could improve their work. If a student saw him in the hall and offered a kindly "hello," Mr. Boise only snapped back an unfriendly grunt along with some suggestion, such as "You're late to class," or "Why don't you get a haircut?"

Your definition: _____

6. My elderly father had become more *sedentary* than I had originally thought. When I went to visit him, the changes in his behavior were clear. He no longer went for his daily walk. He spent many hours sitting on the front porch watching the birds and listening to the rustle of the trees. He didn't visit friends as he used to. My husband and I became so concerned that we finally suggested he might want to come to live with us.

Your definition: _____

Experience, or Commonsense, Clues

A fifth type of context clue is the *experience clue* or *commonsense clue*. In sentences with this type of clue, the author describes a situation that you are probably familiar with or that you can imagine. By using your experience or by considering what would make sense in the situation described, you will be able to figure out the meaning of the unknown word.

Example:

The low temperatures and cloudy sky *foreshadowed* the snowstorm that was soon to come.

Unknown word: foreshadowed

Experience or commonsense clue: low temperatures; cloudy sky

Meaning of unknown word: suggested; indicated beforehand

Explanation: In this sentence, the reader is told about three things: low temperatures, a cloudy sky, and a coming snowstorm. If the reader asks, "What is the relationship between these three things?" it makes sense to say that the low temperatures and cloudy sky are signs of the storm. Thus, *foreshadowed* must mean they are signs of, they suggest, they indicate beforehand.

ACTIVITY F: Experience, or Commonsense, Clues

For each word in italics, indicate the clue given in the sentence. Then write the meaning of the italicized word.

1. The judge *exonerated* the prisoner after learning that the man whom the prisoner had been found guilty of critically wounding had made several attempts on the prisoner's life while the prisoner was on probation.

    Experience or commonsense clue: _____

    Meaning of unknown word: _____

2. I was *repulsed* by the stories of conditions in the concentration camps during the Holocaust.

    Experience or commonsense clue: _____

    Meaning of unknown word: _____

3. So many employees of the town were going on vacation in July that the mayor had to appoint *surrogate* police officers for the month.

   Experience or commonsense clue: _____

   Meaning of unknown word: _____

4. The *cherished* photographs were wrapped carefully in tissue paper and placed in a velvet-lined trunk, which would be kept safely in the attic.

   Experience or commonsense clue: _____

   Meaning of unknown word: _____

5. Using statistics from last year, the World Wildlife Fund has been able to *conjecture* the rate at which humans will slash and burn tropical forests this year.

   Experience or commonsense clue: _____

   Meaning of unknown word: _____

THINKING ABOUT YOUR READING AND WRITING

ACTIVITY G: Reviewing Context Clues

Review each of the five types of context clues explained in this section. Then answer the following questions.

1. Which of these clues were most familiar to you? _____

_____

_____

2. How can knowledge of these clues help you with your reading? _____

_____

_____

_____

_____

ACTIVITY H: Defining Words without Using a Dictionary

Without the use of a dictionary, define each of the italicized words in the following paragraphs. Then in the space provided, explain how you obtained the definition. In some cases, something other than, or in addition to, context may have helped. If you used context clues, indicate which one(s) helped you.

1. Some people are particularly susceptible to frostbite: the itchy, reddish-blue swellings on fingers and toes that appear in cold weather. They are caused by the superficial blood vessels in the skin constricting excessively, due to poor circulation. Poor diet, insufficient warm clothing, and lack of exercise are also factors. Keeping warm and boosting the circulation by getting exercise will help prevent frostbite, and creams and tablets are available to help treat them. Doctors may describe medication to diabetics, the elderly, or those with arthritis in the hands or feet, to help boost the circulation.

   A. Woodham and D. Peters, *Encyclopedia of Healing Therapies* (New York: Dorling Kindersley, 1997), 249.

   Word to define: *frostbite*
   Your definition: _____
   The process you used: _____

   _____

2. Fat babies have been thought to be healthy ones, which is not necessarily so. Fat babies are sometimes praised for being good babies because they seem to fuss less and are less active than thinner babies. Studies have shown that physical activity is habit forming. If we are in the habit of being active, we feel restless when inactive. If we are inactive and *lethargic,* we feel more comfortable that way. Babies should be encouraged to be active and to play so that they will get into the habit of being dynamic rather than vegetative. This will definitely aid in fat prevention.

   Word to define: *lethargic*
   Your definition: _____
   The process you used: _____

   _____

3. As long as parents don't abuse or neglect their children, U.S. law gives them the authority to make their own decisions about their children's welfare. However, parents' authority is not *absolute.* Children do not have to obey parents who order them to do something dangerous or illegal. Parents who mistreat their children can be charged with child abuse. Moreover, parents cannot allow their children to run wild or do anything they want. If they do, the parents can be charged with contributing to the delinquency of a minor. For example, a father who encourages his son to use drugs could be convicted of this crime.

    Edward T. McMahon et al., *Street Law: A Course in Practical Law,* 3d ed. (St. Paul, MN: West, 1986), 219.

    Word to define: *absolute*
    Your definition: _____
    The process you used: _____

    _____

4. *Palimony* is the name given to support payments made by one ex-lover to another after an unwed couple splits up. In the past when an unwed couple split up, any property went to the person who had legal title to it. In relationships in which one partner was the wage earner and the other was the homemaker, the wage earner got the property. This was because the wage earner "owned" the property acquired through his or her wages.

    Edward T. McMahon et al., *Street Law: A Course in Practical Law,* 3d ed. (St. Paul, MN: West, 1986), 212.

    Word to define: *palimony*
    Your definition: _____
    The process you used: _____

    _____

5. How do animals such as homing pigeons have such an amazing navigational ability? Experiments suggest that many animals use Earth's magnetic field for guidance. People do the same with compasses, and many animals seem to have internal compasses. Embedded in their bodies are tiny crystals of an iron oxide called *lodestone.* Like iron filings attracted to a bar magnet, these

crystals *orient* in the direction of Earth's magnetic poles. By sensing this orientation, homing pigeons can determine the direction to their loft.

Word to define: *lodestone*
Your definition: _____
The process you used: _____

_____

_____

Word to define: *orient*
Your definition: _____
The process you used: _____

_____

_____

6. When a camera with automatic exposure ability is pointed at a subject, the needle of the measuring device of the exposure meter inside the camera will be *deflected* a greater or lesser amount, depending on the brightness. When the release button is *actuated,* a stirrup bar presses against the needle. This holds it immovable and stops the needle. This position of the needle determines the exposure value. Then a scanner arm is moved until it touches the needle. At the other end of the scanner are the devices that set the exposure time and the aperture.

    Adapted from *The Way Things Work: An Illustrated Encyclopedia of Technology* (New York: Simon & Schuster, 1967), 176.

    Word to define: *deflected*
    Your definition: _____
    The process you used: _____

    _____

    _____

    Word to define: *actuated*
    Your definition: _____
    The process you used: _____

    _____

    _____

7. Sooner or later, the *validity* of scientific claims is settled by referring to observations of phenomena. Scientists, therefore, concentrate on getting accurate data. They obtain this evidence by observations and measurements taken in situations that range from natural settings, such as a forest, to completely *contrived* ones, such as the laboratory. To make their observations, scientists use their own senses. They also use instruments that enhance those senses, such as microscopes, and instruments that tap characteristics quite different from what humans can sense, such as magnetic fields. Scientists observe *passively* (earthquakes, bird migrations), make collections (rocks, shells), and actively probe the world (as by boring into the earth's crust or administering experimental medicines).

   Adapted from American Association for the Advancement of Sciences, "The Nature of Science," in *Project 2061: Science for All Americans* (Washington, DC: Author, 1989), 26.

   Word to define: *validity*
   Your definition: _____
   The process you used: _____

   _____

   Word to define: *contrived*
   Your definition: _____
   The process you used: _____

   _____

   Word to define: *passively*
   Your definition: _____
   The process you used: _____

   _____

8. When the street people first appeared in force a decade or so ago, they inspired shouts of *dismay* and calls for action. Cities hurriedly opened shelters; churches converted their basements into temporary dormitories; soup kitchens doubled their seating capacity. When the problem only grew worse, city officials across the nation sought to drive beggars from their tunnels and parks

and public doorways. The homeless became targets; sleeping vagrants were set afire, doused with acid and, in a particularly horrific attack in New York City last Halloween, slashed with a meat cleaver. Finally came *resignation.* After years of running hurdles over bodies in train stations, of being hustled by panhandlers on the street, many urban dwellers moved past pity to *contempt,* and are no longer moved by the suffering they see.

Adapted from Nancy Gibbs, "Answers at Last," *Time,* 17 December 1990, 44.

Word to define: *dismay*
Your definition: _____
The process you used: _____

_____

_____

Word to define: *resignation*
Your definition: _____
The process you used: _____

_____

_____

Word to define: *contempt*
Your definition: _____
The process you used: _____

_____

_____

9. Titles of nobility, or *peerages,* are granted by the king or queen of Great Britain upon the recommendation of the prime minister. In most hereditary peerages, the title passes on to a peer's oldest son, or to his closest male heir if the peer has no son (the other children are considered commoners). The title becomes extinct if there is no male heir. There are some ancient peerages that allow the title to be passed to a daughter if the holder leaves no male descendant. The last hereditary peerage was granted in 1964.

From P. Fargis and S. Bykofsky, eds., *The New York Public Library Desk Reference,* 2d ed. (New York: Prentice Hall, 1993), 391.

Word to define: *peerages*
Your definition: _____

The process you used:_____

_____

_____

WORKING TOGETHER

Compare your responses with those of a partner.

1. Which of your definitions were similar?
2. In what ways were the processes you used for defining words similar or different?
3. What reasons can you give to explain the similarities or differences in the processes you each used for defining words?

Intelligent Use of the Dictionary

Although context clues will enable you to determine the meaning of many unknown words, a good dictionary is still an essential tool for academic success.

There are several different types of "standard" dictionaries, dictionaries that contain alphabetical listings of words along with their pronunciations and definitions. One type, an *unabridged dictionary,* contains a great many words of the language as well as information about the origin and use of words. These huge dictionaries include more than 400,000 words. They are expensive and impractical for everyday use. Libraries typically have at least one unabridged dictionary.

Abridged dictionaries contain about half the number of words as an unabridged one. This type of dictionary serves college students extremely well for a number of reasons. They are usually hard bound, which makes them durable, and they contain all the general vocabulary information you will most likely need for your academic study. Most of the information in this section is based on the typical elements of abridged dictionaries.

There are also *pocket dictionaries.* As the name implies, these are very small and thus are not as useful for students. They have only one-quarter to one-half the number of words found in an abridged dictionary. Because these books are smaller, the definitions are shorter. Pocket dictionaries also contain less information about a word's origin or use. They are a handy spelling reference, though, and students often use pocket dictionaries, along with their own reference materials, when they are writing papers.

There are also *specialized dictionaries.* These are devoted to the language of a particular field, such as music or technology. Such a dictionary may become useful to you when you start to take upper-level courses in your major.

A good dictionary is perhaps the most effective tool to use when you want to:

* Define words that cannot be defined from the context
* Check pronunciation
* Verify spellings
* Verify parts of speech
* Verify word usage

Before looking at each of these intelligent uses of the dictionary, you should review some of the basic facts about this learning tool. What prior knowledge do you have about dictionaries? Complete Activity I to find out.

ACTIVITY I: Identifying Your Prior Knowledge about the Dictionary

In this activity are several questions about standard dictionaries. For each, list any information that you already know. Include any details that come to mind, even if they seem unimportant to you.

1. What are some of the things you can learn about an individual word in a dictionary entry in addition to the word's definition(s)? _____

_____

_____

_____

_____

2. How is the information about a word usually sequenced or ordered in a dictionary entry? _____

_____

_____

3. What is a good strategy for locating words in the dictionary? _____

_____

_____

4. What is a good strategy for figuring out how to pronounce words in the dictionary?_____

_____

_____

5. What should you do when more than one meaning is given for a word in the dictionary?_____

_____

_____

6. What else, besides information about individual words, might you find in a good dictionary? _____

_____

_____

WORKING TOGETHER

Share your knowledge with a partner. Add to your answers any information that your partner helped you recall.

How much were you able to recall? Probably quite a bit. You may have mentioned most of the following facts about dictionaries and dictionary entries:

* The word being defined, the *entry word,* is written in boldface type. It is also written to show *end-of-line divisions.* These indicate where to hyphenate if this word must be broken at the end of a line you are writing.

* Entries give the correct pronunciation for the word being defined. *Diacritical markings* are used to show how it is pronounced. Alternative, acceptable pronunciations are also given. A key to the

diacritical markings usually appears at the bottom of the page, with a more detailed explanation in the front matter (the pages preceding the main section of the dictionary).

❋ Dictionary entries also tell the function and usage of the word. A descriptor explains how the defined word usually functions grammatically. You may find, for instance, that the word is usually used as a noun [*n.*] or as an adjective [*adj.*]. This information usually appears immediately following the pronunciation. Words that are no longer used in a language are noted as *obs.,* meaning obsolete. If a word is seldom used, the entry reads *archaic.* In some cases, the entry about usage may indicate that a word's use is limited to a specific region of the United States (such as [New Eng] or [Northwest]) or to another part of the world (such as [chiefly Irish] or [Brit]). Word usage comments also may inform you that a word is *slang* or *nonstandard.* Words or expressions that are slang, such as the expression *main squeeze,* are used only for very informal writing or speaking situations. If the descriptor *nonstan* appears in the entry, it means that the word is disapproved by many people. Try to avoid using slang and nonstandard words in your formal writing assignments.

❋ Entries also inform you about word origin, or *etymology.* Often, you can understand the current usage of a word by knowing the word's history. Abbreviations are used to show the origins, the most common of which are [Gk.] Greek; [Lat.] Latin; [ME] Middle English; [OE] Old English. If the exact date or century when the word was first used in a particular way is known, this information may be shown in parentheses, as in (12c) or (1599). If the word is no longer in use, the period when it was used may be indicated.

❋ The definition, or definitions, of a word is of course also part of the entry. Some words have multiple meanings. The entry gives all of these; you will then need to refer to the context in which the word was used so as to determine the appropriate meaning for your purposes. In some dictionaries, synonyms for the word are noted as well.

❋ *Inflected* forms of the entry word are often included. This part of the entry shows how the word is written in another form, as in a different tense or number. The entire word with the changed inflection is sometimes completely written. For instance, the inflected forms for the word *carry* may be shown as *carried, carrying.* Sometimes, though, only the added portion is shown, as in *-ried; rying.* An inflected form may also be listed as a separate entry.

The following model illustrates how these parts of entries are arranged in one abridged dictionary for the word *collect.* Note that there are two different entries, each for a different part of speech. As you study this entry, note any additional information about dictionary entries that you did not have on your original list in Activity I.

❋ Dictionaries may vary slightly in the order in which the entry contents appear, but the pronunciation, part of speech of the defined word, and word origin are always near the beginning of the entry.

❋ You also probably noted in your answers to Activity I that *guide words* appear at the top of each page of a dictionary. Guide words show the first and last words on the page and enable you to locate words quickly.

❋ Many abridged dictionaries also include some very useful and interesting information in sections that are set apart from the definitions portion of the book. Within a single abridged dictionary, you may find such sections as:

❋ The English language (a history of its development)

❋ Common Abbreviations (this section may also include symbols for chemical elements)

❋ Foreign Words and Phrases

❋ Biographical Names (names of notable persons, both living and dead)

❋ Geographical Names (this section often includes basic information about the countries of the world and their most important regions, cities, and physical features)

❋ Signs and Symbols (especially those used in the sciences and math)

❋ A Handbook of Style (which discusses general rules for punctuation and grammar as well as models for writing bibliographies)

Dictionary entry:

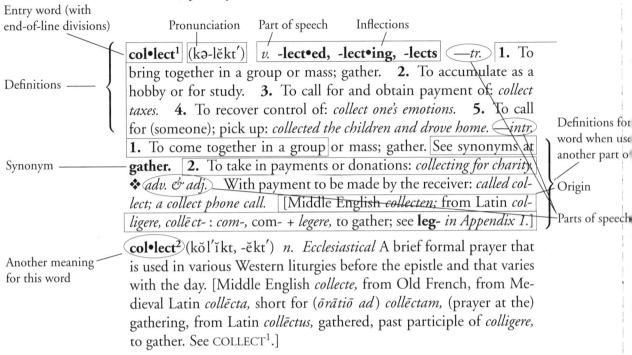

Entry word (with end-of-line divisions)

Pronunciation

Part of speech

Inflections

Definitions

Synonym

Another meaning for this word

Definitions for word when used another part of

Origin

Parts of speech

col•lect¹ (kə-lĕkt′) *v.* **-lect•ed, -lect•ing, -lects** —*tr.* **1.** To bring together in a group or mass; gather. **2.** To accumulate as a hobby or for study. **3.** To call for and obtain payment of: *collect taxes.* **4.** To recover control of: *collect one's emotions.* **5.** To call for (someone); pick up: *collected the children and drove home.* —*intr.* **1.** To come together in a group or mass; gather. See synonyms at **gather.** **2.** To take in payments or donations: *collecting for charity.* ❖ *adv. & adj.* With payment to be made by the receiver: *called collect; a collect phone call.* [Middle English *collecten;* from Latin *colligere, collēct-* : *com-*, com- + *legere*, to gather; see **leg-** *in Appendix I.*]

col•lect² (kŏl′ĭkt, -ĕkt′) *n. Ecclesiastical* A brief formal prayer that is used in various Western liturgies before the epistle and that varies with the day. [Middle English *collecte*, from Old French, from Medieval Latin *collēcta*, short for (*ōrātiō ad*) *collēctam*, (prayer at the) gathering, from Latin *collēctus*, gathered, past participle of *colligere*, to gather. See COLLECT¹.]

❖   Forms of Address (which show the title to use in letters to officials in various capacities, such as an archbishop or ambassador)

ACTIVITY J: Recognizing Functions of Entries in Dictionaries

Here are some dictionary entries from an abridged dictionary. Several items on the entry have been labeled with a letter. In the space provided, identify the function of each lettered item.

(a)

1. **tres•pass** (trĕs′pəs, -păs′) *intr.v.* **-passed, -pass•ing, -pass•es**
   1. To commit an offense or a sin; transgress or err. **2.** *Law* To commit an unlawful injury to the person, property, or rights of another, with actual or implied force or violence, especially to enter onto another's land wrongfully. **3.** To infringe on the privacy, time, or attention of another: *"I must . . . not trespass too far on the patience of a good-natured critic"* (Henry Fielding). ❖ *n.*

(trĕs'păs', -pəs) **1.** Transgression of a moral or social law, code, or duty. **2.** *Law* **a.** The act of trespassing. **b.** A suit brought for trespassing. **3.** An intrusion or infringement on another. See synonyms at **breach.** (Middle English *trespassen,* from Old French *trespasser* : *tres-,* over (from Latin *trāns-*; see TRANS-) + *passer,* to pass; see PASS.] —**tres'pass•er** *n.*

(b)

(c)

a. _____

b. _____

c. _____

(a)

2. **in•ta•glio** (ĭn-tāl'yō, -täl'-) *n., pl.* **-glios** **1a.** A figure or design carved into or beneath the surface of hard metal or stone.
b. The art or process of carving a design in this manner. **2.** A
gemstone carved in intaglio. **3.** Printing done with a plate bearing an image in intaglio. **4.** A die incised so as to produce a design in relief. [Italian, from *intagliare,* to engrave : *in-,* in (from
Latin; see IN–²) + *tagliare,* to cut (from Vulgar Latin **talliāre,*
from Late Latin *tāliāre;* see TAILOR).]

(b)

(c)

a. _____

b. _____

c. _____

(a) (b)

3. **har•mo•ny** (här'mə-nē) *n., pl.* **-nies** **1.** Agreement in feeling
or opinion; accord: *live in harmony.* **2.** A pleasing combination
of elements in a whole: *the order and harmony of the universe.* See

(c) synonyms at **proportion.** **3.** *Music* **a.** The study of the struc-
ter, progression, and relation of chords. **b.** Simultaneous combination of notes in a chord. **c.** The structure of a work or passage
as considered from the point of view of its chordal characteristics
and relationships. **d.** A combination of sounds considered pleasing to the ear. **4.** A collation of parallel passages, especially from
the Gospels, with a commentary demonstrating their con-
sonance and explaining their discrepancies. [Middle English
armonie, from Old French, from Latin *harmonia,* from Greek
harmoniā, articulation, agreement, harmony, from *harmos,* joint.
See **ar-** in Appendix I.]

a. _____

b. _____

c. _____

Using the Dictionary to Define Words

Intelligent use of the dictionary for the purpose of defining words means that you can make choices about which words to look up. If you have searched for context clues to meaning within the material you are reading but have not found any, perhaps you should refer to a dictionary. This does not mean that you should look up *every* word you do not know. Your decisions should be guided by your answers to these two questions.

1. Is the word essential to your comprehension of the material? Essential words usually (a) are repeated often in the material, (b) have specific technical definitions, or (c) are important to the main ideas in the material.

   As a general rule of thumb, look up words that cannot be defined through context whenever the flow of ideas is interrupted for you because you do not know the word's meaning or whenever the word is a technical term.

2. Does your text have a glossary that can provide the definition? Glossaries of technical terms are often included in textbooks. When they are, you are better off using the glossary, instead of the dictionary, because the author tells you precisely how a term is being used in *that* text.

Using the Dictionary to Check Pronunciation

Do you need to be able to pronounce every word you read? If your goal is to read material quickly and to obtain meaning, you can temporarily ignore your questions about pronunciation. Keep your reading going and use a temporary pronunciation for the unpronounceable word. When you complete your reading, you can decide whether you should check pronunciation. If you believe that it will be important for you to be able to use the word in class discussions, you should learn how to pronounce it. Knowing the pronunciation of a word will also help you spell it.

Using the Dictionary to Check Spelling

Your instructors will grade your papers, in part, on your spelling and grammar. If too many words are misspelled, the value of your ideas may be overlooked. The dictionary is a wonderful spelling reference. Use it to check spellings whenever you are in doubt. Some students have begun to rely on spelling checkers that are included in many computer word processing programs. Spelling checkers compare the words in a document you write with words in an electronic dictionary that contains as many as 100,000 words. Additional words usually can be added by the user. The spelling checker runs through your document, comparing each word to the words in the dictionary. If a match is found, it moves on to check the next word. If it does not find a match, the spelling checker either marks the word for later correction or asks the user to correct the error immediately. Some programs even offer suggested corrections, guessing at what the word is supposed to be. Spelling checkers have limitations, though, and should be used with caution. For instance, if the word *are* was typed instead of *art,* the spelling checker would not catch the error because both are legitimate words.

Adapted from Helene G. Kershner, "Using the Dictionary to Check Spelling," in *Computer Literacy,* 2d ed. (Boston: Heath, 1992), 302.

Using the Dictionary to Check Word Usage

Every adult has four vocabularies: speaking, reading, listening, and writing. As adults, our speaking and writing vocabularies tend to be smaller than our reading and listening vocabularies. Thus, the words we use in our writing are ones we already have in our listening vocabulary. If you are uncertain whether a word can be used in a particular form, perhaps as an adjective, you will need to decide if this use of the word is correct. The first way to verify usage is to listen to how the word sounds in the sentence and form you intend to use. If it sounds correct to you, it probably is. If you are still uncertain, though, check the dictionary. A pocket dictionary may not give you this information; you may need to use either an abridged or an unabridged one.

THINKING ABOUT YOUR READING AND WRITING

ACTIVITY K: Personal Use of the Dictionary

Under what circumstances might you use a dictionary, even if you can define a word from the context? List any situations you can think of.

Word Structure: A Clue to Word Meaning

Anyone who is learning a second language knows the advantages of studying a new language that contains some words similar to ones in his or her native language. When words of different languages share a common *root,* it is easier to predict the meaning of the foreign word. Similarly, if you know the most common roots of your own language, as well as the most common *prefixes* and *suffixes,* you can often use this information to correctly guess the meaning of unknown words.

You are probably already familiar with the terms *root, prefix,* and *suffix;* these are the elements of a word's structure. To determine some of your knowledge, and to see how this information can be useful to you, complete Activity L.

ACTIVITY L: Recognizing and Using Word Structure

For each word listed, (a) identify the prefix, root, and suffix, as indicated, and provide a definition for the word. Then (b) think of another word with the same prefix and write its definition; then think of another word with the same root and write its definition. Your definitions may be approximations. If you can't answer one part of the question, continue to the next. Answers to later questions may help you with earlier ones you did not know. Write your answers in the space provided.

Example: *autograph*

    a. ***Prefix:*** auto [Gk.]

       Prefix meaning: self; same

       Root: *graphein* [Gk.]

       Root meaning: to write

       Suffix: ing

       Suffix: an action meaning

       Definition of this word: writing one's own signature or handwriting

    b. ***Another word with the same prefix:*** automobile

       Its definition: a self-propelled passenger vehicle

       Another word with the same root: photograph [noun]

       Its definition: an image, especially positive print, recorded by a camera and reproduced on a photo-sensitive surface

1. *monotonous*

a. Prefix: _____

  Prefix meaning: _____

  Root: _____

  Root meaning: _____

  Suffix: _____

  Suffix meaning: _____

  Definition of this word: _____

b. Another word with the same prefix: _____

  Its definition: _____

Another word with the same root: _____

Its definition: _____

2. *invisible*

a. Prefix: _____

Prefix meaning: _____

Root: _____

Root meaning: _____

Suffix: _____

Suffix meaning: _____

Definition of this word: _____

b. Another word with the same prefix: _____

Its definition: _____

Another word with the same root: _____

Its definition: _____

3. *prediction*

a. Prefix: _____

Prefix meaning: _____

Root: _____

Root meaning: _____

Suffix: _____

Suffix meaning: _____

Definition of this word: _____

b. Another word with the same prefix: _____

Its definition: _____

Another word with the same root: _____

Its definition: _____

4. *tricycle*

a. Prefix: _____

Prefix meaning: _____

Root: _____

Root meaning: _____

Definition of this word: _____

b. Another word with the same prefix: _____

Its definition: _____

Another word with the same root: _____

Its definition: _____

THINKING ABOUT YOUR READING AND WRITING

ACTIVITY M: Your Conclusions about Word Structure

What conclusions can you now draw about using word structure to help you with meanings of unknown words?

_____

_____

_____

_____

You probably now realize the importance of prefixes, suffixes, and roots. The root is the basic unit of a word. It determines the meaning of the word. Many root words have their origins in Greek and Latin. The combination of prefixes and suffixes that are attached to the root create other words. These are always some variation of the root word. Note how, in the example that follows, the meaning of the root *scribere* remains central to the meaning of a wide number of other words in which it appears. All of the words, in one way or another, have to do with writing.

root:	*scribere* [Lat.], to write
scribe	[n.] a public clerk or secretary, especially in ancient times; a professional copyist of manuscripts
	[v.] to work as a scribe; write
transcribe	to make a full written or typewritten copy of
subscribe	to pledge or contribute a sum of money; to sign (one's name) at the end of a document
inscribe	to write, print, carve, or engrave (words or letters) in or on a surface
describe	to give an account of, in speech or writing
prescribe	to set down as a rule or guide; to order the use of (a medicine or other treatment)

All the examples above have one prefix before the root. It is also possible for a word to have more than one prefix. When this occurs, the meaning of each prefix is needed to arrive at the complete meaning of the word. Note how the prefixes are combined for meaning in the following examples. The original root word is also indicated.

redistribute	to distribute again in a different way; reallocate
	re: again; anew
	dis: not; undo; the opposite of
	root: *tribuere* [Lat.], to pay
undiscernible	unable to perceive with the eyes or intellect; unable to recognize as distinct
	un: not; opposite of
	dis: not; undo; the opposite of
	root: *cernere* [Lat.], to see; to perceive
preadmit	to entitle to early entrance (as to a concert)
	pre: earlier; before; prior to

                ad: to; toward

                root: *mittere* [Lat.], to send

inconclusive   not conclusive

                in: not

                con: together; with; jointly

                root: *claudere* [Lat.], to close

The suffix appears at the end of a word. Suffixes often serve to change the form of the word, as in this example:

animate	to give life to; fill with life
animated	having life; filled with activity, vigor or spirit
animation	the act, process, or result of imparting life, interest, spirit, motion, or activity
animatedly	in a lively or active way

When you are reading, you may find a word that is unfamiliar to you but that has a familiar word part. Your knowledge of word parts can help you determine the unknown word's meaning. Certain academic subjects, particularly some of the sciences, have many words that share a common prefix or root. If you learn some of the most common prefixes and roots in the subjects you study, you will have a good start at defining many unfamiliar words. For instance, the prefix *gen* is used often in biology or in courses dealing with the human body. The examples that follow illustrate how this prefix is sometimes used.

prefix: *gen;* also *gene* [Fr.]; also *genes* [Gk.]

words: **gene**   a hereditary unit that occupies a specific location on a chromosome and determines a particular characteristic in an organism

genetic engineering   scientific alteration of the structure of genetic material in a living organism

genetic map   a graphical representation of the arrangement of genes or mutable sites on a chromosome

genetics   the branch of biology that deals with the heredity

genotype   the genetic constitution of an organism or a group of organisms

Some roots, prefixes, and suffixes appear quite often in academic texts. These word parts can be combined into a small number of *master words* that, if memorized, can serve as a reference tool for you for new words.

The following list contains fourteen master words, each of which has a prefix and a root that form a part of many words in the English language. In fact, if you learn this chart, you will have the key to unlocking the meanings of more than 100,000 words!

ACTIVITY N: Applying Your Knowledge of Word Structure

Review the Key to 100,000 Words on page 77. Then in the space provided, write any other words you know that have the same prefix or root as the master word. Write your definitions for each word. Develop your definitions from your knowledge of word parts as well as from your prior experience with using each word.

MASTER WORD	DEFINITION	WORD YOU KNOW	DEFINITION

KEY TO 100,000 WORDS

Prefix	In Other Spellings	Its Meaning	Master Words	Root	Its Other Spellings	Its Meaning
1. *de-*	—	down or away	detain	*tain*	*ten, tin*	have, hold
2. *inter-*	—	between	intermittent	*mitt*	*miss, mis, mit*	send
3. *pre-*	—	before	precept	*cept*	*cap, capt, ceiv, cip, ceit*	take or seize
4. *ob-*	*oc, of, op*	to, toward, against	offer	*fer*	*lat, lay*	carry, bear
5. *in-*	*il, im, ir*	into	insist	*sist*	*sta*	stand endure
6. *mono-*	—	one, alone	monograph	*graph*	—	write
7. *epi-*	—	over, upon, beside	epilogue	*log*	*ology*	speech science
8. *ad-*	*a, ad, ag, al, an, ap, ar, as, at*	to, toward	aspect	*spect*	*spec, spi*	look
9. *un-* *com-*	— *co, col, con, cor*	not with, together	uncomplicated	*plic*	*play, plex, ploy, ply*	fold bend
10. *non-* *ex-*	— *e, ef*	not out, formerly	nonextended	*tend*	*tens, tent*	stretch
11. *re-* *pro-*	— —	back, again forward, in favor of	reproduction	*duct*	*duc, duit*	lead, make shape
12. *in-* *dis-*	*il, im, ir* *di, dif*	not apart from	indisposed	*pos*	*pound, pon, post*	put place
13. *over-* *sub-*	— *suc, suf, sur, sus*	above under	oversufficient	*fic*	*fac, fact fash, feat*	make, do
14. *mis-* *trans-*	— *tra, tran*	wrong(ly) across, beyond	mistranscribe	*scribe*	*script, scriv*	write

Source: Paul D. Leedy, "Key to 100,000 Words," in *A Key to Better Reading* (New York: McGraw-Hill, 1968), 19.

▶ Chapter Summary

Based on your reading of this chapter, list at least five ideas that you believe will help you with future reading assignments. Write in complete sentences.

1. _____

_____

_____

_____

2. _____

_____

_____

_____

3. _____

_____

_____

_____

4. _____

_____

_____

5. _____

_____

_____

_____

▶ *Extended Application*

Now that you have worked with the strategies necessary for using contextual clues and other strategies for increasing vocabulary, you can practice applying them to full-length reading selections. Choose (or your instructor may choose) a reading selection from Part 2 of this book that is typical of what you will be expected to read for your other college courses, such as an essay or a textbook chapter. Use this selection to practice:

- ❋ Identifying a variety of contextual clues
- ❋ Getting meanings of words from context
- ❋ Using the dictionary for a variety of purposes
- ❋ Determining meanings from word structure

Decide on the practice strategies you will use. Apply them to your selection. Then, in a few paragraphs, write a description of what you did and how the strategies you used worked for you.

Name of material used: _____

Page numbers: _____

Your description: _____

CHAPTER THREE

Strategies for Recognizing and Remembering Subtopics and Main Ideas

HAVE YOU EVER TRIED TO put together a jigsaw puzzle? Some people find them extremely frustrating. There are so many pieces! The key to success is to figure out the relationship of each piece to all the other pieces of the puzzle. For instance, if your puzzle is a seascape, some pieces will be part of the sky, others part of the ocean. One major help provided is the puzzle box cover. This gives you the whole picture; it tells you what the final product should look like. Some puzzlers use the box cover picture to help them cluster the pieces in piles related to a particular section of the puzzle, such as the sky.

In some ways, comprehending texts is like working a jigsaw puzzle. There are many details, topics, and main ideas. Good readers need to figure out how the various parts of the text are related to each other. To do this, they usually sort out the topics and main ideas and think about how the details within the text are related to these. This chapter and the next introduce you to strategies for accomplishing this task.

What's the first thing you do when you turn on your television? Do you start your viewing by switching channels? If you do, you are not alone. You probably want to know the different possibilities on TV and how much they interest you before you make your final choice. Most of us channel-surf our TVs to find the topic most appealing to us. A channel that has few viewers will probably go off the air. Authors, like television producers, must find ways to appeal to their audience. When authors choose topics that are interesting to their readers, their readers stay tuned to the text a little longer. Sometimes, though, it is difficult for readers to figure out what the topic is. When this occurs, how can you know if the text will interest you? This section shows you some strategies for identifying topics in any type of reading material. You will then be able to make more informed choices about your reading.

What is the Topic of a Reading Selection?

The *topic* is essentially the subject matter the author has chosen to write about. It can be a situation, a feeling, an event, a person, a hobby, a scientific principle, a belief, a particular country, a design element of a piece of art, an exercise routine, a type of plant. Anything. The list is endless. Anything you think about, feel, touch, read about, experience, or hear about can be the topic of a reading selection.

Some topics that college students often read and write about include:

Career choices

Genetic engineering

The economy

Relations with foreign countries

AIDS

Peer pressure

The Underground Railroad

Global warming

Public education

Race relations

Art history

What are some topics you might like to read or write about that aren't listed here? _____

_____

_____

_____

How Can Knowledge of the Topic Help Readers Comprehend?

Knowing the topic of a piece of writing you are preparing to read will help you in a number of ways. First, it will help you stay focused. If you remind yourself periodically of the topic while you are reading, you will have little difficulty staying focused. Even if your mind wanders, it will be easy for you to get back on track. Second, if you know the topic, you will be better able to see how several ideas in a reading selection are connected. All the important ideas will be saying something about the same topic. This will make it easier for you to pick out important ideas from less important ones. Ideas that have little relationship to the topic may have been included to add interest to the material or to serve as examples, but they are of less importance than those ideas that have a clear relationship to the topic. When you know the topic, you are also in a better position to make predictions about the content. You may be able to anticipate some of the subtopics, the smaller but related parts of the topic, that will be discussed. Then you can mentally prepare yourself for your reading. Each of these advantages of knowing the topic is explained more fully in the following sections.

Recognizing Topics and Subtopics

Narrowing the Topic

Topics can be very broad. To write all there is to write about a single topic might take many pages, even volumes. Therefore, writers must decide the general topic to discuss, but they also must choose what aspect of the topic to focus on; that is, they must decide how to narrow the topic. For instance, instead of writing a book about myths from all over the world, one might be written that concentrated only on *Native American Myths.* The author writing this book could then further divide this topic into smaller units, or chapters, such as these:

Tales of Human Creation

Tales of World Creation

Tales of the Sun, Moon, and Stars

Monsters and Monster Slayers

War and the Warrior Code

Tales of Love and Lust

Stories of Animals and People

Ghosts and the Spirit World

As another example, instead of writing a text on all facets of photography, an author might choose to narrow the topic of the book to unique photography tricks. The author might divide this text, titled *Creative Photography,* into the following chapters:

Viewpoints: Wide Angles, Telephotos, and Composition

Color, Grain, and Contrast

Color Effects

Filter Effects

Mixing Images

Adding Color

Photographic Tricks

Even when the topic of a book title sounds very broad, the author narrows the topic by dividing the contents so that there is a particular focus to the book. Not everything about the topic is discussed in the single text. A book titled *American Government,* for instance, is divided into the following chapters. Despite the broad title, the author discusses primarily the *structure* of American government; there is, for example, no chapter with the title "Corruption in American Government," "Women in American Government," or "Government Controls on American Businesses."

Book Title

American Government

Chapters

1. What Should We Know about American Government?
2. The Constitution
3. Federalism
4. Civil Liberties and Civil Rights
5. Public Opinion and the Media
6. Political Parties and Interest Groups
7. Campaigns and Elections
8. Congress
9. The Presidency
10. The Bureaucracy
11. The Judiciary
12. American Government: Continuity and Change

In the preceding examples, a very broad topic has been narrowed to become the topic of an entire book. Further, each chapter focuses on a smaller part of the larger topic. The divisions within books are usually called *chapters*. Divisions within the chapter itself, or within a single article, are usually called *subtopics*.

Recognizing Topics by Previewing

Recall our discussion of previewing in Chapter 1. Previewing is a particularly useful strategy when you begin a new reading assignment. As the examples above illustrate, previewing titles and subtitles of a textbook chapter, essay, or magazine article will provide you with an outline of the author's focus and give you direction for your reading. For example, one chapter title from a text on American government is called "Civil Liberties and Civil Rights." This title is quite broad. Based on it, the chapter could discuss such things as what these terms mean, what the civil rights and liberties of individuals are, how the civil rights and liberties have changed over time, and landmark cases that have given people civil rights and liberties. But the subtitles, listed below, tell you the specific parts of the topic that will actually be discussed in this chapter.

Once you know the title and subtitles, or topic and subtopics, you can identify their connection to each other. Then you are better prepared to do an in-depth reading. This preparation for reading should also be done quickly. Your goal is to be able to answer the question "What about this topic is going to be discussed in this material?" Once you identify the topic, you can use your knowledge of the relationship between title and subtitles, or topics and subtopics, to help you predict the contents of the material.

Example:

Chapter Title
_____

Civil Liberties and Civil Rights

Subtitles
_____

Freedom of Expression

Church and State

Crime and Due Process

Equal Protection of the Laws

As you can see from these subtitles, each mentions one area or aspect of civil liberties or civil rights. We can safely predict that in the "Freedom of Expression" section, the author will discuss the connections between civil liberties and civil rights and freely communicating your ideas to others. Most probably the "Church and State" section will discuss such rights as the freedom of religion. The title and subtitle work together and enable us to predict the nature of the contents we will be reading.

This next example is from a magazine article. Here, too, the topic is fairly broad. We know that the topic is *nutrition*. Consider, though, how the subtitles help you better understand and prepare for the contents of the article because they direct your attention to particular parts of the topic. The explanation following the outline describes the relationship between the topic and subtopics, which is what you will want to think about each time you look at a chapter outline.

Example:

Article Title
_____

Treat Yourself to Nutrition

Subtitles:
_____

From Scarcity to Plenty

The Food We Eat

Nutrition and Disease

Nutrition at Every Age

Everyday Nutrition

Since the article is about how you can enjoy nutrition, you can expect that each subtitled section will say something about that. You may not be certain what the first section is about, but the others are pretty clear. The section titled "The Food We Eat" will probably discuss the typical diets we have and may mention their nutritional value (or absence of it). The section on "Nutrition and Disease" will obviously give information about the role good eating plays in staying healthy. By looking for these connections, even before you begin reading in depth, you can have a good idea of the direction the text will take, and you can prepare mentally for the rest of it.

There are many other clues to a topic of a selection that you can look for while you preview, in addition to the title and subtitles. These are introductory and concluding paragraphs, chapter questions, and visual aids. Previewing a chapter or article for the purpose of identifying the topic should be done at a rapid reading rate. You are not trying to learn the details or even the main idea. Your goal at this point is to be able to answer the question "What is this about?"

ACTIVITY A: Identifying Topic and Subtopic Relationships

Below are lists of topics and subtopics that might be found in textbook chapters. For each list, identify the topic (T) and subtopics (S). In your own words, explain how the topic and subtopic are related to each other.

List 1

____ Sole Proprietorships   ____ Corporations

____ Partnerships   ____ Other Forms of Ownership

____ Forms of Business Ownership

In your own words, explain the relationship between the topic and subtopics in the list.

_____

_____

_____

List 2

____ African Music   ____ Visual and Musical Arts

____ Figurines and Other Objects   of West Africa

____ Masks and Headpieces   ____ Festival of the Tohossou

In your own words, explain the relationship between the topic and subtopics in this list.

_____

_____

_____

List 3

____ The Importance of Memory   ____ Uncommon Memory

____ Aging and Memory   Conditions

____ Memory   ____ Improving Memory

____ Why People Forget

In your own words, explain the relationship between the topic and subtopics in this list.

_____

_____

_____

THINKING ABOUT YOUR READING AND WRITING

ACTIVITY B: Chapter Subtopics

You have already seen how the chapter on civil liberties was divided for a political science book. What are some subtopics the author might use for the chapter titled "Campaigns and Elections"?

_____

_____

_____

The source from which this chapter is taken actually divides the chapter into the following sections: Political Participation, Historical Voting Patterns, Explaining—and Improving—Turnout, Political Campaigns, The Effects of Campaigns, Opinion and Voting, Election Outcomes, Modern Technology and Political Campaigns, Elections and Money, The Effects of Elections on Policy. Were you able to predict any sections similar to these?

Using Your Prior Knowledge to Make Predictions

Another strategy for identifying topics and subtopics is to use your prior knowledge to make predictions. For instance, if your instructor assigns you to read an article on homelessness, you can use your prior knowledge about this topic before you begin your reading to guess how the author might have narrowed the topic. The chart that follows illustrates the thinking process that might have occurred. On the left are things you might already know about homelessness. You might have spent some time using your prior knowledge to consider how each of these ideas could have been developed into a narrower topic. On the right are some narrowed topics that might have occurred to you. Any one of these topics, or any several of them, might actually be the topic of the assigned reading. Once you begin to read, you will be able to verify your predictions.

Topic: Homelessness

WHAT YOU ALREADY KNOW	NARROWED TOPICS
It is a big problem.	Seriousness of the problem
It occurs in most major cities.	
There is not enough low-income housing.	Cause of the problem
There are not enough places for the mentally ill to live.	
Some of the homeless are drug abusers.	Effects of the problem
Many homeless people have left their families.	
More cities are building shelters for the homeless.	Solutions to the problem

Thinking about all these issues related to homelessness before you read gives you momentum, or intellectual energy, for reading. Once your mind is charged with information, you are ready to go.

This process is similar to starting your car on a cold morning. You can press on the gas pedal immediately, in which case you'd probably experience the sluggishness of your car's cold start. You might even have a number of false starts. Or you can leave your car in park and let the engine idle for a while until it warms up. Then, after a few minutes, you can press on the gas and take off to a smooth start. If you warm up to your reading assignments by tapping into your prior knowledge first, your in-depth reading will go more smoothly.

Looking for Repetition

Even in short reading selections, or those without subtitles or other aids, identifying the topic and subtopics is fairly easy because the author keeps repeating the idea, person, place, or feeling being discussed. For instance, in the paragraph that follows, notice how many times the author refers to *conservation*. Notice, too, that the word *resources* occurs twice.

Conservation involves practicing the most effective use of resources, considering society's present and future needs. One way of conserving is by limiting use of scarce resources. We are now trying to do this with energy sources. Because of legislation and competition, automakers are now producing more fuel-efficient cars, and we are using them less, thus petroleum use is increasing only slightly. Another aspect of conservation is recycling, which is reprocessing used items for further use. Many companies use stationery printed on recycled paper. Alcoa and Reynolds Aluminum pay for used cans, from which new aluminum products can be made more cheaply than from raw materials.

L. Megginson, L. Trueblood, and G. Ross, *Business* (Lexington, MA: Heath, 1985), 47.

The same principle of repetition also applies to longer selections. Thus, a textbook's structure might look like this:

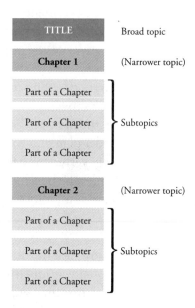

ACTIVITY C: Recognizing Topics in Paragraphs

Read each of the following paragraphs and identify the topics. Use the strategies suggested so far in this chapter.

1. Latitude, or distance from the equator, is measured in degrees. Each parallel of latitude is 1° degree from the parallel next to it. One degree of latitude equals about 69 miles of the earth's surface. Since latitude measurement starts at the equator, the equator is marked 0°. Every other line of latitude is numbered from 1° to 90°. This represents one-fourth of a circle, or one-fourth of 360°. There are 90° between the equator and the North Pole and 90° between the equator and the South Pole. As a result, 90 lines of latitude could be drawn north of the equator or south of the equator on a map of the earth. But this could make the map too crowded, so maps and globes generally show only some lines of the latitude.

    Adapted from G. J. Pelisson, *Mastering Social Studies Skills* (New York: Amsco School Publications, 1982), 198.

Topic: _____

2. If the goverment tries to entrap a person into committing a crime, even if the person commits it, he or she will be found not guilty of the crime. Such was the case of John DeLorean, a wealthy car manufacturer. In 1982 DeLorean was arrested on charges of trying to smuggle cocaine. Videotapes were even made showing DeLorean participating in a criminal act. But in DeLorean's case, government agents had set him up; they devised a plan and then got DeLorean to participate in it. Because the government had deliberately tried to get DeLorean on these charges, he became a victim of entrapment. DeLorean was found not guilty.

Topic: _____

3. "Many Americans are eating out six or seven meals in a week," especially at lunchtime, says Ms. Liebman, author of a study on the nutritional and caloric content of restaurant food. She found that a restaurant meal often has double the number of calories and fat as a similar home-cooked meal. A serving of kung pao

chicken, for instance, contains a hefty 1,620 calories and 76 grams of fat. That's a colossal amount, considering that in an entire day a moderately active adult should consume only 2,000 calories and a maximum of 30 grams of fat. In contrast to the Chinese food, Ms. Liebman says, an average home-cooked dinner of chicken breast, potatoes, and vegetable weighs in at 700 to 800 calories.

R. Alsop, ed., *The Wall Street Journal Almanac* (New York: Ballantine Books, 1998), 768.

Topic: _____

4. In 1968, Arthur Mitchell was at the peak of a successful career as leading dancer with the New York City Ballet. Conscious of the fact that he was still the company's "token" black dancer and that opportunities for others of his race in American ballet were limited, Mitchell decided to devote himself to teaching ballet in Harlem, where he was born, and to create those opportunities by forming a company of his own. This became the Dance Theatre of Harlem. For Mitchell, the Dance Theatre came first; its earliest premises were in a garage whose doors were left open so that passersby could watch and, if they liked, enter and join in. Starting with thirty students, by the end of the first summer, the school had 400.

Adapted from Mary Clarke and David Vaughan, ed., *The Encyclopedia of Dance and Ballet* (New York: Putnam, 1977), 105.

Topic: _____

ACTIVITY D: Composing Questions to Check Comprehension before and during Reading

Based on what you now know about topics, narrowed topics, and subtopics, what are some questions you could ask yourself before reading and during reading? You should ask questions that you believe would be beneficial. That is, the answers to your questions should provide enough information to let you know whether you are comprehending what you are reading.

Before reading, I could ask: _____

_____

_____

_____

During reading, I could ask: _____

_____

_____

_____

WORKING TOGETHER

Compare your ideas with those of a partner. Add any questions that you feel would improve your list.

Being able to identify the topic and subtopics of what you are reading is a good starting point for effective comprehension, but anything you read is *more* than just a listing of topics and subtopics. For example, you are probably familiar with the play *Romeo and Juliet.* If you were asked what it was about and you replied "the deaths of two young lovers," you would be naming the topic, but think about how much you would be leaving out! Authors have major points they want to make about topics. These major points are often called *main ideas.* In this section, you will learn how to identify and restate main ideas in text and how to infer them and create your own main idea sentences when the author doesn't directly state them for you.

Just What is the Main Idea?

Perhaps the most important thing to remember about the main idea is that it is an *idea,* not a single word or phrase. It is *at least one sentence that contains a particular point of view or theory.* Most ideas cannot be stated in a single word. Notice, in the list that follows, the difference between the single word (topics) and the statements (main ideas) about the topics.

Topic	Statement (main idea)
Writing poetry	a. Poetic style and theme are closely related. b. Many different poetic forms can be used to express an idea. c. Good poetry is difficult to write.
Washington, DC	a. There are some wonderful places to visit in Washington, DC. b. Washington, DC has undergone major demographic changes in the last twenty years. c. Some residents of Washington, DC would like their city to have full status as the fifty-first state.
Taking photographs	a. Different lenses will create different photographic effects. b. Photography can be an expensive hobby. c. Doing fashion photography is quite different from taking photos on a trip.

THINKING ABOUT YOUR READING AND WRITING

ACTIVITY E: Distinguishing between Topics and Main Ideas

1. What are some differences that you notice between topics and main ideas? _____

_____

_____

2. What does an author have to think about in order to get from the topic to the main idea? _____

_____

_____

Progressing From Topics to Main Ideas

If your answer to question 2 in Activity E suggested that an author's thinking has to progress from a broad topic to a narrowed topic to the main idea, you are correct. You learned earlier that a broad topic is narrowed when the author selects the part of the topic to discuss. Once that choice is made, the author needs to determine the major or key point to make about it. The result is the main idea. This is the author's *focus.*

If you are able to identify the narrowed topic or focus, you have the starting point for figuring out the author's main idea. This is true no matter what type of material you are reading. To further clarify the relationship between broad topic, narrowed topic, and main idea, let's look at this process from the reader's rather than the author's perspective.

Suppose you read an article whose main idea was that Roseanne Barr's childhood was a difficult one. If someone asked you what you had read about and you said, "Roseanne Barr," you would have stated only the *topic.* If you said "Roseanne Barr's childhood," you would have stated the *narrowed topic* or *focus* and given more information.

But if you went a step further and said you had read about "some of the difficulties Roseanne Barr had when she was growing up," your listener would have a much more accurate picture. You would have been very close to stating the *main idea* of the selection.

Here are two more examples of how broad topics are narrowed, followed by a particular statement about the narrowed topic—that is, the main idea. A different focus is also suggested.

Topic: Sports events

Focus: Pay-per-view television

Author's main idea: Cable television companies benefit considerably from pay-per-view sports events.

Another suggested focus: Ticket scalping

Topic: Commuting to work

Focus: Car pools and commuting to work

Author's main idea: Companies that arrange car pools for their employees have made it easier for people to commute to work.

Another suggested focus: Public transportation

Activity F: Identifying Topics of Main-Idea Sentences

A number of main-idea sentences follow. For each, indicate the broad topic and focus. Then suggest another focus for the same broad topic. It should be one that you think would make for interesting reading.

Example:

Main idea: Antiquing has become an enjoyable pastime for millions of Americans.
Topic: Antiquing
Focus: enjoyable pastime
Your suggested focus: making costly mistakes

1. *Main idea:* Some experts agree that drinking one glass of red wine each day can be beneficial to your health.
   Topic: _____
   Focus: _____
   Your suggested focus: _____

2. *Main idea:* Computer experts can change jobs frequently without risking unemployment.
   Topic: _____
   Focus: _____
   Your suggested focus: _____

3. *Main idea:* Democratic government cannot be based solely on constitutions.
   Topic: _____

Focus: _____

Your suggested focus: _____

4. ***Main Idea:*** _Different parts of the brain serve different functions._

Topic: _____

Focus: _____

Your suggested focus: _____

5. ***Main idea:*** _The Internet is providing new opportunities for teaching and learning._

Topic: _____

Focus: _____

Your suggested focus: _____

6. ***Main idea:*** _Recent investigations into domestic violence have increased the willingness of husbands and wives to file charges against each other._

Topic: _____

Focus: _____

Your suggested focus: _____

ACTIVITY G: Summing It Up

In a sentence or two, explain what you have learned about the relationship between focus and main ideas.

_____

_____

_____

_____

Purposes for Creating Main–Idea Sentences

In Chapter 1 you learned about the importance of putting the author's complicated sentences into your own language. This strategy also applies to main ideas. Main ideas that are directly stated in the material you are reading are sometimes worded in formal language. This can make it hard to remember the main ideas. By restating the main ideas in your own words, you are more likely to retain the information. This is partly because the language is your own and partly because creating a new sentence requires that you think about the meaning of the original statement of the main idea. The following example shows how a main idea can be simplified:

Original main idea:

Many adolescents would like to get through their teen years quickly in order to gain entry into adulthood and many of its benefits.

Student's reworded version:

Many teens are in a great hurry to grow up and gain the benefits of adult life.

Creating your own main-idea sentences will be important in other academic reading situations, including:

* *Reading situations where the main idea is not stated.* Writers frequently state their main ideas in a sentence, sometimes referred to as a *topic sentence.* These often appear as the first or second sentence of a paragraph, but they may be located elsewhere. Sometimes, however, the main idea is not stated at all. When there is no main-idea sentence, you will need to create one to be sure you can explain how the details in the selection are related to one another. The process you use to create a main-idea sentence gives you a chance to verify that you understand what you are reading.

* *Reading situations in which several paragraphs relate to a single main idea.* In these cases, even if the main idea is stated, it will probably appear in only one of the related paragraphs. The other paragraphs may give illustrations or descriptions to support the main idea. In this situation, you should first try to create a main-idea sentence on

your own. Then reread the material to see whether a sentence in the text actually states the main idea. If there is such a sentence and if it has the same meaning as your own sentence, you have verified your comprehension.

❋ *Reading situations where your goal is to comprehend a lengthy essay or article.* In this type of situation, the author may have several main ideas, all of which are tied together by a single *thesis,* or controlling idea. The *thesis statement,* like the main idea, consists of a particular slant, angle, or point of view about the narrowed topic. In fact, thesis statements sound much like main ideas. But the author may discuss the thesis over a number of pages, and it may be developed through a discussion of several main ideas with supporting details for each. In such cases, you will need to look at the entire array of main ideas in the article to see how they are related to one another; then you will need to create your own thesis statement if the author hasn't directly stated one.

The Process for Creating Main-Idea Sentences

The process for creating main-idea sentences is not complicated. To create a main-idea sentence,

1. Identify the narrowed topic or focus of the topic.
2. Decide what is the most important idea the author wants to tell you about this topic or focus.
3. Create a sentence that describes the most important idea the author wants to tell you about this narrowed topic or focus.

You've already practiced the first step in several of the previous exercises. Just keep in mind that identifying the focus is a critical part of creating main ideas.

How do you determine what is most important? The example paragraph that follows also contains several important ideas, all related to a single topic. The paragraph map drawn on page 101 illustrates the relationship. Study the map and then read the explanation beneath it, which describes the connection between the ideas.

Example:

A unique advantage of small businesses is that they develop people as well as goods and services. Their freer, less specialized environment enables employees to strive for more balanced, well-rounded development than they could hope for in larger firms. People in small firms have to be more versatile, and they have a greater variety of work activities than they would if they were working in specialized jobs in larger companies. Instead of just being cogs in the corporate machine, employees have greater freedom to learn by making decisions and living with the results. This freedom, in turn, lends zest and interest to work, trains people to become better leaders, and encourages more effective use of individual talents and energies.

Adapted from Leon C. Megginson, *Business* (Lexington, MA: Heath, 1984), 97.

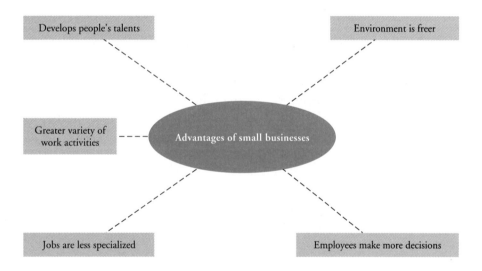

Look at the map and ask yourself: How are these ideas connected? What do they have in common? They obviously have the topic *advantages of small businesses* in common. But the author could have gone in several different directions with this topic. For instance, the author could have discussed the economic advantages of small businesses by describing some of the profit benefits that small businesses have; the author could have focused on the interpersonal relationship advantages that result for people who work in small businesses; or the author could have emphasized the advantages to consumers when they patronize small businesses. Instead, the author has chosen to discuss the advantages of small businesses to the *employees*. The first sentence of the paragraph states this main idea, along with some additional information. The sentence reads, "A unique advantage of small businesses is that they develop people as well as goods and services." Note that the rest of this sentence is not necessary to the main idea. "Goods and services" are not discussed in the paragraph, only the development of people.

You are now ready to create a main-idea sentence for this paragraph. We will use a "main-idea starter" to help you with this. Notice that the starter is a partial sentence that you will complete.

Main-idea starter:

What the author really wants me to understand about the narrowed topic is that_____.

For our example paragraph, your main-idea starter might read this way: *What the author really wants me to understand about the narrowed topic is that* small businesses offer many advantages to their employees. This sentence works as the main idea. In fact, if you put this sentence at the center of the map, instead of the topic that is now there, you would see that it connects to all the other sentences; it ties them together, as this map illustrates.

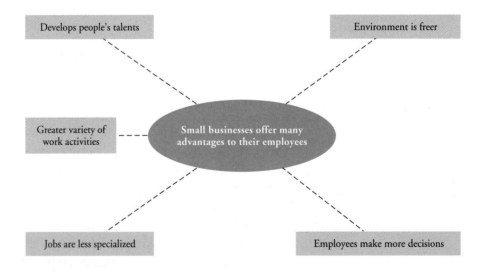

Other Considerations for Creating Main-Idea Sentences

✳ Your main-idea sentence must contain both the topic and the statement the author is making about the topic. This requires that you keep an open mind when you read. If the author's main idea is unusual, or if it differs significantly from your own views, keeping an open mind might be difficult. Your prior knowledge should be used to help you understand the material. And your viewpoints, whether they agree or disagree with the author's, can help you evaluate the author's ideas. But a major goal for students is to learn the information, ideas, and viewpoints presented by the author. At least initially, you will need to set aside your own attitudes and concentrate on determining those of the author.

✳ Since a main idea is an *idea* about the narrowed topic or focus and since ideas are complete thoughts, your main-idea sentence must be a *complete* sentence. Your main-idea sentence, including the starter portion, should read as a complete sentence. A complete sentence should result when you fill in the space that follows the main-idea starter.

What the author really wants me to understand about the focus of the topic is that_____.

This will work only if what you write to follow the main-idea starter fits grammatically with the starter. When you read the entire sentence aloud, including the starter, it must flow naturally, as though you were speaking it. It must sound grammatical. If you begin your completion with a question word (*how, what, why,* and the like), you will not have a complete sentence.

Example:

The author wants me to understand that *many wealthy Americans are choosing to put their money into foreign investments.*

(Not: The author wants me to understand that *how many wealthy Americans are choosing to put their money into foreign investments.*) Remember that whatever you write on the line should be able to serve as a sentence by itself. Using the starter will help you avoid fragments and incomplete sentences.

In summary, to identify main ideas and create main-idea sentences:

1. Identify the broad topic being discussed.
2. Identify the focus.
3. Decide what is the most important thing the author wants to tell you about that focus.
4. Complete the main-idea starter: What the author really wants me to understand about the selected focus of the topic is that:

_____

THINKING ABOUT YOUR READING AND WRITING

ACTIVITY H: Main Ideas in Longer Selections

Finding main ideas is more complicated in longer reading selections than shorter ones. Why do you think this is so?

_____

_____

_____

_____

In your answer, you may have correctly noted that longer reading material often has several main ideas. Or you may have said that sometimes the main idea is not stated, so it must be inferred. (Remember, the main idea might not be stated in shorter essays, either.) Finally, you may have suggested that longer essays could have several main ideas, all or most of which are related to a single thesis. For all these reasons, identifying main ideas in longer selections it is sometimes more difficult. On the other hand, readers are given more information in longer selections than in shorter ones, and this extra information gives you more material to use to verify your thinking about the main ideas.

ACTIVITY I: Creating Main-Idea Sentences

For each of the following paragraphs, identify the broad topic and the focus. Then create a main-idea sentence for each paragraph.

1. The first thing to do when looking for quality child care is to research your state's licensing requirements for child care facilities. If your potential caregiver meets these, you will then want to inspect the child care site. Check for cleanliness, light, noise levels. See if the toys, equipment, and materials are safe and well organized. You will also want to take a peek at the bathrooms, kitchen, playground, and sleeping areas to see that there is no easy route for children to get outside the building without an adult. You should see how other parents relate to the caregivers, too, to see if there is a healthy relationship. In some states, you can call the department that regulates child care to see if the state has been out to inspect the day care site and whether any complaints have been filed against the provider(s). Finally, after you make your selection, ask for a three- or four-week trial period. During this time make an unannounced visit to observe how the child care center operates and how your child is responding in the new environment.

   Adapted from R. Black, "Taking the Fear Out of Choosing a Child Care Provider," *Newsweek Special Advertising Section*, 28 September 1998, 5.

   Topic: _____

   Focus: _____

   Main-idea sentence: _____

   _____

2. The Haymarket incident took place on May 4, 1886, at Chicago's Haymarket Square. It occurred during a peaceful rally to protest the killing three days earlier of six workers who were striking for the eight-hour day. Two hundred policemen were sent in to break up the rally. Before they could, a dynamite bomb of unknown origin exploded. It killed 8 policemen and wounded 65 others. In addition, an undetermined number of civilians were killed. Seven labor leaders were held responsible

and condemned to death. Two had their sentences commuted to life; four were hanged; one killed himself.

Adapted from Barbara Berliner, *The Book of Answers*, (New York: Prentice-Hall, 1990), 11.

Topic: _____

Focus: _____

Main-idea sentence: _____

_____

3. Since biblical times, the branch from the olive tree has been a symbol for peace and prosperity. It is also an extremely useful plant. The leaves have been used to reduce fever and as a mild tranquilizer. The precious oil is an excellent laxative. The pit also stimulates the production of bile in the liver. Externally, it can be used to soothe insect bites, itching, and bruises. Warm olive oil makes a terrific conditioner for dry hair and scalp. Olive oil, high in monounsaturated fats, has received attention recently because of its ability to reduce "bad" cholesterol in the blood-LDLs— without reducing good cholesterol, HDLs. Studies show that people who eat diets high in olive oil have a lower incidence of heart disease than those who eat diets high in other forms of fat.

    Adapted from Earl Mindell, *The Herb Bible* (New York: Simon & Schuster, 1992), 137.

Topic: _____

Focus: _____

Main-idea sentence: _____

_____

4. There was no record of eruptive activity on Tristan da Cunha during historic time, so it was not on the list of active volcanoes. Then in the summer of 1961, some mild earthquakes began shaking in the village. By mid-September they had become more severe. The people began keeping track of them. In one five-day period, they counted eighty-nine shocks. They also found that

the shocks seemed to be localized near the settlement. At the same time, they began to notice other effects. Doors jammed tight and then were released. Walls cracked, then closed. Cracks appeared in the ground, grew bigger, and then closed. Some of the ground cracks were within 600 feet of the nearest house. One crack was rather startling: on one side the ground remained stationary while on the other, it lifted more than ten feet, creating a cliff. The villagers thought some enormous pressure must be forcing up the ground. They were right.

Dan L. Leet and Florence Leet, *Earthquake: Discoveries in Seismology* (New York: Dell, 1964) 111.

Topic: _____

Focus: _____

Main-idea sentence: _____

---

5. Periodontal disease, or pyorrhea, is a bacterial infection. It affects the gum and the bone supporting your teeth. This infection also allows bacteria to enter the bloodstream. In addition to the well-recognized possibility of heart infection in those persons with damaged heart valves, it can also have other serious health effects. It has been demonstrated that in the presence of periodontal disease, there is an increased incidence of coronary artery disease due to an increased clogging of these arteries. Periodontal disease can cause a heart attack! In addition, pregnant women with periodontal disease have an increased incidence of low-birth-weight babies.

Adapted from S. R. Firestone, "Advanced Research Helps Take the Fear Out of Dentistry," *Newsweek Special Advertising Section,* 15 June 1998, 8.

Topic: _____

Focus: _____

Main-idea sentence: _____

---

6. Subtle messages about a culture often appear in the books children read and the stories they hear. For instance, what messages about achievement appear in a culture's literature? Does the story's main character work hard and overcome obstacles (creating expectations of a payoff for persistence)? Or does the character loaf and then win the lottery (suggesting that rewards come randomly regardless of effort)? If the main character succeeds, is this outcome the result of personal initiative, typical of an individualist culture? Or does it illustrate ties to a cooperative and supportive group that is typical of a collectivist culture? Such themes appear to act as blueprints for reaching the goals one should aspire to. In one study, individuals from Saudi Arabia and from the United States were asked to comment on short stories describing people succeeding at various tasks. Saudis tended to see the people in the stories as having succeeded because of the help they got from others. Americans, on the other hand, tended to attribute success to the internal characteristics of each story's main character.

    Adapted from Douglas A. Bernstein and Peggy W. Nash, *Psychology,* 4th ed. (Boston: Houghton Mifflin, 1997), 358.

    Topic: _____

    Focus: _____

    Main-idea sentence: _____

    _____

7. Unlike true physical disabilities, *conversion disorders* tend to appear when a person is under severe stress. They also often help to reduce that stress by enabling the person to avoid unpleasant situations. A third distinction between conversion disorders and true physical disabilities is that the person with the conversion disorder may show remarkably little concern about what is apparently a rather serious problem. Finally, the symptoms may be organically impossible or improbable. For example, one university student experienced visual impairment that began each Sunday evening and became total blindness by Monday morning. Her vision would begin to return on Friday evenings and was

fully restored in time for weekend football games and other social activities. She expressed no undue concern over her condition.

Adapted from Douglas A. Bernstein and Peggy W. Nash, *Psychology*, 4th ed. (Boston: Houghton Mifflin, 1997), 506.

Topic: _____

Focus: _____

Main-idea sentence: _____

_____

8. Pablo Picasso and Georges Braque started adding stuff from the real world to their pictures innocently enough. They stenciled letters in their paintings around 1910. But soon they were adding sand, rope, paper, and anything short of roadkill to their artworks. In 1912, Braque invented *papier colle* (or "glued paper"), using cut-out bits of decorative paper or words or images clipped from newspapers or sheet music. In *Guitar, Sheet Music and Glass,* 1912, Picasso used old wallpaper, fake woodgraining, and colored papers to simulate a guitar; the soundhole of the guitar is just a cutout circle. Active elements—music, drinking, and current events—are suggested by scraps of sheet music, newspaper, and Picasso's own Cubist drawing of a glass. In other collages, Picasso actually glued pieces of rope or imitation chair caning to the canvas. Soon everybody was incorporating real objects into their art, and as the century progressed, things started to get out of hand.

Walter Robinson, *Instant Art History: From Cave Art to Pop Art* (New York: Fawcett Columbine, 1995), 179.

Topic: _____

Focus: _____

Main-idea sentence: _____

_____

9. Law-enforcement officers overheard roughly 2.4 million conversations in 1994 alone, according to an annual government assessment of wiretap activity. (Since all calls on a tapped line are monitored, many if not most of these conversations likely involved no criminal wrongdoing.) The number of federal wiretap orders has lately been increasing by 30 to 40 percent each year, officials estimate. And the government is expanding its surveillance efforts into new areas. In 1996, as part of its settlement of a price-fixing investigation, the Justice Department forced Wall Street securities firms to begin taping a random sample of their traders' conversations. The government also obtains "millions and millions" of records detailing calls made to and from certain phones, "on a very casual basis," according to David Burnham, an investigative journalist, who notes that federal investigators can often obtain the information without the formal court proceedings required for wiretaps.

Adapted from Karim Reed, "The Invasion of Privacy," *Civilization,* 3(5) (1996): 76.

Topic: _____

Focus: _____

Main-idea sentence: _____

_____

10. While the assumption of marriage is permanence, couples who choose to live together but not to marry usually agree to remain together for "as long as it works out." Marriage requires public vows; a judge is needed to authorize its termination. Cohabitation, adults living together in a sexual relationship without being married, has increased about seven times in just over two decades, and about half of the couples who marry have cohabited. Cohabitation requires only that a couple move in together and move out when the relationship sours. Sociologists have found that couples who cohabit before marriage are more likely to divorce than couples who do not first cohabit. The reason, they conclude, is that cohabiting couples have a weaker commitment to marriage and to relationships.

Adapted from James M. Henslin, (1995) *Sociology : A Down-to-Earth Approach,* 2d ed. (Boston: Allyn & Bacon, 1995), 449–50.

Topic: _____

Focus: _____

Main-idea sentence: _____

_____

ACTIVITY J: Creating Main-Idea Maps for Paragraphs

Either on your own or with a small group, select two paragraphs from those in Activity I and create a map that shows the relationship between the main idea and several other sentences in the paragraph. To recall how this is done, refer to the model earlier in this chapter. If you work with a group, you will first need to agree on the main-idea sentence for each of the two paragraphs you choose. You may also see that you need to revise your topic and focus.

1. Paragraph being used _____

Map

2. Paragraph no. _____

Map

♟ WORKING TOGETHER

With a partner, discuss the following chart. What do you think it shows? Write your response in the space beneath the chart.

TOPIC	FOCUS	MAIN IDEA
1. AIDS	1. Prevention	1. People are not practicing safe sex.
2. AIDS	2. Research	2. The money spent on AIDS research significantly increased in the 1990s.
3. AIDS	3. Epidemic	3. AIDS is a global problem.

_____

_____

_____

Testing Your Main-Idea Sentences

Good readers use certain strategies to verify that a main-idea sentence they created really states the main idea of the selection. Making maps, such as you did in Activity J, is a good starting point. But there is even more you can do to make sure your sentence is *a statement of the most important thing the author wants to tell you about the narrowed topic.* You can test your sentence in this way:

1. Determine what questions are raised by your main-idea sentence.
2. Determine whether most of the reading selection's details provide answers to those questions.

A main-idea sentence must be fairly general for it to cause the reader to ask questions. For instance, a sentence such as "It is 93 million miles to the Moon" does not generate many questions. It is too specific. On the other hand, a sentence such as "Scientists have learned much about the relationship of the Moon to Earth" is much broader. It generates questions in the reader's mind such as "What is the relationship?" and "What have scientists learned?" Your ability to distinguish between general and specific statements obviously plays a major role in the quality of the main-idea sentences you create.

ACTIVITY K: Distinguishing between General and Specific Sentences

For each pair of sentences, indicate which is general (G), because it raises questions, and which is specific (S), because it provides at least a partial answer to a question raised by the sentence you said was *general*.

1. Establishing well-baby clinics in every community was one of the suggestions that was under serious consideration. _____
   At a meeting in the White House, the president's top national security advisers considered alternative options for improving health care for infants._____
2. The report said there was substantial evidence that peer pressure can cause students to do better in school than they would do without such pressure._____
   Friends can influence us both negatively and positively._____

3. The college was trying to find a remedy for the shortage in student housing._____
A twelve-story student housing complex was being built in the downtown area._____

4. Just as there are popularity cycles in fashion, there are similar cycles in literature._____
During the last few decades, the "tell-all" story about famous people has been popular._____

5. Most of the advances in electronics, including the ever-smaller chips and faster computers, have been made possible by a process called *photolithography.*_____
Photolithography involves etching intricate electronic circuit designs on microchips by passing a light through a stencil-like mask cut into the shape of the circuit._____

6. Abandoned by his mate shortly after the laying of their egg, the male emperor penguin sits on the egg for two beak-chilling months, huddled together with other forlorn males against the shrieking Antarctic winds._____
Nature is not kind to the male emperor penguin._____

7. Japanese economists were pessimistic about their country's prospects for economic recovery this year._____
Fifty-one percent of the heads of Japan's 100 largest corporations predict that land prices, already down 30 percent in some areas from the previous year, will continue to fall.

8. The act of writing helps people understand things better._____
If you are a student of history and you write about historical theories, data, issues, and problems, you will begin to sort out those theories, data, issues, and problems more clearly._____

The second step for testing your main-idea sentences is to determine whether most of the details of the reading selection provide answers to the questions raised by your sentence. In the next paragraph, the main idea has been underlined. See what questions it brings to mind.

Mobile homes have become more popular as single-family homes have risen in price. However, there are certain drawbacks to mobile home ownership. First, mobile homes are financed more like cars than houses. Mobile home loans are typically for a shorter period than are home mortgages, and buyers are usually charged a higher rate of interest. Second, after buying a mobile home, the owner must find someplace to put it. This is sometimes a problem because many cities restrict the areas where mobile homes may be located. Finally, because some mobile homes are poorly constructed, buyers should carefully check out the dealer's reputation for service and the warranty that accompanies the mobile home.

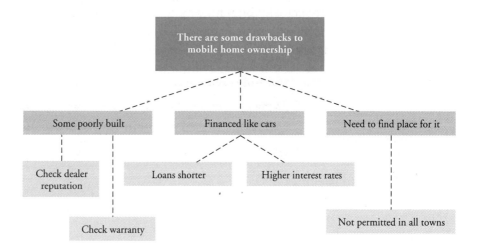

This main-idea sentence raises several questions, including "What are mobile homes?" and "What are the drawbacks to mobile homes?" In the main-idea map for this paragraph, note that the phrases connected directly to the main-idea answer the second question. They are major details that support the main idea. This map verifies that the main idea has been correctly identified. Also included on the map are some minor details that elaborate on the major details. In Chapters 4 and 5, you will learn more about details, as well as some other mapping formats.

You can use the same process for verifying stated main ideas to check any main-idea sentences you infer or create. In the following paragraph, there is no main-idea sentence. One that the reader has inferred and then created has been written beneath the paragraph. In the space provided, write the questions that this main-idea sentence brings to your mind. Then look at the supporting sentences in the paragraph. Ask yourself whether they answer most of the questions generated by the main-idea sentence. Write the answers you find.

Many retailers use handheld tag readers that enter sales information into the register automatically. Some firms are using newer systems that can use the data entered to update inventory and automatically print out purchase orders when new merchandise is needed. Large supermarkets use laser scanners to read the universal product codes printed on almost all grocery items. The sales tape prints out for the customer the items that were actually bought. Simultaneously, the data entered in the computer system help management analyze which products are selling well. Some of the latest systems are even saying, "Thank you for shopping with us."

Main-idea sentence:

Many retailers are using computer-based sales registers.

Questions (based on main-idea sentence):

_____

_____

_____

Answers to your questions provided by this paragraph:

_____

_____

_____

WORKING TOGETHER

Compare your questions with those of a partner. Are they similar? Refer to the paragraph to see whether each of your questions was answered.

What about the main-idea sentences you created in Activity H? Do they raise questions? Are the questions answered by the details in the passage? To test some of your own main-idea sentences, complete Activity L below.

ACTIVITY L: Testing Your Main-Idea Sentences

Return to Activity I, in which you created some original main-idea sentences. Select two of your main-idea sentences. Then, in the spaces provided, (1) indicate the paragraph you are using; (2) write the main-idea sentence you created for that paragraph; (3) write the questions raised by your sentence; (4) write at least two details from the passage that provide answers to your sentence; and (5) if your main-idea sentence does not meet the test, revise your sentence, repeating steps 1 through 3.

1. Paragraph being used _____
   Your original main-idea sentence for that paragraph.

   _____

   _____

   Questions raised by your main-idea sentence.

   _____

   _____

   Answers to your questions provided by the paragraph.

   _____

   _____

   _____

   _____

   Do you need to revise your main-idea sentence? Yes_____ No_____
   (If you answered yes, return to the paragraph and create a new one.
   Then repeat the preceding steps.)

2. Paragraph being used _____
   Your original main-idea sentence for that paragraph.

   _____

   _____

   Questions raised by your main-idea sentence.

   _____

   _____

   Answers to your questions provided by the paragraph.

   _____

   _____

Do you need to revise your main-idea sentence? Yes_____ No_____
(If you answered yes, return to the paragraph and create a new one.
Then repeat the preceding steps.)

THINKING ABOUT YOUR READING AND WRITING

ACTIVITY M: Using Main Ideas to Raise Questions

In your own words, explain the reasons why your main-idea sentence
should raise questions.

_____

_____

_____

_____

_____

_____

▶ *Chapter Summary*

Based on your reading of this chapter, list at least five ideas that you believe will
help you with future reading assignments. Write in complete sentences.

1. _____

_____

_____

2. _____

_____

_____

3. _____

_____

_____

_____

4. _____

_____

_____

_____

5. _____

_____

_____

_____

▶ *Extended Application*

Now that you have worked with the strategies necessary for identifying and re-membering topics and main ideas, practice them with full-length reading se-lections. Choose (or your instructor may choose) a reading selection from Part 2 of this book that is typical of what you will be expected to read for your other college courses, such as an essay or a textbook chapter. Use this selection to practice

  ❋ Composing questions before reading
  ❋ Identifying topics and subtopics
  ❋ Identifying main ideas
  ❋ Creating main ideas
  ❋ Mapping main ideas
  ❋ Composing questions during reading

Decide on the practice strategies you will use. Apply them to your selection. Then, in a few paragraphs, write a description of what you did and how the strategies you used worked for you.

Name of material used: _____

Page numbers: _____

Your description: _____

CHAPTER FOUR

Understanding Details

Your first response to an attractive person might be based on an overall impression; that is, the person may seem well groomed or appear to have a good personality. After a while, you might notice *particular* features of the person, such as an interesting way of dressing, a hairstyle that is particularly suited to the person, or a laugh that has some special sparkle. Readers may experience main ideas and details in much the same way. At first, the reader gets the big picture, the main idea. Then the details might be examined for how they contribute to the total effect of the text. In this chapter, we explore connections between main ideas and details.

Why Are Details Needed?

If you have ever had a conversation with friends who have just returned from a trip, you know that their excitement about their trip is expressed when they give you the details of what they saw, where they went, and so on. Without these details, you might not be convinced that the trip was so terrific. The details are necessary to give the fullest meaning to the statement, "Our vacation was really wonderful." The main idea is supported by the details as the following outline illustrates. Notice how each detail mentions some "wonderful" aspect of the trip.

Main idea:	Our vacation was really wonderful.
Details:	The weather never went above 80 degrees, and it was always sunny.
	Our hotel room overlooked the bay.
	There was so much unusual and delicious food that it was hard to decide what to eat.
	The prices on gold jewelry were so much better than the prices back home.
	The museums and galleries had exhibits of work of the natives from nearby villages

The same principles that apply to sharing information when you speak apply to most of the writing assignments you will have in college, including when you write personal narratives about your experiences, theoretical papers in which you give researched evidence for some idea, and argumentative or persuasive papers in which you provide arguments for or against something. In all cases, support for your ideas is provided by the details. Without the details, your readers would have only the basic statement (the main idea or thesis). Your readers would never fully understand your theory or your experience, nor would they be able to agree or disagree with your arguments. When you read, you want to notice the details and how they contribute to developing the main idea.

Sentences that provide details are usually referred to as *supporting sentences.* They may provide facts and statistics, offer reasons, give examples, add description, give steps or procedures, or in some other way answer questions about the main idea.

ACTIVITY A: Adding Supporting Sentences to Paragraphs

In each of the following paragraphs, the main idea is underlined. To each paragraph, add a sentence of details that you think would lend support for the main idea. Draw an arrow to where in the paragraph this additional sentence of details would go. It should not go at the end or you may find your sentence is a concluding sentence and not a detail. (*Note:* What you add does not have to be true. Use your imagination.)

Example:

Visitors to Hawaii are often surprised to hear that English is not the only language spoken there. Even today, Hawaiians include much of their mother tongue, Hawaiian, in their speech. It is an interesting language to study. It is very musical. It is a dialect of the Polynesian language. Hawaiian contains only twelve letters. Each vowel in a word is pronounced separately and distinctly.

*A **detail** you could add:* The language also uses one of the letters, the letter *h,* in 50 percent of its words.

1. People tend to overrely on doctors for advice about the care of newborns. One study showed that new mothers leaving the hospitals with their babies asked their doctors an average of nine questions about caring for their newborn. Questions ranged from concerns about how to change diapers, to how often to feed the baby. Some parents wanted to know about the proper dress for the infant in various types of weather conditions. A very popular question was "How often shall I feed my baby?" Let's hope these new parents remembered what they were told or sought help elsewhere once they left the hospital.

   *A **detail** you could add:* _____

   _____

2. Sales of hair color for men hit $113.5 million last year, reports Information Resources Inc., triple the amount a decade ago. One in twelve American men today color their hair, according to NFO Research, and they defy the usual stereotypes. A disproportionate number of guys who dye are in their thirties and forties, single or divorced, and lead active social lives. They're more likely than average Americans to work out, go to bars, attend the theater, and take adult education courses (like painting and drawing). They tend to be upper middle class, but not rich enough to let money alone make a first impression.

   From "Father's Day Special: Guys Who Dye," *American Demographics* 21(5) (1999): 20.

   *A **detail** you could add:* _____

   _____

3. Until the Industrial Revolution, workers in Europe were mostly independent. Then they became dependent on someone else— especially absentee owners—for their livelihood. This arrangement led to many abuses since employees were forced to work long hours at hard labor in dingy, windowless, and unventilated factories in return for low pay and no job security. Children

were also unfairly exploited. Children as young as seven years of age were forced to lift heavy loads and work twelve to fourteen hours a day. When workers were hurt in an accident or became too old or sick to work, they were fired, with no pension.

A detail you could add: _____

_____

4. There is a 200-inch telescope at Mount Palomar. Attached to it is a piece of modern genius, a special magnifier called the Charge Coupled Device, or CCD. The CCD improves images or objects in space by gathering light more effectively. For instance, it is possible to see Uranus with its five moons in the distant night sky. The best portrait we have of Neptune was also made with a CCD. It shows major features such as the bright ice-crystal clouds in that planet's northern and southern hemispheres.

A detail you could add: _____

_____

5. Rose Anderson is face down on the examining table. Her blouse is off, her back and shoulders bare except for a purple butterfly hovering over a rose on her right shoulder blade. Poised above her, Dr. Suzanne Linsmeier Kilmer holds what looks like a big black electric toothbrush. As the doc steps on a foot pedal, staccato pulses of green light from the black wand leave BB-size white circles where the butterfly's tiny wing was a second ago. Anderson flinches in pain every time the green laser zaps her flesh. Ten years ago she was sure it would still be cool to have a tattoo when she was 80. "But I didn't think about how I'd feel about it in my late 20s and 30s," says the 32-year-old Sacramento, Calif., education lobbyist. Just a few more sessions of laser torture and the last visible trace of her feral, rebel youth will be a distant memory.

Rick Marin and Dogen Hannah, "Turning In the Badges of Rebellion," *Newsweek,* 6 February 1995, 46.

A detail you could add: _____

_____

THINKING ABOUT YOUR READING AND WRITING

ACTIVITY B: Describing the Process

Describe the process you used to create sentences of details for the paragraphs in Activity A.

_____

_____

_____

_____

WORKING TOGETHER

Share your additional sentences of details with those of a partner. Decide if your sentence and your partner's sentence could both be added to the same paragraph. Could they both be used in the same paragraph? Why or why not? What do you think accounts for this result?

Understanding Types of Details

Important details in an article or textbook chapter may serve different purposes. Depending on the main idea, authors may include details to

* Offer reasons or arguments
* Provide description
* Outline steps or procedures
* Give single or multiple examples or illustrations
* Cite facts or statistics

It is also possible that within a single paragraph, the author will use a combination of these types of details in order to lend support to the main idea. Notice how these various alternatives have been applied in the following example paragraphs. The main ideas have been underlined.

Details That Offer Reasons or Arguments

According to a new survey, 90 percent of the nation's workers admit to surfing recreational sites during office hours, and bosses are taking a dim view of this. They see it as a profit-eating virus, costing corporate America more than $1 billion a year in wasted computer resources, according to SurfWatch, a maker of software to police cyberabuse. And that doesn't even count the billions of dollars in lost productivity. Along with the time wasting, executives worry that the new technology increasingly helps workers to steal trade secrets in the blink of an e-mail. Personal surfing and e-mailing can also seriously strain a company's computer network. And workers who consume a steady diet of porn in their offices may expose their employers and themselves to sexual-harassment lawsuits. Even short of lawsuits, many co-workers are being placed in uncomfortable situations when they walk in on colleagues who are viewing pornograpy. "As more people get access to the Internet, it's becoming an area of abuse on a wider scale," says Patrick Gnazzo, vice president of business ethics at United Technologies. The Hartford, Conn.–based manufacturing conglomerate has instituted a "rat fink" policy that requires workers to tattle on colleagues who are misusing their computers.

Keith Naughton, Joan Raymond, Ken Shulman, and Diane Struzzi, "Cyberslacking," *Newsweek,* 29 November 1999, 62.

Details That Provide Description

Looking out my window, I clearly knew that I was a long way from home. Outside my window the skyscrapers stood side-by-side against the gray sky. The marble edifice of the art museum I had briefly visited yesterday faced me, and to its left was the post office from which I had mailed the fateful postcard to Sandy saying, "I won't be coming back." Down the street, I could see the shopkeepers beginning to open their stores—so many of them. Not at all like the small-town Main Street to which I had become so accustomed.

Details That Outline Steps or Procedures

Homeowners can do home repair work themselves and save a great deal of money. For instance, hanging wallpaper is not difficult. The first step for hanging wallpaper is to select your pattern. You want to be sure that it does not clash with your floor design. After you have made your selection and it has been delivered to you, you will have to gather the tools you will need for hanging. For prepasted paper, you will need a sponge, scissors, a ruler, an edge roller, and an edge cutter or single-edge razor blade. Next, you should be sure you have a large bucket or a tub filled with water for dipping the paper. You will also need a large table on which you can cut the paper to the proper sizes. Once you have gathered your materials, you can finally begin to hang the paper, starting with an edge of a door and working your way around a room until all the areas have been covered. The process is easy, and the results are very satisfying.

Adapted from Ed Ezor and Jill Lewis, *From Paragraph to Essay: A Process Approach to Beginning College Writing* (New York: McGraw-Hill, 1984), 89.

Details That Give Single or Multiple Examples or Illustrations

SINGLE.   The Swiss psychologist Jean Piaget found that around the age of seven or eight, children reach the step of "concrete operations." This stage is marked by the appearance of an ability that Piaget called *conservation.* An example of conservation is demonstrated with an activity using some beakers and water. Before age seven or eight, children believe that the amount of water in a short, wide glass changes when it is poured into a tall, thin beaker—they think there is more water in the beaker because it is higher, or less because it is thinner. An eight-year-old is able to "conserve" the amount of water and understands it remains constant despite the change in shape.

MULTIPLE.   Social Security has relieved children of the obligation to support their parents. Public schools and various public agencies have taken over many traditional parental responsibilities. In general, the social and economic ties between parents and children and grandchildren have loosened a great deal in America. People are far less likely than they once were to live in extended family units. Age groups have segregated themselves: children in the suburbs, single adults in fashionable city enclaves, older people in the Sunbelt retirement communities. Generations are less dependent on one another than in past decades, and this has allowed Americans pursuing their dreams to focus much more sharply on the present—on their own problems and interests.

Details That Cite Facts or Statistics

In 1986 nearly 11,000 people were employed as registered Washington lobbyists, with 3,750 of these serving as officers of 1,900 trade and professional organizations, including labor unions; another 1,500 employed by individual corporations; and about 2,500 representing organizations ranging from the National Right to Life Association to the Sierra Club. In addition, the six major national political-party committees, three Republican and three Democratic, headquartered in Washington, now employ roughly 1,200 people. And the creation and expansion of such ideological think tanks as the Heritage Foundation, the Center for National Policy, the Urban Institute, the American Enterprise Institute, the Cato Institute, and the Hoover Institution on War, Revolution, and Peace have established whole networks of influential public policy entrepreneurs specializing in media relations and in targeted position papers. The number of special interest groups that have set up offices in Washington, DC, is simply astounding.

Paragraphs That Combine Types of Details

Recent reports indicate that two out of every five women over age thirty-five who are pregnant are now opting for genetic screening. Just ten years ago, this figure was one out of every five. Increasingly, women are opting for genetic screening during pregnancy, screening that enables physicians to detect some fetal abnormalities. The reasons for such increases are perhaps best understood by examining what can be learned from the tests that are done. Tests can reveal the condition of fetuses carried by women known to be at risk for specific diseases—such as women in their late thirties, who are more likely to have a child with Down syndrome, a mental retardation caused by an abnormal number of chromosomes. Another disease that can be detected is Tay-Sachs disease, a fatal degenerative disorder of the nervous system. Doctors can use a number of procedures to make these genetic determinations, including blood examinations, ultrasound imaging, and amniocentesis. One woman reported that because of the early testing her son was able to have a prebirth lifesaving heart operation.

ACTIVITY C: Recognizing Types of Details

In each of the following paragraphs, identify the type of support provided by each of the numbered sentences as

Reasons or arguments

Steps or procedures

Description

Single or multiple examples or illustrations

Facts or statistics

If sentences provide more than one type of support, indicate what combination is being used. Be prepared to justify your answers. The main-idea sentence has been underlined in each case, and an example has been done for you.

Example:

(1) Until the mid-1980s, most states and the federal government had no formal statutes focusing on computer crime. (2) Most computer criminals were charged with illegal use of phone lines. (3) In 1984, at least partially in response to the computer invasions caused by the Milwaukee 414ers, the Federal Computer Fraud and Abuse Act was passed, making it illegal to tamper in any way with the federal government's computer systems. (4) This act was expanded in 1986 to include computer crimes against most private computers. (5) In addition, the 1986 Electronic Communications Privacy Act was passed, making it illegal to intercept electronic information including bank transactions and electronic mail. (6) This new law also made it a federal crime to transfer information obtained through computer

break-ins. (7) Providing others with computer information such as phone numbers, passwords, and the like, became the equivalent of trafficking in stolen goods.

Helene G. Kershner, "Specialized Technology," in *Computer Literacy*, 2nd ed. (Springfield, IL: Heath, 1992), 243.

Type of support provided by sentence (3): Example (of what has happened since the mid-1980s) and reason (why law was passed)

Type of support provided by sentence (5): Example (of what has happened since the mid-1980s)

Type of support provided by sentence (7): Reason (why it is considered a crime)

1. (1) Many questionable claims have been made for vitamin C that haven't been proved entirely. (2) Probably the most widely acclaimed value for vitamin C is that it is a preventive and cure for the common cold when taken in massive doses. (3) Famed chemist Linus Pauling, who wrote a small book on the subject, was largely responsible for this claim. (4) He recommended taking one or two grams of vitamin C a day to prevent colds and four grams a day to cure them. (5) His work was based mainly on subjective feelings about how he felt after he took the vitamin.

Adapted from Norman S. Hoffman, *A New World of Health,* 2d ed. (New York: McGraw-Hill, 1977), 185.

Type of support provided by sentence (2): _____
Type of support provided by sentence (4): _____

2. (1) Many European nations have taken a hard-line approach to cloning and genetic technology. (2) These nations do not even allow genetically engineered food to be imported. (3) In Paris, 19 European nations signed the first international treaty on cloning, agreeing to prevent efforts "to create human beings genetically identical to another human being, whether living or dead." (4) Germany refused to sign. (5) It already had stricter laws forbidding all human embryo research in response to the legacy of Nazi genetic experimentation. (6) Britain, which has traditionally upheld the freedoms of scientific research and is the homeland of Dolly, also refused to sign. (7) It found the terms

of the treaty too restrictive. (8) And in October 1999, the European Union moved to adopt a plan requiring companies to provide information levels on foods if the genetic content of any ingredient contained more than one percent GM material.

Amit Majithia, "The Politics of Cloning," *Harvard International Review* 21(4) (1999): 36.

Type of support provided by sentence (5): _____

Type of support provided by sentence (8): _____

3. (1) In *United States v. Roby,* the Eighth Circuit Court of Appeals allowed the use of a drug detection dog to sniff a hallway of a motel where a suspected narcotics dealer was staying. (2) The police walked the dog through a hallway where they suspected the dealer's room to be located. (3) When the dog alerted on a door, a search warrant was issued for the motel room based on the dog's alert. (4) Ten kilos of cocaine were discovered in the room, and the defendant was convicted of possession with intent to distribute. (5) He appealed, claiming that his expectation of privacy in his room had been violated by the dog sniff. (6) The court found that because no expectation of privacy exists in common areas such as motel hallways, no illegal search occurred.

Adapted from Michael J. Bulzomi, "Drug Detection Dogs," *FBI Law Enforcement Bulletin* 69(1) (2000): 27.

Type of support provided by sentence (2): _____

Type of support provided by sentence (4): _____

4. (1) Does the key to who we are lie in our genes or in our family, friends, and experiences? (2) Studies of twins and advances in molecular biology have uncovered a more significant genetic component to personality than was previously known. (3) This can be traced to a 1979 meeting between a steelworker named Jim Lewis and a clerical worker named Jim Springer. (4) Identical twins separated five weeks after birth, they were raised by families 80 miles apart in Ohio. (5) Reunited 39 years later, they would have strained the credulity of the editors of *Ripley's Believe It or Not.* (6) Not only did both have dark hair, stand six feet tall, and weigh 180 pounds, but they spoke with the same inflections, moved with the same gait, and made the same gestures. Both loved stock car racing and hated baseball. (7) Both married

women named Linda, divorced them, and married women named Betty. (8) Both drove Chevrolets, drank Miller Lite, chain-smoked Salems, and vacationed on the same half-mile stretch of Florida beach. (9) Both had elevated blood pressure, had severe migraines, and had undergone vasectomies. (10) Both bit their nails. Their heart rates, brain waves, and IQs were nearly identical. (11) Their scores on personality tests were as close as if one person had taken the same test twice.

Adapted from George Howe Colt et al., "Were You Born That Way?" *Life,* April 1998, 38.

Type of support provided by sentence (2): _____

Type of support provided by sentence (3): _____

5. (1) Dr. George Cierny III, orthopedic surgeon at Atlanta's St. Joseph's Hospital studied the time it took twenty-nine patients to recuperate from leg-bone surgery. (2) His findings: Patients who smoked regained their ability to walk an average of six months later than nonsmokers. (3) "It may be that people smoking a pack a day mend their broken bones only while they sleep," says Cierny. (4) Research indicates that when a bone fractures, cells near the break produce a fibrous substance called collagen that patches the fissures. (5) The carbon monoxide and nicotine in cigarette smoke limit the amount of oxygen that reaches those cells, hindering their collagen-making ability.

Type of support provided by sentence (1): _____

Type of support provided by sentence (3): _____

Type of support provided by sentence (5): _____

6. (1) As if flying foxes needed any more problems! (2) The bats in Australia have been blamed for creating intolerable levels of noise, a crisis in tourism, blackouts, water contamination, and destruction of municipal parks and reserves. (3) Although members of the bat family, and thus branded forever with the bloodthirsty vampire image, they are gentle, sweet-toothed nectar, blossom, and fruit eaters. (4) Their size doesn't help their image: Flying foxes are the largest of all bats, with wingspans of four feet and bodies the size of small cats. (5) The long and elegant snout of the flying fox resembles its namesake's, but it is not related to the fox, except perhaps by its reputation for cunning.

(6) Their size, odd looks, nocturnal behavior, and sheer numbers have long made humans uneasy. (7) Early 20th-century accounts tell of flying fox "camps" measuring four miles long and a half-mile wide and containing millions of animals. (8) When the large bats took to the air, the sky would blacken, and no human could help but feel frightened.

Adapted from Derek Grzelewski, "Batty about Flying Foxes," *Smithsonian,* May 2000, 100.

Type of support provided by sentence (4):_____

Type of support provided by sentence (6):_____

7. (1) Lionell Portell is eight years old. (2) He has spent 4 hours every day watching TV for seven days per week, since he was two. (3) This is a total of 8,760 hours he has already spent viewing cartoons, sitcoms, and whatever else has attracted his eye. (4) There ought to be a limit on how much television a kid can watch. (5) It's bad for the eyes. (6) It's bad for the brain. (7) Little mental exercise is required. (8) There is an absence of problem solving and creative thinking, and communication is all one way. (9) There are better ways for kids to spend their out-of-school time.

Type of support provided by sentence (2):_____

Type of support provided by sentence (8):_____

Type of support provided by sentence (9):_____

Details as Answers to Questions

In Chapter 3 you learned that main-idea sentences are fairly broad sentences; they are more general than sentences whose primary purpose is to provide details as support for the main idea. Recall also that these broad sentences raise questions in the mind of the reader and that the details often answer them. In Chapter 3 you were able to verify the accuracy of the main-idea sentences you created by comparing details in the paragraphs to the questions raised by your main idea. You knew your main-idea sentence was usable if the details answered some or most of the questions that resulted from your sentence.

You can also use the questions raised by main ideas to predict the content of the details in a reading passage. Since the main idea is often stated near the beginning of a reading selection, after you identify it, spend a few moments thinking about the information that probably will follow. In the next example, the main idea is stated in the first sentence. Before you read the remainder of the paragraph, predict what will follow. What type of information can you expect to proceed from this main idea? Then read the rest of the paragraph to verify your predictions.

Example:

> You may be surprised to learn that Buenos Aires resembles a European capital. At first glance, the comparisons are evident: There are tidy plazas with Rodin statues in them, sidewalk cafés, *prêt-à-porter* windows where beautiful women gaze simultaneously at the clothes and their own reflections. A huge obelisk looms in the middle of the Avenida Nueve de Julio, and on either side are heavy-limbed subtropical trees and Parisian-style office buildings. You are in the heart of South America, but you can drink tap water and eat raw salads, and buy almost any new magazine or exquisite cosmetic. Throughout her convulsive and sometimes bloody history, Buenos Aires has kept her eyes fixed lovingly on Europe.

If you predicted that the example paragraph would contain details about Buenos Aires that illustrate its similarity to European cities, you were of course correct. Your prediction prepared you for the reading ahead and kept you focused while you read.

When you read with a questioning attitude, your goal is to find the relationship between some of the more general sentences in the material you are reading and the remaining sentences. You search for those details that elaborate on the questions raised by the more general sentences. And you understand how those details provide support for the main idea. In Activity D, you will have an opportunity to think about this aspect of the reading process.

ACTIVITY D: Predicting Details from Main-Idea Sentences

In these exercises, the main-idea sentence appears above the paragraph. Beneath this is a space for you to make predictions about the content of the details. Base these on the questions that the main idea raises for you. Make as many predictions as you can. After you read the paragraph, decide how accurate your predictions were. Note this in the space provided below the paragraph. An example has been done for you.

Example:

> *Main-idea sentence:* Francis Bacon was known for his writing, his politics, and his influence on the scientific community.
> *Predicted content of details:* The paragraph will discuss his writing and his politics, as well as how he influenced the scientific community.
>
> Francis Bacon was known for his writing, his politics, and his influence on the scientific community. He was a gifted writer and was recognized as an outstanding essayist. Some scholars also consider him as the true author of the plays attributed to William Shakespeare. Bacon is reported to have been an ambitious and unscrupulous politician. Between 1618 and 1621, he was lord chancellor of England, under James I of England. Convicted of accepting bribes, he was dismissed and died in disgrace. Bacon is perhaps best remembered, however, as an early propagandist for the Scientific Revolution. His *New Organon* (1620), designed to replace Aristotle's logical works (collectively called the *Organon*), called for a new approach to the study of nature. Science for Bacon was the means by which men could gain power over nature and use it for their own purposes. To do this, they needed a new instrument, a new method of approach. This new method was *empiricism.*
>
> Adapted from Mary Ann Frese Witt et al., *The Humanities,* 3rd ed., Vol. 2 (Lexington, MA: Heath, 1989), 8–9.
>
> *Accuracy of your prediction:* The details did discuss what had been predicted.

1. *Main-idea sentence:* How a person handles space in dating others is an obvious and very sensitive indicator of how he or she feels about the other person.

   Predicted content of details: _____

   _____

   How a person handles space in dating others is an obvious and very sensitive indicator of how he or she feels about the other person. On a first date, if a woman sits or stands so close to a man that he is acutely conscious of her physical presence inside the intimate-distance zone, the man usually construes it to mean that she is encouraging him. However, before the man starts moving in on the woman, he should be sure what message she's really sending; otherwise, he risks bruising his ego. What is close to someone of northern European background may be neutral or distant to someone of Italian heritage. Also, a woman sometimes uses space as a way of misleading a man, and there are few things that put men off more than women who communicate contradictory messages, such as women who cuddle up and then act insulted when a man takes the next step.

Edward T. Hall and M. R. Hall, "The Sounds of Silence," *Playboy,* June 1971, 138ff.

Accuracy of your prediction: _____

2. *Main-idea sentence:* The branches of the United States military have well-defined career paths.

   Predicted content of details: _____

   _____

   _____

The branches of the United States military have well-defined career paths. The army, for example, has soldiers visit schools to speak about careers and use videos to introduce young people to the army. After young people have been recruited and enter basic training, they are exposed to a variety of career exploration activities to determine their job choices. As they learn a skill, they are challenged with more advanced training and are able to focus on specific areas. As they progress, the opportunity for promotion, management training, and college courses is available. People entering and progressing in the military model know what is expected at each level of development.

Adapted from Richard Ray, "Four Ways to Save a Floundering Workforce," *Techniques: Making Education & Career Connections* 73(4) (1998): 45.

Accuracy of your prediction: _____

3. *Main-idea sentence:* Today we are most familiar and most comfortable with the quantitiative meaning, for that is the way today's culture initially teaches us to appreciate numbers.

Predicted content of details: _____

_____

_____

As symbols, numbers are unique in that they embody two distinct kinds of meaning. One is quantitative; the other is qualitative. Both meanings give numbers power, but different kinds of power. Today we are most familiar and most comfortable with the quantitative meaning, for that is the way today's culture initially teaches us to appreciate numbers. Early on we learn to count, and that simple accomplishment opens up a conceptual world that we share with other creatures only on the most rudimentary of levels. By the time we complete elementary school, we can add, subtract, multiply, divide, and otherwise put numbers to work for us. We continue thereafter to use the power derived from the quantiative nature of numbers to help us with the practical aspects of our lives. We shop, cook, conduct business, keep track of time, take appropriate amounts of medicine, drive cars, fly airplanes, map out (and pay for) vacations, plant crops, and check our e-mail all because the quantitative power of number assists us. What's more, we pretty much take this power for granted. Sometimes we even complain about it. Ask a struggling college student, for instance, whether she's taking "statistics" or "sadistics" and see what answer you get.

Sarah Voss, "Sacred Qualities," *Parabola* 24(3) (1999): 32.

Accuracy of your prediction: _____

4. *Main-idea sentence:* It is obvious that Yom Kippur is a day that Jews anxiously await.

Predicted content of details: _____

_____

_____

To the Jewish people, Yom Kippur, the Day of Atonement, is the most solemn religious holiday of the year. It is a day of great importance, the day they "heed the call of the shofar" and ask God to forgive them for their sins and transgressions. It is obvious that Yom Kippur is a day that Jews anxiously await. Sociologist David Phillips discovered something extremely interesting about

Yom Kippur and the people who observe it. Studying the mortality records for Jews in New York and Budapest, he found a notable drop in the death rate just before the Day of Atonement. There was no such drop among non-Jews before the High Holy Day. Carrying his investigation further, Phillips also examined the mortality patterns around people's birthdays. What he discovered tied in nicely with his Yom Kippur findings: There was a significant dip in deaths before birthdays and a significant peak in deaths thereafter—which all means, according to Phillips, that "some people look forward to witnessing certain important occasions and are able to put off dying in order to do so."

Lewis Andrews and Marvin Karlins, *Psychology, What's in It for Us?* 2d ed. (New York: Random House, 1975), 147.

Accuracy of your prediction:_____

Major and Minor Details

Have you ever stopped to ask for directions when you were driving to an unfamiliar location? If you have, you are surely aware that some people are better direction givers than others. One factor that can distinguish a good set of directions from a poor set is the kind of information provided. Two different sets of directions for the same destination, a local movie theater, follow. They are being given from the same location, a local gas station. As you read each set, think about which set you prefer, and why.

1. As you leave the station, make a right. Turn left after you pass the Fiesta Food store, which you'll see because it has a new brick facing on it and the prices are really low, and then you go past a school for grades two through five; keep going, but don't turn left yet. You see there's a large ballfield, and across from that is the Central gas station. After that, you come to a red house on the right and a bowling alley next to it. Then there's the first traffic light. Turn left here. Go up about three blocks. You'll see a white mailbox and a sign reading "Katie's Kennels" on the first block. An ice cream store and drug store are on the next block. When you get to the third block, you'll see a big sign saying, "Theater Parking." Go in there, and you'll be at the theater.

2. As you leave from the station, make a right. Turn left at the first traffic light. Go up about three blocks. Then you'll see a big sign saying "Theater Parking." Go in there, and you'll be at the theater.

If you are like most people who ask for directions, you would prefer the second set. It is short, to the point, and easy to remember. In fact, most of the information given in the first set is unnecessary. It is interesting and does help create a picture for you of the town, but to get to the theater all you need to know is what is mentioned in the second set. It contains only the major details, whereas the first set contains many minor details.

WORKING TOGETHER

What are some of the minor details in the first set of directions? With a partner, underline all that you can locate.

A sophisticated reader of textbook material spends time sorting out important details from unimportant ones. As you know, the main idea raises questions in the mind of the reader. Sentences that provide answers to those questions are usually the major-detail sentences. Detail sentences might also raise questions, and answers to them can usually be considered minor details. That is, the major details contribute directly to the main idea. The minor details usually elaborate on some other detail that supports the main idea. The next paragraph illustrates this distinction. In this example, the sentence that states the main idea is underlined. The major details are in italics. Other details are only minor. The major details provide answers to the questions "How?" or "What Ways?" The remaining sentences give specific examples. The map following the paragraph illustrates this relationship.

Example:

The government of post–Soviet Russia owns all health care facilities and all medical equipment and determines how many students will attend the medical schools that it also owns and operates. *The physicians,* most of whom are women, *are government employees,* earning about the same salary as factory workers and high school teachers. *Physicians are not trained well,* and the health of the population has declined in the past two decades.

At this point, the health of post–Soviet Russians is closer to that of China than to first world nations. The only hospitals comparable with those of the United States are the hospitals reserved for the elite. In the rest, basic supplies and equipment are in such short supply that surgical scalpels are resharpened until they break. Sometimes even razor blades are used for surgery. *Although health care is free,* patients have no choice about which doctor they see or where they will be treated. Some hospitals do not even have a doctor on staff. The length of the average hospitals stay is three times longer than it is in the United States. Medical care is so inefficient that the majority of X-ray films are uninterpretable because of poor quality. Some of the radical changes now being introduced in the former Soviet Union include employer-based health insurance.

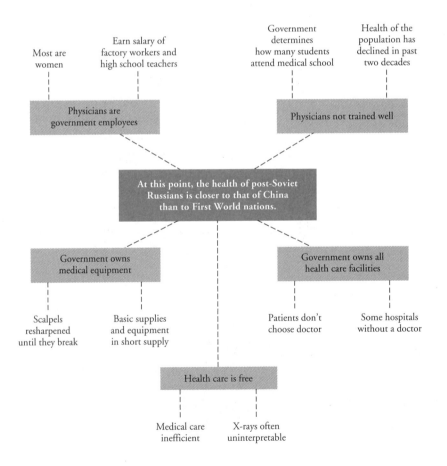

ACTIVITY E: Recognizing Major and Minor Details

Each paragraph includes a stated main idea, which is underlined, as well as sentences containing either major or minor details. In the spaces following the paragraph, write whether each detail listed is major (MAJ) or minor (MIN). Be prepared to justify your answer.

1. When used strategically, camera movement at different angles can enhance the quality and effects of a film. A *pan* (short for panorama) or *panning shot* is a revolving horizontal movement of the camera from left to right or right to left. To achieve this shot, the motion picture camera is mounted on a tripod and simply pivots sideways in either direction to follow the subject. A *tilt* or *tilt shot* is similar to a pan except that the camera moves up and down. In a *tracking shot* (also referred to as a *dolly shot* or *trucking shot*), the camera moves with the subject. The camera is mounted on a *dolly,* a special cart, or on any moving device or vehicle. For a *boom shot,* the camera and its operator are usually placed on a *boom,* a large supporting arm or pole that can move in any direction. Boom shots were used in *Field of Dreams* (1989), so that the audience could see the baseball field from a high angle. In *Honey, I Shrunk the Kids* (1989), directors Joe Johnston and Rob Minkoff used a boom shot to peer through giant blades of grass at shrunken kids struggling to find their way out of their backyard.

   Jan Bone and Ron Johnson, *Understanding the Film,* 5th ed. (Lincolnwood, IL: NTC Publishing Group, 1996), 90.

   a. A *pan* shot involves revolving, horizontal movement. _____

   b. In a *pan* shot, the camera is mounted on a tripod. _____

   c. The *tilt* shot is similar to the *pan* shot. _____

   d. In the *tilt* shot, the camera moves up and down. _____

   e. A *tracking* shot is also referred to as a dolly or trucking shot. _____

   _____

   f. In a *tracking* shot, the camera moves with the subject. _____

   g. A *boom* is a large supporting arm or pole that can move in any direction. _____

   h. Boom shots were used in *Field of Dreams.* _____

2. Nightmares are vivid and terrifying nocturnal episodes in which the dreamer is abruptly awakened from sleep. Typically, the dreamer wakes from REM sleep and is able to describe a detailed, associative, often bizarre dream plot. Usually, the dreamer has difficulty returning to

sleep. Nightmares are also common. In a two-week prospective study of college students, 47 percent described having at least one nightmare. Results of a general population study of 1,049 persons with insomnia revealed that 18.3 percent had nightmares. In this study, nightmares were more common in women and were associated with increases in nocturnal awakenings, sleep-onset insomnia, and daytime memory impairment and anxiety following poor nocturnal sleep. Studies of the general population reveal that 5 to 8 percent of the adult population report a current problem with nightmares. Contrary to popular belief, frequent nightmares in children do not suggest underlying psychopathology.

> Adapted from J. F. Pagel, "Nightmares and Disorders of Dreaming," *American Family Physician* 61(7) (2000): 2037.

a. Nightmares often involve bizarre dream plots. _____

b. The dreamer has difficulty returning to sleep. _____

c. Forty-seven percent of college students described having at least one nightmare. _____

d. Nightmares are more common in women. _____

e. Five to eight percent of the adult population reports current problems. _____

f. The dreamer wakes from REM sleep. _____

g. Nightmares do not suggest psychopathology in children. _____

3. The federal government has initiated no programs for battered women since 1984; and Minnesota, which has one of the most progressive and best-funded abuse prevention programs in the country, spends less to help battered women than to kill mosquitoes. Federal and state funding for battered women's shelters and related services is pitifully short-lived and small. One result is that there are only about a thousand shelters for battered women in the United States. Everywhere, women in need are turned away. In Philadelphia, Women Against Abuse rejects 75 percent of the women who seek shelter. In New York City, Sanctuary for Families turns away one hundred battered women and their children every week. In Seattle, five hundred men are arrested for battering every month, but only thirty-nine shelter beds are available for battered women. In Massachusetts, women's shelters turn away 71 percent of the women in need of shelter and 80 percent of the children. In all areas of the country, demand for temporary shelter, court advocacy, and peer support groups is rising, and budgets are being cut. Some

shelters have had to discontinue support programs for children, while others have had to drop court advocates. Everywhere paid workers have cut their own salaries to make the money stretch farther; many carry on as volunteers. One Midwestern shelter laid off its custodian for lack of funds; later, when the shelter was criticized publicly for being dirty and unsanitary, she wrote to the local newspaper: "Until government and society commit themselves to ending violence in the home, there will always be battered women's shelters, they will always be full and there will always be dishes to wash and bathroom floors to mop. Token laws and band-aid funding are the real problem. If we're looking for solutions, why aren't we putting batterers in shelters and letting the women and children stay at home?"

Ann Jones, *Next Time, She'll Be Dead: Battering and How to Stop It* (Boston: Beacon, 1994), 229–231.

a. There have been no new federal programs for battered women since 1984. _____

b. In New York City, Sanctuary for Families turns away 100 battered women and their children every week. _____

c. In all areas of the country, demand for temporary shelter is rising.

_____

d. Some shelters have had to discontinue support for children. _____

e. One midwestern shelter laid off its custodian for lack of funds. ____

f. Minnesota spends less to help battered women than to kill mosquitos. _____

g. There are only about a thousand shelters for battered women in the United States. _____

h. Everywhere, women in need are turned away. _____

4. Since the beginning of time, it seems, roses have been the flowers of love, the true flowers of Venus. Cleopatra carpeted a room with red rose petals so that their scent would rise above Mark Antony as he walked toward her. Dionysius, the tyrant of Syracuse, filled his house with roses for the frequent compulsory orgies he held with the young women of his city; Nero used millions of the blooms to decorate a hall for a single banquet, and rose water–saturated pigeons fluttered overhead to sprinkle the guests with scent. In fact, roses were so popular in ancient times that they actually became a symbol of the degeneracy of later Roman emperors, and it took the Church, to which the rose became a symbol of purity, to rescue it from oblivion during the Dark Ages. According to

one ancient story, a number of noble Romans were suffocated under tons of rose petals dropped on them during one of Emperor Heliogabalus's orgies. The Romans so loved the flower that they imported bargefuls of rose petals and hips from Egypt, where the growing season was longer, and they believed in the flower's powers so fervently that they used rose water in their fountains. Long before this, the Greek physician Galen had used a full pound of rose oil in a facial cosmetic he invented, and "attar of roses" remains a much-valued cosmetic ingredient to this day. For centuries, the rose has been employed to invoke love in some rather strange ways. Persian women thought that rose water was a philter that would bring back straying lovers; one old Chinese love recipe drunk during the four-month-long rose festivals consisted of prunes, sugar, olives, and rose petals; and colonial ladies made "rose wine" to stimulate their lovers by marinating rose petals in brandy. Finally we have Napoleon's empress Josephine, who, when her teeth turned bad, always carried a rose in her hand with which to cover her mouth when she laughed.

> Robert Hendrickson, *QPB Encyclopedia of Word and Phrase Origins* (New York: Facts on File/Quality Paperback Book Club, 1997), 578–79.

a. Dionysius filled his house with roses for his orgies. _____

b. Roses became a symbol of the degeneracy of later Roman emperors.

_____

c. The Church rescued the rose from oblivion during the Dark Ages.

_____

d. Romans imported rose petals and hips from Egypt. _____

e. Galen used a full pound of rose oil in a facial cosmetic he invented.

_____

f. For centuries, the rose has been employed to invoke love. _____

g. There is a Chinese love recipe that uses rose petals. _____

h. Persian women thought rose water would bring back straying lovers.

_____

5. Joining the migration to the West Coast were "Okies" and "Arkies," many of whom were evicted from their tenant farms during the Depression. They also took to the road to escape the drought that plagued the southern Plains states of Kansas, Colorado, New Mexico, Oklahoma, Arkansas, and Texas, known in the mid-1930s as the Dust Bowl. The Dust Bowl was the result of an environmental tragedy.

For fifteen years, farmers on the southern Plains had bought tens of thousands of tractors and ploughed under millions of acres. In 1930, for instance, there were 66,000 tractors in just one state—Kansas. When the rain stopped in the 1930s, millions of acres of plowed land became vulnerable to the strong winds that caused the dust storms. From 1935 through 1938, 241 dust storms hit the southern Plains. One storm in 1934 carried 300 million tons of dust from the Plains and dropped it on East Coast cities and into the Atlantic Ocean. The tragedy of the Dust Bowl has been ranked as one of the three worst eco-logical mistakes in history.

> Mary Beth Norton, et al., *A People and a Nation: A History of the United States,* brief ed., 4th Ed. (Boston, MA: Houghton Mifflin, 1996), 487.

a. Many "Okies" were evicted from their tenant farms during the Depression. _____

b. The Dust Bowl occurred by droughts in the Plains states. _____

c. The Dust Bowl occurred in the 1930s. _____

d. In 1930 Kansas had 66,000 tractors. _____

e. From 1935 to 1938, 241 dust storms hit the southern Plains. _____

f. One storm carried 300 million tons of dust to East Coast cities and the Atlantic Ocean. _____

g. The plowed land became vulnerable to the strong winds. _____

6. Marie Curie's work began in an unheated, damp, abandoned shed with a roof that leaked in the frequent Paris downpours. Her first notes were dated December 16, 1897, when she began using the piezoquartz elec-trometer invented by her husband, Pierre, and his brother, Jacques, a mineralogy professor. The piezoquartz electrometer measured the feeble electric current emanating from uranium and other substances. Pierre was head of the laboratory at the newly founded School of Industrial Physics and Chemistry in Paris and worked closely with Marie on her research. However, it was Marie who first developed the theory that the *emission of the rays must be a phenomenon coming from within the atom of uranium itself.* That is, the rays were part of the matter, unlike X rays, which are now known to be a form of electromagnetic radiation, and not something absorbed and returned in the form of phosphorescence. She coined the term *radioactivity* from the Latin *radius,* meaning "ray." This simple hypothesis was to become Marie Curie's most important contribution to science, for it opened up the structure of the atom for

others to build on, leading to the unfolding of that structure in the early 20th century.

David Eliot Brody and Arnold R. Brody, *The Science Class you Wish You Had* . . . (New York: Perigee, 1997), 72.

a. Curie began her work in an unheated, damp, abandoned shed. ____

b. Curie first began using the piezoquartz electrometer in 1897.   ____

c. The piezoquartz electrometer measured the electric current emanating from uranium. _____

d. Her husband and his brother invented the piezoquartz electrometer.

_____

e. Marie's husband headed the laboratory at the School of Industrial Physics and Chemistry in Paris. _____

f. Her husband worked closely with Marie on her research. _____

g. Marie coined the term *radioactivity.* _____

h. The term *radioactivity* comes from the Latin *radius,* meaning "ray."

_____

THINKING ABOUT YOUR READING AND WRITING

ACTIVITY F: Understanding Your Thought Process

Describe the thought process you used to determine whether a detail in Activity E was major or minor.

_____

_____

_____

_____

WORKING TOGETHER

With a partner, return to the paragraphs in Activity E. Create maps for two paragraphs that show the relationships between the major and minor details in each.

▶ *Chapter Summary*

Based on your reading of this chapter, list at least five ideas that you believe will help you with future reading assignments. Write in complete sentences.

1. _____

_____

_____

2. _____

_____

_____

3. _____

_____

_____

4. _____

_____

_____

5. _____

_____

_____

▶ *Extended Application*

Now that you have worked with the strategies necessary for understanding details, you can practice applying them to full-length reading selections. Choose (or your instructor may choose) a reading selection from Part 2 of this book that is typical of what you will be expected to read for your other college courses, such as an essay or a textbook chapter. Use this selection to

* ❋ Recognize supporting sentences
* ❋ Understand types of details
* ❋ Understand relationships between main ideas and details
* ❋ Distinguish between major and minor details

Decide on the practice strategies you will use. Apply them to your selection. Then, in a few paragraphs, describe what you did and how the strategies you used worked for you.

Name of material used: _____

Page numbers: _____

Your description: _____

CHAPTER FIVE

Patterns of Organization in Academic Texts

T HINK ABOUT THE LYRICS OF A SONG you enjoy hearing. Is there a clear-cut beginning, a middle, and end to the song? How does one part connect to the next? How does this structure affect your enjoyment of the song?

As composers write music, they consider each section of their musical composition and how it contributes to the total effect that they want to achieve. Certain patterns for organizing music are associated with classical music, others with jazz, rap, and so on. These patterns give the musical score unity. The parts fit together to create a well-coordinated whole.

Writers of prose also need organizational patterns so that the different sections of their text fit together in a way that makes sense. Such a plan is often referred to as the *writer's organization.* In this chapter you learn how writers achieve organization and how this helps them convey their messages to their readers.

Reviewing What You Already Know

You have already learned that a relationship exists between the main idea and the remainder of the text you are reading. You now know that the main idea or thesis provides the focus of the reading material and that details essentially explain, describe, support, or in some other way elaborate on the main idea. Authors of expository text organize their main ideas and details around patterns.

The design of an essay or paragraph, then, might look like the following illustration.

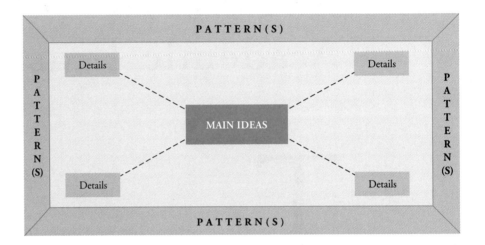

Organizational patterns are extremely beneficial to writers. They provide the framework for connecting the main idea and details of an essay. They help writers assist readers in understanding the development of ideas and stay on the main point. Patterns also help writers achieve variety in their writing and keep audience interest. Writers can choose to organize their ideas in a number of ways. There are six common organizational patterns:

1. Simple listing
2. Definition and explanation
3. Comparison and contrast
4. Thesis and proof *or* opinion and reason
5. Cause and effect
6. Problem and solution

ACTIVITY A: Recognizing What You Already Know about Patterns

In this exercise list any pattern(s) from the list above with which you are familiar. For each one you list, indicate what you know about it or in what kinds of writing situations it might be useful. Also note any signal words you can recall that are associated with the particular pattern. Don't worry if you can't do too much with this activity. Each pattern is explained in this chapter.

1. Pattern I know: _____

   What I know about it: _____

   _____

   Signal words I know for this pattern: _____

   _____

2. Pattern I know: _____

   What I know about it: _____

   _____

   Signal words I know for this pattern: _____

   _____

3. Pattern I know: _____

   What I know about it: _____

   _____

   Signal words I know for this pattern: _____

   _____

A single essay may be structured around one pattern, such as thesis and proof, or comparison and contrast. This is the primary pattern of the essay. But within such an essay, individual paragraphs may have their own patterns or arrangements of details. One paragraph may also contain several patterns, but one pattern may seem more dominant. As you will learn later in this chapter, the author's purpose for writing, along with the main idea or thesis to be developed through the essay, plays a key role in determining what and how many patterns he or she will use.

The patterns discussed in this chapter are used more frequently in expository writing (such as essays or informative writing like textbooks) than in narrative writing (such as plays, novels, short stories, and poems). Narrative writing most often uses other mechanisms, such as dialogue and plot, for creating unity.

Knowledge of patterns of organization also offers benefits to readers. If *before* and *during* your reading you search for the organizational structure, you may be able to

* Follow the development of an author's ideas
* Stay focused on the main ideas
* Make predictions about what might be the next topic of discussion or next set of details
* See relationships between details
* Remember information (using the pattern as the organizing structure for memory)
* Create visuals to help you remember the information

How Can Patterns Be Identified?

The following sections contain more detailed explanations of each pattern. You will learn about *signal words* that are often associated with each pattern, sample sentences that suggest the pattern the author will probably use, and example paragraphs. A signal word does not need to be used every time a new pattern begins. However, be alert to these words because, when they are used, you will be able to predict the way the material will be organized and to follow the author's thinking while you read.

Simple Listing

In this pattern, a number of details are given in list order. The list may be written in order of importance, chronologically, spatially, or enumerated in no particular order.

Signal Words for Simple Listing

Order of importance: Most important, less important, least important

Chronological: First, second, and so on; next, then, today, yesterday, finally; 1991, 1992, and so on; after, before, previously, once, meanwhile

Spatial: To the right, to the left, on top, inside

Enumeration: Also, in addition, further, another, furthermore, moreover, besides, a number of, several

EXAMPLES OF SENTENCES THAT SUGGEST A SIMPLE LISTING PATTERN

1. Over the last five years, New Jersey taxpayers have expressed increasing dissatisfaction with the state government. *You would expect a listing of the dissatisfactions, perhaps in chronological order.*

2. There are several important steps to take when you are planning to apply for a job. *You would expect a listing of the steps, perhaps in order of importance.*

WORKING TOGETHER

With a partner, write one sentence that you believe could suggest a simple listing paragraph.

Sample paragraph: simple listing pattern [chronological] **(with signal words underlined)**

Several days before every press conference, members of the president's staff compile a list of every possible question that might be asked. They then create a well-worded response to each one. The president studies the answers carefully, trying to memorize the content and the exact language. This helps him appear informed and concerned about all issues. When he <u>finally</u> meets the press, the president is well-armed for even the most hostile reporter.

Sample paragraph: simple listing pattern [order of importance] **(with signal words underlined)**

Since the 1970s, some interesting studies have been done on teachers' attitudes toward girls in the classroom. Perhaps <u>the most important</u> finding is that stereotypes about girls influenced teacher expectations about acceptable classroom behavior and academic performance. Girls were expected to be "ladylike" and to "control themselves." Aggressive behavior by girls was discouraged. <u>Also significant</u> were the findings concerning specific subject areas. Many teachers believed that girls are likely to "love" reading and to "hate" mathematics and science. Girls were not expected to think logically or to understand scientific principles. It was also noted in <u>many studies</u> that if there were student-organized activities, boys were typically in charge, with girls assisting, in the stereotyped role of secretary. Today's educators have worked hard to eliminate these sex biases in the classroom.

Definition and Explanation

This pattern is used to define a new term or concept or to explain or describe a topic, idea, or process that the author thinks may be unclear to the reader. An entire paragraph may be written in this pattern. The definition may be straightforward and may sound almost like a dictionary entry. Or the definition may include *classification* of the unknown term or concept. For instance, an author might define the musical style of a new group by defining the type of music it plays, such as *techno*. Or an animal may be defined by such classifications as its *phylum, genus,* and *species.* Readers can understand a new term or concept by associating it with one they already know when the classification is given.

This pattern also refers to paragraphs of elaborate explanation, such as an explanation of how personal computers work or how to use a high-speed drill.

Signal Words for Definition and Explanation

this is

for example

in other words

such as

for instance

which means

EXAMPLES OF SENTENCES THAT SUGGEST A DEFINITION AND
EXPLANATION PATTERN

1. Before the breakup of the Soviet Union, *perestroika* was thought to be the answer to that nation's economic problems. *You would expect a definition of* perestroika. *Then you would expect to learn why this was thought to be the answer to the economic problems.*

2. It is not difficult to use a single-lens reflex camera. *You would expect a definition of single-lens reflex camera. Then you would hope for an explanation of how to use it, perhaps in a chronological, spatial, or order-of-importance listing pattern.*

WORKING TOGETHER

With a partner, write one sentence that you believe could suggest a definition and explanation paragraph.

Sample paragraph: definition and explanation pattern (with signal words underlined)

The control unit is the computer's internal police officer. This CPU component maintains order and controls all the internal activities of the machine. The control unit sends out electronic signals directing the computer to perform specific tasks such as moving data between memory and the CPU, activating the ALU, receiving data and sending information. The control unit manages the flow of data throughout the machine based on the instructions it receives from programs. No instructions are processed by the control unit. Rather, it directs other parts of the computer to perform their functions in a specific order, at a specific time.

Helene G. Kershner, *Computer Literacy,* 2d ed. (Lexington, MA: Heath, 1992), 77.

What term in this paragraph did the author think needed to be defined for readers?_____

Explain what the author did to help the reader understand this term. _____

_____

_____

_____

_____

Comparison and Contrast

This pattern is used to show similarities (comparisons) or to show differences (contrasts). Writers use this pattern when they want to show how something or someone is similar to or different from something or someone else. Often, both similarities and differences are included within a single comparison and contrast paragraph. Signal words associated with this pattern are then used to let the reader know a shift in focus is occurring.

Signal Words for Comparison and Contrast

COMPARISON	CONTRAST	
in the same way	although	on the contrary
similarly	on the other hand	instead
likewise	however	yet unlike
both	but	conversely
in comparison	nevertheless	in contrast

EXAMPLES OF SENTENCES THAT SUGGEST A COMPARISON AND CONTRAST PATTERN

1. The Padres fans behaved better than those who were rooting for the Yankees. *You would expect a contrast to be made between the two groups of fans.*

2. Moderate exercise for a few minutes every day is more beneficial than doing a whole day of strenuous physical exercise once a week. *You would expect a contrast between the two exercise regimens to be made in order to show why one is better than the other.*

WORKING TOGETHER

With a partner, write one sentence that you believe could suggest a comparison or contrast paragraph. Indicate what type of paragraph will result from your sentence.

Sample paragraph: comparison pattern (with signal words underlined)

Roberto Corelli, the main character in the story "Rise Up and Fall Down," reminds me of my maternal grandfather in several respects. Roberto came to America in 1900, a penniless nine-year-old orphan. He was apprenticed to a brutal uncle in Chicago who kept him out of school and put him to work in a blacksmith's shop. My grandfather sailed to America in steerage just a few years after 1900. Like Roberto, he had little chance for formal education. As soon as he had learned to read, write, and add, he was taken out of his second-grade class by his impoverished parents and made to sell newspapers on the Boston streets. Roberto ran away, joined a circus, and at the age of twenty-one became the Strong Man in a sideshow set. My grandfather started to practice boxing at the YMCA and by the age of eighteen was a promising light heavyweight. Both Roberto and my grandfather eventually fell in love with immigrant girls, married, and settled down as local shopkeepers—Roberto as a butcher and my grandfather as a newsdealer. Similarities such as these continued to occur to me as I read "Rise Up and Fall Down," making it easy for me to give Roberto the understanding and compassion that his life's story was intended to evoke.

Ed Ezor and Jill Lewis, *From Paragraph to Essay: A Process Approach for Beginning College Writing* (New York: McGraw-Hill, 1984), 255.

Sample paragraph: contrast pattern (with signal words underlined)

The new Surveillance and Destiny cars have surprisingly little in common. They're comparable in size—inside and out—<u>but</u> the Surveillance has front-wheel drive with a strut-type suspension, <u>whereas</u> the Destiny uses rear-wheeled propulsion and control-arm front-and-rear suspension. Inside, the Surveillance relies on leather and wood-paneled elegance. The Destiny, <u>in contrast</u>, gives more attention to functional details. Bucket seats in the Destiny slide forward automatically for rear entry. Its center console is artfully twisted toward the driver for a handier reach to sound-system and climate-control switches. During the test drive, the Surveillance demonstrated a tighter grip on the road during steady cornering, <u>unlike</u> the Destiny, which occasionally wagged its tail at the time of adhesion. Both on and off the test track, there's a significant <u>difference</u> in the sensations delivered to the driver through the steering wheel.

Sample paragraph: comparison-and-contrast pattern (with signal words underlined)

Shamika's college adviser told her that she possessed many of the traits <u>similar</u> to those of successful businesswomen, and he suggested that she should consider majoring in business. Shamika had excellent rapport with other people. She was a good public speaker and had shown leadership skills when she served as one of the key organizers for the college's first Environmental Awareness conference. <u>On the other hand</u>, she had some traits that her adviser thought <u>might hinder</u> her chances for success. For instance, she was often late with her assignments, and she was impatient with herself when things took longer to do than expected. She also needed to improve her math skills. Her adviser suggested that Shamika consider all that he had said before she selected a major.

Thesis and Proof or *Opinion and Reason*

This pattern is used to persuade readers to accept an idea. The idea may be one that is factual or well researched, supported by substantial evidence, or supported by information drawn from authoritative sources. The author may have conducted a research study and have cited evidence or findings from this study to support the thesis. Or the material may be a statement of opinion, supported by unresearched reasons, personal beliefs, or information from unauthoritative sources. The sentence that states the opinion or the thesis serves as the main idea for the paragraph or essay. The author offers proof for the thesis and reasons for the opinion. The proof or reasons are intended to convince the reader that the author's view is correct. These arguments may be enumerated and may be listed in ascending or descending order.

Signal Words for Thesis and Proof or Opinion and Reason

it is widely known	one must consider
the reasons for this	in my opinion
there is evidence	evidently
it should be accepted as proof	it is believed

EXAMPLES OF SENTENCES THAT SUGGEST A THESIS-AND-PROOF OR OPINION-AND-REASON PATTERN

1. The city council argued that the town pool should be built immediately. *You would expect several sentences to give the reasons that the council argued this way.* This suggests an opinion and reason pattern.
2. It has been established that dinosaurs were both herbivores and carnivores. *You would expect sentences to show how this has been "established."* This suggests a thesis-and-proof pattern.

WORKING TOGETHER

With a partner, write one sentence that you believe could suggest either a thesis-and-proof or opinion-and-reason paragraph. Indicate which type of paragraph your sentence suggests.

Sample paragraph: opinion-and-reason pattern (with signal words underlined)

Dog owners <u>ought</u> to accept more responsibility for their animals. They <u>should</u> not let their dogs run wild because dogs can be very destructive to other people's property. Further, dogs sometimes carry rabies, and if they bite another dog, or worse, a human, the dog or human can develop rabies and die. Dog owners also have responsibility for their pets' own welfare. If dogs are allowed to run loose, they can get killed by cars or hurt by wild animals such as raccoons and squirrels.

Sample paragraph: thesis-and-proof pattern (with signal words underlined)

Although we used to believe that "folk" medical remedies were merely forms of superstition, now <u>we know</u> otherwise. Biomedical research has shown that the active ingredient in many folk remedies is the same as in the medicines doctors prescribe. There is also new <u>evidence</u> that <u>supports the view</u> that many prohibited foods in folk medicine were based on sound biological principles.

Cause and Effect

Authors might want to tell their readers what made something happen, the *cause* of something. Or they might wish to tell the outcome, results, or *effects* of some action. A paragraph might include both *cause* and *effect,* or they might be written as two separate paragraphs; one paragraph will state the *cause,* and the other will give the *effects.* The terms *cause* and *effect* are often confused. It may help you remember the distinction between them if you keep in mind that <u>the *cause* results in the *effect*.</u> The *cause* may show what led up to the event or idea—that is, what *caused* it to become what it is now. The consequences of the event or idea are the *effects* of it.

Signal Words for Cause and Effect

CAUSE	EFFECT	COMBINED
because	as a result	if (cause), then (effect)
since	thus	(cause) resulted in (effect)
as	consequently	because of (cause), (effect)
the reason for this	so	happened
a cause	hence	
	therefore	
	one outcome	
	an effect	

EXAMPLES OF SENTENCES THAT SUGGEST A CAUSE-AND-EFFECT PATTERN

1. Once she read the news report, the hotel manager understood why the hotel's occupancy rate had significantly increased. *This sentence suggests a* cause *pattern. You would expect a discussion of the reasons for the increase.*

2. The sudden rise to fame and fortune for some professional athletes may result in financial and personal problems for them. *This suggests an* effect *pattern. You would expect a discussion of the effects of sudden fame and fortune on the finances and personal lives of athletes. The* cause *is given.*

3. Advances in technology have caused some major changes in the way industries operate today. *You would expect a discussion of the advances (causes) and the changes (effects) of technology on business.*

WORKING TOGETHER

With a partner, write one sentence that you believe could suggest a cause-and-effect paragraph. Indicate whether it will result in a cause, effect, or a combined cause-and-effect paragraph.

Sample paragraph: cause pattern (with signal words underlined)

Farming has become a much easier occupation in recent years. One reason for this is that cows are now milked by automatic pumps rather than by hand. Eggs are hatched in incubators instead of by the hens themselves, which <u>also results</u> in less work for the farmers, who no longer have to <u>keep</u> nesting hens warm or watch over them to make sure they don't damage the eggs. The temperature and humidity in the hen houses are controlled by thermostats, not by nature's whim; and the amount of feed chickens get each day is determined by a computer rather than by a farmhand's estimates. <u>Another factor</u> that <u>makes</u> farming easier is that the farmhouse itself probably features an electronic range in place of the old coal kitchen stove. Unlike farmers of olden days, today's farmer can actually take a vacation and leave all the work to the brain of a computer, which will sense when each chore must be done and will signal the technological innovation that will accomplish it.

Adapted from Ed Ezor and Jill Lewis, *From Paragraph to Essay: A Process Approach for Beginning College Writing* (New York: McGraw-Hill, 1984), 255.

This paragraph gives causes of

_____

_____

Two causes mentioned are

1. _____

_____

2. _____

_____

Sample paragraph: effect pattern (with signal words underlined)

Looking at the 1998 election *results,* many Republicans realized how their party's actions during the previous eight months had <u>affected</u> political conditions. A major <u>outcome</u> of this election was that Republicans lost the size of the majority they had once enjoyed. They gave up five seats to Democrats. The Speaker of the House, Newt Gingrich, resigned. He knew he could not win election to another term as speaker. Polls showed that the American public was dissatisfied with the accomplishments of the past two years of the Republican-controlled Congress. And powerful Republican representatives who had been very outspoken about the Clinton–Lewinsky affair had lost the elections in their states. It seemed that what was once predicted to be a 1998 "election party" for the Republicans had really become an election nightmare.

This paragraph gives effects of

_____

_____

Two effects mentioned are

1. _____

_____

2. _____

_____

Sample paragraph: cause-and-effect pattern (with signal words underlined)

Until World War I, the United States had always been a debtor nation. This means we owed more money to foreign nations than they owed us. This was partly because the value of the goods and services we imported often exceeded the value of goods we sold to foreigners. Also, foreigners were investing far more in the United States than Americans were investing in other countries. Thus, we had to pay interest and dividends to investors abroad. During World War I, the situation was reversed. The war-torn nations of Europe needed U.S. goods, so our exports more than doubled, while the value of the goods we imported declined. By 1919 we had become a creditor nation—

foreign nations owed more to the United States than the United States owed to them. This position continued until 1985, when the United States once again became a net debtor nation. The value of our imports greatly exceeded the value of our exports, and foreigners were investing heavily in U.S. securities, largely because of the relatively high interest rates here. [*Note:* A chronological listing is also evident in this paragraph, but the cause-and-effect relationship of the events is the major emphasis.]

Adapted from Sanford D. Gordon and George G. Dawson, *Introductory Economics,* 7th ed. (Lexington, MA: Heath, 1991), 433.

This paragraph gives causes of

_____

_____

Two causes mentioned are

1. _____

   _____

2. _____

   _____

This paragraph gives effects of

_____

_____

Two effects mentioned are

1. _____

   _____

2. _____

_____

Problem and Solution

This pattern is used to explain a problem and to offer recommendations. Most often the causes and effects of the problem are also stated, which means this pattern may not be clear until you have read several sentences or paragraphs. The statement of the problem is usually at or near the beginning of the paragraph or essay, and this should alert you to look for this pattern in the text that follows.

Signal Words for Problem and Solution

PROBLEM	SOLUTION
unfortunately	clearly
the problem	obviously
a difficulty	to solve
	one solution

EXAMPLES OF SENTENCES THAT SUGGEST
A PROBLEM-AND-SOLUTION PATTERN

1. People who rent apartments must find ways to deal with landlords who sometimes ignore tenants' needs. *You would expect an explanation of the solutions to the problem already stated.*
2. Multinational corporations must regain support from customers after being accused of taking advantage of workers in third world countries. *You would probably expect some suggestions for regaining support and a more detailed explanation of the accusations.*

WORKING TOGETHER

With a partner, write one sentence that you believe could suggest a problem-and-solution paragraph.

Sample paragraph: problem-and-solution pattern (with signal words underlined)

Parents often have <u>difficulty</u> determining how much allowance to give their children. <u>One reason</u> for this is that they are torn between believing their children should have an opportunity to budget their money and the feeling that their children will not use their allowance wisely and will continue to ask for additional money. Parents also have trouble deciding what to include in the child's list of items that the allowance must pay for. The result of such dilemmas is that children are often given too little or too much allowance, with little clear guidance about how it is to be spent. The rules keep changing. One way <u>to solve</u> this problem is for parents and children to confer regularly about how the allowance is being spent and to establish clear guidelines. Revisions can be made every so often, as the child's needs and interests change.

The problem that is stated is

_____

_____

The cause(s) given for the problem is (are)

_____

_____

The effect(s) of the problem is (are)

_____

_____

The solution(s) offered is (are)

_____

_____

Note that each part you've listed could be developed into its own paragraph. If you added introductory and concluding paragraphs, the result could be a complete essay.

Relationships Between Main Ideas, Details, and Patterns

In the preceding section, you saw how single sentences could indicate the pattern that would probably be used by the author. These sentences could have been main-idea sentences for paragraphs or entire essays. The main idea often suggests how the material will be organized—what pattern(s) will be used. The writer's choice of organizational patterns is often based on a decision about which questions raised by the main idea, or thesis statement, will be answered. The example main-idea sentence that follows illustrates this point.

Example:

There are at least three good reasons people should participate in community service activities.

The author of this sentence will certainly need to give at least three reasons for this belief about community service activities. The sentence suggests two patterns: (1) *opinion and reason* and (2) *simple listing.* The next example suggests a different pattern of organization even though the sentence is about the same topic as the previous example.

Example:

Teenagers who participate in community service activities have greater self-esteem than those who don't.

Although the author will probably be giving opinions again, the comparison and contrast introduced in the main-idea sentence needs elaboration. This sentence lends itself to a *comparison-and-contrast essay,* which may easily incorporate a simple listing format. In the next example, also on the same topic, the author will probably use a different pattern of organization to develop the idea.

Example:

Community service means different things to different people.

Very likely, this author will use a *definition* or a *comparison* pattern to explain the different meanings.

To some extent then, the main idea controls the way the essay will be written. This is similar to how a movie theme, such as love or suspense, suggests a particular type of background music. And, just as knowing the theme of a movie would help you predict the type of music you might hear, so too, once you identify the main idea or thesis of what you are reading, you should be able to predict the primary pattern that will be used. Use your knowledge of patterns to help you follow the development of the main idea or thesis while you read; you will know to look for certain kinds of information, such as definitions, reasons, and comparisons. If there is no main idea or thesis statement, you will be able to create one that suits the organization of the reading material. Your knowledge of patterns will also help you remember the information and comprehend how the different details are related to each other and to the main idea.

Recognizing Patterns of Organization

Four steps will help you recognize what pattern is being used, whether it provides the organizing structure for an entire essay or is the basis for a single paragraph.

1. Identify the stated main idea or thesis, or create one.
2. Make a prediction about the pattern that might be used as the author elaborates on this main point.
3. Locate key words within the supporting sentences that suggest a pattern.
4. Verify your prediction. For example, if you had predicted an opinion-and-reason pattern, you should be able to find opinions or reasons in the content. If you had predicted a problem-and-solution pattern, you should find each of these as well as, perhaps, some causes and effects of each.

Keep each of these steps in mind as you complete Activities B and C.

ACTIVITY B: Predicting Patterns

Read each main-idea sentence. Make a prediction about the pattern(s) that the author will most likely use in elaborating on this main idea. Be prepared to explain your predictions. Your choices of patterns are listed below. Be as specific as possible in your identification.

Simple listing (chronological, order of importance, spatial, enumeration)

Definition and explanation

Comparison and contrast

Thesis and proof *or* opinion and reason

Cause and effect (or one of these)

Problem and solution

1. One psychologist's research shows that people who visit an aquarium experience a sense of peace and security.

   Pattern(s) the author will probably use: _____

   Reasons for your prediction: _____

   _____

   _____

2. The best way to begin a research paper is to have an organized plan of attack.

   Pattern(s) the author will probably use: _____

   Reasons for your prediction: _____

   _____

   _____

3. *Neoteny* can change an animal's evolutionary course.

   Pattern(s) the author will probably use: _____

   Reasons for your prediction: _____

   _____

   _____

4. Gun control laws must be strengthened.

   Pattern(s) the author will probably use: _____

   Reasons for your prediction: _____

   _____

   _____

5. Ricky Martin's sudden rise to fame can be easily understood.

   Pattern(s) the author will probably use: _____

   Reasons for your prediction: _____

   _____

   _____

WORKING TOGETHER

Compare your answers to Activity B with those of a partner. Make any changes to your answers that you believe are justified as a result of your comparisons.

ACTIVITY C: Identifying Patterns in Text

For each paragraph, decide the pattern(s) of organization being used. Consider the main idea of the paragraph as well as the details when making your decision. Circle any signal words within the paragraph that are associated with the pattern(s) you select. Then write a sentence below each paragraph in which you explain the reasons for your selection.

Pattern Choices

a. Simple listing	d. Thesis and proof	g. Problem and solution
b. Definition and explanation	e. Opinion and reason	h. Combination (list each pattern name)
c. Comparison and contrast	f. Cause and effect	

1. Despite their shortcomings, DNA databases have dramatically proven their value, solving scores of old murder and rape cases by matching DNA evidence from those crimes to DNA profiles. Florida claims to have made some 200 "cold hits" using the databases, and Virginia reports 78. A "cold hit" occurs when po-

lice who have no leads find a suspect by checking the DNA from a crime scene against the DNA profiles in the databases. Great Britain was an early innovator in DNA profiling, and British police claim to solve 300 to 400 crimes per week using DNA databases. DNA databases are effective because many criminals make a career of crime: In two studies, one in 1991 and another in 1995, political scientist John Dilulio reported that, based on interviews with prison inmates, they had committed an average of 12 crimes in addition to the ones for which they were caught and convicted.

Adapted from Ronald Bailey, "Unlocking the Cells," *Reason* 31(8) (2000): 50.

Pattern(s): _____

Your explanation: _____

_____

_____

2. One unusual region of the smallest of Uranus's five major satellites, Miranda, is a dark rectangular feature measuring 100 miles by 70 miles. It frames a bright, **V**-shaped patch, dubbed "the Chevron" by mission scientists. Two adjacent sides of the rectangle are aligned with what appear to be long, straight faults that extend at least halfway around Miranda, while a third side falls off precipitously into a deep canyon. *Voyager 2* also revealed an unusual series of concentric, oval grooves on Miranda that resembles a racetrack. Mission scientists informally named this feature the "Circus Maximus," after the famous chariot race course in ancient Rome. Closer inspection of the photographs showed that concentric, oval grooves also surround the Chevron.

Adapted from Richard Golob and Eric Brus, eds., *The Alamanac of Science and Technology: What's New and What's Known* (Boston: Harcourt Brace Jovanovich, 1990), 22.

Pattern(s): _____

Your explanation: _____

_____

_____

3. Nationwide, 4.4 percent of preschoolers—890,000 children—suffer from lead poisoning, a condition that has been linked to learning disabilities, reduced IQ and attention span, stunted

growth, and aggressive behavior. While industrial facilities such as the ASAP, CO, plant—and 70 percent of Superfund sites— pollute surrounding communities with lead, most children are poisoned by lead-based paint and lead-contaminated dust in their own homes. Lead paint was banned for residential use in 1978, but it persists in almost two-thirds of U.S. houses.

Jennifer Hattam, "Get the Lead Out," *Sierra,* May–June 2000, 21.

Pattern(s): _____

Your explanation: _____

_____

_____

4. I was following the crest of a ridge along one of the many old elephant trails that crisscrossed the bamboo. Soon the tracks became fresh. The toenails were still clearly defined, and swarms of tiny black flies hovered about the heaps of dung. I pushed my fingers into some dung. It was still warm. Clouds drifted in and grey fog crept from stem to stem, reducing my visibility to about fifty feet. I continued on silently and carefully, straining my senses, trying to see the bulky grey forms of the elephants in this shadowless dusky world, trying to smell their musky odor. But the only sound was the pounding of my heart.

G. B. Schaller, *The Year of the Gorilla,* (Chicago: University of Chicago Press, 1964), 78.

Pattern(s): _____

Your explanation: _____

_____

_____

5. In May of 1779, the First Company of Philadelphia Artillery petitioned the Assembly about the troubles of the "midling and poor" and threatened violence against "those who are avariciously intent upon amassing wealth by the destruction of the more virtuous part of the community." That same month, there was a mass meeting, an extralegal gathering which called for price reductions and initiated an investigation of Robert Morris, a rich Philadelphian who was accused of holding food from the market. In October came the "Fort Wilson riot," in which a

militia group marched into the city and to the house of James Wilson, a wealthy lawyer and Revolutionary official who had opposed price controls and the democratic constitution adopted in Pennsylvania in 1776. The militia were driven away by a "silk stocking brigade" of well-off Philadelphia citizens.

H. Zinn, *A People's History of the United States* (New York: Harper & Row, 1980), 79.

Pattern(s): _____

Your explanation: _____

_____

6. Rice University researchers have reported that the electronic properties of clusters of copper or silver atoms depend on the number of atoms making up the cluster. They measured the ionization potentials of the clusters—the energy required to remove an electron from an atom—and found that the potential decreases sharply as the number of atoms in a cluster increases from 2 to about 10. The potential then falls more slowly until the characteristic ionization potential of an atom in a bulk metal is reached at about 80 atoms. In general, however, the researchers found that clusters with odd numbers of atoms have lower ionization potentials than the even-numbered clusters on either side of them.

Richard Golob and Eric Brus, eds., *The Alamanac of Science and Technology: What's New and What's Known* (Boston: Harcourt Brace Jovanovich, 1990), 169.

Pattern(s): _____

Your explanation: _____

_____

7. In early 1936, at the Firestone rubber plant in Akron, makers of truck tires, their wages already too low to pay for food and rent, were faced with a wage cut. When several union men were fired, others began to stop work, to sit down on the job. In one day the whole of plant #1 was sitting down on the job. In two days, plant #2 was sitting down, and management gave in. In the next ten days there was a sit-down at Goodyear. A court issued an injunction against mass picketing. It was ignored, and 150

deputies were sworn in. But they soon faced ten thousand workers from all over Akron. In a month the strike was won.

H. Zinn, *A People's History of the United States* (New York: Harper & Row, 1980), 390.

Pattern(s): _____

Your explanation: _____

_____

8. Formal education in psychology, sociology, and communication help college-educated officers avoid many complaints. Their advanced education provides them with a better understanding of the world and their place in society. College campus life provides an excellent environment to learn interpersonal communication skills and experience cultural diversity. Officers possessing police-work experience, maturity, and higher education appear better equipped to handle stressful situations without offending individuals.

    Adapted from Richard R. Johnson, "Citizen Complaints," *FBI Law Enforcement Bulletin* 67(12) (1998): 1.

    Pattern(s): _____

    Your explanation: _____

    _____

9. Clarence Birdseye was in Labrador on a hunting trip in the early 1920s. He was hunting for bears. During his trip, he noticed how fish that were kept outside in the subzero temperature froze immediately and tasted delicious months later. When he returned to the United States, Birdseye experimented with ways of freezing fish as quickly as possible to preserve their flavor. People thought he was crazy for spending so much time and energy on this. But he continued to experiment over the next several years. Eventually, he worked out methods of freezing food so fast that it went through the zone of maximum crystallization in a few minutes instead of taking the usual several hours. This way, the large dangerous crystals had no time to form. Birdseye developed his own machinery to do this quick freezing, and by the

end of the 1920s, the first packages of frozen food were available at the grocery store.

Pattern(s): _____

Your explanation: _____

_____

10. The soaring growth of the Hispanic business community is not only lifting Hispanic incomes. It is also revitalizing neglected areas of cities where Hispanics have established a strong presence. Along Florence Avenue in South Central Los Angeles, a once predominately black community, many of the storefronts destroyed during the 1992 riots have been replaced by small, Hispanic-owned retail stores and mini-marts. In Chicago, Hispanic jewelers, restauranteurs, and clothing retailers control commerce along 26th Street, generating sales-tax revenue second only to Michigan Avenue, Chicago's wealthiest retail strip. And, as Peter Beinart reported in the *New Republic* in 1997, Roosevelt Avenue in Queens, New York, is lined with the small shops established by Ecuadorean, Dominican, Colombian, and Mexican immigrants who have moved in only during the past two decades.

Tyce Palmaffy, "El Millonario Next Door," *Policy Review* July–August 1998, 30.

Pattern(s): _____

Your explanation: _____

_____

11. The term *personal computer,* or *PC,* was originally coined by IBM to describe its microcomputer. It has come to refer to a flexible and memory-rich microcomputer, not necessarily an IBM. Other words that originated as brand names have taken on more general definitions, such as Kleenex for tissue and Xerox for photocopy. Personal computers are relatively inexpensive, single-user machines most often found in business settings. Increasingly, they are used in the home. Some businesses even supply their employees with computers to take home so that their work can be continued out of the office. This probably benefits

the business quite a bit. Personal computers can solve very sophisticated problems. They can process between 1,000 and 6,000 instructions per second, depending on processor design and layout. Newer processors will increase these speeds. Personal computers frequently have color monitors and a laser printer attached.

Adapted from H. G. Kershner, *Computer Literacy,* 2d ed. (Lexington, MA: Heath, 1992), 15.

Pattern(s): _____

Your explanation: _____

_____

_____

12. Is gender a factor in group tasks or maintenance? Generally, the studies on leadership and group process indicate that differences do occur in the way the genders operate in a group. For example, "women tend to be more process-oriented than men. Men are more goal-oriented. For women, the process is as important, or more important, than the product." Other studies indicate that "individuals prefer managers who possess masculine characteristics." This carries over into courtrooms, where men are more likely than women to be selected as foreperson of a jury. Research in educational groups indicates that students believe classes led by women to be more discussion-oriented, and classes taught by men to be more structured and emphasizing content mastery more. In addition, male college professors are perceived to be less supportive and less innovative than are female instructors.

Roy M. Berko, et al., *Communicating* (Boston: Houghton Mifflin, 1998), 253.

Pattern(s): _____

Your explanation: _____

_____

_____

13. In the last few decades, several styles of leadership have been identified. The authoritarian leader holds all authority and responsibility. Communication usually moves from top to bottom within the organization. At the other extreme is the laissez-faire

leader, who does not accept any responsibility and allows subordinates to work as they choose with a minimum of interference.

Pattern(s): _____

Your explanation: _____

_____

_____

14. Opponents of capital punishment have many reasons for opposing the death penalty. They say that anyone who values life cannot approve this form of punishment. They argue that it is morally wrong and that it is not constitutional. Another point they make is that it does not deter crime, as some who favor it would have you believe. Minority offenders are more likely to be executed, which, opponents argue, means this penalty is applied unfairly.

Pattern(s): _____

Your explanation: _____

_____

_____

15. Even though all uniformed patrol officers have a high probability of receiving a citizen complaint, some officers' characteristics slightly elevate this chance. Officers under age 30, with less than 5 years of police experience and only a high school education, suffer the greatest risk for receiving a citizen complaint. In contrast, few complaints are lodged against more mature, older officers who have learned to communicate with people through years of life experience. By trial and error, they have learned various ways to understand and effectively deal with various individuals. Seasoned officers have gained experience negotiating in various situations, and officers with over 5 years of police experience have learned to handle people in stressful situations.

Adapted from Richard R. Johnson, "Citizen Complaints," *FBI Law Enforcement Bulletin* 67(12) (1998): 1.

Pattern(s): _____

Your explanation: _____

16. There are many choices of colleges in the United States, and they vary in size, academic program, and quality of life offered to students. At one college, the fine arts program may be very strong. It may also have wonderful athletic programs and lots of options in the humanities. But the science facilities may not be as good, and the business programs may be weaker than those found at other colleges. Unless students know what they want, they may have difficulty choosing which college to attend. Students today have so many options—what music to listen to, what movies to see, what books to read—they can end up feeling overwhelmed and unable to make a decision. Some colleges provide a small, closely knit community in which students live in the dorms and know practically everyone on campus. At other institutions, the campus is so big that buses transport students from one class in one building to another. Tuition also varies quite a bit from college to college. The cost of tuition is not always a reflection of the quality of the academic program, either. Every year, one popular magazine lists those campuses that give students the most for their money.

    Pattern(s): _____

    Your explanation: _____

    _____

17. The word *population* derives from the Latin *populus,* "people." Like most verbal nouns, a "population" once designated either a process or a state. One of the charges made against Britain's King George III in the American Declaration of Independence was that he "endeavored to prevent the population of these states," but in this sense of "growth in numbers" the word has become archaic. The English language never developed a full equivalent of the French *peuplement:* "peopling" is not standard professional usage, and the usual term in geography, "settlement," has special connotations.

    Adapted from William Petersen, "Population: The Fundamentals," *Society* 37 (1) (1999): 48.

Pattern(s): _____

Your explanation: _____

_____

18. The basic reason for failure of the Edsel was the curiously unscientific approach of Ford's management. For instance, the car was designed in group sessions with too many fingers leaving their marks on its identity. Also, it was ordered into production without research to determine whether or not there was a need for it. To compound the error even further, it was pushed through production so rapidly that there were more than the usual number of flaws and defects. And once produced, the Edsel was undermined by Ford executives, who almost immediately wrote it off after a disappointing introduction to the market. Perhaps no product could have survived with all these handicaps, and certainly not one called Edsel, the name of the deceased son of Henry Ford, the founder of Ford Motor Company.

    Adapted from L. Megginson, L. Trueblood, and G. Ross, *Business* (Lexington, MA: Heath, 1985), 333.

Pattern(s): _____

Your explanation: _____

_____

Activity D. Patterns in Multiparagraph Essays

Essays often use a variety of patterns. This adds interest to the writing and lets the writer accomplish a number of purposes within a single essay. In a single essay, for instance, an author may wish to present a problem, along with solutions; give a number of examples; compare one aspect of the problem with some other aspect; and describe in chronological order how the problem developed. Multiparagraph essays usually have an introductory paragraph that introduces the topic and, perhaps, states the main idea to be developed. They often also have a concluding paragraph that restates the main idea and summarizes major points.

Read the following multiparagraph essay to see how many different patterns within it you can find. Look for signal words. See also whether there is an introductory or concluding paragraph.

(1)   The pace of economic growth in the United States during the 1800s was uneven. Prosperity reigned during two long periods, from 1823 to 1835 and from 1843 to 1857. But there were long stretches of economic contraction as well. Between Jefferson's 1807 embargo and the end of the War of 1812, the growth rate was negative—that is, fewer goods and services were produced. Contraction and deflation (decline in the general price level) occurred again during the hard times of 1819–1823, 1839–1843, and 1857. During these periods, banks collapsed, businesses went bankrupt, and wages and prices declined. For workers, the down side meant lower wages and higher unemployment rates.

(2)   Hard times were devastating for workers. In 1857, the Mercantile Agency—the forerunner of Dun & Bradstreet—recorded 5,123 bankruptcies, nearly double the number of the previous year. Comtemporary reports estimated that twenty to thirty thousand people were unemployed in Philadelphia, and thirty to forty thousand in New York City. Female benevolent societies expanded their soup kitchens and distributed free firewood to the needy. In Chicago, charities reorganized to meet the needs of the poor; in New York, the city hired the unemployed to repair streets and develop Central Park. And in Fall River, Massachusetts, a citizens' committee disbursed public funds on a weekly basis to nine hundred families. The soup kitchen, the bread line, and public aid had become fixtures in urban America.

(3)   What caused the boom-and-bust cycles that brought about such suffering? Generally speaking, they were a direct result of the new market economy. Prosperity stimulated greater demand for staples and finished goods, such as clothing and furniture. Increased demand in turn led not only to higher prices and still higher production but also, because of business confidence and expectation of higher prices, to speculation in land and to the flow of foreign currency into the country. Eventually, production surpassed demand, causing prices and wages to fall; in response, inflated land and stock values collapsed. The inflow of foreign

money led first to easy credit and then to collapse when the un-happy investors withdrew their funds.

(4)   Some contemporary economists considered this process bene-ficial—a self-adjusting cycle that eliminated unprofitable eco-nomic ventures. In theory, people concentrated on the activities they did best, and the economy as a whole became more effi-cient. Advocates of the system also argued that it enhanced indi-vidual freedom, because theoretically each seller, whether of goods or labor, was free to determine the conditions of the sale. But in fact the system tied workers to a perpetual roller coaster; they became dependent on wages—and the availability of jobs—for their very existence.

Adapted from Mary Beth Norton et al., *A People and a Nation,* Brief edition, 4th ed. (Boston: Houghton Mifflin, 1996), 187.

What patterns did you find? List the patterns and the paragraphs in which you found them. Circle the signal words that support your findings.

_____

_____

_____

WORKING TOGETHER

Compare your answers with those of a partner. Make any revisions to your answers that you believe are needed.

Using Patterns to Help You Remember

You can use the knowledge you now have about the relationships between main ideas, paragraph patterns, and details and about distinctions be-tween major and minor details to help you create visual displays of the in-formation you read. These displays, sometimes referred to as *graphic organizers,* are frameworks that illustrate the important conceptual rela-tionships between ideas in text. They will help you organize and recall information, and they are valuable study aids. The process of creating them will give you an opportunity to verify that you have understood the connections between ideas. (In Chapter 7, you will learn how to interpret and create graphic organizers that are used primarily for displaying statistics.)

There are different types of graphic organizers. We discuss several types in the following sections. The patterns used in the text direct you toward the type of organizer to create.

Concept Maps (for Key Vocabulary)

Recall that the definition-and-explanation pattern introduces new terms or concepts. Once you establish that the primary purpose of a section of the material you are reading is to define or explain a new term or concept, you can think about preparing a *concept map* for it. The basic layout for a concept map is shown in the figure. Notice that the term, or concept, is placed in the middle of the map. The broad definition for it appears at the top. On the right is space for indicating characteristics or properties of the term or concept. At the bottom is room for examples of it. On the left is space for writing another term or concept that is different from the one in the center but that will help you make comparisons with the new term.

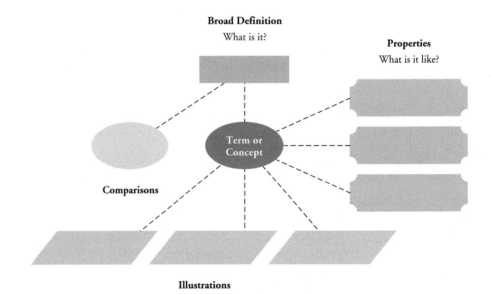

Broad Definition
What is it?

Properties
What is it like?

Term or Concept

Comparisons

Illustrations
What are some examples?

Here is an example of material for which a concept map could be created. Read the material, and while you do so think about what such a map would look like for this selection. Then study the example map that follows.

Example:

Optical Fibers

The revolution in ground-based communications is partly due to the development of the *optical fiber.* An optical fiber is a hairthin, flexible thread of ultra clear glass one-tenth of a millimeter in diameter. Optical fibers also are known as *lightguides* because they serve as pipelines or conduits for laser light.

A glass optical fiber is made from silicon. This material is also used to make microchips. Silicon is the main ingredient in sand, so it is very plentiful. An optical fiber has a glass inner *core* with an outer layer called the *cladding.*

The cladding is composed of a slightly different glass from the core. It acts like a mirror, totally reflecting the light beam traveling through the optical fiber back into the core of the fiber. The trapped light beam cannot escape from the optical fiber until it comes to the other end. For this reason, laser light traveling through an optical fiber does not lose its brightness.

Optical fibers have many advantages over copper wires for voice, information, or data transmission. Much more information can be sent by laser beam over a single optical fiber than by electricity over one copper wire. A single optical fiber can carry the same amount of information as a telephone cable containing 256 pairs of wires. A spool of optical fiber weighing only four and one-half pounds is capable of transmitting the same number of messages as 200 reels of copper wire weighing over eight tons!

Optical fiber looks fragile, but it is stronger than steel. It can withstand over 600,000 pounds of pulling force per square inch. Unlike ordinary glass, optical fibers are not brittle or easily broken. An optical fiber is flexible enough to be tied into a loose knot and still transmit laser light flawlessly.

The first commercial application of lasers and optical fibers to connect telephones in the United States was in 1978 at Disney World in Orlando, Florida. Vista-United Telecommunications

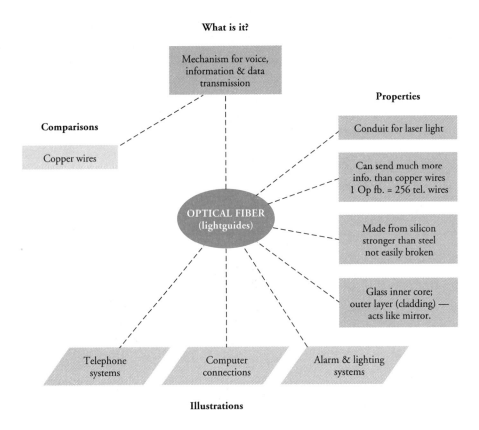

linked telephones throughout the thousands of acres of the park using fiber optic trunk lines. In addition, alarm systems and lighting systems in the park use optical fibers.

Adapted from Charlene Billings, *Lasers: The New Technology of Light* (New York: Facts on File, 1992), 34–39.

Semantic Webbing

If you decide to create a *semantic web* from text, it means that you believe the author's purpose for the material you are diagramming is to give a considerable amount of information about an event, process, or situation. The semantic web is useful as a self-monitoring tool, particularly if you create your web immediately after reading the material and without referring to the text. The semantic web is especially useful when several patterns are evident or for the problem-and-solution pattern. Once you have drawn it, you can verify that your web contains the important points made in the selection and that the relationship between these points has been clearly drawn. To identify prior knowledge they have on a topic, students sometimes create semantic webs before reading new material. This is always a good idea.

Read the example text. Then study the web above it. Notice how the lines drawn on the web show how the ideas are connected.

Example:

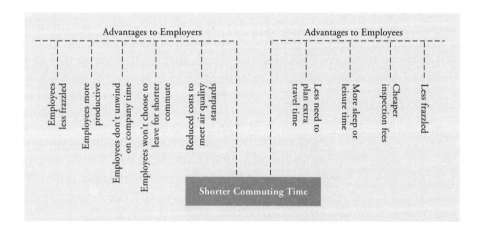

There are plenty of reasons for companies to shorten their employees' communting distances as much as possible. For example, waiting out accidents, negotiating construction, and dealing with other delays can force employees to build a "cushion" into their average drive time. As a result, they must leave home earlier to provide that cushion, eroding possible leisure or sleep time.

Commute-frazzled employees may arrive at work with a couple of hours' worth of tension in them; they either aren't as productive as they ought to be, or they unwind on company time when they do get to work. When the drive becomes too harried, some of these employees may opt to work for organizations closer to their homes.

In addition, auto emissions and other air pollutants directly affect businesses because noncompliance with air quality standards leads to restrictions on building additional highway lanes or expanding roads. For example, metropolitan Atlanta is not in compliance with air quality standards, so there are now strings attached to its $475 million in federal transportation funding. The city can repave roads or make safety improvements if needed, but it cannot build additional road capacity until it regains compliance.

What's more, when cities fail to meet air quality standards, drivers also begin paying relatively expensive emissions inspection fees for their vehicles, which can hurt lower-wage employees who drive older cars. Cities may also require fees from manufacturing companies that want to move into the area to offset the costs of pollution containment. These and other measures can affect where a company can cost-effectively relocate.

Carla Joinson and Laurie Case, "Suburbs vs. Cities," *HR Magazine,* 44(3) (1999): 34.

Notice that the topic is in the middle of this map. Each important point (main idea) that is discussed and that is related to the topic is noted separately, and a line is drawn from it to the topic. The major details pertaining to each main idea have also been noted; lines extend between the detail and main idea. Minor details are drawn on lines that extend from the major details. Even someone who had not read the text would be able to see the relationship between the ideas on this web.

Hierarchical Array

When an author presents ideas in order of importance, you can diagram these relationships on a *hierarchical array*. This type of visual display is illustrated in two figures. In the example text, on which both displays are based, signal words tell you to expect that some details will have greater importance than others. This should alert you to read actively and to try to visualize the hierarchy while you read so that you are prepared to create the array immediately afterward.

Example:

Death aboard Slave Ships

Death in the crossing was due to a variety of causes. The biggest killers were gastrointestinal disorders, which were often related to the quality of food and water available on the trip, and fevers. Bouts of dysentery were common and the "bloody flux," as it was called, could break out in epidemic proportions. The increasing exposure of the slaves to dysentery increased both the rates of contamination of supplies and the incidence of death. It was dysentery that accounted for the majority of deaths and was the most common disease experienced on all voyages. The astronomic rates of mortality reached on occasional voyages were due to outbreaks of smallpox, measles, or other highly communicable diseases that were not related to time at sea or the conditions of food and water supply, hygiene, and sanitation practices. It was this randomness of epidemic diseases that prevented even experienced and efficient captains from eliminating very high mortality rates on any given voyage.

Although time at sea was not usually correlated with mortality, there were some routes in which time was a factor. Simply because they were a third longer than any other routes, the East African slave trades that developed in the late eighteenth and nineteenth centuries were noted for overall higher mortality than the West African routes, even though mortality per day at sea was the same or lower than on the shorter routes. Also, just the transporting together of slaves from different epidemiological zones in Africa guaranteed the transmission of a host of local endemic diseases to all those who were aboard. In turn, this guaranteed the spread of all major African diseases to America.

From Herbert S. Klein, "Profits and the Causes of Mortality," in *The Atlantic Slave Trade,* ed. David Northrup (Lexington, MA: Heath, 1994), 118.

In Model A, the hierarchy is noted by the size of the print as well as the order in which the items have been placed beneath the heading. In Model B, the distance of each item from the heading indicates its relative importance.

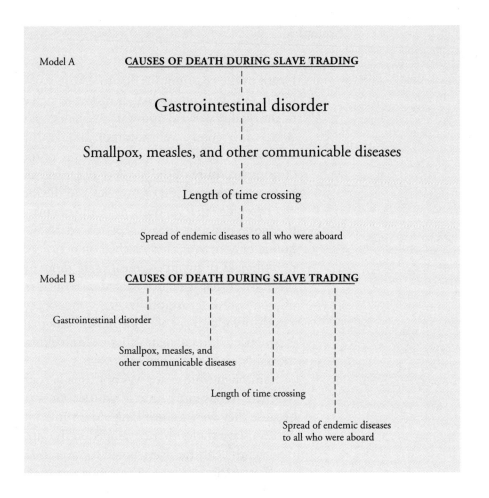

This type of diagram also works well for material that includes classifications. An essay about Indo-European languages, for instance, might result in your creation of a hierarchical array similar to the one shown on the next page.

Linear Array

A linear array, sometimes called a *flowchart,* may also be used to show a sequence of events, as in the simple listing chronological pattern, or a process, as in the definition-and-explanation pattern when used to explain how something occurs. The example text discusses a process, and

Indo-European Languages Today

the linear array for the details appears beneath the text. Notice that the connections between the parts of the array are made clear by lines and arrows. It would be possible to understand the information on this visual without reading the text. When you create a visual such as this, be sure that you have included all the steps of the process.

Example:

> Organizational communication is a complex system involving people's feelings, attitudes, relationships, and skills as well as the goals of management and the process of change, adaptation, and growth. Individuals can both send and receive information. Both the receiver and sender have their own personal frame of reference, developed over time. Each also uses his or her own communication skills, such as reading, writing, and listening abilities, that either strengthen or lessen understanding.
>
> In the communication process between a manager and another organizational member, the receiver accepts the message and transmits either verbal or nonverbal feedback, thereby becoming the sender. Verbal feedback is a written or spoken response. Nonverbal feedback is a body movement or actions. Noise is the interference or the barriers that may occur at any point in the process, distorting understanding. The

organizational environment also affects sending, receiving, and interpreting the message. The communication process is successful only when the sender and receiver understand the message to the same degree. Feedback permits clarification and repetition until the message is fully understood.

Adapted from Jerry Kinard, *Management* (Lexington, MA: Heath, 1988), 349.

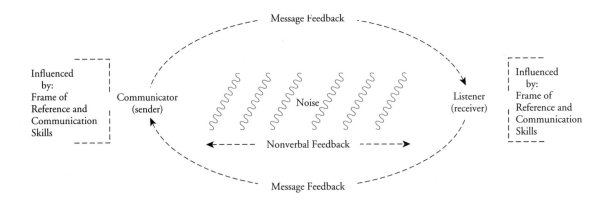

Visual Aids to Show Comparisons and Contrasts

You can also use visuals to illustrate comparison-and-contrast patterns. This will help you determine whether you really know the comparisons or contrasts made. If you do not know them, you will not be able to complete all parts of the visual aid, which would indicate that you need to reread the material. In this section we show two ways to prepare visuals for text that includes comparisons and contrasts.

COMPARISON-AND-CONTRAST BOX.   Read the example text to note the contrasts being discussed. Think about the specific points made and try to visualize how you might place this information inside a box. Then look at the model to see how it has been done.

Example:

The Family in Agricultural Societies

In most agricultural societies the family is *patriarchal* and *patrilineal:* the male is the dominant authority and kinship is determined through the male line. The family is an economic institution, as well as a sexual and child-rearing one; it owns land, produces many artifacts, and cares for its old as well as its young. Male family heads exercise power in the wider community; patriarchs may govern the village or tribe. Male authority frequently means the subjugation of both women and children. This family arrangement is buttressed by traditional moral values and religious teachings that emphasize discipline, self-sacrifice, and the sanctity of the family unit.

Women face a lifetime of childbearing, child rearing, and household work. Families of ten or fifteen children are not uncommon. The property rights of a woman are vested in her husband. Women are taught to serve and obey their husbands and are not considered as mentally competent as men. The husband owns and manages the family's economic enterprise. Tasks are divided: men raise crops, tend animals, and perform heavy work; women make clothes, prepare food, tend the sick, and perform endless household services.

The Family in Industrialized Societies

Industrialization alters the economic functions of the family and brings about changes in the traditional patterns of authority. In industrialized societies the household is no longer an important unit of production, even though it retains an economic role as a consumer unit. Work is to be found outside the home, and industrial technology provides gainful employment for women as well as for men. This means an increase in opportunities for women outside the family unit and the possibility of economic independence. The number of women in the labor force increases; today in the United States more than 60 percent of adult women are employed outside the home.

The patriarchal authority structure that typifies the family in an agricultural economy is altered by the new opportunities for women in an advanced industrial nation. Not only do women acquire employment alternatives, but their opportunities for education also expand. Independence allows them to modify many of the more oppressive features of patriarchy. Women in an advanced industrialized society have fewer children. Divorce becomes a realistic alternative to an unhappy marriage. The trend in divorce rates in industrialized societies is upward.

At the same time, governments in industrialized societies assume many of the traditional functions of the family, further increasing opportunities for women. The government steps into the field of formal education—not just in the instruction of reading, writing, and arithmetic, but in support of home economics, driver training, health care, and perhaps even sex education, all areas that were once the province of the family. Governmental welfare programs provide assistance to dependent children when a family breadwinner is absent or unable to provide for the children. The government undertakes to care for the aged, the sick, and others incapable of supporting themselves, thus relieving families of still another traditional function.

Despite these characteristics of industrial society, however, *the family remains the fundamental social unit.* The family is not disappearing; marriage and family life are as popular as ever. But the father-dominated authority structure, with its traditional duties and rigid gender roles, is changing. The family is becoming an institution in which both husband and wife seek individual happiness rather than the perpetuation of the species and economic efficiency. Many women still choose to seek fulfillment in marriage and child rearing rather than in outside employment. The important point is that now this is a *choice* and not a cultural requirement.

Thomas R. Dye, *Power and Society: An Introduction to the Social Sciences* (Belmont, CA: Wadsworth, 1993), 49–51.

Notice that the information in the box that follows is written in short phrases; not everything has been written—just the most important points.

Types of Families	
Agricultural	**Industrial**
Patriarchal	Less patriarchal
Economic	No longer the unit of production
Sexual	Divorce is higher
Child-rearing function	Having children is a choice
Owns/works land	Women work outside the home
Cares for old and young	Government provides more
Women are subjugated	Women can be educated
Traditional moral values	Women have greater independence
Women have primarily childbearing role	Many women work

VENN DIAGRAMS.   A second way to illustrate comparison and contrast information from text is by creating a diagram that illustrates both points of commonality and points of difference. This diagram, called a *Venn diagram,* is shown following the example text.

Example:

The one thing that all crystals have in common is that they are built up of repeated patterns. In other ways, crystals may differ widely. Some shatter easily. Others do not. Some are very hard. Some crumble at a touch.

These different properties of crystals are due to many causes. Let's look at some of them.

The way the atoms are arranged in a crystal affects its properties. Two crystals may be made up of the same kind of atom and yet have very different properties. The difference is caused by the way the atoms are arranged in each crystal.

The "lead" in a pencil is really a kind of crystalline material called graphite. Graphite is a form of the element carbon, so graphite crystals are made up entirely of carbon atoms.

Diamond is another form of carbon. Diamond crystals are also made up entirely of carbon atoms.

Diamond and graphite appear to be as different as Dr. Jekyll and Mr. Hyde. Or, as one scientist has put it, they are "beauty and the beast among crystals."

Diamond is the hardest material known. This is another way

of saying that diamond will scratch or cut through all other materials. Diamond drills and saws are used to cut through rock. Diamond dust is used to grind and shape metal tools. Diamond crystals when cut and polished make brilliant gems.

Graphite is usually dull black in color and has a greasy feel. It is a very soft material. Like mica, graphite can be sliced easily into very thin sheets. The fact that thin sheets of graphite slide past each other very easily makes it useful for "oiling" moving parts in machines and makes it work in a pencil.

The difference between graphite and a diamond is the result of one extra atom of carbon in the building block of the diamond. Let's take a look at the building block of graphite first.

Malcolm E. Weiss, *Why Glass Breaks, Rubber Bends, and Glue Sticks* (New York: Harcourt Brace Jovanovich, 1974), 24.

The center part of the Venn diagram below shows how the two types of crystals are similar; hence, the circles overlap. The left and right parts list the differences. This diagram could not have been prepared unless the reader understood the material.

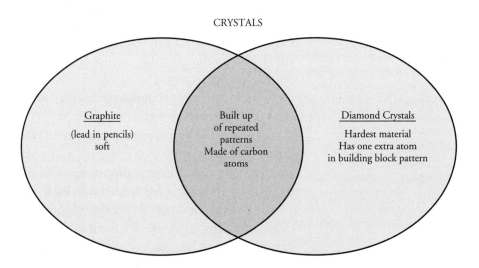

CRYSTALS

Graphite
(lead in pencils)
soft

Built up
of repeated
patterns
Made of carbon
atoms

Diamond Crystals
Hardest material
Has one extra atom
in building block pattern

WORKING TOGETHER

With a partner, decide which type of visual aid would be best for each of the following passages. Then work together to create a visual aid for one of them.

1. Smoking

Smoking is the single most preventable risk factor for fatal illnesses in the United States. Cigarette smoking accounts for more deaths than do all other drugs, car accidents, suicides, homicides, and fires *combined.* Even nonsmokers who inhale "secondhand" smoke face an elevated risk for lung cancer and other respiratory diseases. The American Cancer Society has estimated that, if people did not smoke cigarettes, 400,000 fewer U.S. citizens would die in the next twelve months, and 25 percent of all cancer deaths and thousands of heart attacks would never occur.

Although smoking is on the decline in the United States overall—about 26 percent of adults now smoke—the habit is actually increasing among adolescent women. Poorer, less educated people are particularly likely to smoke. High smoking rates are also found among certain American Indian tribes in the northern plains, among Hispanic-American males, and among African-Americans generally. Conversely, some American Indian tribes in the Southwest and most Asian groups are less likely than other groups to smoke. In many other countries, especially those of the Third World, smoking is still the rule rather than the exception.

Breaking the smoking habit is difficult. Only about 35 percent of those participating in the stop-smoking programs available today show long-term success. Improving this success rate and preventing adolescents from taking up smoking remain among health psychology's greatest challenges.

Adapted from Douglas A. Bernstein and Peggy W. Nash, (1999). *Essentials of Psychology* (Boston: Houghton Mifflin, 1999), 396.

Type of visual aid to create for this text: _____

2. HIV: Where We Are Today, What Tomorrow May Bring

Although people with HIV now have treatments that can prolong their lives, it is not an easy way of life. Protease inhibitors are now part of "the AIDS cocktail," a carefully balanced mix of several drugs, which fights HIV. Patients need to take as many as 30 pills a day, some with food, some without, and always on a strict time schedule. While protease inhibitors suppress the virus and allow the immune system to become strong again, they are not cures. For one thing, the body can become resistant to the drugs so that they no longer work. For another, doctors have found that HIV "hides" in various places in the body, such as the brain and eyes. "The virus is eliminated from the blood but it's still in the body, and it's still able to infect new cells," says Dr. Lawrence Friedman.

Will there ever be a cure for AIDS? Maybe, but it's not likely to happen soon.

Right now, researchers are looking at different methods of killing the virus that hides in the body. One method, for example, involves removing a few of a patient's killer T-cells (white blood cells that kill invading germs) and growing them in a laboratory. Massive numbers of the cells are then reinjected into the patient to destroy his or her infected blood cells. They do, but the effect is temporary.

Methods such as this are so expensive and complicated that they're not practical for use in the general population. To complicate things even more, HIV, like any microbe, has the amazing ability to mutate, or change. The medicines that help one person may not help another who has a slightly different strain of the virus.

For now, say doctors, the best protection against HIV is prevention. Avoid getting it in the first place.

Typically, a vaccine contains a weakened virus, or a protein from a virus. It's injected into a healthy person so that his or her body will produce the antibodies or killer immune system cells needed to fight that virus. If that person comes into contact with the virus in the future, the antibodies will be ready and waiting to destroy it.

That's the way a vaccine works. Now the big question: Will there ever be a vaccine to protect people from AIDS? "Scientists are looking at more than two dozen different approaches to developing an AIDS vaccine," says Victor Zonana, vice-president of the International AIDS Vaccine Initiative (IAVI) in New York. "Right now, none is even close to being ready for use in the general population."

Finding a protein or antigen that looks as if it could be the basis for a vaccine is just the beginning, explains Jorge Flores, M.D., chief of the Clinical Development Branch of the AIDS

Vaccine Prevention and Research Program at the National Institutes of Health. "From there, we do a series of progressive studies, starting with testing the antigen on small animals and then monkeys. If the vaccine looks hopeful, it would then be ready to test on humans. These multiple studies take years to complete." Only one vaccine has reached the stage of being tested for efficacy (effectiveness) on volunteers.

Developing a vaccine is a long and tedious process, but that doesn't mean it won't happen. The way scientists are working, there just may be one available in your lifetime.

Adapted from Nina Riccio, *Current Health 2* 26(6), (2000): 21.

Type of visual aid to create for this text: _____

3. T'ai Chi

One of the best-known of the martial arts, t'ai chi is both a self-defense strategy and, more commonly in the West, a gentle exercise technique. In Chinese the words *t'ai chi chuan* mean "supreme ultimate fist," a reference, in part, to its lofty status among the martial arts.

T'ai chi consists of a series of postures performed in sequences. Known as forms, they vary in complexity, with some involving 18 postures and others more than 100. Students move from one posture to the next in a flowing motion that resembles dance. While not as physically demanding as karate and judo, t'ai chi takes a long time to master. Movements are learned slowly and carefully, creating a state of restful action in which the mind can concentrate on every motion. But the pace of class may quicken as students acquire proficiency and agility.

Tracing T'ai Chi's Roots. The origins of t'ai chi are obscure. There are reports that it was being practiced some 5,000 years ago, and ancient Chinese drawings depict monks performing movements that look similar to t'ai chi. Some accounts of its origins describe the founder as a monk and kung fu student at a monastery in China in the thirteenth century. After witnessing a fight between a bird and a snake, the man noticed that the snake managed to avoid the bird's attack using swift but subtle movements; from these observations, he developed the art of t'ai chi. Newer theories credit a Chinese general who, in the seventeenth century, improvised t'ai chi by combining martial arts with theories of traditional Chinese medicine.

Like aikido, the Japanese martial art, t'ai chi was influenced by the idea of Tao, which means "the way" or "the path," described by the Chinese philosopher Lao-tze. His philosophy, known as Taoism, stresses that humankind must attain harmony with nature and the universe. When in perfect harmony, things function effortlessly and spontaneously, according to natural laws. So, too, the body operates by the same principles. "When people are alive," Lao wrote, "they are soft and supple. When a plant is alive, it is soft and tender." T'ai chi practitioners believe that the qualities of softness and suppleness can be developed by cultivating the life force, qi, that flows through the body.

Clarity through Contradiction.   Among the most intriguing aspects of t'ai chi are its various contradictions and seeming paradoxes. These are rooted in the Chinese notion of yin and yang, the law of complementary opposites. For instance, alert relaxation is essential to each movement. The body should remain supple and at ease, but not to the extent of going limp. Movement likewise entails opposition or contradiction. To move to the right, for example, you must first turn slightly leftward; to rise up, you must first sink slightly. The movement called push can be performed most effectively *without* the application of force: the arms and shoulders relax, the elbows hang loose, and the palms of the two partners meet without touching. All movement in t'ai chi describes circles, spirals, or arches. To achieve this effect is sometimes termed "curved seeking straightness." This refers to the necessary curvature of limbs.

Al Guinness, *Family Guide to Natural Medicine* (Pleasantville, NY: Reader's Digest, 1993), 230–31.

Type of visual aid to create for this text: _____

▶ Chapter Summary

Based on your reading of this chapter, list at least five ideas that you believe will help you with future reading assignments. Write in complete sentences.

1. _____

_____

_____

_____

2. _____

_____

_____

_____

3. _____

_____

_____

_____

4. _____

_____

_____

_____

5. _____

_____

_____

_____

▶ *Extended Application*

Now that you have worked with the strategies necessary for understanding paragraph patterns, you can practice applying them to full-length reading selections. Choose (or your instructor may choose) a reading selection from Part 2 of this book that is typical of what you will be expected to read for your other college courses, such as an essay or a textbook chapter. Use this selection to practice

※ Identifying paragraph patterns
※ Predicting paragraph patterns
※ Using patterns to create visual aids

Decide on the practice strategies you will use. Apply them to your selection. Then, in a few paragraphs, write a description of what you did and how the strategies you used worked for you.

Name of material used: _____

Page numbers: _____

Your description: _____

CHAPTER SIX

Strategies for Critical Reading and Thinking

WHAT MADE YOU DECIDE TO attend this school? You may have considered other colleges before making your choice. In the process, you may have reviewed such facts as costs, programs of study, housing, and tuition assistance opportunities. Sources of information for this choice may have included talking with college representatives and reading college catalogs. Perhaps you also sought opinions from students already attending this school. Once you had all this information, you could weigh the advantages and disadvantages and sort out reliable from unreliable sources. Then you made your decision. This process required you to do critical reading, thinking, and listening. All critical reading, thinking, and listening experience involves similar analytical and reflective processes: you make judgments about what you read, see, or hear. In this chapter, you will learn the types of criteria to use for making these judgments and how to apply these criteria to academic situations.

What Is Critical Reading?

There are many definitions of critical reading, but all of them involve evaluating what you read for:

Logic

Truth or accuracy

Merit of the ideas

Usefulness of the ideas

Evaluating text material in this way requires that you analyze what you read, that you do more than simply identify main ideas and details. Authors select the information they will give readers, and they decide how this information will be presented. They also determine which ideas to state directly and which to suggest indirectly. When you read critically, you:

* Draw conclusions and form judgments about what you read on the basis of what you are told, as well as how the information is presented.
* Examine the underlying ideas that are suggested by both of these.
* Consider the logic of the ideas.
* Think about how the information coincides or conflicts with your prior knowledge and personal beliefs.

Critical readers are aware that a single subject or event can be discussed from many viewpoints. If you hear only one side of an argument or read about an event that is written from only one perspective, you are limiting your understanding and your ability to analyze it critically. The critical reader is an investigative reader. The value of being able to read with a critical eye is illustrated in Activity A.

ACTIVITY A: Critical Analysis of Three News Articles

Three accounts of the same event, each from a different newspaper, follow. Read all three news stories, and then answer the questions.

1. Queens Woman Is Stabbed to Death in Front of Home (*NY Times*)
A 28 year old Queens woman was stabbed to death early yesterday morning outside her apartment house in Kew Gardens.

Neighbors who were awakened by her screams found the woman, Miss Catherine Genovese of 82-70 Austin Street, shortly after 3 a.m. in front of a building three doors from her home.

The police said that Miss Genovese had been attacked in front of her building and had run to where she fell. She had parked her car in a nearby lot, the police said, after having driven it from the Hollis Bar where she was day manager.

The police, who spent the day searching for the murder weapon, interviewing witnesses and checking automobiles that had been seen in the neighborhood, said last night they had no clues.

New York Times, 14 March 1964, 26 © 1964 by the New York Times Company.

2. "Help" Cry Ignored, Girl Dies of Knifing (*NY Herald Tribune*)
Robert Parrella

The neighbors had grandstand seats for the slaying of Kitty Genovese.

And yet, when the pretty diminutive 28 year old brunette called for help, she called in vain.

It wasn't until she had been stabbed 12 times and had crawled into a vestibule, that somebody called police, and even then Kitty lay for 10 minutes, bleeding and unbefriended, before they arrived.

"I wonder how many lives could be saved in this city if people who ask for help were not ignored?" Magistrate Bernard J. Dublin mused yesterday in Queens Criminal Court. "How many people could have been saved from death if when they call for help other persons did not run away."

Karl Ross, 31, a poodle clipper, of 82-65 Austin Street, Kew Gardens, a neighbor of Kitty's, finally did call police.

Mr. Ross had just testified that he recognized the girl, bleeding profusely after she had staggered into the vestibule of his apartment house. He returned to his apartment, he said, and called the police, and remained in the apartment until he heard them arrive, some ten minutes later.

A charge of breach of the peace was leveled against Mr. Ross later in the day by Detective Mitchell Sang, who said Mr. Ross tried to prevent him from questioning one of Miss Genovese's roommates, Mary Ann Zielonko.

Mr. Ross was sentenced to pay a $25 fine and serve five days on the breach of peace charge which was reduced from interference with an officer. The jail term was suspended.

Detectives on the case say that at least half a dozen neighbors heard Miss Genovese scream for help on Austin Street at about 3:30 a.m.

yesterday. Several of the witnesses told police they saw a man bending over the girl, straighten up and run away.

The girl, they said, then staggered around the corner onto 82nd Street. Her slayer reappeared at that point, and then, not finding his victim, disappeared again. Finally, Miss Genovese returned to Austin Street and collapsed in the vestibule about 30 yards from her own apartment door.

Police, called by Mr. Ross, summoned an ambulance, and the girl was taken to Queens General Hospital, where she died a short time later. Assistant Queens Medical Examiner, Dr. William Bennison, said she had suffered 12 stab wounds in the chest, abdomen and back, inflicted by a very strong killer armed with a slender knife.

Police said Miss Genovese was manager of Ev's 11th Hour, a tavern at 1293-14 Jamaica Avenue, Hollis, and shared her apartment with Miss Zielonko and another waitress from the establishment.

Detectives are seeking to question a patron at the tavern with whom Miss Genovese had had dinner earlier in the evening. Although the girl's wallet was not found at the stabbing scene, investigators said they did not believe the motive was robbery.

New York Herald Tribune, 14 March 1964, 10.

3. Queens Barmaid, Stabbed, Dies (*NY Daily News*)

Thomas Pugh and Richard Henry

An attractive 28 year old brunette who had given up a more prosaic life for a career as a barmaid and residence in a tiny Bohemian Section of Queens was stabbed to death early yesterday.

Catherine (Kitty) Genovese, 5 feet 1 and 105 pounds was stabbed eight times in the chest and four times in the back and she had three cuts on her hands, probably inflicted as she tried to fight off her attacker near her apartment in an alley way, at 82-70 Austin Street at Lefferts Boulevard, Kew Gardens.

Late yesterday, police said the 30 detectives assigned to the case had not come up with any clues or a possible motive for the savage murder.

Had Teen Nuptial Annulled

Police of the Richmond Hill Precinct said Kitty had had her teenage marriage annulled two months after her wedding and, when her large family moved to Connecticut, she stayed in New York on her own.

She worked for an insurance firm, but gave that up for a barmaid's career. In August 1961, her travels with a "fast crowd" contributed to her arrest on a bookmaking rap.

Police pieced together this account of her last hours at 6 p.m. Thursday; she left Ev's Eleventh Hour Tavern, 193-14 Jamaica Avenue, Hollis, where she had been a barmaid and co-manager for one and a half years.

She and a male patron went on a dinner date to Brooklyn, and returned to Ev's at midnight. Her escort left (he was questioned by cops yesterday and his alibi freed him of suspicion in the crime).

Three Girls Shared Apartment

Kitty left the bar at 3 a.m. and drove her Fiat sports car seven miles to her home. She parked in the Long Island Railroad's parking lot next to the group of buildings where she and two other girls shared an apartment.

She walked along Austin Street, instead of going more directly to the apartment via a walkway at the rear of the building. Police said she apparently walked out front to have the protection of the street lights.

Gasps *"I've Been Stabbed!"*

Neighbors suddenly heard screams and the roar of an auto driving off. Leaving a trail of blood, Kitty staggered back toward the parking lot, around the rear of the structures, and collapsed in the doorway of 892-60 Austin Street, next to her home.

***"I've Been Stabbed! I've Been Stabbed!"* the Brunette Gasped**

Kitty died in an ambulance en route to Queens General Hospital, Jamaica.

New York Daily News, 14 March 1964, 10.

1. How does each author want you to feel about the event?

Article 1: _____

_____

Article 2: _____

_____

*Article 3:*_____

_____

2. What does each author do to get you to feel this way?

*Article 1:*_____

_____

*Article 2:*_____

_____

*Article 3:*_____

_____

3. What does the author of each article want you to feel about the person who is primarily involved?

*Article 1:*_____

_____

*Article 2:*_____

_____

*Article 3:*_____

_____

4. How do you know the author wants you to feel this way?

*Article 1:*_____

_____

*Article 2:*_____

_____

*Article 3:*_____

_____

5. Which article has left the biggest impression on you? Why do you think it has?

_____

_____

_____

☗ WORKING TOGETHER

With a partner, discuss how a reader's reactions to this event might differ, depending on which news story he or she has read.

THINKING ABOUT YOUR READING AND WRITING

ACTIVITY B: Your Conclusions about Content and Language
What does Activity A tell you about how an author's content and language can influence a reader's beliefs and knowledge?

_____

_____

_____

_____

It is not wrong for an author to try to influence others. Authors write because they have something to say. They expect their readers to understand their ideas and, they hope, to agree with them. But critical readers and listeners will evaluate the ideas before accepting them. In the remainder of this chapter, you will learn strategies for making such evaluations, including strategies that will enable you to recognize

* when an author's content and language suggest unstated ideas
* when an author's content and language suggest certain biases
* when these biases and ideas are justified by reasons and evidence

   ✴   how the author's attitudes are similar to or different from your own
and those of others

   ✴   what conclusions reasonably follow from ideas that you accept

These strategies are explained separately so that you can have a clear
picture of how to use each. However, these features of communication
work simultaneously, in combination with one another, to produce the final effect on the reader or listener. For instance, if the newspaper articles
in Activity A had differed from one another by only one sentence, the effect of any single article on you would probably not have been very different from that of any other single article. It was the totality—the
headlines, the events discussed, the descriptions—that caused the striking
contrasts.

Distinguishing Statements of Fact from Statements of Opinion

Text material and lectures contain both factual information and opinions.
Statements of opinion in academic text and lectures are also sometimes
referred to as *thesis statements, theories,* or *hypotheses.* Your knowledge of
the distinctions between these and statements of fact will help you evaluate the ideas of others. As a critical reader and listener, you will recognize
ideas that are accurate, logical, and worthy of serious consideration, as
well as those that you must question because they are unsupported, illog-
ical, or seem inaccurate. Further, you will be more aware of whether the
judgments you make about the ideas of others are grounded in fact or
opinion or in a combination of these.

Factual statements are distinguished from statements of opinion in several ways:

   ✴   Facts can be proved to be true.

   ✴   Facts cannot be disputed. There is evidence to prove their truth.

   ✴   Facts are easily agreed-on ideas or are concepts that are held by
everyone or that can easily be proved, such as, "The sun sets in the
west" or "Maine is in the northeastern part of the United States."

* Facts are based on direct evidence or actual observation. Examples, statistics, original documents, reports from research experiments, or eyewitness accounts are used to verify them.

* Facts are things that have occurred. They are not predictions.

* Factual statements often begin with such expressions as, *The evidence for this is* _____ ; _____ *found; Statistical evidence for this appeared in a study by* _____

Opinions, on the other hand, are not clear cut or right or wrong, as are facts. Your academic reading and experiences in classrooms will expose you to many areas of controversy where opinions are voiced strongly. People may disagree endlessly about an opinion and never reach a conclusion. For instance, one person might say capital punishment is a good idea; another might say capital punishment should be abolished. Opinions are one person's view of the truth.

Frequently, academic writing will express opposing viewpoints. For example, there is disagreement over such issues as how the earth was first created and the seriousness of global warming. Psychologists and others have disagreed over the extent to which a person's genetic makeup influences his or her personality and intelligence, compared to his or her environment. (These are called nature–nurture theories.) Critical readers recognize there can be such disagreements and will draw conclusions based on whatever evidence and facts they can find. Statements of opinion, then, have several features that will help you distinguish them from facts:

* Statements of opinion cannot be conclusively verified. Even if you agree with the author's opinion, it is still just an opinion, although there may be good evidence for that opinion.

* Statements of opinion often express one person's values, beliefs, attitudes, or feelings. These are frequently based on hunches, inferences, or guesses. It is when you agree with the author's point of view that it is more difficult to distinguish between a fact and an opinion. Try to avoid letting your own opinions influence your ability to determine which is which.

  ❉ Statements of opinion are subjective. The language of opinion statements is often vague or persuasive. The words used to convey the opinion may be open to many interpretations, like *love, peace, beneficial, dangerous.*

  ❉ Opinion statements often begin with such expressions as *I believe, It appears, It seems, All would agree, I think* _____ *is true because, In my opinion . . .*

  ❉ A single word can turn a statement of fact into a statement of opinion. For example, the phrase *sixteenth-century music* is a factual phrase. The descriptor, *sixteenth-century,* is factual because one could prove whether the music was of that period. However, the phrase *beautiful music* is a statement of opinion. Its descriptor, *beautiful,* is a matter of opinion to the listener.

ACTIVITY C: Creating Fact and Opinion Descriptors

For each pair, write one descriptor that makes a phrase factual and one that makes it an opinion. An example is done for you. Be prepared to justify your answers.

FACTUAL		OPINION	
Sunday	picnic	*enjoyable*	picnic
_____	damage	_____	damage
_____	country	_____	country
_____	parents	_____	parents
_____	law	_____	law
_____	highway	_____	highway

THINKING ABOUT YOUR READING AND WRITING

ACTIVITY D: Evaluating What You Know

What are some features of facts and opinions that you think will be useful for you to remember as you listen to lectures and do your reading assignments?

_____

_____

_____

_____

_____

_____

ACTIVITY E: Writing Personal Facts and Opinions

In the space provided, write some factual and some opinion statements about yourself. As you do this, think about the criteria you are using to distinguish between fact and opinion.

Factual statements about you:

_____

_____

_____

_____

_____

Opinion statements about you:

_____

_____

_____

_____

_____

WORKING TOGETHER

Have a partner look at your personal factual and opinion statements in Activity E. Discuss whether they meet the criteria for each.

ACTIVITY F: Recognizing Statements of Fact and Opinion

Read each sentence and determine whether it is a statement of fact (F) or opinion (O). Mark your answer in the space provided. Be prepared to justify your answers.

1. Life on Earth depends on two fundamental processes: matter cycling and the one-way flow of high-quality energy from the sun. _____

2. Terminally ill patients can be kept alive hooked up to respirators, dialysis machines, and other devices that keep their vital organs functioning. _____

3. The tight end's personality changed for the worse when he made the varsity team. _____

4. The six-year-old girl was very mature for her age. _____

5. Smoking makes some people more sociable. _____

6. Smoking makes some people sick. _____

7. High school classes are a waste of time. _____

8. The score you achieve on some intelligence tests is called your IQ. _____

WORKING TOGETHER

Compare your answers to Activity F with those of a partner. If you disagree, try to reach agreement by reviewing the criteria for factual statements.

At this point, you are ready for some good news and some bad news. The good news is that by now you have developed some useful strategies for determining whether an idea is a statement of fact or opinion. The bad news is that many statements that appear in academic text are neither all fact nor all opinion. Very often a statement contains some fact *and* some opinion. This is a particularly useful technique for writing an argumentative or persuasive essay, one in which you are trying to convince the reader to accept a certain idea or viewpoint. The opinions are mingled with the facts, so the sentence sounds factual. But, in reality, only that portion that states a fact is verifiable. The rest of it must be considered opinion and open to disagreement.

For example, a sentence may read: *The World Trade Center in New York City, which was bombed in 1993, is very likely targeted for more attacks in the future.* The part of this sentence that is fact is *The World Trade Center in New York City, which was bombed in 1993.* The rest, which reads *is very likely targeted for more attacks in the future,* is the author's opinion.

Here's another example: *Although the Navajo have written many myths, none is as popular as that of the Big Fly, which has been part of the culture for centuries.* Which part is fact? You should have recognized that there are two factual parts in this sentence: *the Navajo have written many myths* is a fact. Further, the segment of the sentence that reads *which has been part of the culture for centuries* is a fact. One can check to see whether the Navajo have indeed written many myths and whether this particular myth has been part of the culture for so long. The rest of the sentence is definitely opinion. It would be hard to prove that one myth is more popular than another, and views on methods to use to judge popularity would vary.

Fact and opinion also can become intermingled when someone else's opinion is quoted. The quotation marks give the opinion the appearance of fact, and it is a fact that someone made the quoted statement, but often the idea within the quotation marks is an opinion. For example, consider the statement, *"The United States should consider a complete halt in nuclear power plant construction because of unresolved safety questions," an Atomic Energy Commission safety expert said on September 21, 1974.* An individual made this statement when he resigned from the Atomic Energy Commission because he felt the Commission was ignoring questions of safety. It is a fact that the AEC safety expert made this statement, and perhaps one could argue that it is a fact that there were *unresolved safety questions* when the statement was made. But the solution recommended, *a complete halt in nuclear power plant construction,* is an opinion.

In Activity G, you will have a chance to identify those parts of sentences that are fact and those that are opinion.

ACTIVITY G: Recognizing Segments of Fact and Opinion in Sentences

In each sentence, *underline* those portions that you believe to be fact. Remember that you are claiming that what is not underlined is opinion. More than one part of a sentence may be factual. Be prepared to justify your answers.

1. Although everyone feels sad now and then, 4 to 8 million Americans are treated yearly for clinical depression, and about 250,000 of these require hospitalization.
2. By 1885 fewer than 1,000 buffalo were left on the Midwest plains, and clearly there was little concern that the once-numerous quadrupeds were facing an inevitable complete extermination.
3. Ten years ago, John Graves Fletcher, a distinguished painter, designed the colorful, expressive murals in our student union building, which houses all clubs, fraternities, and sororities, as well as a number of auditoriums and conference rooms.
4. Today's adolescents graduate from high school with a diploma and feelings of optimism about their future.
5. Some scholars have spent decades studying the unplanned effects of social reform, and they have now reached the conclusion that everything has been tried, but nothing has worked.

THINKING ABOUT YOUR READING AND WRITING

ACTIVITY H: Reviewing Your Decision-Making Processes

Describe the thought process you used in Activity G to distinguish between fact and opinion. List as many of the steps you used in this procedure as you can.

_____

_____

_____

_____

_____

_____

_____

Evidence for Statements of Opinion

An opinion cannot be absolutely verified, but it can be supported with evidence that strengthens its force and makes it more believable. Critical readers will examine the type of evidence given for such statements to determine its value as support for the opinions or theories that are suggested. Several types of evidence commonly used in academic writing are discussed below.

Expert Opinion

Expert opinion differs from other opinions because the person expressing the opinion knows quite a bit about the subject being discussed. Examples include Eastern European historians discussing the end of communism in Eastern Europe, music historians discussing the influence of the Beatles on contemporary music, economists discussing a recession, and a physician giving medical testimony. When support for an opinion or theory is provided by an expert rather than by someone who knows little about the subject, that opinion carries more weight.

Informed Opinion

Authors and speakers preparing arguments or developing a thesis frequently conduct research or seek information from other sources that will help them prove their points. Informed opinions may include statistical reference, historical reference, the use of visual aids, and the use of personal experience.

REFERERENCE TO STATISTICS OBTAINED THROUGH RESEARCH. For instance, if someone has the opinion that gun control legislation deters crime, statistics from states that have passed gun control legislation may be used to provide evidence that in these states there has been a reduction in crime. If someone wants to argue that one method of teaching mathematics to children is superior to another, the argument can be bolstered by citing mathematics test scores of the children using the favored method or by comparing these test results to those of children who were taught by a different method.

There is one caution, however. Since in both examples a number of factors affect the situation being discussed, the facts cited as evidence are only partially useful. They do not give the whole picture. For example, crime might have dropped in cities that had passed gun control laws because the economy in those states was up. Or children who were using the favored math approach might have been in school systems that also had very small classes. When statistics are used to support arguments, they must be considered carefully. The one voicing the opinion has chosen to include only particular statistics. Other statistics may support an equally strong argument against it.

HISTORICAL REFERENCE.   The use of history to prove one's point is a fairly common strategy for creating the impression of an informed opinion. Phrases such *as history tells us* or *we know from the past* convince us that the opinion expressed is based on fact. Reference to historical documents, diaries, or speeches may be used as well. Critical readers will notice such references and will try to verify that the history as presented is both factually correct and unbiased.

THE USE OF VISUAL AIDS.   Photographs, charts, and diagrams give arguments an air of validity. After all, the reasoning goes, if it can be graphically depicted, it must be so. Consider, however, the photos on the covers of supermarket tabloids. Wonderful graphics can be made on computers as well. But how valid is what they portray? Further, you must analyze whether there is any relationship between what is on the graphic display and the idea under discussion. For instance, if one is arguing in favor of gun control legislation, a photo of a baby who has just been caught in the cross-fire between two drug dealers might be used. The impact on you is powerful. But how much support, beyond emotional appeal, does this photo lend to the key point? The critical reader will examine the source of the visual aid as well as the relationship between it and the argument or theory itself.

THE USE OF PERSONAL EXPERIENCE.   How often have you remarked that you knew something to be true because you experienced it yourself? Perhaps you have said this when expressing such opinions as the food in a particular restaurant is bad, a certain band has a great sound, or someone you know is a terrific athlete. When you gave your opinion, did everyone agree with you? It is very common to use personal experience as evidence for one's own theories or opinions, but critical thinkers will not rely too heavily on this type of evidence for judging the merit of ideas. People interpret their experiences differently. Personal experience is subjective, as are opinions themselves. When personal experience is used as evidence, it is really a case of using subjective evidence to support a subjective idea.

Unsupported Opinion

Unsupported opinions often consist of *sweeping generalizations* and *stereotypes.* These are even less reliable than opinions based on personal experience. For example, to give support to the argument that towns ought to have curfews for teenagers, one might say: *Today's parents have little time for disciplining their children.* This statement is not backed by any statistical evidence or facts. It is a personal opinion intended to give strength to the argument that towns need curfews. Or if one is arguing that the news media should be controlled by the government, one might also say: *The stories in many local newspapers encourage crime.* This claim is unsupported. It is merely an unsupported personal opinion. Even a seemingly noncontroversial view, such as that the Industrial Revolution had a major effect on the family life of Americans, would not be well defended if the only support given for such a statement was: *Men worked in factories for long hours and came home too tired to pay attention to their wives and families.* How is this known? It remains just an unsupported opinion unless some evidence is offered, such as statistics, entries from diaries of people living at the time, or findings from other research studies.

ACTIVITY I: Identifying Support for Opinions

Several statements of opinion follow. Beneath each opinion statement are two other sentences that provide support for the opinion. Based on the type of support given, indicate whether the opinion is an expert opinion

(EO), informed opinion (IO), or unsupported opinion (UO). Be prepared to justify your answers.

1. Sexual harassment in the workplace is far more common than most people suppose. _____

   ❊ One worker said she was sexually harassed by her boss nearly every day for six years.

   ❊ The American Civil Liberties Union noted that more than 200 cases of sexual harassment are reported to them every day.

2. Politicians have become extremely self-centered. _____

   ❊ Elected officials are more occupied with their own plans for reelection than with the public interest.

   ❊ Senators obviously spend more time campaigning in their home states than voting on important issues in Congress.

3. Prior to 1870, American children were not encouraged to think independently. _____

   ❊ One popular children's magazine I investigated, *Youth's Companion,* published from the mid-1800s until 1910, told children in 1856 to spend their time "thinking of ways they could achieve salvation."

   ❊ Another American periodical I examined, *Juvenile Miscellany,* first published in 1826, contained numerous stories of children who lived in fear of the dire consequences they would face if they did anything contrary to religious teachings.

4. Some actors and actresses pay a heavy price for stardom._____

   ❊ It is rumored that the legendary Greta Garbo once said she never married because "all those damn photographers would just follow us around then, maybe even to the bedroom."

   ❊ The public craves all the latest gossip on their favorite stars, making them the target of tabloid smear campaigns.

5. Single-parent families can no longer be viewed as nontraditional families. _____

❋ According to a study done by a Pennsylvania research group, more than 25 percent of American families are headed by either a mother or a father.

❋ Cincinnati school administrators report that nearly 30 percent of the children in its public schools live in single-parent homes now, as compared with 15 percent ten years ago.

6. Boredom is a serious problem in our society. _____

❋ Twenty-one percent of Americans say that they are regularly bored, and many researchers think the number is much higher.

❋ Studies have linked boredom to accidents, drug use, pathological gambling, and even street violence.

7. Photographers of children have to be more skilled than those who photograph other subjects. _____

❋ Children are less likely to stay still during a photo shoot than other subjects, such as mountains or trees.

❋ Children's personalities are difficult to capture on film.

WORKING TOGETHER

With a partner, provide different types of support to make each of the following statements an expert opinion, informed opinion, and unsupported opinion. Write your support in the space provided. (Be creative. Make up the support for an expert opinion and informed opinion if you wish.)

Statement 1: Small businesses provide service for their customers that larger businesses just cannot offer.

Support to make this an expert opinion: _____

_____

Support to make this an informed opinion: _____

_____

Support to make this an unsupported opinion: _____

_____

Statement 2:   People who watch their diet will be happier than people who eat whatever they choose.

Support to make this an expert opinion: _____

_____

Support to make this an informed opinion: _____

_____

Support to make this an unsupported opinion: _____

_____

Additional Criteria for Judging Facts and Opinions

As you evaluate ideas presented in texts and lectures, you should consider some additional factors.

The Author's Qualifications

Some authors are more knowledgeable about a subject than others because of the length of time they have been doing research, the experience they have had in the subject, and/or the formal training they have received in the subject. In textbooks, information about the author can often be found in the introduction or the foreword. Periodicals sometimes offer a brief biography of the author.

The Source of the Material

Hundreds of articles appear monthly in magazines, journals, and newspapers that are published by special-interest groups: religious organizations, groups with particular leanings, senior citizens' organizations, women's rights associations, labor unions, environmental protection organizations, and so on. Such affiliations are identified in the editorial box, usually found in the first few pages of the publication. The critical reader understands that an article that discusses whether parents should be concerned about the type of music listened to by today's teenagers would be very different if it appeared in *Good Housekeeping* magazine than if it appeared in *Spin.* The special interests of the publisher and the audiences for those two magazines are different; they play an important role in the content and method of presentation of information. Critical readers consider this when they evaluate the ideas presented.

The *recency of the information* must also be considered. If the material was published some time ago, its age may affect its value. In many fields, such as the sciences, history, and anthropology, new information continually updates older theories and research findings.

The Author's Bias

An author's opinion on an issue is a particular *bias, slant, position, perspective,* or *point of view.* The facts and opinions included are usually those that support that perspective. Thus, the details will reflect a particular slant. They will have been chosen because they support the author's point of view. At times, other positions are stated, but only to give the author a chance to show what is wrong with them. When you determine the extent to which the information is factual or subjective, as well as the source of the facts and opinions, you will be able to recognize author bias. Knowing the source of the material will also help you establish the author's bias, even before you begin your reading. If an author appears to be particularly biased, you may want to read additional material on the same subject written from another point of view. This will give you a fuller picture of the issues involved and the different sides of the argument. This aspect of critical reading is discussed more thoroughly in the next section.

Recognizing Point of View

An author's writing often reflects personal beliefs about a subject. When readers identify these beliefs, they are finding the author's point of view or bias. A point of view may concern a very controversial topic, such as whether there should be mandatory testing for AIDS in the workplace. Or an author may express a point of view on something less controversial that is still a topic about which people may have differing opinions, such as the best way to make chocolate chip cookies. This bias usually results from the author's perspective on a subject. For example, an author may use one of several perspectives to discuss a plan by New York City's mayor to overhaul the mass transit system:

* The perspective of someone who lives in the city and who regularly uses the system
* The perspective of a Rochester, New York, resident who would have to pay toward the system but who does not use it
* The perspective of a senior citizen who doesn't use the system but lives in New York City and would pay increased taxes

Whatever the author's perspective, the result is a particular bias toward the subject that reveals itself in the content.

Readers may sometimes recognize that an author's point of view differs from their own. It is always useful to consider how an author's own experience and background have influenced his or her point of view and to assess how your own experience and background influence your position on the same subject. You also need to consider other possible points of view.

A single word can suggest much about your attitude or point of view toward a person or situation. For instance, if you refer to a person as a *dedicated worker,* you are saying something positive. But if you call that same person a *workaholic,* you are conveying a negative attitude about the same set of behaviors. Following a class debate, you might comment to a friend that the class debate was *stimulating,* or you might call it *argumentative.* One city dweller visiting a small town might call it *dull;* another person visiting the same town might describe it as *peaceful.* In each case the descriptive word suggests a reaction to the same experience, and in each case the reaction is clearly different.

In the example that follows, we illustrate a point of view on a controversial subject. Several questions about the paragraph are asked and then answered.

Example:

> In sixteen of the past seventeen Gallup polls on education, poor student discipline has been the most frequent criticism of public schools. Are better discipline codes and more homework adequate remedies for our current school problems? Or are the problems more profound? Should they be treated with more sensitive and complex remedies? Literacy and student effort are certainly worthy goals, but they are only part of the process of communicating serious morality. If we want to improve the ways we are now transmitting morality to students, we need to ana-

lyze the way morality used to be transmitted, before youth disorder became such a distressing issue.

❋ *What is the author's point of view?* Behavior problems in school are a distressing issue. They are related to morality, and they cannot be solved simply by stricter discipline codes.

❋ *What evidence is there that this is the author's point of view?* The author says that more old-fashioned methods of teaching morality to children should be used. The author refers to Gallup polls to prove the point that people are concerned about the behavior of today's youth.

❋ *How does this point of view compare with your own on this subject?* This question calls for a personal reaction. You may agree or disagree with the author's point of view for your own reasons.

❋ *What other points of view are possible?* Even if you agree with the author, others might not. Some might suggest that it is parental neglect in the home that causes problems in the school, not the methods we use to communicate morality. Others might suggest that stricter discipline policies in school would solve the problem.

Notice that in the example the author uses specific words that suggest the point of view. Words such as *remedies, criticisms, problems,* and *distressing* all convey the author's bias.

ACTIVITY J: Determining Point of View

Read each paragraph to identify the point of view and then answer the questions that follow. Where you are asked to give evidence to support your own point of view, it may be from some source other than the paragraph.

1. A report released by the U.S. Bureau of Justice Statistics in 1997 indicated that in 1994, 29 percent of persons whose most serious conviction offense was a drug-trafficking felony got probation instead of incarceration; so did 31 percent of those whose most serious conviction offense was a weapons crime felony. Weapons offenders were thus slightly more likely than drug merchants to escape incarceration and get probation. In Massachusetts and several other states, about half of probationers are

under supervision for a violent crime, while half of those in prison for drug law violations have no official record of violence. From a crime control perspective, forcing drug-only offenders behind bars while violent offenders beat feet to the streets is just plain batty.

John J. DiIulio Jr., "Against Mandatory Minimums," *National Review* 51(9) (1999): 46.

What is the subject? _____

_____

What is the author's point of view toward this subject? _____

_____

What evidence is there that this is the author's point of view? ___

_____

How does this point of view compare with your own? _____

_____

What evidence do you have to support your viewpoint? _____

_____

What other points of view are possible? _____

_____

2. Over the past decade, 68 new ballparks have been constructed throughout the United States. Among the leagues affiliated with Major League Baseball, four new ballparks opened in 1999, and four more are opening this year. Many Tulsans have been to the magnificent new Bricktown Ballpark in Oklahoma City and have seen not just a first-class stadium but also the millions of private dollars that have been invested in the commercial development surrounding the ballpark. This phenomenon is creating real economic growth in our city.

Adapted from Terry Simonson, *Urban Tulsa Weekly Online,* 15–22 June 2000.

What is the subject? _____

_____

What is the author's point of view toward this subject? _____

_____

What evidence is there that this is the author's point of view?

_____

How does this point of view compare with your own? _____

_____

What evidence do you have to support your viewpoint? _____

_____

What other points of view are possible? _____

_____

3. The corporation is a relatively new form of business ownership
    that didn't become really popular until about a century ago. Yet
    today it's the best-known and most powerful form of business
    ownership in the country. Although less than 15 percent of all
    U.S. businesses are corporations, they account for over 86 per-
    cent of revenues each year and receive 75 percent of all profits.
    This staggering financial record gives corporations tremendous
    economic and political clout. Corporations even influence cam-
    paigns by forming political action committees (PACs) to con-
    tribute to favored candidates.

    Leon C. Megginson et al., *Business* (Lexington, MA: Heath, 1985), 66.

What is the subject? _____

_____

What is the author's point of view toward this subject? _____

_____

What evidence is there that this is the author's point of view?

_____

How does this point of view compare with your own? _____

_____

What evidence do you have to support your viewpoint? _____

_____

What other points of view are possible? _____

_____

4. Today there seems to be an indifference to the flag. In the United States, changes in the values of the average citizen and permissive legislators have tended to reduce patriotic days and holidays to just an extra day off, no more than a long weekend. Flag Day is not a holiday in the United States. Although it is marked on calendars, it is merely observed by a few people with little or no fanfare, and for most Americans, the day passes without knowledge of the significance of the date.

    Adapted from Richard Skidmore, *San Francisco Examiner,* 16 June 2000.

    What is the subject? _____

    _____

    What is the author's point of view toward this subject? _____

    _____

    What evidence is there that this is the author's point of view?

    _____

    How does this point of view compare with your own? _____

    _____

    What evidence do you have to support your viewpoint? _____

    _____

    What other points of view are possible? _____

    _____

5. Driving or riding in a car is one of the most dangerous things Americans do. We may worry about flying in jets or swimming in the sea, but being on the road is where we are most likely to be injured or killed. And in more than nine of 10 accidents, somebody wasn't paying close enough attention.

    In 1997, a study appeared in the *New England Journal of Medicine* which examined the risks of driving while using a cell phone. The conclusion: "The use of cellular telephones in motor vehicles is associated with a quadrupling of the risk of a collision during the brief period of a call." It's comparable to being drunk.

    Steve Heilig, "S.F. Should Ban Cell Phone Use by Drivers," *San Francisco Examiner,* June 16, 2000: A23.

What is the subject? _____

_____

What is the author's point of view toward this subject? _____

_____

What evidence is there that this is the author's point of view? ____

_____

How does this point of view compare with your own? _____

_____

What evidence do you have to support your viewpoint? _____

_____

What other points of view are possible? _____

_____

WORKING TOGETHER

Compare your responses to Activity J with those of a partner. Look for differences in point of view.

THINKING ABOUT YOUR READING AND WRITING

ACTIVITY K: Personal Response to Point of View

Do you think it is more interesting to read ideas that are similar to or different from your own? Explain your answer.

_____

_____

_____

_____

_____

_____

Reading to Make Inferences

Have you ever decided whether or not to see a movie based on the reactions of people coming out of the theater? Many people find this a useful way to judge whether or not to spend their money on seeing a film. Since strangers coming out of the theater most likely won't just come out and tell you their opinions, it is useful to know what to look for as audience indicators of a good movie: people laughing or crying (depending on the movie content) or people excitedly talking about it. Similarly, authors often don't tell you everything. Critical readers look for ideas that are *suggested* in text as well as for those that are directly stated. When you identified the author's point of view, you looked for words or phrases that suggested bias, as well as at the particular content the author chose to discuss. This was *inferential reading*. In this section, we discuss strategies for making other types of inferences: inferences about events, characters, or ideas that are suggested by the information stated in the text.

Inferences in Everyday Life

We are constantly making guesses, or *inferences,* about things we see, hear, and read. Imagine, for instance, that your attention is caught by a front-page photo in this morning's newspaper: A Jeep is turned over; shattered glass is all around it. The middle of the Jeep looks crushed. A car is close behind it. Standing beside the car is a young man looking off into the distance. Also next to the car is a firefighter. Across the street is a fire truck, its hose extending to the Jeep. Without reading the caption, you can already infer what has happened: a serious accident. Clearly, this was not some stunt being performed or some advertising ploy designed to capture the attention of Jeep buyers. Only one driver is in the photo, near the car; maybe the driver of the Jeep is trapped inside or has been taken to a hospital. That driver probably didn't survive. You wonder if there were any passengers. You also guess that there was a fire in the Jeep, caused when it flipped over. The man standing by the Jeep may have driven the car and may have caused the accident. It is hard to tell. But he doesn't look hurt.

You are hypothesizing all this information through your interpretation of the picture. You still have not read any text. Now you read the article beneath the photo. It confirms some of your hypotheses and denies others: there was an accident and a fire; a young boy, not the driver, had been killed. Making inferences from text, without photos, works in much the same way.

Finding Support for Your Inferences

An inference is an "informed guess" you make about something you read or experience. Your guess is based on what you know from your *prior experience*. You also use *information given* in the text, photograph, cartoon, letter, situation, or dialogue about which you are making inferences. What you know (the factual details in the text as well as your prior knowledge) provide the evidence or support for your guess. The inferences you make must follow logically from the available information. As more information becomes available, you may need to modify your original thinking. The following example illustrates how the process of making inferences works and how new information may cause you to reject inferences you made earlier. Read sentence 1. Then decide which statements beneath it could be appropriate guesses, based on the information in that sentence, as well as on your prior knowledge.

> **Sentence 1:**   The surgeon quickly removed his gloves and scanned the chart on the wall.
>
> **Possible inferences:**   [Decide which inferences are logical. More than one can be selected. Put the letter(s) of your choice(s) in the space provided.]
>
> a. The surgeon had just completed surgery.
>
> b. The surgeon felt the surgery had gone poorly.
>
> c. The surgeon was getting ready for his next patient.
>
> d. The surgeon was in a hurry.
>
> e. The surgeon had been cold.
>
> f. The surgeon was an experienced pilot.
>
> ***Supported inferences:*** _____

There is evidence that supports sentences a, c, d, and e. For sentence (a), the evidence is that he was taking off gloves. You know that surgeons wear gloves. For sentence (c), the evidence is that he is looking at a chart, which might be a chart of patients and surgery schedules. You know that hospitals use charts for patients. For sentence (d), the evidence is the word *quickly,* which describes how the gloves were removed. For sentence (e), the evidence is that the surgeon was wearing gloves. He might have come inside from where he had been cold and then taken off the gloves.

Now read sentence 2, which gives additional information. From your choices of inferences that seemed logical based on sentence 1 and your prior knowledge, eliminate those that no longer make sense. In the space provided, list only those inferences that can now be supported.

Sentence 2:   The airport where he was now waiting for his departure was freezing cold.

Supported inferences: _____

The sentences to be eliminated as logical inferences are (a) and (c). In both cases, the sentences are contradicted by the fact that the surgeon is at an airport. You know that surgery is not performed at airports.

The sentence to be added as a logical inference is (f). Sentence (f) is a logical inference because he is at an airport, and it is possible he will fly a plane. The charts he is looking at in sentence 1 might be connected to his flight. You know that airports keep various charts and records of flight schedules. We now have sentences (d), (e), and (f) as inferences that can be supported based on the information from the first two sentences.

Now read sentence 3, which gives additional details. Repeat the procedure you used with sentence 2.

Sentence 3:   From the chart, he learned which instructor he had been assigned to for his first flying lesson.

Supported inferences: _____

What sentences did you say are now suitable as inferences? Only (d) and (e) remain as logical inferences. Sentence 3 contradicts choice (f), which, based on sentence 2, initially seemed possible.

You can see how important it is not to jump to conclusions. Every sentence *before and after* the sentence from which you make an inference contains information that will assist you in determining the extent to which your inference is valid. Reject your inference if you can't find support for it in the material and if you have no prior knowledge to support it.

This process of making inferences while you read is applicable to any kind of text, regardless of length or subject matter. It works for both nonfictional (expository) and fictional (narrative) reading material. Activity M offers additional practice in applying this reading and thinking strategy.

THINKING ABOUT YOUR READING AND WRITING

ACTIVITY L: Understanding How to Make Inferences
In your own words, explain the process for making inferences.

_____

_____

_____

_____

_____

ACTIVITY M: Identifying Possible Inferences
Beneath each paragraph are several possible inferences. For each possible inference, indicate whether it is supported (S) or contradicted (C) by the information given in the paragraph. If there is no information either supporting or contradicting the possible inference, write (?) to indicate that the inference is neither supported nor contradicted by the paragraph. Be prepared to cite evidence for your answers. Your evidence may include

your prior knowledge but should also include information from the passage.

Example:

> Major advertisers, eager to tap the estimated $134 billion in spending power wielded by Spanish-speaking Americans, have ventured into "Spanglish" to promote their products. In some cases, attempts to sprinkle Spanish through commercials have produced embarrassing mistakes. An ad for now-bankrupt Braniff Airlines that sought to tell Spanish-speaking audiences they could settle back *en* (in) a luxurious *cuero* (seat), for example, mistakenly said they could fly without clothes (*encuero*).

Possible inferences:

<u> S </u>   a. Corporations will write specific ads for specific audiences. (The first sentence supports this inference.)

<u> S </u>   b. Large corporations are willing to spend huge sums of money on advertising.
(The first sentence also supports this inference.)

<u> ? </u>   c. Spanish-speaking Americans object to ads designed to appeal especially to them.
(There is no information about this in the paragraph.)

<u> S </u>   d. It is sometimes difficult to translate concepts from one language to another.
(The example given illustrates this inference.)

<u> C </u>   e. Braniff intended its ad to be humorous.
(It is suggested that this was an "embarrassing mistake.")

1. Benedict Arnold had long considered himself unjustly treated by Congress. Time and again, his brilliant gifts had been overlooked and less able officers promoted over his head. But such had also been the lot of other competent commanders in the army, yet none turned traitor to his country. Arnold, however, feeling mistreated and suffering financial embarrassment due to his own reckless expenditures and the extravagances of his pretty wife, the former Peggy Shippen, entered into secret negotiations

with Sir Henry Clinton. On the promise of a large sum of money and a command in the British army, he agreed to surrender West Point, key fortress to the Hudson River Valley and vital to communication lines between New England and the other states.

Possible inferences:

_____   a. Benedict Arnold easily forgave people.
_____   b. Benedict Arnold knew that his negotiations with the British army were wrong.
_____   c. Benedict Arnold's wife encouraged him to be a traitor.
_____   d. Benedict Arnold was guided by his feelings more than by his intellect.
_____   e. Sir Henry Clinton knew of Benedict Arnold's financial problems.

2. Web sites have to maintain a high degree of integrity with every transaction, and they should be independently tested for compliance against a stringent set of standards. Many a Web site loses sales when the buyer has to struggle to complete a transaction. Nothing alienates shoppers more often than order-entry glitches that cause the loss of entered information, computer freezes, or being bounced off the site. A site's lack of full disclosure regarding actual costs is also a big turnoff. Online shoppers want to know all costs before going through detailed registration in order to avoid surprises and significant changes to the online price. An order-tracking system that allows online shoppers to review orders and/or maintain addresses and credit card information is also very helpful in building trust in a site.

"Best Practices for Building Consumer Trust," *Journal of Accountancy* 189 no. 6 (2000): 32.

Possible inferences:

_____   a. Online shoppers expect shopping on the Web to be easy.
_____   b. Prices of goods that can be bought on the Web are often higher than the price of the same item in a retail shop.

_____ c. Customer privacy is the major reason people don't shop online.

_____ d. Online shoppers might become repeat customers at good Web sites.

_____ e. Companies that sell on the Web have increased their overall sales volume.

3. The ethical code that all physicians recite when the join the medical profession today goes back at least 2000 years. The Hippocratic oath defines what ethical behavior is when a physician works with his or her patients. The oath describes not only the methods that physicians should and should not use in treating the ill but also the code of conduct they should follow in working with patients. One part of the code says, for example, "Whatever, in connection with my professional practice, or not in connection with it, I see or hear, in the life of men which ought not to be spoken of abroad, I will not divulge as reckoning that all such should be kept secret."

Possible inferences:

_____ a. Ethical problems in medicine have concerned men and women for a long time.

_____ b. The concern for ethics in medicine originated in the United States.

_____ c. Some patients prefer physicians who have not taken the Hippocratic oath.

_____ d. Part of the ethical behavior of physicians is to respect a patient's right to privacy.

_____ e. Today, graduates of medical schools in Europe do not have to take the Hippocratic oath.

4. Flying solo isn't necessarily a lonely ride, says Duane Alwin, a University of Michigan expert on single living and mental health. A large body of research indicates that unmarried people suffer more from depression, anxiety, and ill health than those who are married—the theory being that close relationships protect the married against stresses the unmarried face alone. But Alwin argues that solitary living itself can't be held responsible. People need strong ties with others to be happy, he says, but it

can't be assumed that living alone prevents those ties from forming.

J. Seligman, "The Art of Flying Solo," *Newsweek,* 1 March 1993, 70.

Possible inferences:

_____ a. Duane Alwin is married.
_____ b. The longer a person is married, the less he or she will feel depressed.
_____ c. Unmarried people are incapable of forming strong ties with others.
_____ d. Flying solo refers to being unmarried.
_____ e. Sometimes there is disagreement about psychological theories.

5. Full-service gas stations are all but extinct in the U.S. Today about 90 percent of gasoline purchases—some 16 billion transactions a year, according to the American Petroleum Institute in Washington, D.C.—are made by customers willing to pump for themselves. Self-serve technology has changed relatively little since 1947, when two Californians seem to have come up with the idea almost simultaneously. Although self-serve stations saved customers money (the first ones charged five cents less per gallon), they were thought to be a fad, something Americans would eventually tire of. But by the 1970s they were clearly here to stay. New Jersey and Oregon, however, still allow only station attendants to pump gas.

Marguerite Holloway, "Fill 'Er Up," *Scientific American* 282 no. 5 (2000): 92.

Possible inferences:

_____ a. Americans like to do things for themselves.
_____ b. It saves gas stations money when customers do self-serve.
_____ c. Extensive research is being done to improve self-serve technology.
_____ d. Self-serve stations will probably lose popularity in the next decade.
_____ e. New Jerseyans have fought vigorously to keep self-serve stations out of their state.

6. Fire escapes are wonderful tools for firefighters—they get us up to, down from, at, into, out of, and down. But they cause injuries, too. They have disappeared from the new construction in our cities and towns. They have been legislated out of existence by new building codes. They have become forgotten as inspection areas. They are left unattended, cluttered, and unmaintained! They come loose from support assemblies, come apart from corrosion, and are loaded with tripping hazards. But the hazard most often associated with roof teams is the gooseneck ladder—the one that gets you on or off the roof and from or to the top-floor balcony of the fire escape system. The weakest point is where the fire ladder is connected to the roof boards. Before you use it, shake it. When you are on that vertical ladder, "hook" your hand tools on the rungs so that you have both hands free, and anticipate what you will do if the ladder weakens and begins to fail. Remember, no surprises in this game!

Tom Brennan, "Roof 'Safely,'" *Fire Engineering* 153(4) (2000): 1.

Possible inferences:

_____ a. Firefighters have no way to protect themselves from fire escapes that are poorly maintained.

_____ b. Fire escapes are viewed as a necessary part of new buildings.

_____ c. Fire escapes can become damaged by the weather.

_____ d. Some parts of the fire escape system are more dangerous than others.

_____ e. Changes in building codes can have unintended consequences.

THINKING ABOUT YOUR READING AND WRITING

ACTIVITY N: Contrasts in Processes for Inferences and Main Ideas

In a few sentences, explain how the thought processes you use to make inferences differ from those you use to find main ideas.

_____

_____

_____

_____

_____

_____

Identifying Author's Style, Mood, and Tone

Critical readers are aware that several other features of a written work contribute to its overall effect. These features include the author's *style, mood,* and *tone.* We discuss each separately in this section, but as with all the elements of an article or essay, they work together to create a single effect on the reader. Style, mood, and tone describe *how* something has been written. *How* something has been written affects the reader's response to the text.

Identifying Style

The author's style refers to the *types of words* and *sentence construction* the author uses in order to appeal to a particular type of audience. Some writers want to appeal to a wide audience. They will use fairly common expressions, slang, or easy-to-read sentences. Other authors are addressing their comments to a more informed group. Their sentences tend to be longer, and their choice of words more sophisticated. If a writer expects the audience to have a great deal of knowledge of the subject, he or she may use more technical language. Authors who want to persuade their audience to respond in a certain way will use emotional language; others will not make any effort to appeal to their readers' emotions. Authors' purposes, then, influence the language they use.

Writers, of course, generally do not tell their readers what style they are using. The reader must know what to look for within the text itself in order to determine the author's style. The process is similar to the one you used to search for evidence to make other types of inferences.

Example 1:

> Long-haul drivers, away from family and hearth for weeks at a time, put in longer hours to make a decent living than any other workers in America. From up high in a big truck we can look down into your little cars and scope out the "seat covers" (passengers). Despite what we sometimes see, we often wish we were in this other, more normal world. We can watch couples argue with each other, watch ladies try to drive to work and paint their faces at the same time, watch the less affluent people with their windows rolled down in the summer (no AC) but looking so proud: black T shirt, the driver's beefy arm hanging out the window with the radio blasting. (It's amazing how healthy the males look and how sparky the females in those noisy, hot cages.) Our TV screen is the windshield and yes, we male drivers do leer sometimes, enjoying the view as we observe the multiethnic, sultry femucopia of south Florida, the aggressive, preening go-getters driving the D.C. beltway, the Chicago working girls as we pass the train platforms alongside I-94, or the sunbathers along any beach highway. But what every driver likes even more, when he can get it, is a little respect.
>
> J. Aalborg, "The View from the Big Road," *Newsweek,* 20 December 1993, 10.

The author of this paragraph does not use a very extensive vocabulary, and the language is informal. Words such as *scope out* and *AC* contribute to this informality. The sentences are not complicated, either. They are short and easy to read. The intended audience is probably, then, a large general audience—perhaps all of us who have wondered about the life of the long-haul driver. The style is very natural, down to earth. The examples that illustrate what the drivers see—all of us—connect the author to all of us. By relating so personally to us, the driver is able to keep our attention to the end when he asks for *respect.* The author's style, then, helps accomplish his purpose.

Example 2:

> When an external magnetic field is applied to a diamagnetic substance, such as bismuth, the only magnetic moments included in the substance are aligned *against* the external field. Correspondingly, a diamagnetic substance has a *negative* suscep-

tibility. Furthermore, one finds that a diamagnetic sample is *repelled* when placed near the pole of a strong magnet (in contrast with a paramagnetic sample, which is *attracted*). Although the effect of diamagnetism is present in all matter, it is weak compared with paramagnetism and ferromagnetism.

The language of this passage is extremely technical. The author assumes that readers are familiar with the subject already. The sentences are fairly long and complex, but the author believes that this educated audience will be able to follow. Since the language is unemotional, the author's intention is probably just to convey information. By writing with a straightforward style, the author is able to accomplish this purpose.

Critical readers who are sensitive to an author's style will have another measure by which to evaluate the usefulness of an author's ideas. You will be able to select material that is suitable for your own purposes. For instance, if you are writing a research paper, you would want to use material that has itself been researched and has used authoritative sources to support personal opinions. On the other hand, if you are reading for pleasure, you might prefer material written for a wide general audience rather than a specialized one. Many authors are sensitive to their audiences. A textbook author who is aware that students are taking an introductory course in the particular discipline, for example, will often use examples they can relate to in order to help them comprehend the subject matter. This is often not the case in textbooks written for advanced students, who are expected to have more knowledge of the field.

Keep in mind, too, that an author's style should have a bearing on your reading rate. If the language is very technical, you will need to slow down. If the writing style is more like that of the first example, you can go at a faster pace.

ACTIVITY O: Identifying Author's Style

Read each paragraph, noting the style in which it is written. Then answer the questions that follow.

1. Our nation's economy today is a far cry from what the classical economists envisioned. In Chapter 9, we will survey and discuss the changes in size and influence of our various levels of government. Today, a third of the market value of all the production in

the United States, called the *gross national product* (GNP), is spent by our local, state, and national governments.

Who is the intended audience? _____

How do you know? _____

Is there any evidence that the author is trying to appeal to your emotions? If so, what is it? _____

_____

2. Prague is beautiful year-round, but avoid midsummer (especially July and August) and the Christmas and Easter holidays, when the city is overrun with tourists. Spring and fall generally combine good weather with a more bearable level of tourism. During the winter months you'll encounter few other visitors, and have the opportunity to see Prague breathtakingly covered in snow; but it can get very cold. The same guidelines generally apply to traveling in the rest of Bohemia and Moravia, although even in August the peak of the high season, the number of visitors to these areas is far smaller than in Prague. The Giant Mountains of Bohemia come into their own in winter (December–February), when skiers from all over the country crowd the slopes and resorts. If you're not a skier, try visiting the mountains in late spring (May or June) or fall, when the colors are dazzling and you'll have the hotels and restaurants nearly to yourself.

Matthew Lore, ed., *Fodor's Eastern and Central Europe* (New York: Fodor's Travel Publications, 1996), 27.

Who is the intended audience? _____

How do you know? _____

Is there any evidence that the author is trying to appeal to your emotions? If so, what is it? _____

_____

3. Many people came in contact with Elinor, including some people of power and influence. Many tried to assist her. Could not someone, some agency, have done something to alter the course of her seemingly inevitable destruction? In many ways,

Elinor chose the way she lived, she chose to stay in the terminal. But that's just too simple: she was a victim.

Who is the intended audience?_____

How do you know?_____

Is there any evidence that the author is trying to appeal to your emotions? If so, what is it?_____

_____

4. Cotton was grown in the American South, sold to English factories, where it was made into clothing, and then sent back to the United States, where it was bought by Americans. By the 1850s, tariffs on the clothing that was brought into the country greatly reduced the profits that the English could make on their products. As a result, the English naturally bought less cotton from the South. Southerners complained bitterly about the tariffs but could do nothing about them.

Who is the intended audience?_____

How do you know?_____

Is there any evidence that the author is trying to appeal to your emotions? If so, what is it?_____

_____

5. Any viewer of the United States who watched regularly the television reporting from Vietnam—and it was from television that 60 percent of Americans got most of their war news—would agree that he saw scenes of real-life violence, death, and horror on his screen that would have been unthinkable before Vietnam. The risk and intrusion that such filming involved could, perhaps, be justified if it could be shown that television had been particularly effective in revealing the true nature of the war and thus had been able to change people's attitudes to it. Is there any evidence to this effect?

Phillip Knightley, "The First Televised War," in *Fields of Writing*, 3rd ed., ed. N. R. Comley et al. (New York: St. Martin's, 1975), 632.

Who is the intended audience?_____

How do you know? _____

Is there any evidence that the author is trying to appeal to your emotions? If so, what is it? _____

_____

WORKING TOGETHER

Compare your answers to Activity O with those of a partner. Did you agree on which paragraphs made emotional appeals to readers?

Identifying Mood and Tone

Words can be powerful descriptors of feeling. Mood and tone refer to the emotional atmosphere created by written language. When readers analyze narrative text (short stories, poetry, plays, and novels), the terms *mood* and *tone* may be used interchangeably. A character's dialogue, for instance, may simultaneously suggest a tone and create a mood, as in the case of a dying soldier who bids a passionate farewell to his lover. However, when readers analyze expository text (essays, newspaper or periodical articles, and textbook chapters), the term *tone* is generally used. Once again, you will need to infer the author's meaning. The author may not tell you directly what mood or tone is present in the writing. You will need to analyze the word choice and the details of the writing to understand its mood or tone. You will be able to further appreciate and understand mood and tone by looking at some everyday examples of them.

Your experiences communicating with others have no doubt made you sensitive to differences in tone of voice. If a friend is troubled, you might listen and talk sympathetically. If you are speaking to someone who has damaged your property, you probably sound angry. If a new co-worker asks you to explain some work-related procedure, you probably use an instructional or serious tone of voice. If you have very strong feelings in an argument, you may be passionate when you explain your point of view. We adjust our tone of voice to suit the situation and our purpose, as well as to convey our feelings in the situation. Authors of expository text, or narrators of a literary work, use tone to reflect serious, angry, sympathetic, instructional, argumentative or persuasive, humorous, or ironic attitudes.

Tone can influence our personal reactions to a piece of writing or toward a character. Consider, for instance, the difference in your reactions to someone who requests a favor and sounds sweet and grateful, compared with someone who sounds demanding and insistent. You should recognize that your response to what you read may be similarly influenced by its tone. Thus, to read critically, you will need to be able to separate the content of what is said from the manner in which it is said. Then you will be able to honestly assess whether the ideas have merit.

As a critical reader, try to match your purpose for reading to the author's purpose for writing. Doing this will help your comprehension. For instance, if an author writes an essay suggesting that people should never own pets and does so in a humorous vein, the reader who recognizes the humor will read it as a humorous piece and won't criticize the author for having outrageous ideas. However, readers who think this author is serious will misinterpret the entire essay. To accomplish this reader–writer match in purpose, it is essential to determine the author's tone.

The mood of a written work may refer to the frame of mind of a character, as reflected through the character's actions, dialogue, and tone of voice. Mood also refers to the general atmosphere that surrounds an incident or scene; it is created by description and details or events. To further understand this element of a writer's craft, imagine that you are getting ready for a first date with someone you find pretty exciting. Your date has planned the entire evening. You hope for candlelight and champagne; instead, you are treated to hot dogs and a football game. Obviously, there is a difference in the mood or atmosphere created by the details used to describe each of these situations.

Authors of narrative text use details for a variety of purposes. One of these is to create a particular mood for their story. The details work together to create an overall effect. Some examples of mood that you might find in narrative text are suspense or mystery, horror, gaiety or joyfulness, sadness, gloominess, anticipation or adventure, romance, loneliness, hopefulness, and frustration.

If an author has been successful at creating a particular mood, the reader will feel it. Notice the contrast between the following two example paragraphs, both of which are about the same event. One has been written with carefully chosen details so as to create a certain mood; the other seems flat by comparison. Note the difference in the effect each has on you, the reader.

Example 1:

> It was unbelievably wonderful to be home. The first thing she did was to race upstairs, tear off her uniform, and put on some proper clothes—an old cotton skirt, a well-worn white shirt left over from school, her favorite red sweater. Nothing had changed; the room was just the way she had left it, only tidier and shiningly clean. When, bare legged, she ran downstairs again, it was to go from room to room, a thorough inspection, just to make sure that there, as well, everything was exactly the same. Which it was.

Example 2:

> It was good to be home. She first went upstairs, took off her uniform, and put on some proper clothes—a cotton skirt, a white shirt left over from school, a red sweater. Her room was as she had left it, only cleaner. After dressing, she went downstairs again to go through the house to make sure that there, as well, everything was the way she had left it. Which it was.

*What mood or tone is created by Example 1?*_____

*What details contribute to its effectiveness?*_____

_____

_____

There is an air of excitement in the first example that isn't present in the second. Some of the details that help create this mood are the phrases *unbelievably wonderful* and *nothing had changed*. We can tell how glad the girl is to be home and to be putting on her *favorite red sweater*. These details, and others you may have noticed, work together to create the mood.

ACTIVITY P: Identifying Author's Mood and Tone

In the space provided, indicate the tone or mood that has been used in each paragraph. Then explain why you believe this is the tone or mood of the passage.

Example:

> All health-care workers must follow universal precautions and established infection-control procedures to reduce infection risks to patients and themselves. Appropriate use and disposal of needles and sharp instruments are the most important risk-reduction strategy. In addition, universal precautions include the use of gloves, masks, eye protection, and other barriers as needed for procedures that involve contact with blood and body fluids.

Mood or tone: informative; serious

Explanation: A good deal of information is given. There is not much emotional language.

1. Every new advance in medicine—every new drug, new operation, new therapy of any kind—must sooner or later be tried on a living being for the first time. That trial, controlled or uncontrolled, will be an experiment. The subject of that experiment, if not an animal, will be a human being. Prohibiting the use of live animals in biomedical research, therefore, or sharply restricting it, must result either in the blockage of much valuable research or in the replacement of animal subjects with human subjects. These are the consequences—unacceptable to most reasonable persons—of not using animals in research.

   Mood or tone: _____

   Explanation: _____

   _____

2. I speak from experience when I say that cigar smokers have suffered the scorn of Americans who think our habit is vile. We have seen the steady disappearance of places where cigar smoking is acceptable. Now we are being told that the federal government wants to raise taxes on our cigars to help finance health care. Eventually, cigars will cost nothing because if the prices keep going up and there's nowhere to smoke them, nobody's going to smoke them. The whole thing makes me nauseous.

   Mood or tone: _____

   Explanation: _____

   _____

3. As terrible as the fear of existence is, the fear of nonexistence is even worse. Maybe if we only knew what happened to us after we died, it would all be easier.

    One speculation is that we go to the Land of the Umbrellas. You've probably seen them at the end of every rainstorm. Lying in the gutter, crumpled, skeletal, inside-out, bereft of personal history. Who did these umbrellas belong to? Where are they going? What use are they now?

    Others say that after death we go to the Land of the M&M's—the place where the M&M's go after they fall behind the cushions on the sofa. Or some say it's the Land of the Other Shoe. (Ever drive along the road and see only one shoe lying on the pavement and wonder how it got there? You never see *both shoes;* the other shoe has gone to join the umbrellas and the M&M's.)

    In the end, it is probably foolish to speculate about such matters. In ancient times, the biggest fear was that you would have a terrible life and be reincarnated, and the next life would be even worse. Nowadays, life is Hollywood, and if your life's been bad, you don't have to worry about there being a sequel. Not if Part I didn't make any money.

    Stephanie Brush, "Life: A Warning," in *The Big Book of North American Humor,* ed. W. Novak and M. Waldoks (New York: HarperCollins, 1990), 178.

    Mood or tone: _____

    Explanation: _____

    _____

4. He sat on a bench here, watching the leafy trees and the flowers blooming on the inside of the railing, thinking of a better life for himself. He thought of the jobs he had had since he had quit school—delivery boy, stock clerk, runner, lately working in a factory—and he was dissatisfied with all of them. He felt he would someday like to have a good job and live in a private house with a porch on a street with trees. He wanted to have some dough in his pocket to buy things with, and a girl to go

with, so as not to be so lonely, especially on Saturday nights. He wanted people to like and respect him.

Bernard Malamud, "A Summer's Reading," in *Best Short Stories: Advanced Level,* 2nd ed., ed. R. Harris (Providence, RI: Jamestown Publishers, 1990), 91.

Mood or tone: _____

Explanation: _____

_____

5. She looked up at him, the wide, young eyes blazing with light. And he bent down and kissed her on the lips. And the dawn blazed in them, their new life came to pass, it was beyond all conceiving good, it was so good, that it was almost like a passing-away, a trespass. He drew her suddenly closer to him.

Mood or tone: _____

Explanation: _____

_____

6. Alfred lowered the gun. One shot, and he would be cornered like a rabbit at harvest time. If he was going to kill the man, he would have to do so silently. With the Colt in his right hand, he pulled off his shoes and crept cautiously across the tiles. A chimney stack obstructed his view for part of the way. By the time he rounded it, Snits had raised the rifle to his shoulder and was settling himself into a firing position.

Mood or tone: _____

Explanation: _____

_____

7. It should not be necessary for grandparents to resort to legal action in order to see their grandchildren. Neither should parents be ordered by the courts to grant, against their personal wishes, visitation rights to grandparents. Divorce, for whatever reason, is an unhappy and distressful event in the lives of two people who once shared a loving relationship, and leaves in its wake heartache and acrimony. These hurts and ill feelings spill over into their respective families and thereby set up a scenario of accusations and revengeful actions. Where children are involved the situation may quickly evolve into a battle between the

custodial parents and the grandparents. No outsider can possibly know the extenuating circumstances, the cruel words or divisive behavior that may have occurred between the parents and grandparents during the marriage or afterwards. This is not a perfect world inhabited by perfect people. But it would seem reasonably clear [that] thinking adults could put aside their anger and animosity toward one another to reach a compromise for the sake of the children who are the helpless victims in this bitter tug of war. Kids can benefit from a relationship with loving grandparents whose experience, knowledge, and time are limitless. However, in the final analysis the parents of the children, unless abusive or irresponsible, should have the final word regarding visitation privileges of grandparents.

Gladys Oetter, Letter to the Editor, *Tinley Park* (Illinois): *Daily Southtown,* 17 June 2000.

Mood or tone: _____

Explanation: _____

_____

THINKING ABOUT YOUR READING AND WRITING

ACTIVITY Q: Mood and Tone in Films

Think about some movies or videos you have seen. In a few sentences, discuss what you notice about how filmmakers create mood.

_____

_____

_____

_____

_____

_____

_____

WORKING TOGETHER

With a partner, discuss some films you have seen where the mood has been an important part of the film's effect on you. Compare the types of moods you prefer.

Drawing Conclusions from Your Reading

Critical readers often draw conclusions from what they read. Some of these conclusions are probability statements based on the information in the text. Others are suggestions of how an author's ideas can be applied to different situations. In this section, you will learn how to form conclusions and how to decide whether your conclusions reasonably follow from the text and from your prior knowledge.

What Are Conclusions?

We draw conclusions about our everyday experiences all the time. For instance, we go into Sam's Music Store and notice that the price of a popular CD is $17.99, which is $2 higher than in Lonny's Music Store. From this, we might conclude that Sam's has high prices on CDs. Our conclusion is verified by other instances of higher prices on CDs at Sam's. We try to remember whether Lonny's was having a sale when we looked at its prices. If it was not, we can predict, or conclude, that anytime we come to Sam's the prices on CDs will be higher. If a sale was being held at Lonny's, however, we cannot conclude this.

In drawing conclusions about CD prices, we are stating that something is a *probable outcome* based on evidence we have gathered. Drawing conclusions from texts or lectures uses the same process:

1. We look at the facts or reasons (which may include opinions).
2. We judge how accurate and unbiased they are.
3. We eliminate particularly biased or irrelevant information.

A conclusion may explain or predict what will probably happen or what will result, based on what you already know. It is a *reasonable guess* about an outcome. Conclusions are based on facts and well-supported opinions. For a conclusion to be probable, it should follow logically from this information. When you draw a conclusion, you are tying together the various pieces of information you have into a broad statement of probability. The information you use to draw your conclusion may come from several sources, as in Example 1. Or it may come from a single source, as in Example 2.

Example 1:

> **Conclusion:** In your search for a family dog, you have decided that *the golden retriever is the best kind of dog for a family to own.* Your reasons are:
>
> a. The American Kennel Club rates the golden retriever as the dog with the best disposition.
> b. A friend of yours says his golden retriever has never destroyed any of his property.
> c. You have read a newspaper account of a golden retriever who rescued a baby who had fallen into a pool.

Example 2:

> **Conclusion:** As a result of your reading about the code of medieval chivalry, you have concluded that *the honor of being called a chivalrous gentleman could be bestowed on only a few men.* The basis for this conclusion is the information in the following passage:
>
> A chivalrous gentleman was brave, straightforward, and honorable; loyal to his monarch, country, and friends; unfailingly true to his word; ready to take issue with anyone he saw ill-treating a woman, a child, or an animal. He was a natural leader of men, and others unhesitatingly followed his lead. He was fearless in war and on the hunting field and excelled at many sports, but however tough with the tough, he was invariably gentle to the weak; above all, he was always tender, respectful, and courteous to women regardless of their rank. He put the needs of others before his own.

In each example, the conclusion logically follows from the information gathered. They are acceptable conclusions. It may be that at a later date some other information will become known that will refute these conclusions, but since it is not now available, these conclusions are considered probable or likely to be true.

ACTIVITY R: Identifying Conclusions

Select the conclusion that *logically follows* for each paragraph. Underline the information in the paragraph that you believe supports your conclusion. Be prepared to justify your answers.

1. The skillful blending of different textures in a room is just as important to the success of the scheme as the choice of colors and the mixing and matching of patterned and plain surfaces, yet it is often a neglected subject. Textures are all too often put together haphazardly even when the rest of the scheme has been carefully balanced. The selecting of textures needs even more care and attention when a room is being decorated with mostly plain colors on the larger areas of walls, floor, windows, and on upholstered furniture. If all these surfaces are of the same texture, even if the colors are different, the final effect will be boring. Just as a successful scheme in mainly warm or cool colors needs a sharp contrast from the opposite side of the color wheel to bring it to life, so textures need contrast for emphasis.

   Adapted from Jill Blake, *Colour and Pattern in the Home* (London: Design Council, 1978), 50.

   a. The textures in a room can have a major impact on the final effect of its appearance.

   b. When colors in a room are of the same hue, the effect is dramatic.

   c. Textures and colors can be used to reflect certain period styles.

   d. To give rooms a lavish appearance, you should use velvet and satin textures.

2. During World War II, when great numbers of trained technicians were in demand, it was assumed that those who had mechanical aptitude would make good airplane mechanics. A careful analysis of this assumption proved otherwise. It turned out that a good shoe clerk in civilian life would become a better

mechanic for military purposes than someone who had fixed cars most of his life and learned on a Model-T Ford. The critical trait was not mechanical aptitude but the ability of the trainee to follow instructions. The Army then worked out its instruction manuals so meticulously that the best recruit turned out to be a mildly obsessional person who could read and follow directions. The last thing they wanted was someone with his own ideas on how to fix equipment.

Edward T. Hall, *The Silent Language* (New York: Anchor, 1981), 71.

a. The Army is not a good place for a dentist.

b. Instruction manuals printed by the Army are designed for people who do not read very well.

c. Specialized skills are not needed by the Army.

d. The Army gives careful consideration to job requirements.

3. Concept testing is a phase of marketing in which a small sample of potential buyers is presented with a product idea through a written or oral description (and perhaps a few drawings) to determine their attitudes and initial buying intentions regarding the product. For a single product idea, an organization can test one or several concepts of the same product. Concept testing is a low-cost means for an organization to determine consumers' initial reactions to a product prior to investing considerable resources in product research and development. Product development personnel can use the results of concept testing to improve product attributes and product benefits that are most important to potential customers. The types of questions asked vary considerably depending on the type of product idea being tested.

    Adapted from William M. Pride, Robert J. Hughes, and Jack R. Kapoor, *Business,* 4th ed. (Boston: Houghton Mifflin, 1993), 370–71.

    a. Concept testing can save companies a great deal of money.

    b. Consumers have difficulty being honest during concept testing.

    c. Concept testing is seldom useful to companies.

    d. Few companies use concept testing.

4. Toward the end of March, Alice Manfred put her needles aside to think again of what she called the *impunity* of the man who killed her niece just because he could. It had not been hard to do; it had not even made him think twice about what danger he was putting himself in. He just did it. One man. One defenseless girl. Death. A sample-case man. A nice, neighborly, everybody-knows-him man. The kind you let in your house because he was not dangerous, because you had seen him with children, bought his products and never heard a scrap of gossip about him doing wrong. Felt not only safe but kindly in his company because he was the sort women ran to when they thought they were being followed, or watched, or needed someone to have the extra key just in case you locked yourself out. He was the man who took you to your door if you missed the trolley and had to walk night streets at night. Who warned young girls away from hooch joints and the men who lingered there. Women teased him because they trusted him. He was one of those men who might have marched down Fifth Avenue—cold and dignified—into the space the drums made. He knew wrong wasn't right, and did it anyway.

Toni Morrison, *Jazz* (New York: Knopf, 1992), 73–74.

   a. Alice Manfred thought her niece had been unwise.

   b. The man who killed Alice Manfred's niece had escaped.

   c. Alice Manfred felt very unsafe after her niece's death.

   d. Alice Manfred felt that the courts were ignoring the horror of her niece's death.

5. Years ago, when refrigerators were still unknown and the iceman came every day to keep your icebox filled, you had to be pretty particular about what you put in your mouth, especially in the summer months, when food spoilage was a common occurrence. In those days lovers of shellfish developed a fairly reliable rule of thumb to remind themselves when to be wary. You could eat oysters and other shellfish in any month with an "r" in it; months without an "r" (that is, the summer months, May through August) were taboo. This was a pretty good rule then, at least in the northern hemisphere, but it became obsolete with

the advent of modern refrigeration. No oyster now travels cross-country in anything but an air-conditioned car, and as a result, you can enjoy them just as safely in June as in March.

Ashley Montagu and Edward Darling, *The Prevalence of Nonsense* (New York: Harper & Row, 1967), as reported in *Tuleja, Fabulous Fallacies,* 1982 (New York: Stonesong Press, Galahad Books edition, 1999), 174.

a. People would like a return of old-fashioned iceboxes.

b. New refrigeration technology has changed our diets.

c. In California during "icebox" days, people could eat oysters in July.

d. Shellfish lovers ignore health warnings.

6. Total casualties of the northern and southern armies of the Civil War equaled American casualties in World War II; but when the Civil War occurred, the nation was only one-third as large as it was during the latter conflict. There were few families that did not suffer the loss of a loved one during the Civil War. In addition to military casualities, the toll in lives and property among civilians was enormous. A great deal of domestic violence also occurred both before and after the war. Beginning in 1856, proslavery and antislavery forces fought in "bleeding Kansas." The guerrilla war that took place in the West during the Civil War has seldom been equaled for savagery. Moreover, after the war, racial strife and Ku Klux Klan activity became routine in the former Confederate states.

Adapted from Thomas R. Dye, *Power and Society,* 6th ed. (Belmont, Calif.: Wadsworth, 1993), 309.

a. The Ku Klux Klan knew that Confederate soldiers would join them in great numbers once the Civil War ended.

b. The Civil War was the bloodiest war the United States ever fought.

c. War seldom affects anyone except the soldiers who fight in them.

d. The end of the Civil War saw the beginning of greater racial harmony.

7. Now, even before a new employee is hired, he or she embarks on an electronic journey. We receive 600 to 900 resumes from job

applicants every day by postal mail, by e-mail, or via our Resume Builder on the Microsoft Web site. Seventy percent of the resumes arrive electronically via e-mail or the Web, up from 6 percent two years ago and rising. Our software automatically acknowledges every electronic submission. Our recruiting database, from Restrac of Lexington, Massachusetts, directly accepts information from resumes created at our Resume Builder Web site; e-mail submissions are parsed to deliver candidate information to Restrac. A paper resume is scanned and converted into text that can go into the database. All resumes are electronically matched with open job positions within twenty-four to forty-eight hours of receipt.

Bill Gates, *Business @ the Speed of Thought* (New York: Warner Books, 1999), 41.

a. Both job seekers and employers benefit from job-search technology.

b. Job applicants are reluctant to use technology to apply for jobs.

c. Job seekers who don't use technology to apply for jobs should realize their paper applications will be ignored.

d. Microsoft is developing new job-recruitment technology.

THINKING ABOUT YOUR READING AND WRITING

ACTIVITY S: Reflecting on Drawing Conclusions

In a few sentences, describe the thought process you used to reject or accept conclusions in Activity R.

_____

_____

_____

_____

_____

_____

_____

ACTIVITY T: Evidence for Conclusions

The sentences that follow offer conclusions that could have been drawn from academic texts or lectures. In the space provided, indicate what type of evidence you would want to have before you accepted this conclusion. Be specific.

Example:

> **Conclusion:** Increasingly, the Mundurucu people of the Amazon's rain forest are becoming westernized.
>
> **Evidence you would need to accept this conclusion:**   Reports from anthropologists who have been there.

1. **Conclusion:** Women have an easier time moving into executive positions today than they did twenty-five years ago.

   Evidence you would need to accept this conclusion: _____

   _____

2. **Conclusion:** Lee Harvey Oswald was acting alone when he assassinated John F. Kennedy.

   Evidence you would need to accept this conclusion: _____

   _____

3. **Conclusion:** America's wilderness and sensitive animal life are not threatened by big business, but by government.

   Evidence you would need to accept this conclusion: _____

   _____

4. **Conclusion:** Young men and women living in wealthy communities have similar attitudes about premarital sex.

   Evidence you would need to accept this conclusion: _____

   _____

5. **Conclusion:** Children who are adopted by gay couples fare as well in life as those who grow up with heterosexual couples.

Evidence you would need to accept this conclusion: _____

_____

WORKING TOGETHER

Compare your answers to Activity T with those of a partner. What differences were there in the evidence you each wanted? Add any of your partner's ideas that you liked to your own.

THINKING ABOUT YOUR READING AND WRITING

ACTIVITY U: Your Conclusions about Conclusions

What are some conclusions you can draw about how critical reading and thinking will benefit you in your college career?

_____

_____

_____

_____

_____

_____

_____

_____

_____

▶ Chapter Summary

Based on your reading of this chapter, list at least five ideas that you believe will help you with future reading assignments. Write in complete sentences.

1. _____

_____

_____

_____

2. _____

_____

_____

_____

3. _____

_____

_____

_____

4. _____

_____

_____

_____

5. _____

_____

_____

_____

▶ *Extended Application*

Now that you have worked with the strategies necessary for critical reading and thinking, you can practice applying them to full-length reading selections. Choose (or your instructor may choose) a reading selection from Part 2 of this book that is typical of what you will be expected to read for your other college courses, such as an essay or a textbook chapter. Use this selection to practice:

- ❋ Distinguishing between fact and opinion
- ❋ Evaluating evidence for statements of opinion
- ❋ Identifying point of view
- ❋ Making inferences
- ❋ Drawing conclusions
- ❋ Locating evidence for conclusions

Decide the practice strategies you will use. Apply them to your selection. Then in a few paragraphs, write a description of what you did and how the strategies you used worked for you.

Name of material used: _____

Page numbers: _____

Your description: _____

CHAPTER SEVEN

Strategies for Reading Visual Aids in Texts

DO YOU LIKE TO TAKE PHOTOGRAPHS? Why? Why do so many people take cameras with them when they go on vacation or to special events? Most say they enjoy taking photos because then they can share with others what they've seen. It also helps them remember the places they've visited and the people they've met. Although reading a textbook isn't exactly like going on vacation, authors often include visual information in their texts for some of the same reasons: to help explain information to the readers and to help them remember what they have read. In Chapter 5, you were shown how to make visuals, or graphic organizers, for your own purposes. In this chapter, you will learn strategies for reading visual aids that authors provide and how these strategies can help you with reading comprehension.

What Are Visual Aids?

Pictorial displays, or visual aids, are often included in textbook chapters. They can be of great assistance to readers who know how to use them effectively.

ACTIVITY A: Determining the Value of Visual Aids

Read Selection 1 and Selection 2. Then answer the questions that follow under the heading Reflection.

Selection 1

It's that decision-making time of the year: Rehoboth Beach, Del., or Duck, N.C.? Motel or rental house? Sun protection factor 15 or 30? And the biggest question of all: How much of your precious vacation time do you want to use?

The vacation equation has generally improved for most workers nationally in recent years, particularly those employed full time at medium-size or large companies. Until the past decade, most companies gave workers two paid weeks off each year, with some allowing three weeks after five years. Workers typically needed to invest 20 years with a company before they got four weeks, according to benefits consultants.

That's one reason federal employment has been appealing to many workers over the years. Federal workers, according to the Office of Personnel Management, get 13 paid vacation days during the first three years of service, a bit more than 2½ weeks; four weeks after three years and up to 15 years; and five weeks and a day after that point.

But private employers have learned that time off is a prized commodity, and many firms have been sweetening their vacation policies, according to the Hay Group, a Philadelphia-based benefits consulting firm. About half of all large firms start workers at three paid weeks of vacation, with the other half clinging to the old two-week standard. And most increase vacation time faster than in the past, with many workers getting up to four weeks' paid leave at 15 years' tenure. At 25 years, they typically get five weeks, which is just slightly less than federal workers receive.

Consequently, federal employment doesn't look quite as appealing on the vacation front as it did in earlier decades, says Michael Carter, senior benefits consultant at the Hay Group. "Then it was a clear advantage to working in the federal government," he says.

"It's still true, but it's not as true as it was 25 or 30 years ago," Carter says.

Most striking now, amid a globalizing world economy, is the vacation gap between the United States and the rest of the world. In most other industrialized countries, vacation periods and holidays are mandated by the government. In Belgium, for example, workers are given 30 days off each year by law.

The French get 36 days, and Italians get up to 42 days off a year. Japanese workers get 24, Australians get 30 and Venezuelans get 28. And some companies add more paid days off on top to reward longtime workers, giving employees in some countries up to seven or eight weeks of paid vacation a year.

Europeans, in particular, view American leave policies as "horrible, terrible," Carter says. ". . . They think our practices are barbaric, and they don't know how our people can bear having only two or three weeks a year."

There are no U.S. requirements regarding vacation time. Some companies offer no paid vacation, particularly to part-time workers, seasonal help or independent contractors. But for permanent, full-time workers, most companies voluntarily offer, on average, 27 to 29 paid days a year, including vacation and holidays, according to the Hay Group. Workers in the Mountain states and on the West Coast on average get about two extra vacation days a year compared with workers in the South and Plains states.

Cultural differences explain part of the gap between the U.S. and European countries, Carter says. "It's the American work ethic," he says. "It's generally accepted that Americans are the hardest-working, except for the Japanese perhaps."

Kirstin Downey Grimsley, "Sweetening the Vacation Equation," *Washington Post,* 6 July 1998, 316.

Selection 2

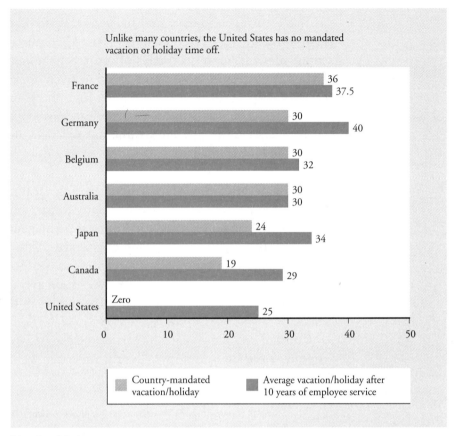

Unlike many countries, the United States has no mandated vacation or holiday time off.

Country		
France	36	37.5
Germany	30	40
Belgium	30	32
Australia	30	30
Japan	24	34
Canada	19	29
United States	Zero	25

Country-mandated vacation/holiday

Average vacation/holiday after 10 years of employee service

Mandated Leisure

Source: Hay Group; appeared in *The Washington Post National Weekly Edition,* 6 July 1998, 35.

Reflection:

What are some differences between the approaches you used to read Selection 1 and Selection 2? _____

Which presentation of this information do you prefer? Why?

_____

_____

Which presentation do you think will help you remember this information longer? Why? _____

_____

In what way was the visual aid helpful? _____

_____

WORKING TOGETHER

Compare your answers to Activity A with those of a partner. What differences do you find in your responses?

What Are the Various Types of Visual Aids?

There are several common types of visual aids. Each type has its own unique features and purposes.

Charts

Charts summarize information through a combination of words and graphics. Often they show relationships between the items on the chart or comparisons between them. Charts enable the writer to explain complex ideas more concretely, and they enable the reader to visualize the relationship between abstract concepts.

TREE CHARTS. *Tree charts* look like trees with branches. A tree chart showing the relationship between the sales division of a large company and the rest of the company might look like the one that follows:

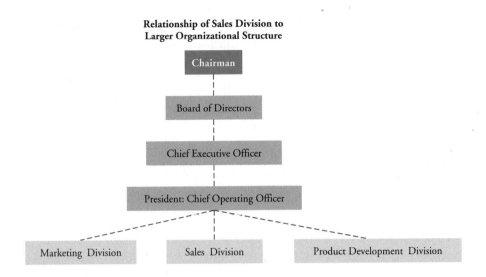

Relationship of Sales Division to Larger Organizational Structure

FLOWCHARTS. *Flowcharts* show movement between events (a process) and may depict stopping out or correction points in this process. A flowchart designed to show the process for answering the phone might look like the diagram on the next page. Notice that several decision points can cause the flow to stop or to continue. These *stopping* or *rerouting points* are common on flowcharts and are one reason they are useful for depicting processes.

Sample Flowchart

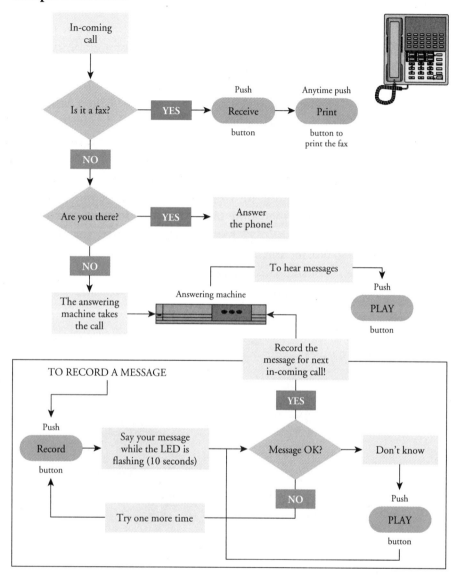

Graphs

Graphs, especially *circle* (or *pie*), *bar,* and *line* graphs, are also commonly found in textbooks. The purpose of a graph is most often to show comparisons of quantitative information. There is always text, either directly on or surrounding the graph, and this information tells the reader what is being depicted. The reader then needs to see the relationship between the different pieces of information and determine the significance of it. For instance, by looking at the *circle graph* below, we can see the differences in the amount of carbon dioxide emitted from fossil fuels in 1997 in different parts of the world. The information outside the graph tells us what we are looking at. We can draw several conclusions from the data, for instance, that some parts of the world emit significantly more carbon dioxide from fossil fuels than other parts; that the Far East, Oceania, and North America are responsible for more than half of it; and that a relationship exists between how industrialized a part of the world is and the amount of carbon dioxide from fossil fuels it emits.

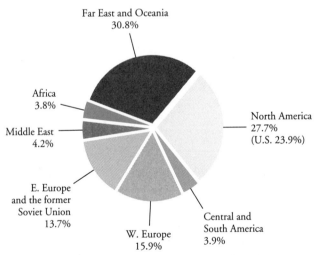

World Carbon Dioxide Emissions from the Use of Fossil Fuels, 1997

Source: Energy Information Administration, 1999.

Bar graphs depict information that would be difficult for readers to follow in a textual discussion; they also make it easy for the reader to compare data, as the bar graphs shown here illustrate. Notice that the meanings of the various shadings are provided in the legend to the graph. On the bar graph about debit cards, the graph shows several relationships. The reader can compare growth in card use between 1990 and 2005 in two-year intervals, popularity of particular cards, and the billions of dollars spent or projected to be spent at each interval.

Bar graphs can also be drawn horizontally, as in the example on the next page. Once again, several comparisons are shown. One is a comparison by age. Another is the comparison by race, namely, black and white males. In addition to the bar itself, which illustrates differences, the specific numbers of persons are provided by the notations along the bottom of the chart.

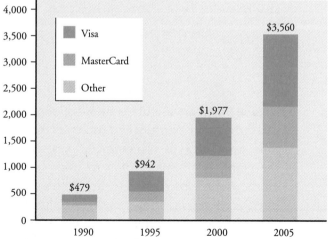

Projected Growth of Credit and Debit Card Volume in the U.S. ($ billions)

The Nilson Report

Source: Appeared in Ronald J. Alsop, ed., *The Wall Street Journal Almanac* (New York: Ballantine Books, 1998), 424.

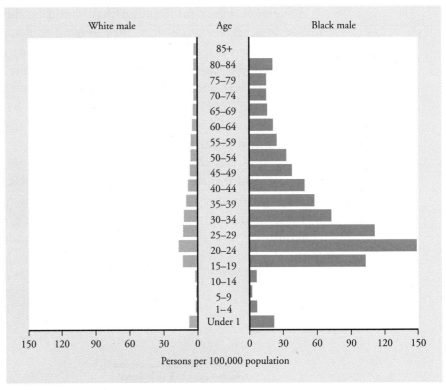

Male Homicide Rates, by Race and Age: 1996

Source: U.S. Census Bureau, *Statistical Abstract of the United States* (Washington, DC: Government Printing Office, 1999), 72.

Line graphs are useful for showing trends over time. Because line graphs can show small increases and decreases, they are sometimes considered the most accurate type of graph. As in all graphs, the information outside the graph is critical for you to read. It explains what the information on the graph represents. The line graph shown on the next page has three lines, each representing a particular kind of population growth in the United States: rural growth, urban growth, and a total for the entire country. On this graph, different line thicknesses are used to represent the different areas of growth. The information to the left and on the bottom of the graph informs the reader that the line placements represent millions of people between the years 1900 and 1990.

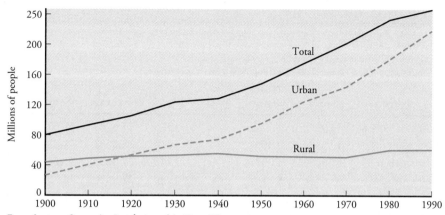

Population Growth, *Population of the United States, 1900–1990*

Source: Richard Lachmann, ed., *The Encyclopedic Dictionary of Sociology,* 4th ed. (Guilford, CT: Dushkin, 1991), 224.

Tables

Tables are used to classify or categorize information, particularly when there are many numbers or several categories. The information on a table is usually arranged in columns, with the categories listed horizontally across the top and the items falling into each category listed vertically. As in the example (on page 272), often several comparison points are being made on a single table. Footnotes also frequently appear on tables to give further explanation for some of the items.

POPULATION SHIFTS BY REGION

Shown below is the percentage of the total U.S. population living in each region of the country, according to the results of the decennial censuses. Initially, almost all Americans lived in the Northeast and the South. Before long, however, the North Central region began to attract large numbers of settlers and was growing in importance, and by the mid-19th century the West had begun its steady growth. By 1990 it had a larger share of the population than the Northeast.

	Northeast	South	North Central	West		Northeast	South	North Central	West
1790	50.09%	49.91%	—	—	1900	27.62%	32.18%	34.55%	5.65%
1800	49.66%	49.39%	0.96%	—	1910	28.05%	31.87%	32.41%	7.68%
1810	48.16%	47.80%	4.03%	—	1920	27.98%	31.24%	32.09%	8.69%
1820	45.24%	45.85%	8.91%	—	1930	27.94%	30.73%	31.33%	10.00%
1830	43.07%	44.36%	12.51%	—	1940	27.22%	31.53%	30.37%	10.88%
1840	39.61%	40.72%	19.64%	—	1950	26.09%	31.19%	29.38%	13.34%
1850	37.20%	38.73%	23.30%	0.77%	1960	24.91%	30.66%	28.79%	15.64%
1860	33.69%	35.41%	28.93%	1.97%	1970	24.12%	30.89%	27.93%	17.12%
1870	31.90%	31.87%	33.67%	2.57%	1980	21.67%	33.28%	26.00%	19.07%
1880	28.90%	32.91%	34.60%	3.59%	1990	20.43%	34.35%	23.99%	21.22%
1890	27.64%	31.80%	35.58%	4.98%					

Source: U.S. Bureau of the Census

Timelines

To show how something has progressed in stages or how something has evolved over time, a *timeline* is particularly effective. Timelines often appear in scientific writing and may illustrate how scientific discoveries progressed from one stage, perhaps the stage where an illness is first identified, to a later stage, perhaps when a cure is found. More frequently, timelines are used to show progressive events in chronological order, as in the timeline shown here.

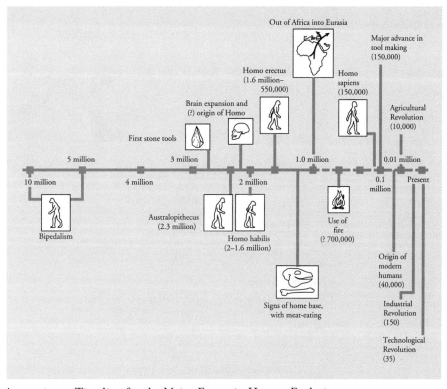

Approximate Timeline for the Major Events in Human Evolution

Source: Philip G. Zimbardo and Ann L. Weber, *Psychology* (New York: HarperCollins, 1994), 41.

Photographs

Another popular type of visual aid in texts is the *photograph*. Some photographs depict situations that are true to life, such as urban street scenes, children in classrooms, or athletes in training. Art books depend heavily on photos of paintings. Other photos may be the result of special effects, such as photos of cells as seen from under a microscope or photos that are the result of computer graphic effects.

Diagrams

Technological or scientific writing often includes *diagrams* to explain complicated processes, structures, or sequences discussed in the text. In

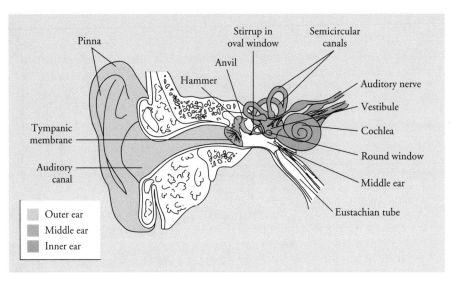

Phonoreceptors

Source: Sylvia Mader, *Biology: Inquiry into Life*, 5th ed. (Dubuque, IA: Brown, 1988), Figure 17.16, 364.

this example, a drawing has been used to help the reader understand the structure of the ear. Each part is clearly labeled.

THINKING ABOUT YOUR READING AND WRITING

ACTIVITY B: Your Prior Experience with Visual Aids

In the past, what types of visual aids have you found the most useful?

_____

What types have been most difficult for you to read?

_____

What do you do when you encounter a difficult one?

_____

_____

ACTIVITY C: Creating a Visual Aid Reference Table

Using the information from the preceding section, create your own table for handy reference to visual aids. In the space provided, create separate columns to list (1) the type of visual aid, (2) why it is used, and (3) its distinguishing features. Give a title to your table. When you have completed it, compare your table with a partner's.

How Do Visual Aids Facilitate Comprehension?

Perhaps you commented in Activity A that it would be easier for you to recall information when it was presented in table format rather than in paragraph form. Most people would agree with you. Even when the paragraphs and sentences give valuable information, visuals allow us to organize that information in a way that is often easier to remember.

Another advantage of visuals is the effect they have on reader response to the information. The visual impact of an idea can be much more impressive than an idea stated in words. An author who wants to impress the reader with an idea, to make a more powerful statement, might want to use a visual aid. Notice the difference in the effect between the two presentations of the same idea that follow.

Example 1:

> **Numbers, Origins, and Location**   The second-largest ethnic group in the United States is the *Latinos* or Hispanic Americans, people of Spanish origin. In addition to the fourteen to twenty million **Chicanos** (those whose country of origin is Mexico), Latinos include about three million Puerto Ricans, a million Cuban Americans, and about three million people from Central

or South America, primarily Venezuela and Colombia. Officially tallied at twenty-two million, the actual number of *Latinos* is considerably higher, perhaps twenty-seven million.

James M. Henslin, *Sociology: A Down-to-Earth Approach,* 2nd ed. (Needham Heights, MA: Allyn and Bacon, 1995), 331.

Example 2:

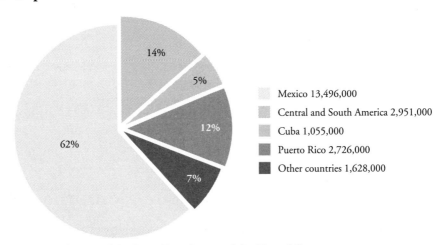

Country of Origin of the *Latino* Population of the United States

Source: Statistical Abstract of the United States (Washington DC: Government Printing Office, 1993), Tables 32, 53.

THINKING ABOUT READING AND WRITING

ACTIVITY D: Responding to Visual Aids

What is the visual impact of the preceding visual (Example 2) on you? Why do you think this graph has this impact?

_____

_____

Visual information can also help clarify material that sounds complex when stated in sentence form. Read the following paragraph. Then look at the diagram accompanying the text. Notice how the diagram helps the reader understand the complex process described in the text.

Example 1:

> The tick vector of Lyme disease has a two-year life cycle in which it requires three blood meals. The larval form becomes infected from small animals, usually field mice, then enters a dormant stage until the following spring. Then it molts into a nymph, which is still infected. This is the stage at which it is most likely to infect humans. It is crucial to the maintenance of the cycle in the wild that the spirochete be able to remain viable in small animals to reinfect the larvae the following year. The field mouse is well adapted to this. The third feeding, by the infected adults that develop from the nymph, is taken from the deer. After this, the adults lay eggs, which are uninfected, that over winter develop into larvae the following spring.

Example 2:

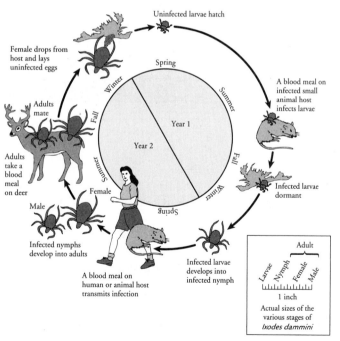

Source: Gerard J. Tortora, Berdell R. Funke, and Christine L. Case, *Microbiology: An Introduction,* 4th ed. (Redwood City, CA: Benjamin/Cummings, 1992), 570.

Visual aids can also substitute for written information. There is a saying that "a picture is worth a thousand words." For readers, pictures often can convey much more than words could ever describe. See how this saying might apply to the photo shown here.

Source: Deborah Gibert (Boston: The Image Bank), n.d.

THINKING ABOUT YOUR READING AND WRITING

ACTIVITY E: Assessing the Impact of a Photo

Do you think this visual aid is "worth a thousand words"? Why or why not?

_____

_____

What Are Effective Strategies for Reading Visual Aids?

For successful reading of visual aids, you should

1. Preview the visual aid to get an overall impression and to make predictions.
2. Note details to gain more information and to verify your predictions.
3. Make connections between the visual aid and the text to see how each part is supported or extended by the other.
4. Make inferences from the visual aid to elaborate on your interpretation of the data and look for confirmation of your inferences in the rest of the text.
5. Draw conclusions from the visual aid to determine any wider application of the information and to see how your conclusions are further supported by information anywhere else in the reading selection.

In the remainder of this chapter, you will note that the strategies for reading visual aids differ somewhat from those you use for reading texts that do not contain visual aids. There are also common techniques, however, and so you will also be able to apply your prior knowledge about reading strategies to the activities in this section.

Previewing Visual Aids

Visual aids, like information conveyed through sentences and paragraphs, can be previewed. During your preview, your goal is to obtain an overall idea of the purpose of the visual and to determine how the data on it are organized. You also hope to be able to predict what sort of details you will find once you examine the visual aid more closely.

Previewing Graphs

To preview a graph, you need to

1. Read the title of the graph. Treat it in the same way you would treat the title of a chapter or article.

2. Examine the lengths of the bars, divisions of a circle graph, or shape of the line(s). These features of a graph are similar to subtitles in texts. They convey an overall impression of the information that will be provided through the details.

3. Look along the sides and bottom of the graph for any headings or labels that tell you more about the details displayed.

4. Look for any keys, legends, or footnotes on the graph that identify codes the author is using.

5. Make predictions about what you will find when you read the information on the graph more closely.

On the first bar graph, some details have been eliminated. Follow the steps for previewing a graph to see what information you can obtain and what predictions you can make about the contents of the rest of the graph.

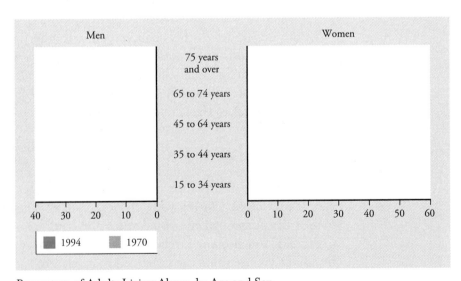

Percentage of Adults Living Alone, by Age and Sex

Source: Adapted from Ronald J. Alsop, ed., *The Wall Street Journal Almanac* (New York: Ballantine Books, 1998), 707.

What information can you obtain from the graph in its present form?

_____

_____

_____

Now look at the second version of this graph, below, which has added details.

What additional information do you learn about percentages of adults living alone?

_____

_____

_____

During your preview, you were able to recognize that this graph would be about the percentage of adults living alone, by age and sex, and that you

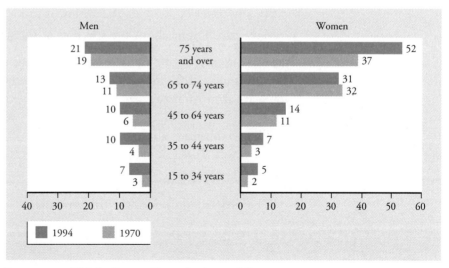

Percentage of Adults Living Alone, by Age and Sex

Source: Ronald J. Alsop, ed., *The Wall Street Journal Almanac* (New York: Ballantine Books, 1998), 707.

would see differences between 1970 and 1994. You should have been able to tell that the groups were divided into ten-year clusters, starting at age 35, but the 15–34 age group and the 75-and-over age group included more years.

One prediction you might have made is that there were fewer people living alone in the first age group because few 15-year-olds live alone and because many people in this group would also be living at college or getting married. You also might have predicted that percentages would have increased for all age groups because of the improved economy.

Previewing Tables

The aids for previewing that you will find on tables include the title of the table (often appearing at the top) and the subheadings that appear above each column on the table. These parts of the table should be treated in the same way as titles and subtitles in texts. Thus, to preview a table:

1. Read the title.
2. Read the subheadings.
3. Use the title and subheadings to determine the focus of the table.
4. Look for any keys, legends, or footnotes on the table that identify any codes or symbols the author is using.
5. Make predictions about the specifics of the data in the table.

In the next example, you are first presented with a table that contains only the title and vertical and horizontal subheadings. Examine it to see what you learn from your preview. Then answer the questions that follow.

What is this table about?

_____

What information does the title provide?

_____

_____

How are the title and the subheadings on this table related to one another?

_____

_____

What kinds of details will you most likely find on this visual?

_____

_____

MATERNITY LEAVE

Percentage of women, 15 to 44 years of age, by use of maternity leave for the most recent birth

Characteristic of the Mother	Not Employed	Took Maternity Leave	Did Not Take Maternity Leave		
			Not Needed	Not Offered	Other Reasons
All women					
Age at time of birth					
15–19 years					
20–24 years					
25–29 years					
30–44 years					
Year of child's birth					
1991–95					
1981–90					
1980 and before					

Source: Centers for Disease Control and Prevention, National Center for Health Statistics; appeared in and adapted from Ronald A. Alsop. ed., *The Wall Street Journal Almanac* (New York: Ballantine Books, 1998), 317.

Based on your prior knowledge, what do you expect the data to show (for instance, increases, decreases)? Why do you expect this?

_____

_____

Look now at the complete table, which includes all the previously missing details. How accurate were your predictions?

_____

_____

What additional information have you learned now that you have studied the details of this table?

_____

_____

During your preview, you no doubt recognized that this title would be about women who go on maternity leave between the ages of 15 and 44 and their reasons for doing so. From the information beneath the title, you could tell that the details would be percentages by age groups. You would also know that any differences would be shown between these percentages for children born in 1980 or before, between 1981 and 1990, and between 1991 and 1995. One prediction you might have made, based on your prior knowledge of this topic, is that more women between the ages of 15 and 19 would not be working and thus would not be taking maternity leave. You might also know that more women are going to work now and this might result in an increase in percentages taking maternity leave between 1980 and 1995.

MATERNITY LEAVE

Percentage of women, 15 to 44 years of age, by use of maternity leave for the most recent birth

			Did Not Take Maternity Leave		
Characteristic of the Mother	Not Employed	Took Maternity Leave	Not Needed	Not Offered	Other Reasons
All women	48.0%	37.3%	2.3%	0.9%	11.6%
Age at time of birth					
15–19 years	71.9	14.8	0.7	0.1	12.5
20–24 years	52.8	29.8	1.3	1.3	14.9
25–29 years	44.8	41.1	2.7	0.8	10.5
30–44 years	38.3	48.3	3.5	0.8	9.1
Year of child's birth					
1991–95	43.2	43.5	2.2	0.9	10.3
1981–90	47.4	37.2	2.7	0.8	11.8
1980 and before	61.5	22.0	1.6	0.9	14.0

Source: Centers for Disease Control and Prevention, National Center for Health Statistics; appeared in Ronald A. Alsop, ed., *The Wall Street Journal Almanac* (New York: Ballantine Books, 1998), 317.

WORKING TOGETHER

Compare your findings with those of a partner. Did you notice the same details? What information did your partner find that was also important?

Previewing Other Types of Visual Aids

All visual aids contain elements that can be studied for making predictions before you make a closer inspection. In previewing timelines and flowcharts, for instance, you can first read the major headings and the beginning and ending notations to see the period covered or the starting and finishing points of the process that are included in the visual aid. With a diagram or photo, you should first identify those features that stand out from the rest; then these can be used to make predictions about the remaining details.

When you are reading a tree chart, you will want to notice the overall organization of the chart—such as how the hierarchy is arranged and how many branches stem from each of the major branches—before you read the individually boxed headings. You will always want to look for keys, legends, or footnotes to the visual aid and to take note of any special effects the author has used to make distinctions, such as colors or shadings.

Whenever and whatever you preview, your goal is to obtain a general sense of the material before you do more extensive analysis. In this way, you are mentally preparing yourself for the detailed reading and analysis ahead. Try this with the pie chart that follows.

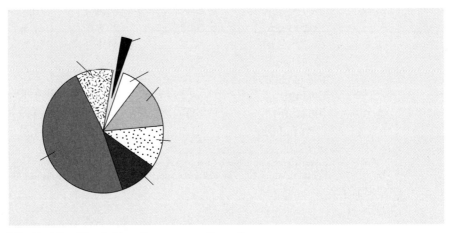

Who Do You Think State Government Serves?
Source: Boston Globe, 3 September 1990, 1, 8–9.

Predictions:

Based on your prior knowledge, what information do you expect to find next to the lines by each section of the circle?

_____

What significant points do you expect this new information to prove?

_____

_____

How are the different sections of the circle related to one another?

_____

_____

The pie chart below includes all the previously missing details. How accurate were your predictions?

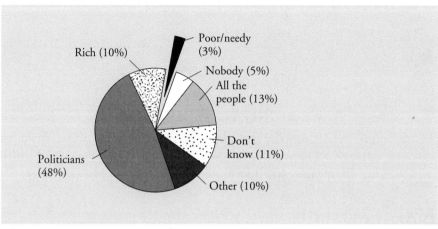

Who Do You Think State Government Serves?

Source: Boston Globe, 3 September 1990, 1, 8–9.

Closer Analysis:

What additional information have you learned now that you have studied the details of this visual aid?

_____

_____

THINKING ABOUT YOUR READING AND WRITING

ACTIVITY F: Sharing What You Know with Others

What advice can you now offer to another student about strategies to use when previewing visual aids?

_____

_____

_____

_____

_____

_____

_____

_____

♦♦♦♦ WORKING TOGETHER

Compare the advice you have written in Activity F with that of a partner. Discuss the value of each suggestion. Make any additions to your original thoughts that you now think should be included.

Noting Details

When you complete your preview of a visual aid, your next step will be to analyze all its details. As you do this, you will want to:

1. Identify any special effects the author uses to make distinctions between the various elements on the visual aid. Consider some of the methods used in the previous section:

   Colors, shadings, or patterns. The bar graph on page 281 showing the percentage of adults living alone, by age and sex, illustrate how various colors are used to separate one year from another. You may recall maps you have read that use different colors to reflect different temperature zones or topographical features.

   Broken or solid lines. If a line graph contains several lines, the author may distinguish what each line represents by using a combination of broken and solid lines or by varying line thicknesses. In this chapter, the graph on population growth in the United States between 1900 and 1990 uses different types of lines to make distinctions.

2. Establish the nature or types of details included. Details may be names, dates, percentages, whole numbers, qualities, or almost anything. Often a combination of these details is provided. As you have seen in this chapter, when numbers are too large to ex-

press completely, the author may use a shortened form, which is then explained in the key.

3. Determine how the details are related to one another. In diagrams, each label may represent part of a whole. On a tree graph, they may show a hierarchy of importance. Details on a timeline or flowchart show a sequence over time. Numbers may be used to show comparisons such as those between cities, ethnic groups, gender, age, or years.

4. Determine whether the details are presented in any particular order. This is obvious on tree charts or flowcharts and timelines, but on tables, you often must determine an order for yourself, such as size, chronology, increases, or decreases.

5. Determine whether some details have more significance than others. For example, on the pie chart on state government (page 287), many more respondents thought the government served the politicians than served the poor.

ACTIVITY G: **Understanding Details on Visual Aids**
Preview each visual aid, then answer the questions that follow it.

1.

TWENTY-ITEM CHECKLIST CONSISTING OF REASONS FOR AND REACTIONS TO SHOPLIFTING
PERCENT OF RESPONDENTS CHECKING EACH ITEM PRE- AND POSTGROUP (N = 143)

	Pregroup		Postgroup	
Items	**Number**	**Percent**	**Number**	**Percent**
You felt remorseful when caught.	85	59	76	53
You do not understand why you shoplifted.	73	51	31	22
You shoplifted because you couldn't afford the items.	56	39	48	34
You were surprised that you were arrested for the shoplifting offense.	51	36	45	32
You shoplifted because you were frustrated.	50	35	76	53
You shoplifted because you don't have enough money to support yourself and/or your family.	44	31	39	27
You shoplifted because it was so easy to get away with it.	43	30	45	32
You shoplifted because you felt angry.	38	27	58	41
You knew you were going to be caught shoplifting.	37	26	51	36

Items	Pregroup		Postgroup	
	Number	Percent	Number	Percent
You shoplifted because you felt sorry for yourself.	29	20	55	39
You shoplifted because you didn't see it as a serious crime.	26	18	32	22
You were relieved when you were caught.	25	18	51	36
You are very lonely.	24	17	29	20
You shoplifted because it was exciting.	20	14	32	22
You shoplifted because you wanted revenge.	20	14	33	23
You shoplifted because you felt that stores make too much money anyway.	13	9	17	12
You wanted to be caught.	11	8	26	18
You started shoplifting as a teenager and have continued to shoplift as an adult.	6	4	8	6
You shoplifted because you felt that you wanted to humiliate yourself.	5	4	5	4
You shoplifted because you had been drinking or using drugs.	4	3	9	6

Source: Anita Sue Kolman and Claudia Wasserman, "Theft Groups for Women: A Cry for Help," *Federal Probation* 55, no. 1 (1991): 49.

What is the nature of the details? _____

_____

What special effects, if any, does the author use to make distinctions between details? _____

_____

How are the details related to one another? _____

_____

Which details, if any, give information that you consider to be particularly significant? _____

_____

2.

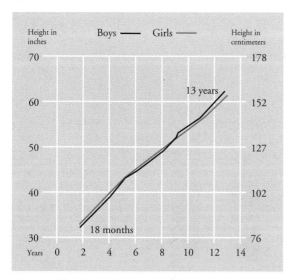
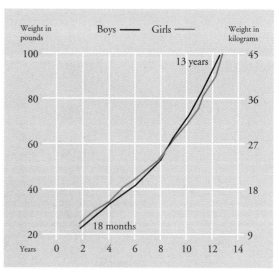

Average Height and Weight for Children

Source: National Center for Health Statistics, U.S. Public Health Service, adapted by *The World Book Encyclope-dia.* © 2000 World Book, Inc. By permission of the publisher. www.worldbook.com.

What is the nature of the details? _____

_____

What special effects, if any, does the author use to make distinctions between details? _____

_____

How are the details related to one another? _____

_____

Which details, if any, give information that you consider to be particularly significant? _____

_____

3.

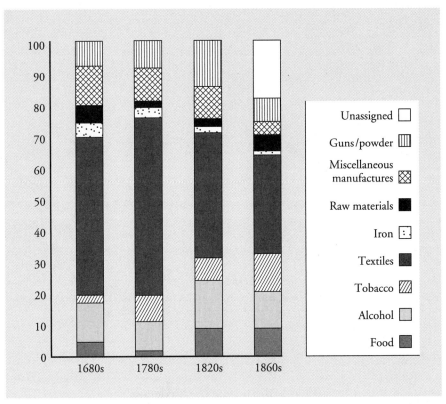

Estimated Relative Value of Imports Into Western Africa in Selected Decades, 1680s–1860s

Source: David Eltis, "The Economics of African Participation in the Slave Trade," *The Atlantic Slave Trade,* ed. D. Northrup (Lexington, MA: Heath, 1994), 166.

What is the nature of the details? _____

_____

What special effects, if any, does the author use to make distinctions between details? _____

_____

How are the details related to one another?_____

_____

Which details, if any, give information that you consider to be particularly significant? _____

Connecting Visual Aids to Text

Visual aids most often accompany text for one of the following reasons:

* *To give evidence for a point made in the text.* For instance, the text may make the claim that poverty rates have increased in urban areas during the last decade. A table with poverty rates in urban areas during the last several decades would illustrate this point.

* *To clarify or explain a complicated idea.* The diagram of the life cycle of Lyme disease, which appeared earlier in this chapter, is an example. The idea presented is complicated because of the number of stages and species involved in the two-year period of the cycle. The visual aid helped clarify the events during the cycle.

* *To add interest to the text.* Sometimes visual aids do not add a great deal of information to the reading material, but they do help maintain reader involvement. Photographs frequently are used for this purpose.

Whenever a visual aid is included in your reading material, you should decide its purpose. Visual aids that give evidence or explain complicated ideas are often as important to know for exams as is the text itself.

ACTIVITY H: Connecting Visual Aids and Text

Look at each visual and read the text that accompanies it. Decide whether the purpose of the visual is to (1) give evidence, (2) clarify or explain a complicated idea, or (3) provide interest.

1. In the figure that follows, we can see the first migration pattern, from the farms to the cities. The most marked population shift occurred during the rapid growth phase of the S-curve, from approximately 1875 to 1905. The popular availability of railroads, telegraphs, and large-scale

power plants made cities the attractive, economical place to live and work. These were *centralizing* technologies. Consumers simply couldn't get cheap power at the farm, nor was it economical to string telegraph wires or lay railroad track between farm and city. Also, the cities offered a different place to live, plentiful entertainment, innovative products and services, and new, higher-paying factory jobs.

In the second wave of migration, from the mid-1930s to the mid-1960s, there was a mass exodus from cities to suburbs. This movement was made possible by the rapid proliferation of cars, phones, and electricity. These were *decentralizing* technologies. They allowed us to travel to and communicate with the cities for business, yet live in uncrowded, affordable suburbs.

The third major population migration will begin its growth phase from the mid-1990s and last into the mid-2020s. During this migration, we will return to smaller towns, called *penturbia,* and to more remote suburbs, called the *exurbs.* A study of past migration trends by Jack Lessinger at Washington State University—who coined the term *penturbia*—suggests that approximately 20 percent of the population will make this shift. That means as many as 70 million people in North America will be on the move in the next 30 years!

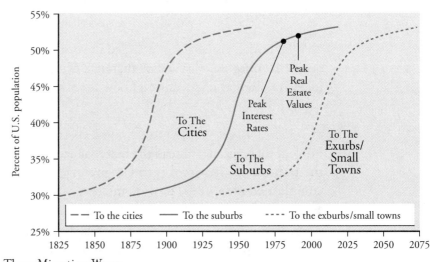

Three Migration Waves

Source: Adapted from Harry S. Dent Jr., *The Roaring 2000s.* (New York: Touchstone, 1998), 211–12.

The purpose of this visual aid is to_____

_____

2. **Mass Extinctions of the Past**

At least five major episodes of mass extinction have occurred since life developed on Earth. Each time, at least one-fourth, and on average one-half, of all species died out within a few million years—a mere moment in Earth's geological history.

The largest mass extinction took place about 240 million years ago, marking the end of the Paleozoic Era. Scientists estimate that during that extinction, from 80 to 96 percent of all species disappeared. Marine organisms, which made up the great majority of species during the Paleozoic, were the hardest hit. Many species that lived on the ocean floor, such as sea lilies, died out. Flat shellfish called trilobites and a group of fish called placoderms, both common during the early Paleozoic, also became extinct.

Two other mass extinctions occurred earlier during the Paleozoic Era. The first marked the end of the Ordovician Period, about 435 million years ago. The next occurred in the later part of the Devonian Period, which ended about 360 million years ago. Tens of thousands of species of marine organisms, particularly tiny creatures such as graptolites, died out during these two episodes of mass extinction.

Another mass extinction occurred about 205 million years ago, ending the Triassic Period. At this time, many species of amphibians and reptiles became extinct. The extinction set the stage for the rise of the dinosaurs, which for a time became the world's dominant animals.

The most recent and best-known mass extinction took place at the end of the Mesozoic Era, about 65 million years ago, when the last living dinosaur species vanished from the Earth. Many other terrestrial species and many marine species also became extinct during this time. The extinctions led to the rise of mammals and marked the beginning of the Cenozoic Era, in which we live today.

Mass extinctions through the ages

Scientists have identified at least five mass extinctions since life began nearly 4 billion years ago. In many cases, these extinctions define the boundaries of periods or eras in the geologic timeline. Scientists compiled the record of extinction based primarily on studies of fossil remains of marine organisms.

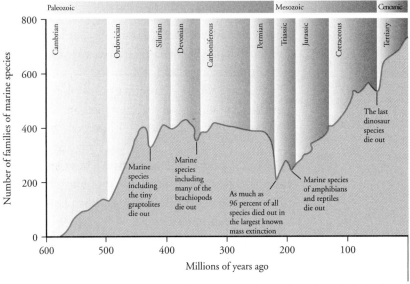

Human beings appear only recently on the geologic timeline. The rise of human beings marks the beginning of a sixth mass extinction, because human activities are directly or indirectly responsible for almost all of the current extinctions.

Source: Norman Myers, *World Book Annual Science Supplement: Science Year* (Chicago: World Book, 1996), 178.

The purpose of this visual aid is to_____

_____

3.

A Multinational Company Must Often Cope With a Wide Variety of Work Customs and Even Languages

Source: Richard Lachmann, ed., *The Encyclopedic Dictionary of Sociology,* 4th ed. (Guilford, CT: Dushkin, 1991).

The purpose of this visual aid is to _____

_____

4. Common Stock

A share of **common stock** represents the most basic form of corporate ownership. A common-stock certificate for Houghton Mifflin Company is shown in the figure on the next page. In return for the financing provided by selling common stock, management must make certain concessions to stockholders that may restrict or change corporate policies. By law, every corporation must hold an annual meeting, at which the holders of common stock may vote for the board of directors and approve (or disapprove) major corporate actions. Among such actions are

1. Amendments to the corporate charter or bylaws
2. Sale of certain assets
3. Mergers and acquisitions
4. Issuing of preferred stock or bonds
5. Changes in the amount of common stock issued

A Common-Stock Certificate
Stockholders provide the company with capital when they purchase shares of stock (equity) in the company. (Used with permission of Houghton Mifflin Company.)
Source: William M. Pride, Robert J. Hughes, and Jack R. Kapoor, *Business*, 5th ed. (Boston: Houghton Mifflin, 1996), 619.

The purpose of this visual aid is to _____

_____

Making Inferences from Visual Aids

THINKING ABOUT YOUR READING AND WRITING

ACTIVITY I: Applying Your Prior Knowledge about Inferences

1. How might the strategies you learned in Chapter 6 for making inferences be applied to reading visual aids?

_____

_____

_____

_____

2. What should the reader of the visual aid do to make an inference?

_____

_____

_____

_____

WORKING TOGETHER

Compare your answers in Activity I with those of a partner. Do you suggest similar strategies? Refer to Chapter 6 after you make your comparisons and see what else you can add. Then make your revisions to Activity I.

In Chapter 6, you learned that inferences are statements about the unknown based on what is known. With your partner, you probably agreed that you can make inferences from visual aids in the same way that you make inferences from text. When you make them from visual aids, of course, the numbers or features on graphs and tables, parts of the diagram, points on the timeline, or details on the photograph become the evidence to support the inference in the same way that details in sentences or paragraphs provide evidence to support an inference about written material. The figure below illustrates this point. Although not stated on the graph, it is obvious that once the measles vaccine was licensed and people realized its value, they took advantage of it, which resulted in the sharp drop in the number of measles cases.

ACTIVITY J: Making Inferences from Visual Aids

Use the details on each visual aid to make at least one inference about it. Beneath your inference, indicate your evidence.

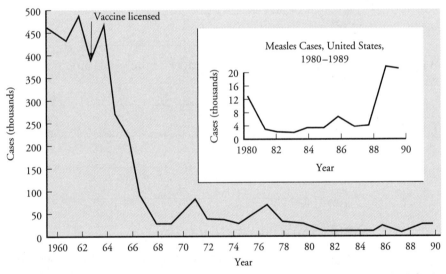

Source: Gerald J. Tortora, Berdell R. Funke, and Christine L. Case, *Microbiology: An Introduction,* 4th ed. (Redwood City, CA: Benjamin/Cummings, 1992), 527.

1.

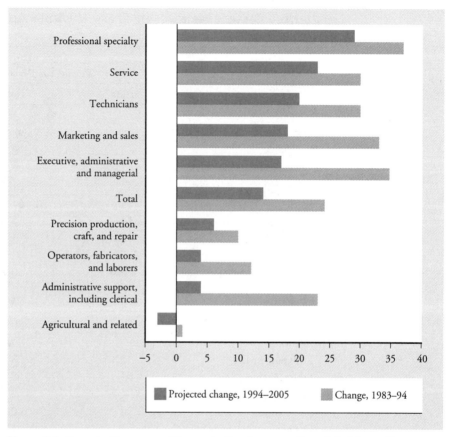

Slower Job Growth: Percentage Change in Employment Growth by Major Occupational Group

Source: U.S.Bureau of Labor Statistics; appeared in Ronald J. Alsop, ed., *The Wall Street Journal Almanac* (New York: Ballantine Books, 1998), 305.

Your inference from this visual aid:

_____

Your evidence:

_____

2.

SELECTED CHARACTERISTICS OF PERSONS UNDER AGE 18 ADMITTED TO STATE PRISON, 1985–97

Characteristics	New Commitments to State Prison for Persons Under Age 18		
	1985	1990	1997
Gender			
Male	97%	98%	97%
Female	3	2	3
Race/Hispanic origin			
White*	32%	21%	25%
Black*	53	61	58
Hispanic	14	15	15
Other	1	1	2
Age at Admission			
14 or under	0%	0%	1%
15	2	3	4
16	18	17	21
17	80	80	74
Education			
8th grade or less	32%	28%	28%
9th to 11th grade	63	68	66
High school graduate	4	3	5
Some college	0	0	0
Other	1	1	1

Note: Figures may not add up to total because of rounding. Statistics include only those with a sentence of more than one year. High school graduate includes GED credential.
*Excludes Hispanics.

Source: Bureau of Justice Statistics, U.S. Department of Justice; *Education Week,* 29 March 2000, 3.

Your inference from this visual aid:

Your evidence:

3.

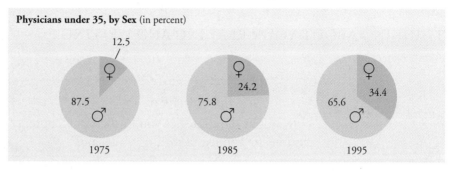

Physicians under 35, by Sex (in percent)

Male and Female Physicians										
	1975		1980		1985		1990		1995	
	Number	%	Number	%	Number	%	Number	%	Number	%
Total	393,742		467,679		552,716		615,421		720,325	
Male	358,106	90.9	413,395	88.4	471,991	85.4	511,227	83.1	570,921	79.3
Female	35,636	9.1	54,284	11.6	80,725	14.6	104,194	16.9	149,404	20.7

Female Physicians in Selected Specialties						
	1975		1985		1995	
Specialty	Number	%	Number	%	Number	%
Total	35,636		80,725		149,404	
Family practice	590	1.7	5,657	7.0	13,971	9.4
Internal medicine	4,006	11.2	14,716	18.2	27,609	18.5
Ob/Gyn	1,777	5.0	5,597	6.9	11,231	7.5
Pediatrics	5,135	14.4	12,440	15.4	22,646	15.2
Psychiatry	3,144	8.8	6,539	8.1	10,392	7.0

Women in Medicine

Source: American Medical Association; appeared in Ronald J. Alsop, ed., *The Wall Street Journal Almanac* (New York: Ballantine Books, 1998), 727.

Your inference from this visual aid:

Your evidence:

Drawing Conclusions from Visual Aids

THINKING ABOUT YOUR READING AND WRITING

ACTIVITY K: Using Your Prior Knowledge about Drawing Conclusions

1. How might the strategies you learned in Chapter 6 about drawing conclusions be applied to reading visual aids?

_____

_____

_____

2. What should someone reading a visual aid do to draw a conclusion?

_____

_____

_____

WORKING TOGETHER

Compare your answers to Activity K with those of a partner. Do you suggest similar strategies? Refer to Chapter 6 after you make your comparisons to see what else you can add. Then make your revisions to Activity K.

As you work with visual aids in texts, you will need to draw your own conclusions from them. You will look for likely outcomes based on the data given. Conclusions move you beyond the text to thinking about applications and logical consequences or results that you can expect in the future, based on the data given. Authors may state their conclusions from the data directly within the body of the text, but the visual aid will help you see how such conclusions were reached. Additionally, you may be able to draw other conclusions that the author does not state explicitly. These are often the most interesting conclusions because they are truly your own ideas, and the visual aid proves why your ideas are logical. The next example illustrates how information on visual aids leads to a variety of conclusions and applications.

Example.

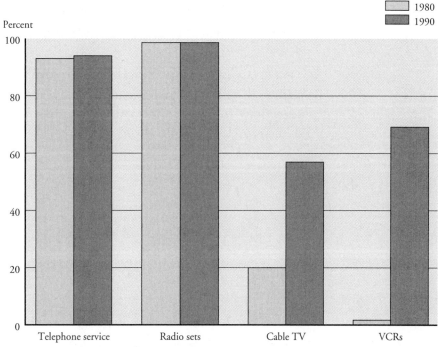

Households with Selected Media: 1980 and 1990

Source: World Almanac, 1992. Chart prepared by U.S. Bureau of the Census.

Your conclusions:

_____

_____

_____

_____

Why is each conclusion logical?_____

_____

_____

_____

It is logical to conclude from this chart that people in the United States felt it was more important to have telephone service and radio sets than cable television and VCRs and that having a radio set was the most important of all. You can also reasonably conclude that American households in the 1980s considered telephone service and radio sets necessities while cable television and VCRs were luxuries.

ACTIVITY L: Drawing Conclusions from Visual Aids

Beneath each of the following visual aids, write as many conclusions as you can draw from the information provided. Then indicate why you think these are logical conclusions.

1.

ADVERTISING EXPENDITURES AND SALES VOLUME FOR THE TOP 20 NATIONAL ADVERTISERS (IN MILLIONS OF DOLLARS)

Rank	Company	Advertising Expenditures	Sales	Advertising Expenditures as Percentage of Sales
1	Proctor & Gamble Co.	$2,397.5	$15,362	15.6%
2	Philip Morris Cos.	1,844.3	38,387	4.8
3	General Motors Corp.	1,539.2	109,668	1.4
4	Sears, Roebuck and Co.	1,310.7	29,565	4.4
5	Pepsico Inc.	1,038.9	18,309	5.7
6	Ford Motor Co.	958.3	75,661	1.3
7	AT&T	812.1	61,580	1.3
8	Nestlé SA	793.7	20,163	3.9
9	Johnson & Johnson	762.5	7,203	10.6
10	Chrysler Corp.	761.6	37,847	2.0
11	Warner-Lambert Co.	751.0	2,747	27.3
12	Unilever NV	738.2	8,550	8.6
13	McDonald's Corp.	736.6	3,931	18.7
14	Time Warner	695.1	4,414	15.7
15	Toyota Motor Corp.	690.4	84,873	0.8
16	Walt Disney Co.	675.7	6,711	10.1
17	Grand Metropolitan PLC	652.9	6,862	9.5
18	Kellogg Co.	627.1	3,784	16.6
19	Eastman Kodak Co.	624.7	8,384	7.5
20	Sony Corp.	589.0	9,127	6.5

Source: Reprinted with permission from *Advertising Age,* September 28, 1994. Copyright © Crain Communications, Inc. All rights reserved.

Your conclusions: _____

_____

_____

_____

Why is each conclusion logical?

_____

_____

_____

_____

2.

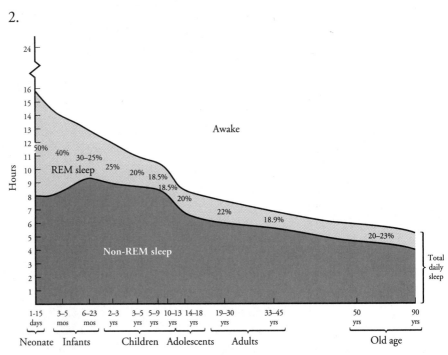

Note: Percentages indicate portion of total sleep time spent in REM.

Sleep and Dreaming Over the Life Span

Source: Douglas A. Bernstein et al., *Psychology*, 4th ed. (Boston: Houghton Mifflin, 1997), 172.

Your conclusions:

_____

_____

_____

_____

Why is each conclusion logical?

3.

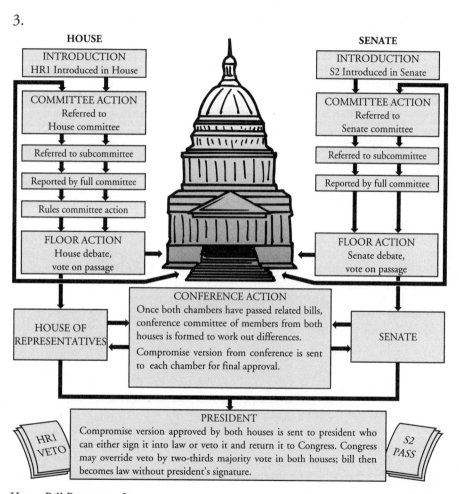

How a Bill Becomes a Law

Source: James Q. Wilson, *American Government*, Brief Version, 2nd ed. (Lexington, MA: Heath, 1990), 201.

Your conclusions: _____

_____

_____

_____

Why is each conclusion logical? _____

_____

_____

_____

4.

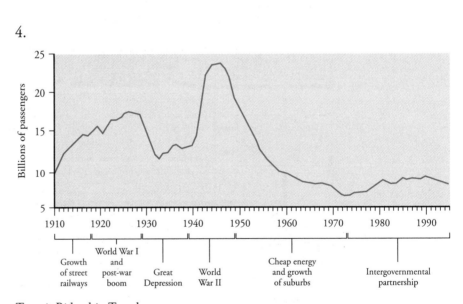

Transit Ridership Trend

Source: American Public Transit Association; appeared in Ronald J. Alsop, ed., *The Wall Street Journal Almanac* (New York: Ballantine Books, 1998), 891.

Your conclusions: _____

_____

_____

_____

Why is each conclusion logical? _____

_____

_____

_____

▶ *Chapter Summary*

Based on your reading of this chapter, list at least five strategies that you believe will help you with future reading assignments. Write in complete sentences.

1. _____

_____

_____

_____

2. _____

_____

_____

_____

3. _____

_____

_____

_____

4. _____

_____

_____

_____

5. _____

_____

_____

_____

▶ *Extended Application*

Now that you have worked with the strategies necessary for reading visual aids, you can practice applying them to full-length reading selections. Choose (or your instructor may choose) a reading selection that is typical of what you will be expected to read for college courses, such as an essay or a textbook chapter, which also contains visual aids. Use this selection to

- ❋ Preview visual aids
- ❋ Note details of visual aids
- ❋ Make connections between visual aids and text
- ❋ Make inferences from visual aids
- ❋ Draw conclusions from visual aids

Decide on the practice strategies you will use. Apply them to your selection. Then, in a few paragraphs, write a description of what you did and how the strategies you used worked for you.

Name of material used: _____

Page numbers: _____

Your description: _____

CHAPTER EIGHT

Strategies for Active Listening and Note Taking

HOW MIGHT YOU EXPERIENCE A FOOTBALL GAME differently if you were a player in the game as compared to a spectator watching it? In which situation would you obtain the greatest inside knowledge about what had happened during particular plays? Which experience would result in more information about why your team won or lost the game? In which circumstance would you have greater connection to the emotions and reactions of the other team members? No doubt you realize that in answer to most or all of these questions, being in the game would give you an advantage over watching it. College students have a choice to make when they attend classes and do their reading assignments—they can be in the game, or they can be spectators. The experiences and knowledge you gain as a student will largely depend on which choice you make. In this chapter, you are introduced to strategies for listening and note taking that will help you become an active player in academic life.

Becoming a Good Listener

Good listening does not come automatically to most people. It is a skill that is learned, practiced, analyzed, and practiced some more. We are constantly bombarded with noises that compete for our attention. We *hear* all these sounds. But when we *listen,* we make a decision about which sounds will get our attention. Hearing that is purposeful and directed is called *listening.*

In your earliest grades in school, your teachers tried to instill in you the habit of being a good listener. Consider, for instance, how many times you sat in a circle in the classroom while the teacher told you and your classmates to "Shhh." Can you recall some special signals your teacher may have used to tell you that it was time to listen? Maybe the lights were momentarily turned off, or two fingers were raised, or perhaps your teacher rang a small bell that sat on his or her desk. These school practices were designed to help children learn that there was time to talk and time to listen. In some families, listening is very important, and children in them are frequently told they must listen to their elders. In other families, it appears that no one listens to anyone else—everyone seems to be talking all the time without concern for whether they are being heard.

In adulthood, our needs and interests in various situations guide our listening habits. We are more aware that listening is a voluntary activity and that we can deliberately tune in or tune out as we choose. When we tune out, communication stops and messages sent to us become undeliverable. But when we choose to listen, all sorts of knowledge and understanding become possible for us. Your decision whether or not to be an effective listener can have a major impact on your success in college and career.

The amount of time college students spend listening in classes, as opposed to other in-class activities, is considerable. Some estimates suggest that students spend more than 50 percent of class time listening to their instructors. Given this situation, you can understand why it is necessary to develop effective listening strategies.

THINKING ABOUT YOUR READING AND WRITING

ACTIVITY A: Your Listening Habits

Think about the listening habits you developed in your early life. How have they helped or hindered your ability to listen in a college classroom?

_____

_____

_____

_____

_____

_____

_____

_____

_____

ACTIVITY B: How Good a Listener Are You?

Here are some characteristics of listeners. Rate yourself on each item by placing a check in the column that most applies to you.

	Always True of Me	Sometimes True of Me	Never True of Me
When I Listen, I			
1. Look at the speaker.			
2. Make predictions about what will be said.			
3. Think about what I already know about the topic.			
4. Look at the speaker's body language.			

(continued)

	Always True of Me	Sometimes True of Me	Never True of Me
5. Intend to understand.			
6. Stay awake.			
7. Ask for clarification when I don't understand.			
8. Select what is important.			
9. Take notes.			
10. Become distracted easily.			
11. Try to restate what the speaker has said in my own words.			
12. Fake attention.			
13. Evaluate my personal biases on the topic.			
14. Focus on the speaker.			
15. Summarize what's being said.			
16. Daydream.			
17. Listen for the speaker's organization.			
18. Use speaker's pauses as time to think.			
19. Try to identify the speaker's purpose.			
20. Concentrate on content, not delivery.			
21. Listen for speaker bias.			
22. Set a purpose for listening.			

THINKING ABOUT YOUR READING AND WRITING

ACTIVITY C: Analyzing Your Listening Strengths

How did you do? Put the item numbers you placed in each category on the following lines:

Always true of me _____

Sometimes true of me _____

Never true of me _____

Only items 10, 12, and 16 suggest *negative listening behaviors.* They are behaviors that interfere with effective listening. All the other statements are *positive listening behaviors.* You can evaluate your own listening behavior by noting the number of the positive behaviors that are true of you sometimes or all the time. We explain the reasons these are considered positive behaviors in the next section.

Indicators of Positive Listening

Connecting with the Speaker

Communication is a two-way process between speaker and listener or reader and author. Speakers often look at their audience for evidence that their ideas are being communicated successfully. One source of evidence is the audience's actions while listening. Listeners who make eye contact with the speaker, who sit in an attentive posture, who nod in recognition of some ideas, or who take notes signal that they are connecting with the speaker and that speaker–listener communication is occurring. Professors are usually aware of those students who try to become involved in the lecture or discussion and those who are dozing off or who seem inattentive. Students may try to fake attention, but they are easily spotted. Even though these students may appear to be looking at the speaker, their eyes are often glazed over, and it is clear to the observer that these listeners' minds are elsewhere.

If you analyze the speaker's body language, it may help you stay focused on the speaker. You might notice particular body language signals that the speaker uses to send important messages to listeners. For instance, if the speaker is pacing back and forth across the front of the room but suddenly stops to face the audience, it probably signals that an important point will be made. If the speaker's hand makes a pounding or other forceful type of motion, this, too, is to emphasize an important idea. Sometimes speakers will move closer to the audience when they really want to get a point across. Arms folded across the speaker's chest may mean that the speaker will later remark or argue against what he or she is saying now. Voice changes, such as increased volume, or a slowed rate of speech, or repetition of an idea, also signal key points.

You will find that many benefits result from effective listening. How well you stay engaged with the speaker can affect the speaker's own enthusiasm and effort to *keep* you interested. This give-and-take between listener and speaker builds mutual rapport. Speakers are more willing to answer questions and to provide requested clarifications for an attentive audience. Further, your efforts to stay involved with the speaker will have a bearing on how much you will remember of what you have heard. In a college classroom, this may have a tremendous impact on your grades; tests often measure what was discussed in class as well as what you have read. The rapport you establish with your professor by being a good listener can also carry over into other classroom activities and may result in your instructor having a positive feeling toward you as a student.

Maintaining Concentration

Positive listeners are able to stay focused on the speaker, no matter what is occurring in the surrounding environment. Often the environment in which a lecture is given is not ideal—construction, bad weather, or loud conversation may be occurring outside the classroom. Imagine how distracting such noise is for someone trying to lead a discussion or to give a lecture. Of course, it is equally difficult for listeners to pay attention to what is happening inside the classroom when distractions such as these are outside. Nevertheless, both speaker and listener must try to stay focused and to ignore the distractions. How can you do this? *Concentration* is the key to success in such a situation. This means you must be able to focus your attention on a single task—in this case, on the speaker.

We have become used to being able to "change the channel" when we watch TV and don't like the program. This can make it difficult for us to concentrate when a lecture seems boring or unrelated to other things that are more meaningful for us. Some strategies to help you keep focused while listening follow.

THINK ABOUT HOW THE INFORMATION YOU HEAR RELATES TO WHAT YOU ALREADY KNOW ABOUT A SUBJECT.   Some instructors assume their students have considerable background on a topic, either because of students' prior knowledge or because they believe students have completed a reading assigned before the lecture. We have discussed the importance of prior knowledge at many points in this text. If you connect new knowledge from a lecture to information you already have, it will help you understand and remember it.

WHILE YOU LISTEN, SORT OUT MAIN POINTS FROM LESSER ONES. We have already mentioned some ways in which you can do this:

1. Look for body clues that are signals to important ideas.
2. Follow the organizational plan to identify shifts in topic or focus or details to support key points.
3. Notice whether the speaker uses a different tone of voice to signal important points.
4. Recognize a speaker's special efforts to point out major ideas. Sometimes visual aids are used to clarify or emphasize these.
5. Note when your professor refers to pages in the text that may further explain some point being made or when you are given such hints as "This would be a good topic of discussion for a test."

STAY FOCUSED BY MAKING PREDICTIONS ABOUT WHAT WILL BE SAID NEXT.   While you follow the speaker's direction of thought, try to make some predictions about key points to be made, types of supporting evidence that will be used, and point of view. You will keep mentally active as you listen for these.

FORM QUESTIONS WHILE YOU LISTEN.   Active listening includes active questioning. Questions might be about points that seem unclear or about which you would like more information or about arguments you might dispute with other evidence.

TRY TO IDENTIFY THE SPEAKER'S POINT OF VIEW, EVEN WHEN IT ISN'T EXPRESSED DIRECTLY.   This will require "listening between the lines." Your speaker's point of view might not be spoken directly, but you can use body language signals, as well as remarks about other points of view on the subject, to determine the speaker's position. You will need to listen actively for evidence of the speaker's biases and to confirm your conclusions.

EVALUATE THE MESSAGE.   Recall how in Chapter 6 you evaluated an author's writing for evidence. In the same way, if the talk is anything more than merely stating facts, you will want to analyze the evidence offered as proof of the speaker's position. As you know, evaluation of messages includes noting whether the proof provided is merely more opinion or whether the factual evidence is available. It also involves asking yourself such questions as "How authoritative is the source? What other opinions on this subject are possible?"

TAKE NOTES.   Note taking is an important skill in college, one that we discuss later in this chapter. It is one of the best ways to maintain your concentration during a lecture and to keep yourself actively involved in what is being said.

Listening with the Intent to Learn

Students who have positive attitudes will enter the lecture hall or classroom each time with an *intent* to listen. This intention requires that several things occur before and during the lecture.

COME PREPARED TO LISTEN AND LEARN.   This means you should do the assigned readings before you arrive in class, and you should have brought the tools necessary for effective listening: your text, a course notebook, and pen or pencil for writing important ideas during the lecture, as well as any other tools needed, such as a calculator.

BE AWARE OF BARRIERS TO EFFECTIVE COMMUNICATION DURING THE LECTURE AND TRY TO REMOVE THESE.   A professor's dialect or accent might be unfamiliar to you. This could pose a listening barrier. The speaker's native language might be different from the listener's, yet the speaker is using the listener's language. It is then up to the listener to make every effort to identify the pronunciation differences that occur regularly and to make listening accommodations.

Another barrier might be the physical appearance of the speaker. If it is somehow disturbing, or if he or she seems very nervous or uncomfortable, you will need to listen hard and to shut out the physical distractions caused by the speaker. Being aware of the distractions is the first step toward ignoring them.

Technical language used by the speaker can also be a barrier to communication. In such cases, advance reading and use of context are the two best strategies for overcoming the difficulty. If you have done these but still are unable to understand some of the language used, try asking for clarification.

It may also be the case that you are unfamiliar with the speaker's style. When the speaker is one of your professors, you do have the advantage of having many class sessions during which you can adjust to the particular approach and language used. One area of difference may be the way in which the speaker organizes the lecture. Chapter 5 introduced you to organizational patterns in writing. These patterns are also often used in speaking situations. Although the speaker might stray from the topic from time to time, you may still be able to find an overall pattern of organization. This will help you follow the speaker's ideas. Another difference you will notice is that some professors will use long, complex sentences with many embedded ideas. You will need to process this information rather rapidly, sorting out important ideas from unimportant ones. Fortunately, rate of speech is slower than rate of thinking, so you will have some time to weigh the importance of each part of the lecture. Some instructors may help you in this by identifying lecture goals at the start of class. This will certainly facilitate communication.

A final barrier to communication may result from the instructional style the speaker uses, particularly if it is different from what you have been used to. Instructors include student activities in their course presentations to different extents. In some classes, there will be a great deal of collaboration, and students will be expected to learn important concepts of the course as a result of these experiences with classmates. At the other extreme, the professor will remain at the center of activity, and the students will participate actively only as listeners. In all instructional settings, you will need to ask yourself, "What is the instructor expecting me to do in order to learn the major concepts of this course?"

LISTEN FOR SPEAKER BIAS BUT KEEP AN OPEN MIND.   The intent to learn requires that the listener believe there is something to be gained from listening. How do you typically respond to a speaker whose ideas are in total disagreement with yours? If you are like most of us, you get angry and want an opportunity to explain to everyone why the speaker is wrong. This tactic does not promote good listening because your mind is so focused on your rebuttal that you really don't listen to what the speaker is saying. In the speaker's ideas, there may be some points you haven't considered, or there may be points that serve your interests because you can easily argue against their logic or significance. But if you don't listen to the speaker, if you are so wrapped up in developing your plan of attack, you will miss the opportunity to hear these other ideas. College students often find that their ideas about things change from when they first enter their academic program to when they graduate. There are many influences on your attitudes. Your personal biases are the result of your experiences and your memories of them. These are valuable sources of evidence for your present perceptions and biases. However, your instructors may have some new insights to offer that will help you rethink your ideas and, perhaps, modify them. By keeping an open mind, you are allowing yourself to find support for your beliefs or to change your ideas to more defensible and logical ones. Intelligent responses are easier when you have listened to what has already been said.

RECOGNIZE CONFUSIONS.   Effective listeners plan to learn from lectures or discussions. This means they must recognize when they are confused and when learning is therefore not occurring. In most classrooms and lecture halls, there is opportunity for students to ask questions. Don't hesitate to do so. Some professors assign "one-minute papers" after a lecture in which students write some of the main ideas they obtained from the lecture as well as any questions they still have about the topic that was discussed. Use this opportunity to give feedback to your instructor and to ask for further explanation. If there is no chance to ask questions during the class session, make an appointment to see your instructor afterward. You will show yourself to be a serious student. You will be respected for seeking clarification, and you will demonstrate that you are working hard at reaching understanding.

THINKING ABOUT YOUR READING AND WRITING

ACTIVITY D: Controlling Your Listening Experience

To what extent are listeners in control of how much they benefit from a learning situation? Write your response in the space provided. Be specific.

_____

_____

_____

_____

_____

_____

WORKING TOGETHER

Compare your ideas in Activity D with those of a partner. How do you differ in your definition of what it means to be in control of a learning situation? Make any changes to your response in Activity D that you feel are appropriate.

ACTIVITY E: Analyzing Instructional Styles

Complete this activity for two of your instructors. For each category, write a few sentences that characterize each instructor. Then explain how this instructional style affects you as a listener.

1. Instructor A (name not required)

Speech complexity: _____

_____

_____

Body language: _____

_____

_____

Assumptions about prior knowledge of students: _____

_____

_____

Clarity of presentation: _____

_____

_____

Organization: _____

_____

_____

Opportunities for student involvement: _____

_____

_____

Listening strategies I should use in this class: _____

_____

_____

Overall characterization of style: _____

_____

_____

_____

How this instructional style affects me: _____

_____

_____

_____

2. Instructor B (name not required)

Speech complexity:_____

_____

_____

Body language:_____

_____

_____

Assumptions about prior knowledge of students:_____

_____

_____

Clarity of presentation:_____

_____

_____

Organization:_____

_____

_____

Opportunities for student involvement:_____

_____

_____

Listening strategies I should use in this class: _____

_____

_____

Overall characterization of style: _____

_____

_____

_____

How this instructional style affects me: _____

_____

_____

_____

Effective Note Taking from Books and Lectures

High school and college differ in the extent to which students are expected to be independent learners. In high school, your teachers may have put a lecture outline on the chalkboard, and they may have deliberately pointed out important points for you. This is often not the case in college. Usually, you must decide for yourself what notes to take and how to write them. Further, in some college courses, outside reading assignments are never discussed in class. Still, you are expected to read, understand, and remember information from them, and these assignments may form an important basis for exams and class lectures on related topics. Thus, your ability to effectively mark your textbooks and to take notes from them can have an impact on your course grades.

Note-taking and textbook-marking skills are seldom taught to students. You may believe that there aren't any specific strategies to use and that some students just have a knack for good note taking, and others don't. This, however, is seldom so. There are many strategies for effective marking of textbooks and taking notes. This section describes those that have been found to be most beneficial to college students. As you work with them, try adapting them to your own purposes and learning needs so that they will be most useful for you.

A Process for Effective Note Taking

Earlier you read that effective listeners think about what they hear before they write anything. A listener can use the *wait time,* the time between a speaker's thought and actual speech, to think about and then to write down the important ideas, as shown here.

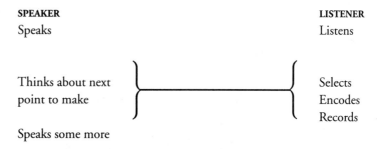

SPEAKER		**LISTENER**
Speaks		Listens
Thinks about next point to make		Selects Encodes Records
Speaks some more		

During wait time, you *select* what is most important from all the information that is spoken. Then you *encode,* or translate, these important ideas into language that is more like your own. Finally, you *record* these ideas. This process of listening, selecting, encoding, and recording continues until the lecture ends.

Identifying Usable Notes

Imagine that you are preparing for a test in the introductory psychology course you are taking. You are studying your lecture notes from a session on memory. Two examples of notes from part of that lecture follow. Which set would you prefer to have available to you as you study?

Example 1:

Memory

Laboratory studies of memory show how much you know later as compared to how much you know right away. Really, memory study is study of forgetting.

In lab studies the subject is given task and then scientist measures how much learning occurred. Subject does activity to keep him/her from thinking about the new information. Later is tested again to see what of the new information is remembered.

Recall is reproduction of the learned material. Sometimes it is rote or verbatim, which means remembering it in the exact form. Recognition is recognizing something that was previously experienced, such as faces of friends. Relearning involves both recall and recognition. Scientist finds out how long it takes to learn the material as measured on a test. After an interval of time, the subject relearns it. (may test subject on it till he can pass the same test equally well on two occasions)

Ebbinghaus did first important studies on retention; used nonsense syllables. List of nonsense syllables had to be remembered in serial order. Found there was a rapid initial loss, followed by a gradual slower decline. (Memory Curve)

Why we forget? trace decay theory says knowledge we have learned just fades away, and the longer it remains unused, the greater we decay. interference theory—other learnings interfere with memory of a previous learning. Trance transformation theory—memory is active process; information stored is automatically transformed to make it more consistent with other knowledge we are remembering. Repression theory—believes that the things we remember and the things we forget are related to their value and importance to us. (Freud)

Example 2:

Memory

11/4/01

Lab studies of Memory
—show how much you know later as compared to how much you know right after learning.
—Mem. study is really a study of forgetting.

Lab procedures
(1) subject given task & scientist measures how much learning occurred.
(2) Subj. does activity—kept from thinking about new info.
(3) Subj. tested again later to see what new info is remembered.

Terms About Memory
Recall—
reproduction of the lrnd material.
Sometimes (rote) or (verbatim) (remembering it exactly)
Recognition—
recognizing something that was experienced before, i.e. faces of friends.
Relearning—
involves both recall and recognition. **see text pg. 247**
(1) Scientist finds out how long it takes to learn the material (may give a test)
(2) Later subj. relearns it. (may be tested till he can pass the same test equally well on two occasions)

STUDIES
Ebbinghaus
—first imp. studies on retention
—used list of nonsense syllables
—syllables had to be remembered in (serial) order
—Found rapid loss at beginning, followed by gradual slower decline.

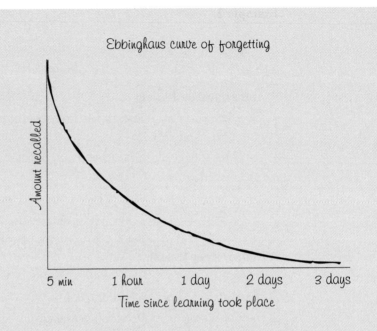

Ebbinghaus curve of forgetting

Amount recalled (vertical axis)

5 min   1 hour   1 day   2 days   3 days

Time since learning took place

THEORIES of WHY WE FORGET

trace decay theory:

what we lrnd just fades away,

the longer it remains unused, the greater it decays.

interference theory:

other lrngs interfere with mem. of previous lrng.

trance transformation theory:

mem is active process

? information stored is automatically transformed to

make it more consistent with other knowledge we are remembering.

repression theory:

things we remember and things we forget are related to their value

and importance to us. (Freud)

Sources: Hermann Ebbinghaus, "Curve of Forgetting," in *Psychology: An Elementary Text-Book* [1908], trans. and ed. M. Meyer (New York: Arno, 1973). Adapted from Floyd L. Ruch and Philip G. Zimbardo, *Psychology and Life,* Brief Version, 8th ed. (Glenview, IL: Scott, Foresman, 1971).

THINKING ABOUT YOUR READING AND WRITING

ACTIVITY F: Your Note Taking Preferences

1. Which set of notes do you prefer? Why?

_____

_____

_____

_____

2. What differences do you see between the two examples?

_____

_____

_____

_____

_____

_____

_____

_____

_____

_____

Note-Taking Basics

If you had considered that the notes you chose were to be used to study for a test, you should have chosen the second example. Perhaps you recognized some of the following features in this example, which are features of a good set of lecture notes.

1. *The notes are dated.* The date is a reference for you. You will be able to compare a set of lecture notes from a particular date with those of another student. Further, if your notes get out of sequence for some reason, it will be easy to put them back in order by date. Ideas from earlier lectures may have a bearing on those of lectures later in the semester.

2. *The notes are organized so that the relationships between ideas are clear.* This clarity results from the student's systematic approach to note taking. Main topics can readily be distinguished from minor ones because they have been placed apart from the details, and the margin of the page serves as the starting place for writing the main topics. Each new important topic is written on a separate line. Details and subtopics are indented under the related main ideas. Major details are distinguished from minor ones by indenting the minor details even further.

3. *Important terms are seen quickly.* A system of circling new terminology has been used. This will make it easy to go back to this notebook and to locate where new vocabulary has been introduced.

4. *Only a few words are used to convey ideas.* It is impossible, and also not a good idea, to write everything that is said word for word. Effective note takers learn to condense whole sentences into shorter phrases that convey the same meaning. This saves time and offers you an additional opportunity to reflect on the meaning. This is part of the process of encoding the material.

5. *There is space for additional information.* Even with the advantage of wait time, other related ideas or information may occur to you well after you have taken your original set of notes. In the second example, space has been left for such entries.

6. *A personal shorthand system has been used for repeated and common words.* The author of these notes recognizes that some words, like *subject* and *memory,* occur over and over again in this course. Having this system of abbreviations (for example, *subj.* and *mem.*) cuts writing time.

7. *Areas of uncertainty are noted.* The question mark for areas needing further investigation shows that the author of these notes has

processed the ideas of the speaker during the lecture; while the lecture is occurring, the note taker has asked, "Am I understanding this?" A question mark enables areas of uncertainty to be easily located later, and you will be able to seek assistance and clarification.

8. *Diagrams have been carefully drawn.* We cannot tell whether the student taking these notes drew the diagram without direction from the instructor to do so or whether it had been copied from the board or overhead. The important point, though, is that all parts are clearly labeled, and it will be a useful study aid during the semester.

9. *References to pages in the textbook have been noted and are easily spotted.* Again, we do not know whether this reference to the textbook was noted by the student or whether it had been pointed out by the instructor. But it is clear that the student will be able to refer to the text for further elaboration on this point. If the instructor made the reference and the student ignored it, an opportunity would have been missed.

10. *The notes are legible.* All the information is easy to read. Some students who incorporate many of the basics of effective note taking into their study skills repertoire still have a serious problem. When they try to study from their notes, they find they can't read what they have written! This might be from writing too fast or trying to write the lecture word for word. Carefully selecting what to write means that you will need to write less so you can write legibly. You will want to keep the doodling to a minimum, too!

THINKING ABOUT YOUR READING AND WRITING

ACTIVITY G: Analyzing Your Note-Taking Processes

1. Which note-taking basics do you already use?

_____

_____

_____

_____

2. Which basics might be hard for you to apply? Why?

_____

_____

_____

_____

Note-Taking Systems

There are more ways than one to take good notes from lectures and textbooks. We describe two of the most popular note-taking systems in this section. Examine each and then decide which system will work best for you, which will most satisfactorily help you achieve your own note-taking objectives. Keep an open mind as you try your selected approach. You might start using one system but later decide that you need to try another approach because your first strategy is not working for you.

The Cornell Method

This note-taking method, developed by Walter Pauk, is highly recommended by study skills experts. Although it is a little more structured than the notes in Example 2 that you reviewed earlier, it is popular with students because it is easy to use and it encourages reflection about the material both during and after the lecture or initial reading. To use the Cornell method, you will need a full-size (8½ × 11-inch) notebook that has an extra-wide left margin (legal ruled or summary ruled). Such notebooks are available in bookstores, or you may rule the margins yourself. The Cornell method involves a two-phase process of note taking. During the lecture or initial reading of the assignment, write information in a right-hand (6-inch) column. Write each main idea on a separate line, and write supporting details beneath each of these. A set of notes written this way for a lecture in a business course is illustrated next.

Cornell method example (phase 1):

February 19, 2001
Careers in Marketing

Mktg. is a broad field; many opportunities
  Can be involved with product any time—from creation til after
    sale, incl. service & maintenance
  1983—demand for sales & mktg. execs. rchd 5 yr. high, esp in
    Southeast & Midwest
  Over 1/2 labor force in service is in some aspect of mktg.
  Career opp. in selling, advertising, sales promotion, publ. rela,
    product mngmnt, mktg resrch, retailing, wholesaling, physical
    distrib, mktg mngmnt.
Selling has many opportunities
  more employees than any other mktg. occup
  some salespeople are own boss; most work for others
  most jobs routine—structured work schedule, regular pay
    ed. & trng vary
      for standardized goods & svcs— only h.s.dip.;
        e.g. Retail trade sales—interest cust. in product;
        demonstrate prod., prep sales slips, receive cash, give
        change and receipt—reg. h.s. dip.
      for manufacturers salespeople—college degree req.
        e.g. sell to factories, banks, wholesalers, schools,
        hospitals, libraries
Advertising jobs very competitive; good starting salary
  Jobs are in advertising depts. of producers and intermediaries; ad
  agencies; w/media firms.
  e.g. adv. mgr—directs program; decides allocation of $, type of
  ad and ad agcy to use.
      rsrch directors—survey cust buying habits; test sample ads.
      production mgr—arranges for printing ads (or film, t.v.,
      radio)
Jobs in Public Relations
        req. college deg. in jrnlism, communications, or pub rela
        helps orgs. build & maintain positive pub image; must
        underst. pub concerns & communicate this info. to mngmnt

Source: Adapted from Leon C. Megginson, Lyle R. Trueblood, and Gayle M. Ross, *Business* (Lexington, MA: Heath, 1985), 420–423.

In the second phase of using the Cornell method, you review the information that is in the center of the page and then edit and summarize it. In editing you may correct spelling, insert punctuation, delete or add words, and improve the organization of the notes, perhaps by numbering ideas. When you summarize, you want to make it easy to find the key topics that were discussed and to state the main ideas. To do this, write on the left-side margin (the remaining one-third page) any key words, phrases, or questions that summarize the main ideas and pull together important facts from the right side of the page. These summary notes will serve as important cues when it is time for you to review for subsequent readings or lectures or to study for exams. As a part of your summary, also write one or two sentences that state the main idea of the lecture. This summary is written at the bottom of your final page of notes. Create the space to write it by drawing an additional line at the bottom of the notebook page, 2 inches up from the edge. When you summarize ideas in this way, you are giving yourself an additional opportunity to review and reflect on the lecture and to organize it into meaningful units of information. The next example illustrates this second step.

Cornell method example (phase 2):

February 19, 2001
Careers in Marketing

Job Opportunities	Mktg. is a broad field; many opportunities Can be involved with product any time—from creation til after sale, incl. service & maintenance
Where are they located?	1983—demand for sales & mktg. execs. rchd 5 yr. high, esp in Southeast & Midwest Over 1/2 labor force in service is in some aspect of mktg.
What type of jobs?	Career opp. in selling, advertising, sales promotion, publ. rela, product mngmnt, mktg resrch, retailing, wholesaling, physical distrib, mktg mngmnt.

Opportunities in Selling	Selling has many opportunities
	    more employees than any other mktg. occup
	    some salespeople are own boss; most work for others
	    most jobs routine—structured work schedule, regular pay
	    ed. & trng vary

variety and requirements	for standardized goods & svcs— only h.s.dip.; e.g. Retail trade sales—interest cust. in product; demonstrate prod., prep sales slips, receive cash, give change and receipt—req. h.s. dip. for manufacturers salespeople—college degree req. e.g. sell to factories, banks, wholesalers, schools, hospitals, libraries
Advertising	Advertising jobs very competitive; good starting salary Jobs are in advertising depts. of producers and intermediaries; ad agencies; w/media firms.
variety	e.g. adv. mgr—directs program; decides allocation of $, type of ad and ad agcy to use. rsrch directors—survey cust buying habits; test sample ads. production mgr—arranges for printing ads (or film, t.v., radio)
Public Relations requirements variety	Jobs in Public Relations req. college deg. in jrnlism, communications, or pub rela helps orgs. build & maintain positive pub image; must underst. pub concerns & communicate this info. to mngmnt

Summary: There are many job opportunities in marketing, including jobs in selling, advertising and public relations. The jobs have different education requirements and involve different types of responsibilities

Source: Adapted from Leon C. Megginson, Lyle R. Trueblood, and Gayle M. Ross, *Business* (Lexington, MA: Heath, 1985), 420–23.

The Outline Method

You may find that in some instances an outline format is more useful for note taking from lectures and texts. This is particularly true when a lecturer or text is very well organized, provided you are comfortable with numbering each topic and detail during the lecture or reading. Outlines may be written using only topics, sentences, or paragraphs. However, outlines often use a combination of main-idea sentences and subtopics supporting each main idea. The importance of each idea in relation to each other is shown on the outline through the use of either a Roman or Arabic number-and-letter system or a decimal numbering system. The first outline, which is based on a class lecture, illustrates the Roman numeral system. The decimal system is illustrated in the second outline.

Example outline A:

The Human Nervous System

I. Divisions
    A. Central Nervous System (CNS)
       1. Housed in skull and vertebral column
       2. Consists of brain and spinal cord
    B. Peripheral Nervous System (PNS)
       1. Distributed throughout the body
       2. Consists of afferent and efferent fibers and sense organs.

II. Interactions
    A. The two systems interact constantly
    B. Both systems are necessary for voluntary actions and involuntary actions

III. Activities of Central Nervous System
    A. Reception
       1. From motor (efferent) divisions of PNS
       2. From sensory (afferent) divisions of PNS
    B. Integration
       1. Of information about internal and external environments
       2. Decides on course of action
    C. Action
       1. Distributes "instructions" to effector organs
       2. Effector organs may be glands, blood vessels, fingers and toes, etc.

Example outline B:

The Human Nervous System

1. Divisions
    1.1 Central Nervous System (CNS)
       1.1.1 Housed in skull and vertebral column
       1.1.2 Consists of brain and spinal cord
    1.2 Peripheral Nervous System (PNS)
       1.2.1 Distributed throughout the body
       1.2.2 Consists of afferent and efferent fibers and sense organs

2. Interactions
   2.1 The two systems interact constantly
   2.2 Both systems are necessary for voluntary actions and involuntary actions
3. Activities of Central Nervous System
   3.1. Reception
       3.1.1 From motor (efferent) divisions of PNS
       3.1.2 From sensory (afferent) divisions of PNS
   3.2. Integration
       3.2.1 Of information about internal and external environments
       3.2.2 Decides on course of action
   3.3. Action
       3.3.1 Distributes "instructions" to effector organs
       3.3.2 Effector organs may be glands, blood vessels, fingers and toes, etc.

THINKING ABOUT YOUR READING AND WRITING

Activity H: Selecting a Note-Taking System

Of the several note-taking systems introduced in this section, which do you believe will be the best one for you? Why have you selected this approach?

_____

_____

_____

_____

_____

_____

_____

_____

_____

_____

_____

WORKING TOGETHER

Compare your responses to the questions in Activity H with those of a partner. How are your note-taking-system needs similar? How are they different?

ACTIVITY I: Creating Notes from Lectures and Textbooks

Select a textbook chapter or a lecture to attend for note-taking practice. Take notes using the note-taking method you prefer. Then write a one-page analysis of how the method worked for you and what changes, if any, you think you should make in your approach.

Using Your Notes Effectively

Once you have a good set of notes, you will want to make the best possible use of them. We outline six strategies for effective use of notes in this section. As you read these strategies, see whether you have used any of them before. Also try to identify any suggestions that you would like to use from now on.

Edit Your Notes

Edit immediately after a lecture or after completing a reading assignment while the ideas are still fresh in your mind. Your goal for editing is to create a set of notes that you will understand weeks, or even months, after you have heard the lecture or completed the reading. When editing, you should:

1. Be sure everything is legible.
2. Add any punctuation that is needed for clarity.
3. Check your abbreviations and write out the complete words for abbreviations that you do not frequently use.
4. Check the spelling of technical terms and proper names.
5. Check the accuracy of dates.
6. Be sure the relative importance of ideas is clearly seen from your layout.

Cross-Reference Text Notes with Class Notes, and Vice Versa

Class and text notes should support each other; that is, one should add more information to the other. Textbook or other assigned readings often address the same subject as lectures. Note in your reading material the lecture dates that address the same subject and write in your lecture notes the related text-page numbers.

Check Your Notes for Accuracy

While you are editing your notes, you may find that you are unclear on some points or that information seems incomplete. In such cases:

1. Get clarification on the ideas and terminology about which you are uncertain. To do this, you can refer to the relevant portions of your text, compare your notes with others, discuss the material with your instructor, or refer to other materials on the same subject.
2. If you are describing a sequence of events, a procedure, or any series that you will need to remember in order, be certain you have included all parts of the sequence. If there appear to be gaps in the sequence you have recorded in your notes, you will again need to check other sources to make your notes complete.

Summarize Key Points

Do this as soon as you feel you have reviewed a chunk of related information. Write down your summaries. When you put ideas on paper, you can see whether you really can state a few sentences that will express the main points of the lecture or reading or whether there are some points on which you are uncertain. Follow these steps to write an effective summary:

1. Consider the entire lecture you have heard or text material you have read. Be sure the meaning is clear to you. Review what you have underlined and highlighted or noted as being a major point.

2. If a thesis was stated that connected the main points of the text or lecture, write it as the first sentence of your summary.

3. Write a sentence that states each key point of the lecture or reading. These are really statements of main ideas. For an hour's lecture, there may be only three or four main points.

4. Identify the major supporting details for each point that the lecturer or author has included. Try to combine these major details into one or two sentences and then add them to your summary, following each main idea. The result will be a paragraph of perhaps seven to ten sentences, written in your own words.

5. Return to the full set of notes you have summarized to compare it to your summary. Be certain you have not omitted key points or changed the essential meaning.

Practice Distributed Review

How much of what you heard in class last week do you still remember? What about what you heard three or four weeks ago? There is so much information coming into the sensory storage area of our brain that it is impossible for it to stay there for more than just a few seconds. During this time, we need to decide whether to retain the information and transmit it to our short-term memory or to discard it. Information that we transfer to short-term memory we will retain for only a few seconds—twenty or less—unless we rehearse it, deliberately, as we might do with a shopping list or telephone number. Information that we wish to keep in permanent

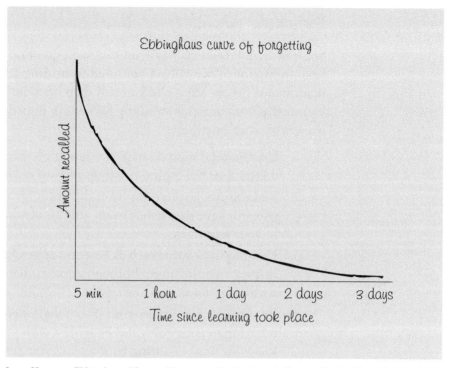

Source: Hermann Ebbinghaus, "Curve of Forgetting," in *Psychology: An Elementary Text-Book* [1908], trans. and ed. M. Meyer (New York: Arno, 1973).

storage for a long time, such as ideas from lectures and textbooks, must be reviewed regularly, or it will be difficult to retrieve. Research shows that without such periodic review we quickly forget what we learned. Three days after learning something, we forget most of it if we make no effort to remember it. The curve of forgetting that appeared earlier in the memory lecture notes is shown again here. It illustrates the point that if you periodically review your notes you will keep the information fresh in your mind and reduce greatly the amount of material you will need to relearn. It will be easier for you to recall the ideas for tests and class discussion or as prior knowledge to help you comprehend later material.

Formulate Questions from Your Notes

See how many different ways you can ask a question that will yield similar information. This will get you used to hearing requests for the information in different ways, and you will then be more likely to know when your instructor's question is calling for certain information. To create and work with your questions:

1. Use the headings you have written in the left column (Cornell method) or the topical headings of your outline.

2. Make as many questions from the headings as you can so that you will have the chance to include all of what you have studied in your responses.

3. Use question words such as *how* and *why*. Questions worded in this way require more thorough answers than those beginning with *what, who, when,* or *where*.

4. Be sure you can answer your questions. Check your answers by referring to your notes and be honest with yourself. If you don't know the answer during your review, you certainly won't know it for an exam.

THINKING ABOUT YOUR READING AND WRITING

ACTIVITY J: Making Personal Decisions about Note Taking

Which of the suggestions for using your notes effectively are new ideas for you? Which of these new suggestions do you think you will try?

_____

_____

_____

_____

_____

_____

ACTIVITY K: Making Notes Usable

Choose a set of notes that you have written from a previous lecture or reading assignment. Make whatever revisions you believe are needed. Keep your original notes. On a separate sheet of paper, explain what you have done to make your notes more usable. Attach your original notes to the revised notes and your explanation.

WORKING TOGETHER

Review your revised notes with a partner. Can your partner suggest anything else to improve them?

Preparing Graphics from Lectures and Texts

One way to record information from lectures and textbooks that we have not yet discussed in this chapter is to make a graphic that shows the relationship between ideas. In Chapters 3–5, you worked with graphics that organized main ideas and details. In Chapter 7, you practiced creating and interpreting graphics that illustrated other types of relationships. You can create any of these graphics, such as timelines, circle charts, tables, flowcharts, semantic maps, or Venn diagrams, to more visually express the ideas from lectures and texts. If you found the work with graphics in the previous chapters to be beneficial, you should consider using this strategy often.

ACTIVITY L: Creating a Graphic from Lecture or Text Notes

Select a set of notes you have taken from a lecture or reading assignment and prepare a graphic to show the relationship between ideas or data. Choose the graphic format that best fits the data or information you have chosen to graphically illustrate. Be prepared to discuss why it is the best type of visual aid for the information.

Underlining and Marking Textbooks

Did you experience "sticker shock" at the bookstore this semester when you purchased your textbooks? Most first-year students have not had to pay for textbooks in the past, and they are usually astonished at the prices.

Once the shock is over, though, you can think about some of the advantages of owning the books, an advantage most students did not have in high school, where the books are typically owned by the school.

Owning your textbooks allows you to underline and make notations in them. If you use effective underlining and textbook-notation strategies, you will be able to find important information and to review it more easily. Study the examples of textbook-page notations that appear in the next three examples. All examples have been taken from the same textbook page, but the notations were made by three different readers. See what differences you can find in how each reader has interacted with the text.

Example A:

The Supreme Court in Action

If your case should find its way to the Supreme Court—and of course the odds are that it will not—you will be able to participate in one of the more impressive, sometimes dramatic, ceremonies of American public life. The Court is in session in its white marble building for thirty-six weeks out of each year, from early October until the end of June. The nine justices read briefs in their individual offices, hear oral arguments in the stately courtroom, and discuss their decisions with one another in a conference room where no outsider is ever allowed.

Most cases, as we have seen, come to the Court on a writ of certiorari. The lawyers for each side may then submit their *briefs,* documents that set forth the facts, summarize the lower-court decision, give the arguments for the side represented by the lawyer, and discuss the other cases that the Court has decided that bear on the issue. Then the lawyers are allowed to present their oral arguments in open court. They usually summarize the briefs or emphasize particular points in them, and are strictly limited in time—usually to no more than a half hour. (The lawyer speaks from a lectern that has two lights on it. When the white light goes on, the attorney has five minutes remaining; when the red flashes, he or she must stop—instantly.) The oral arguments give the justices a chance to question the lawyers, sometimes searchingly.

Since the federal government is a party—as either plaintiff or defendant—to about half the cases that the Supreme Court

for decisions

hears, the government's top trial lawyer, the solicitor general of the United States, appears frequently before the Court. The solicitor general is the third-ranking officer of the Department of Justice, right after the attorney general and <u>deputy attorney general</u>. The solicitor general decides what cases the government <u>will</u> appeal from lower courts and personally approves every case that the government presents to the Supreme Court. In recent years the solicitor general has often been selected from the ranks of distinguished law-school professors.

In addition to the arguments made by lawyers for the two sides in a case, written briefs and even oral arguments may also be offered by "a friend of the court," or *amicus curiae*. An amicus brief is from an interested party not directly involved in the suit. For example, when Allan Bakke complained that he had been the victim of "reverse discrimination" when he was denied admission to a University of California medical school, fifty-eight amicus briefs were filed supporting or opposing his position. Before such briefs can be filed, both parties must agree or the Court must grant permission. Though these briefs sometimes offer new arguments, they are really a kind of polite lobbying of the Court that declares what interest groups are on which side. The <u>ACLU, the NAACP, the AFL-CIO</u>, and the United States government itself have been among the leading sources of such briefs.

involved →

These briefs are not the only source of influence on the justices' views. Legal periodicals such as the *Harvard Law Review* and the *Yale Law Journal* are frequently consulted, and citations to them often appear in the Court's decisions. Thus the outside world of lawyers and law professors can help shape, or at least supply arguments for, the conclusions of the justices.

The justices retire every Friday to their conference room, where in complete secrecy they debate the cases that they have heard. The chief justice speaks first, followed by the other justices in order of seniority. After the arguments they vote, traditionally <u>in reverse order of seniority</u>: the newest justice votes first, the chief justice last. In this process an able chief justice can exercise considerable influence—in guiding or limiting debate, in setting forth the issues, and in handling sometimes temperamental personalities. In deciding a case, a majority of the justices must be in agreement: if there is a tie, the lower-court decision is left standing. (There can be a tie among nine justices if one is ill or disqualifies himself or herself because of prior involvement in the case.)

Though the vote is what counts, by tradition the Court usually issues a written opinion explaining its decision. Sometimes this opinion is brief and unsigned (called a *per curiam* opinion); sometimes it is quite long and signed by the justices agreeing with it. If the chief justice is in the majority, he will either write the opinion or assign the task to a justice who agrees with him. If he is in the minority, the senior justice on the winning side will decide who writes the Court's opinion. There are three kinds of opinions—*opinion of the Court* (reflecting the majority's view), *concurring* (an opinion by one or more justices who agree with the majority's conclusion but for different reasons that they wish to express), and *dissenting* (the opinion of the justices on the losing side). Each justice has three or four law clerks (bright, recent graduates of the leading law schools) to help him or her review the many petitions that the Court receives, study cases, and write opinions.

Example B:

The Supreme Court in Action

If your case should find its way to the Supreme Court—and of course the odds are that it will not—you will be able to participate in one of the more impressive, sometimes dramatic ceremonies of American public life. The Court is in session in its white marble building for thirty-six weeks out of each year, from early October until the end of June. The nine justices read briefs in their individual offices, hear oral arguments in the stately courtroom, and discuss their decisions with one another in a conference room where no outsider is ever allowed.

Most cases, as we have seen, come to the Court on a writ of certiorari. The lawyers for each side may then submit their *briefs,* documents that set forth the facts, summarize the lower-court decision, give the arguments for the side represented by the lawyer, and discuss the other cases that the Court has decided that bear on the issue. Then the lawyers are allowed to present their oral arguments in open court. They usually summarize the briefs or emphasize particular points in them, and are strictly limited in time—usually to no more than a half hour. (The lawyer speaks from a lectern that has two lights on it. When the white light goes on, the attorney has five minutes remaining; when the red flashes, he or she must stop—instantly.) The oral arguments give the justices a chance to question the lawyers, sometimes searchingly.

Since the federal government is a party—as either plaintiff or defendant—to about half the cases that the Supreme Court hears, the government's top trial lawyer, the solicitor general of the United States, appears frequently before the Court. The solicitor general is the third-ranking officer of the Department of Justice, right after the attorney general and deputy attorney general. The solicitor general decides what cases the government will appeal from lower courts and personally approves every case that the government presents to the Supreme Court. In recent years the solicitor general has often been selected from the ranks of distinguished law-school professors.

In addition to the arguments made by lawyers for the two sides in a case, written briefs and even oral arguments may also be offered by "a friend of the court," or *amicus curiae.* An amicus brief is from an interested party not directly involved in the suit. For example, when Allan Bakke complained that he had been the victim of "reverse discrimination" when he was denied admission to a University of California medical school, fifty-eight amicus briefs were filed supporting or opposing his position. Before such briefs can be filed, both parties must agree or the Court must grant permission. Though these briefs sometimes offer new arguments, they are really a kind of polite lobbying of the Court that declares what interest groups are on which side. The ACLU, the NAACP, the AFL-CIO, and the United States government itself have been among the leading sources of such briefs.

These briefs are not the only source of influence on the justices' views. Legal periodicals such as the *Harvard Law Review* and the *Yale Law Journal* are frequently consulted, and citations to them often appear in the Court's decisions. Thus the outside world of lawyers and law professors can help shape, or at least supply arguments for, the conclusions of the justices.

The justices retire every Friday to their conference room, where in complete secrecy they debate the cases that they have heard. The chief justice speaks first, followed by the other justices in order of seniority. After the arguments they vote, traditionally in reverse order of seniority: the newest justice votes first, the chief justice last. In this process an able chief justice can exercise considerable influence—in guiding or limiting debate, in setting forth the issues, and in handling sometimes temperamental personalities. In deciding a case, a majority of the justices must be in agreement: if there is a tie, the lower-court decision is left standing. (There can be a tie among nine justices if one is ill or disqualifies himself or herself because of prior involvement in the case.)

Though the vote is what counts, by tradition the Court usually issues a written opinion explaining its decision. Sometimes this opinion is brief and unsigned (called a *per curiam* opinion); sometimes it is quite long and signed by the justices agreeing with it. If the chief justice is in the majority, he will either write the opinion or assign the task to a justice who agrees with him. If he is in the minority, the senior justice on the winning side will decide who writes the Court's opinion. There are three kinds of opinions—*opinion of the Court* (reflecting the majority's view), *concurring* (an opinion by one or more justices who agree with the majority's conclusion but for different reasons that they wish to express), and *dissenting* (the opinion of the justices on the losing side). Each justice has three or four law clerks (bright, recent graduates of the leading law schools) to help him or her review the many petitions that the Court receives, study cases, and write opinions.

Example C:

The Supreme Court in Action

If your case should find its way to the Supreme Court—and of course the odds are that it will not—you will be able to participate in one of the more impressive, sometimes dramatic cere-

monies of American public life. The Court is in session in its
white marble building for thirty-six weeks out of each year, from
early October until the end of June. The nine justices read briefs
in their individual offices, hear oral arguments in the stately
courtroom, and discuss their decisions with one another in a
conference room where no outsider is ever allowed.

1.   Most cases, as we have seen, come to the Court on a writ of
certiorari. The lawyers for each side may then submit their briefs,
documents that set forth the facts, summarize the lower-court
decision, give the arguments for the side represented by the
lawyer, and discuss the other cases that the Court has decided

2.   that bear on the issue. Then the lawyers are allowed to present
their oral arguments in open court. They [usually summarize the
briefs or emphasize particular points in them,] and are [strictly
limited in time]—usually to no more than a half hour. (The
lawyer speaks from a lectern that has two lights on it. When the
white light goes on, the attorney has five minutes remaining;
when the red flashes, he or she must stop—instantly.) The oral
arguments give the justices a chance to question the lawyers,
sometimes searchingly.

         Since the federal government is a party—as either plaintiff
or defendant—to about half the cases that the Supreme Court
hears, the government's top trial lawyer, the solicitor general of
the United States, appears frequently before the Court. The solicitor general is the third-ranking officer of the Department of
Justice, right after the attorney general and deputy attorney gen-

job of
sol. gen'l

eral. The solicitor general decides what cases the government
will appeal from lower courts and personally approves every case
that the government presents to the Supreme Court. In recent
years the solicitor general has often been selected from the ranks
of distinguished law-school professors.

         In addition to the arguments made by lawyers for the two
sides in a case, written briefs and even oral arguments may also
3.   be offered by "a friend of the court," or *amicus curiae.* An amicus
brief is from an interested party not directly involved in the suit.
For example, when Allan Bakke complained that he had been
the victim of "reverse discrimination" when he was denied admission to a University of California medical school, fifty-eight

amicus briefs were filed supporting or opposing his position. Before such briefs can be filed, both parties must agree or the Court must grant permission. Though these briefs sometimes offer new arguments, they are really a kind of polite lobbying of the Court that declares what interest groups are on which side. The ACLU, the NAACP, the AFL-CIO, and the United States government itself have been among the leading sources of such briefs.

amicus curiae

These briefs are not the only source of influence on the justices' views. Legal periodicals such as the *Harvard Law Review* and the *Yale Law Journal* are frequently consulted, and citations to them often appear in the Court's decisions. Thus the outside world of lawyers and law professors can help shape, or at least supply arguments for, the conclusions of the justices.

4.

order of voting

The justices retire every Friday to their conference room, where in complete secrecy they debate the cases that they have heard. The chief justice speaks first, followed by the other justices in order of seniority. After the arguments they vote, traditionally in reverse order of seniority: the newest justice votes first, the chief justice last. In this process an able chief justice can exercise considerable influence—in guiding or limiting debate, in setting forth the issues, and in handling sometimes temperamental personalities. In deciding a case, a majority of the justices must be in agreement: if there is a tie, the lower-court decision is left standing. (There can be a tie among nine justices if one is ill or disqualifies himself or herself because of prior involvement in the case.)

5.

Though the vote is what counts, by tradition the Court usually issues a written opinion explaining its decision. Sometimes this opinion is brief and unsigned (called a *per curiam* opinion); sometimes it is quite long and signed by the justices agreeing with it. If the chief justice is in the majority, he will either write the opinion or assign the task to a justice who agrees with him. If he is in the minority, the senior justice on the winning side will decide who writes the Court's opinion. There are three

①
②

kinds of opinions—*opinion of the Court* (reflecting the majority's view), *concurring* (an opinion by one or more justices who agree with the majority's conclusion but for different reasons that they

③ wish to express), and *dissenting* (the opinion of the justices on the losing side). Each justice has three or four law clerks (bright, recent graduates of the leading law schools) to help him or her review the many petitions that the Court receives, study cases, and write opinions.

James Q. Wilson, "The Supreme Court in Action," in *American Government,* 5th ed. (Lexington, MA: Heath, 1992), 410–11.

THINKING ABOUT YOUR READING AND WRITING

ACTIVITY M: Evaluating Notations

Which of the three examples do you think has the most effective notations? Why?

_____

_____

_____

_____

You may have noticed some of the following about each example:

Example A: Very little has been marked. Only single words and short phrases have been underlined, and they have little relationship to one another. The meaning of marginal notes is unclear.

Example B: A great deal has been underlined. It is hard to distinguish between important ideas and details.

Example C: Symbols have been used. Technical terms have been circled. Main ideas have been underlined, and related details are numbered. This is the most effectively marked page. This page is useful for study purposes because the important ideas and technical vocabulary stand out from the rest. The reader will not have to reread the entire page to get the most from it.

There are a few guidelines to follow when you are deciding what to mark on textbook pages. These guidelines also apply to any other reading materials that you will later need to reread and study. These guidelines incorporate principles of good textbook reading and good note taking from lectures and textbooks. At this point, they should sound very familiar to you:

1. *Make predictions about chapter content before and while you read the chapter.* You will then know, at the outset, the most important concepts to be discussed. You may want to review the process for predictions and previewing discussed in Chapters 2 through 5. As you preview, be sure that you analyze the introductory and concluding paragraphs, headings, and subheadings, as well as graphics and questions that may appear at the end of the chapter.

2. *Read sections of information before you do any marking.* It is surprising how many students think that if they have highlighted something they've read, they will remember it. The mere act of highlighting does not ensure memorization. Some students' textbooks are filled with highlighted page after highlighted page. It is clear that little reflection actually went into deciding what to mark since all of it was considered important. The three-step process for highlighting or underlining is to:

   Read with your marker or pen down.

   Think which of the many ideas are the most important.

   Mark the ideas you selected as important.

3. *Develop a marking system.* Students use a variety of these, but features of the most popular ones include:

   Double underlining—for main ideas

   Double vertical lines—for very long main ideas

   Single underlining—for important details

   Arrows—to show connections

   Marginal notes—for personal comments on an idea (if these are very long, you may want to write them on an adhesive note and attach this to your page)

   Question marks—to indicate uncertainty

   Brackets or circling—to note important terms

Numbers—to note a sequence or a listing of details related to a main idea

4. *Review your notated pages regularly.* Treat your marked textbook pages as you would your notes from lectures and texts. Review them periodically so that you can easily recall the material when you prepare for tests and class discussion.

ACTIVITY N: Underlining and Marking Textbooks

Select two or three pages of a reading assignment that interests you. Mark the material, following those guidelines described that you believe will be most helpful to you. On another sheet of paper, indicate which guidelines you followed.

WORKING TOGETHER

Review your notations with a partner. See whether your partner can quickly spot the important information on the page. Does your partner have any additional suggestions for making your notations?

▶ Chapter Summary

Based on your reading of this chapter, list at least five points that were made that you believe will help you with future academic assignments.

1. _____

   _____

   _____

   _____

2. _____

   _____

   _____

   _____

3. _____

   _____

   _____

   _____

4. _____

   _____

   _____

   _____

5. _____

   _____

   _____

   _____

▶ Extended Application

Now that you have worked with the strategies necessary for active listening and note taking, you can practice applying them to other academic situations. Choose (or your instructor may choose) a reading selection from Part 2 of this text or a classroom listening experience that is typical in a college setting. Use this selection or lecture to practice:

* Using active and positive listening
* Creating a set of usable notes
* Creating a graphic from lecture or text notes
* Using your notes effectively
* Underlining and marking textbooks

Decide on the practice strategies you will use. Apply them to your selection. Then, in a few paragraphs, write a description of what you did and how the strategies you used worked for you.

Name of material used: _____

Page numbers: _____

Your description: _____

CHAPTER NINE

Assessing Your New Knowledge

C ONGRATULATIONS! YOU HAVE NOW PRACTICED using all the major reading and study strategies necessary for meeting many of the literacy challenges you will face at college. It is time to reconsider how you feel about your ability to meet these challenges. You may recall that you completed the following survey when you started to use this textbook. Complete it again, and then you will have an opportunity to analyze your pre- and poststudy survey results.

Survey of Academic Self-Esteem

Directions: For each item, circle the number that you feel best describes you as you are now (1 = not true of me at all; 4 = very true of me).

1. I can successfully prepare to take exams.	1	2	3	4
2. I can figure out what will be asked on tests.	1	2	3	4
3. I have successful strategies for taking notes on lectures and reading assignments.	1	2	3	4
4. I know how to preview my textbooks.	1	2	3	4
5. I know how to come prepared for class.	1	2	3	4
6. I know how to mark and underline reading material for review purposes.	1	2	3	4
7. I know how to make predictions when I read.	1	2	3	4
8. I can answer questions in a college classroom.	1	2	3	4
9. I can read a college textbook with understanding.	1	2	3	4
10. I know when to slow down my reading rate for better comprehension.	1	2	3	4
11. I know how to use context to get the meaning of unknown words in college-level material.	1	2	3	4
12. I have good strategies for thinking critically about things I have read.	1	2	3	4
13. I can figure out the main ideas of college-type reading materials (for example, sociology, psychology, science).	1	2	3	4
14. I can set purposes for my reading.	1	2	3	4
15. I can read and interpret maps, graphs, and charts.	1	2	3	4
16. I know how to create summaries and visual aids to help me remember what I have read.	1	2	3	4
17. I know how to distinguish between important and unimportant details when I read.	1	2	3	4
18. I can participate successfully in a college classroom.	1	2	3	4
19. I can ask a professor for help when I have a question.	1	2	3	4
20. I believe that I will be admitted to the major of my choice.	1	2	3	4
21. I believe that I have a lot of knowledge to share with others.	1	2	3	4
22. I believe that I will graduate from college.	1	2	3	4
23. I believe that I will have a successful future.	1	2	3	4

Let's analyze the results of this poststudy survey. The following chart shows the category into which different items fall. Place your ratings on the chart. Then respond to the questions in Activity A.

SURVEY ANALYSIS

Category	Question Nos.								
Study Skills		1	2	3	4	6	14	16	
Your ratings:		___	___	___	___	___	___	___	
Reading Skills		7	9	10	11	12	13	15	17
Your ratings:		___	___	___	___	___	___	___	___
Participating in College Classrooms		5	8	18	19	21			
Your ratings:		___	___	___	___	___			
Expecting a Successful Future		20	22	23					
Your ratings:		___	___	___					

ACTIVITY A: Assessing Your Academic Self-Esteem

1. Based on the information you've obtained from this survey, in which area(s) do you seem particularly strong?

_____

_____

_____

_____

_____

2. Look at the responses you gave to these areas in Chapter 1. How have you changed?

_____

_____

_____

_____

_____

3. In a few sentences, describe the academic self-esteem goals you feel you have achieved this term.

_____

_____

_____

_____

4. What are some of the areas of academic literacy you would like to continue to develop?

_____

_____

_____

_____

_____

You should now be able to recognize that you have gained a great deal of knowledge and self-esteem concerning your ability to read and study academic material. You should also realize that these changes would not have occurred if you had not taken responsibility for your learning and had not applied yourself seriously to the material in this text. This is true for any learning situation. It is up to you to decide how much you will get out of it.

Remember: You are in control.

Integrated Practice for Reading and Learning

Cross-Reference to Handbook for Reading and Study Strategies

You may wish to refer to the handbook chapters listed here to help you recall strategies for answering particular types of questions.

CHAPTER TEN

Readings in the Social Sciences

No human emotion can transcend the social conditions around it.

—Zhang Jie (b. 1937), Chinese writer

The Whole World Book of Quotations, comp. Kathryn Petras and Ross Petras (Reading, MA: Addison-Wesley, 1994), 264.

READING

Guidelines for Reading the Social Sciences

What Are the Social Sciences?

According to a dictionary definition, "social science is a branch of science that deals with the institutions and functioning of human society with all the interpersonal relationships of individuals as members of society." Many fields of study are part of social science. Notice how the definition of each of these includes mention of people and their activities and/or behavior. The following fields of study are most often considered part of social science.

ANTHROPOLOGY   Anthropology is the study of human beings in relation to distribution, origin, classification and relationship of races, physical character, environmental and social relations, and culture. There are many branches of anthropology—for example, cultural anthropology, linguistic anthropology, and economic anthropology. In all cases, though, the anthropologist is interested in exploring different aspects of culture and how these have impact on people's lives.

HISTORY   History is a record of explanation of past events. Historians often hope that this record will help societies and individuals understand their connections to generations of the past as well as to those who will come. History offers lessons from the past that will help us make wise choices in the future.

POLITICAL SCIENCE   A social science that analyzes political processes and institutions, political science helps people become effective citizens; learn how to use readily available alternatives that have influence on decisions made by individuals, groups, and governments; and learn how to deal with conflict. Political scientists are concerned with why one group's preferences take priority over those of another group and how compromise is reached.

PSYCHOLOGY   Sometimes considered a pure science rather than a social science, psychology is the science of mind and behavior. Psychologists often look at individual behavior, but they also study behavior of such groups as families and workplaces. The goal is often to help an individual in relationships with others.

SOCIOLOGY   Sociology is the science of societies and their effects on human behavior. Sociologists look at social patterns in the behavior of individuals in order to understand how social forces shape us into various kinds of people. They try to understand the behavior of individuals and groups within a societal context, often to learn how the society's rules, or norms, influenced that behavior. The society might be the family, school, peer group, or government—that is, *any* group that exerts influence over its members.

Specific Strategies

Our reading of social science can help us understand ourselves and others within the context of our culture and society. To read successfully, you must read actively. Stay connected to the text you are reading by thinking about it while you read.

* **Understand that much of what you read in a social science will be based on research.** Therefore, you will need to *look for the organizational structure of the material.*

   The article often begins with a statement about some feature of human behavior. For example, a psychologist might write, "Children who come from homes where there is an alcoholic parent are likely to have periods of depression and to suffer from low self-esteem." This statement states a point of view for which the author will most likely give evidence. It suggests a thesis-and-proof pattern.

   Then the author will provide some evidence, usually starting with what other researchers have found. This evidence—often summaries of research done by others—might be cited, or named, to support this writer's viewpoint. The citation for the supporting research might be written as follows: (Stern, 1987). This tells you the name of the researcher and when the research was published.

   A more complete reference may appear at the end of the reading selection. Evidence to support the idea that children of alcoholic parents are depressed or have low self-esteem, for instance, might include results of interviews a psychologist has conducted with such children or results of questionnaires a researcher has given to them.

Next, the author might give you a detailed description of his or her own research. The author may have looked at a population that was different from those studied by others, may have used different methods of obtaining information, or may have found different results.

Primary, or original, resources might be used for this research. These are resources that provide firsthand knowledge of the event, such as eyewitness accounts. Historians, for example, might find such accounts in letters, diaries, and interviews; courthouse records; original governmental documents; and artifacts at museums or in other collections. Anthropologists and sociologists might become participant observers, temporarily becoming a part of the group being studied.

Secondary sources might also be used. Some examples are governmental statistics, secondhand accounts of events, such as some newspaper articles; texts written by others; and individuals reporting what others have said.

Conclusions are drawn based on findings of the author's research. An author's own study, for instance, may find that children of alcoholic parents have developed sophisticated survival skills.

Finally, the author might make recommendations based on the conclusions. The author might suggest, for instance, that teachers should receive more education on indicators of children growing up in alcoholic homes.

❊ **Look for signals to the various parts of the article.** Subtitles are frequently used to separate hypotheses, related research, methods used in the present study, findings conclusions, and recommendations. Use these divisions to help you follow the discussion.

❊ **Look for key questions being investigated.** Sometimes the writer will include interesting but minor details about social interactions. Good readers will not get lost while reading these.

❊ **Be sure you understand the author's definition of terms used.** Each branch of social science has its own terminology. These terms represent broad concepts. A glossary in your text can help you locate definitions quickly.

❋ **Look for generalizations and the support offered for them.** By combining several ideas into a single statement that shows how these ideas are connected to one another, a social scientist forms a generalization. For example, the sociologist might make the following generalization: As the educational level of a family increases, so does its level of income. You should locate the *empirical* (factual) *evidence* in the reading material that supports such statements. The author might present a number of different statistics to demonstrate correlation between education and income.

❋ **Note the scope of the materials you have been assigned to read.** The range of topics in the social sciences is enormous. Whole texts have been written in anthropology, for instance, on medical practices or wedding traditions in a particular culture. In psychology, entire textbooks are written on what appear to be narrow topics, such as a single emotional disorder like depression, perception, the psychology of language, and learning processes. Introductory courses in these fields, however, usually cover many topics.

❋ **Identify the author's perspective.** In each social science, there are controversies, sometimes referred to as different "schools of thought." In psychology, for instance, the Behaviorist and Humanist schools of thought have different views about how people come to be what they are and how behavior can be changed. Today's historians, many of whom are called "revisionist" historians, look at past events from new perspectives, such as a feminist perspective. And political scientists have preferences for particular forms of government that can influence their interpretation of political events. These differences are important to know because an author's perspective, or theoretical orientation, will influence the approach to the topic that is taken, including what research is cited and what methods for changing behavior are suggested.

❋ **Look for bias.** A good social scientist will often make this bias clear at the start of an article through the thesis statement, or statement of the main idea. When you detect bias, try to consider exactly how it is affecting the writer's interpretation of events, statistics, or even other research. You will want to be sure that the author's conclusions are supported by facts, not as the result of bias. Critical readers will evaluate what is said and will challenge unsupported ideas.

Keep these suggestions in mind as you read the following articles from social science.

What are some fields of social science that interest you?

_____

_____

What additional suggestions can you make for reading the social sciences?_____

_____

_____

_____

_____

_____

~ SELECTION 1
Preview

Is the Miss America pageant more than a beauty contest? What does the contest tell us about ourselves and our culture? This author tries to answer these questions and explain the appeal of the pageant.

To Think About Before You Read

What qualities make the ideal Miss America? In the following space, write the qualities that you believe are most important. You will have an opportunity to reconsider these qualities after you read this article.

Five qualities Miss America should have are

1. _____

_____

2. _____

_____

3. _____

_____

4. _____

_____

5. _____

_____

Terms to Know Before You Read

cacophonous (1) chaotic sounding

penumbra (11) shadow

nurture (15) education; upbringing

paradox (19) contradiction

corollary (29) inference; result

Why We Need Miss America

■ By Jill Neimark

1 Three quarters of a century ago, eight teenage girls came to Atlantic City on Labor Day weekend to compete in a bathing beauty contest. The year was 1921, and they arrived by train at this sequined and cacophonous city, flanked by miles of boardwalk that had originally been built to keep sand off the posh hotel carpets—this resort that had become a kind of Broadway by the beach, packed with diversions and enormous crowds. It was a city of pure contradiction, constructed on a wilderness of swamps and dunes, a place where the average working man could arrive by train and hire a "servant" for a buck to roll him down the boardwalk in a wicker chair. Doesn't it somehow make perfect sense that Atlantic City's swimsuit contest, dreamed up by the Chamber of Commerce to extend the summer holiday, would evolve into the most famous beauty pageant in modern history? A pageant as innocent and corrupt as the city that gave birth to it—and as the country that invented that city.

2 For a skin show, she's been caught in the crossfire of colossal cultural battles: women's rights, pornography, changing racial and religious values. Feminist poet Robin Morgan claimed that the pageant inspired the formal launching of the women's movement in 1968, when a crowd of protesters burned their bras, torched host Bert Parks in effigy, stormed the exhibition hall, and accused the contest of being lily-white, racist, and pro-military. Since then, Miss America has changed with the times: she has been black, deaf, and a social activist with platforms ranging from AIDS prevention to children's self esteem and aging with dignity—although she still struts in a bathing suit.

3 In the last decade, interest in the title has been flagging, and the pageant has had to offer gimmicks like viewer phone-in votes and two-piece swimsuits to boost television ratings. Still, every September, at least 20 million Americans stay home on a Saturday night to scorn or applaud the winner and see the crown passed on. If you're one who observes that annual ritual, you may watch out of simple nostalgia—Miss America as a kind of reminder of days long gone, when you were a girl and she was a queen. Or you may watch for the treacly high camp of it all, or just out of an ambivalent blend of disgust and fascination. Yet somehow, at 78-years-old, this icon still lives.

4 The fact is, Miss America informs us about our culture's ideals and conflicts. That's what all beauty pageants do, according to

From *Psychology Today* (September/October 1998): 40–43, 72–73.

Richard Wilk, professor of anthropology at Indiana University. "They're always about fundamental contradictions in the culture," he declares. "How else could you get millions of people to watch a bunch of relatively untalented women in bathing suits?" The Miss America contest has always knit together in its middle-class queen the deep schisms in American society. Whether her contestants flaunt pierced belly buttons or Ph.D.s in veterinary medicine, wear pants or ballgowns, Miss America is a mirror of America, even now.

5   So what *is* she really saying about us—and why do we need to know, anyway?

6   *We're a big clubhouse, but we're not sure you should be a member.* We may be a melting pot of races and types, but we have a fairly inflexible standard of beauty. Almost all the Miss Americas have been white. Accordng to Frank Deford, author of *There She Is,* the composite contestant in 1971 was 19 years old, 5 feet 6 inches, 119 pounds, with brown hair, blue eyes, and a fair complexion. And she hasn't changed much since then. "Miss America is the official standard of beauty, kind of like the dollar bill," observes Wilk. "The rest of us schlubs are not necessarily ugly. We may be beautiful, but by different standards." As an example, he cites Monica Lewinsky, with her plump curves and formerly big hair. "She is extremely beautiful by the small-town standards of the Midwest, and that big hair is the peak of fashion in southern Indiana where I live. But she does not look like a Miss America."

7   Give the pageant a bit of credit, though.

The first black winner was chosen in 1984—Vanessa Williams (and her replacement, Suzette Charles). Since then, three more African-Americans have worn the crown. Williams, with her fine-boned features, was said to match the "white" ideal, but Marjorie Vincent, the 1991 titleholder, with her very dark skin and full figure, represented a different, and more diverse, vision of beauty. In 1997, the contestant from Colorado was Hispanic and Miss Washington, D.C., was of Indian descent.

8   "More Latina young women and African-Americans are entering the contest, and those audiences are now watching," says New York City psychologist Elizabeth Debold, author of *Mother Daughter Revolution: From Good Girls to Great Women.* "The pageant may be providing a way for immigrant and outsider groups to enter the mainstream."

9   It is at the smaller local contest level that the clash of immigrant culture and mainstream America is most clearly seen. In fact, some local competitions seem to exist precisely on that fault line, providing a stage on which to battle out cultural assimilation in the arena of beauty. "These pageants let immigrants ask who they are," says Wilk, "how much of the American model they want, how much they're going to adapt, how to pass their culture's values on to the next generation." For instance, the Miss India America pageant, held in Atlanta, Georgia, offers teenagers of Asian Indian descent a chance to parade their own standards of beauty and their position in American society. One teen performs an

acrobatic routine to disco music; another does a classical Indian dance.

10   Though such local contests don't feed directly into the Miss America pageant, the conflicts of the microcosm spread ripples that are felt in the macrocosm. Even so, the favored contestant hasn't altered all that much. If beauty does reflect cultural and social values, we—the great democracy—don't know how inclusive we really want to be. Bess Myerson, the first Jewish Miss America, was crowned in 1945. "She meant as much then to Jewish women as Vanessa Williams meant to blacks," says Vicki Gold Levi, co-author with Lee Eisenberg of *Atlantic City: 125 Years of Ocean Madness.* Myerson is still the only Jewish woman to wear the crown. And most of the finalists and winners are still white.

11   *We're still a nation of Yankees and Southern belles.* Miss America unmasks the schism between the North and the South—it never went away—and the penumbra of the Southern belle still holds sway in our national psyche. Only one New England contestant has ever won the Miss America title, Connecticut's Marian Bergeron in 1933, while southern and western states have been overwhelmingly represented. New England women don't seem to cotton to beauty pageants. In Vermont, the Miss America organization has such a hard time dredging up contestants that a few years ago there were only 10 candidates for the state crown. One recent Miss Vermont flaunted a pierced navel—not exactly Miss America's brand of all-American.

12   *Cinderella ought to come from the middle class and go to college.* Miss America gives us a capsule look at middle-class America and its values. After World War II, Miss America became part of the culture of middle-class civic boosterism. The girls who make it to the national pageant start out competing in county or state contests sponsored by community organizations like the Elks or the Rotary Club. "At the local level," says anthropologist Robert Lavenda, a professor at St. Cloud State University in Minnesota, "the community is looking for an appropriate representative. When a girl wins a small-town queen pageant she'll be announced as 'Mary Jo, the daughter of Frank and Suzanne.' The community knows these girls." These days, however, junior contestants are drawn from a different circle than earlier. Where once they came from cheerleading squads and drama clubs, nowadays they're picked off soccer fields and basketball courts.

13   The "bawdy" pageant initiated its scholarship program at the end of the War, and today the organization gives out $32 million in scholarships to young women every year. Many of the early winners of the crown vowed to use the money to enter college. Today's Miss America often has her sights set far higher. Older than earlier candidates, she's likely to already be in college and aiming for medical, law, or graduate school. In fact, many Miss America contestants now say the sole reason they enter the pageant is to finance their education. Practicality—what could be a more middle-class and American virtue?

14   *We've got faith.* She reminds us of our

bottomless sincerity and spirit. Miss Americas say things like "Mental attitude is so important" and "Every day is a gift from God." You might snicker at the platitudes, but who's buying all the self-help books that offer precisely that inspirational message? She comes out of the same cultural spout as that runaway bestseller, *Chicken Soup for the Soul.*

15   *We've got pluck.* Miss America embodies our Horatio Alger can-do spirit. We believe that by dint of hard work we can overcome anything. It's the triumph of nurture over nature. So many aspects of being a beauty queen are beyond personal control—you've got to be between 5 feet 6 inches and 5 feet 10 inches, for instance. "On the other hand," notes Wilk, "everyone always talks about how hard these girls work."

16   Reflecting our preoccupation with fitness, today's Miss America is pumped and streamlined, whereas in 1921 she was soft and plump. Bodybuilding is practically a given for contestants as are strenuous sessions in the gym. One participant in the 1990 pageant, Karrie Mitchell of Colorado, admitted, "I was not a swimsuit winner a year ago, let me tell you." She worked out until she shrank from a size 12 to a size five.

17   Many contestants are willing to undergo extensive cosmetic surgery (which the state pageants sometimes pay for). They also resort to the old stand-bys, mummifying themselves with surgical tape to enhance their cleavage and the curve of their buttocks.

18   *We're all equal, but we love royalty.* Sure, she's just an ordinary American girl, but she wears a crown and is cloaked in celebrity. Norman Rockwell was one of the pageants' original judges, others have ranged from Grace Kelly to Donald Trump. Miss America opens shopping centers and moves in power circles. As a *Boston Globe* editorial recently noted, "In a letter to the President, one icon to another, Miss America asked for federal funds for needle exchange programs [to prevent AIDS]." Icons, of course, gain status when they rub noses with other icons. She's got to be more than a bathing beauty, asking the president for federal funding.

19   Very few Miss Americas have gone on to lasting fame, but that makes perfect sense. To win, she has to be the ultimate paradox, everyday royalty, the thing that every American secretly believes he or she is.

20   *We love to gossip.* It's the corollary to fame. Miss America lets us know we love knowing a secret, no matter how trivial. Journalists have asked competitors about the "firm grip gunk" they spray on their butts to keep their bathing suits from riding up; during one recent pageant, the press rooted out that 37 contestants had been arrested for speeding at some time in their life.

21   *We love glitz.* Let's face it, America has always had a purple-spangled heart, always been genuinely and even naively trashy. From its start, Miss America has been high camp. "The pageant always manages to confuse the wholesome with the wholesale, a clean time with a good time," says Levi.

22   In the late 1940s, Miss Montana rode

her horse onstage and almost fell into the orchestra pit; after that animals were banned; Miss Nevada lamented, "You mean I won't be able to have my cow perform?" Miss Nebraska tossed a flaming baton into the judges' booth; flaming batons were banned. Later, a church choir member did a striptease—and won the crown.

23   Alas, such glorious moments are gone. The highlight of the pageant, though, remains: the declaration of the winner with her requisite burst of tears and careful stroll down the runway, crown slipping from her head.

24   *Superwoman is alive and well.* This pageant tells us what women are supposed to be. "She's the cultural icon of the perfect girl," declares Debold. Today, Miss Americas are asked to be beautiful, to achieve, and to serve. (In the pageant's official parlance, she no longer "reigns.") She has a platform, and it's inevitably for social good. One recent Miss America was a cancer sur-

vivor studying to be a musical therapist for the gravely ill.

25   "It's a totally contradictory model," asserts Wilk. "She should be strong but weak, aggressive but submissive, totally committed to her career and her family, have touches of the social worker, and basically walk on water in high-heeled shoes and make it look easy." Whew.

26   *It's all for one and one for all.* Miss America tells us, finally, one last fact: that we still believe a single person can serve as a living snapshot of an entire country. Like the Mercury astronauts, like baseball's boys of summer, Miss America thrives, simply because we believe in the best and the brightest. What could be brighter than her Vaselined smile, telling us, at the close of that special September evening every year, that we still believe? We're a nation of believers. God Bless Miss America—and does anyone have a handful of popcorn to throw at the TV?

Evaluation of the Article
Difficulty rating □ 1 □ 2 □ 3 □ 4 □ 5
(1 = easy; 5 = difficult)

What reading difficulties did you encounter?_____

_____

How did you handle these difficulties?_____

_____

Postreading Comprehension Development

Rewriting Sentences

To check your understanding of some of the key concepts of this essay, rewrite each of the following sentences in your own words, keeping the original idea. (See Chapter 1.)

1. We may be a melting pot of races and types, but we have a fairly inflexible standard of beauty. (6) _____

    _____

    _____

2. Miss America unmasks the schism between the North and the South—it never went away—and the penumbra of the Southern belle still holds sway in our national psyche. (11) _____

    _____

    _____

    _____

3. After World War II, Miss America became part of the culture of middle-class civic boosterism. (12) _____

    _____

    _____

Author's Main Idea

1. The author's purpose for writing this article is to

    _____a. give a history of the Miss America pageant.

    _____b. explain what the Miss America pageant tells us about our culture.

_____c. argue that more Miss Americas should be minorities.

_____d. discuss the reasons why different Miss America pageant contestants become winners.

2. Which paragraphs introduce the main idea?

_____a. 1 through 3

_____b. 2 through 5

_____c. 4 and 5

_____d. 3 and 4

3. Create a new title for this selection that you think would help a reader predict its major focus.

_____

4. What predictions do you believe that a reader could make from your title?

_____

_____

Inferences, Metaphors, and Vocabulary in Context

1. How do you think the author wants a reader to feel about the Miss America pageant after reading this selection? What are the reasons for your beliefs?

_____

_____

2. Which of the following does the author imply in paragraph 1? Be prepared to justify your answer.

_____a. Atlantic City needed the pageant in 1921 to help its economy.

_____b. The first pageant would not have done as well had it been held in a small, quiet town.

_____c. It was surprising that the 1921 pageant was such a huge success.

_____d. Most people came to Atlantic City in 1921 specifically to see the Miss America pageant.

3. Check each statement with which you think the author would agree. Be prepared to justify your answers.

_____a. Some think the women's movement was formally begun at the 1968 pageant.

_____b. Women of Hispanic descent shouldn't participate in the Miss America pageant.

_____c. State pageants for Miss America are likely to be more biased than the national Miss America pageant.

_____d. The desired traits of Miss America change with the times.

_____e. Current trends have little effect on the type of woman who wins the national pageant.

_____f. Miss America candidates can inspire people.

_____g. The talent segment of the Miss America pageant should be removed.

_____h. Most Miss America contestants come from privileged backgrounds and are out of touch with reality.

4. Which of the following does the author imply in paragraph 9? Be prepared to justify your answer.

_____a. Local beauty pageants will soon end because people disagree over what makes someone beautiful.

_____b. Only someone who looks and acts purely Asian Indian can win the Miss India America pageant.

_____c. In Georgia, women of Asian Indian descent are not permitted to enter the state Miss America pageant.

_____d. Today's teenagers are beginning to find Miss America pageants less appealing than teens of earlier generations.

5. In your own words, explain what the author means when she says, "That makes perfect sense" (19).

   _____

   _____

6. Why do you think Monica Lewinsky was mentioned in this article (6)?

   _____

   _____

7. How do the quotations from Professor Wilk help serve the author's purpose for writing this article (4), (6)?

   _____

   _____

8. The author's tone throughout most of this essay is

   _____a. humorous.

   _____b. persuasive.

   _____c. informative.

   _____d. critical.

9. What attitude is conveyed by the last sentence of this article?

   _____a. Disgust

   _____b. Criticism

   _____c. Approval

   _____d. Ambivalence

10. Why does the author refer to Cinderella (12)?

    _____

    _____

11. How might this article be different if it had been written by a winner of the Miss America pageant?

_____

_____

12. Using only the context, define each of the following words. Do not use a dictionary.

a. schisms (4) and (11) _____

b. microcosm (10) _____

c. macrocosm (10) _____

d. snicker (14)_____

e. pluck (15) _____

f. icon (18) and (24) _____

g. parlance (24) _____

Recalling Details

1. Which of the following are factual statements in this article? Which are opinions? Use (F) or (O) for your response. For those you label opinion, write any support for the opinion that is given in this article.

_____a. The pageant initiated its scholarship program after World War II.

_____b. Miss America lets us know that we love knowing a secret, no matter how trivial.

_____c. Norman Rockwell was one of the pageant's original judges.

_____d. Southern and western states have been overrepresented among the pageant winners.

_____e. This pageant tells us what women are supposed to be.

_____ f. The girls who make it to the national pageant start out competing in county or state contests.

_____ g. We may be a melting pot of races and types, but we have a fairly inflexible standard of beauty.

_____ h. We still believe a single person can serve as a living snapshot of an entire country.

2. The pattern of organization used in paragraph 13 is a

_____ a. simple listing.

_____ b. definition or explanation.

_____ c. comparison or contrast.

_____ d. problem and solution.

3. The pattern of organization used in paragraph 25 is a

_____ a. simple listing.

_____ b. definition or explanation.

_____ c. comparison or contrast.

_____ d. problem and solution.

4. Indicate whether each item is a major (MAJ) or minor (MIN) detail of this article. Be prepared to justify your answers.

_____ a. The first Miss America pageant took place in 1921.

_____ b. In 1968 a crowd of protesters torched host Bert Parks in effigy.

_____ c. Only one New Englander has ever won the Miss America title.

_____ d. The Miss America organization gives out $32 million in scholarships to young women every year.

_____ e. A church choir member did a striptease in the national pageant.

_____ f. The reigning Miss America opens shopping centers.

_____ g. In the last decade, interest in the title has been flagging.

_____ h. Bess Myerson, the first Jewish Miss America, was crowned in 1945.

5. Which of the following components of the pageant was not mentioned in this article?

_____ a. Talent show

_____ b. Swimsuit competition

_____ c. Announcing the winner

_____ d. Miss Congeniality award

Critical Thinking: Reaction and Discussion

1. Review the list you made in the section "To Think About Before You Read." Make any changes to your list, but list no more than five qualities. Share your list with a partner or group to find similarities and differences in the qualities you considered important for Miss America. Then discuss the following:

    a. What do you think accounts for these similarities and differences?

    b. What does this tell you about the judging part of the Miss America pageant?

    c. If possible, can you and your partner or group agree on five qualities?

2. With a group, select for discussion three of the cultural ideals that this author believes are portrayed by the Miss America pageant. With your group discuss the following:

    a. Is this ideal valued by people you know?

    b. Does this ideal contribute to the popularity of the pageant?

    c. Is this ideal an important quality for Miss America to possess?

    Prepare to share your discussion with the class.

3. Either with a group or in an essay of at least 250 words, discuss the following: Should there be a Mr. America pageant that is modeled after the Miss America pageant? What competitions should be included? Who should be the judges? If you do not believe that there should be such a contest, what are your reasons?

USING TECHNOLOGY FOR FURTHER UNDERSTANDING

Visit the Miss America Web site at

http://www.pressplus.com/missam/articles.html

What additional information do you learn about the pageant at this site? From this site, select one article to read. Be prepared to discuss new information that you learned about the contestants or the pageant from reading this article.

READING

~ SELECTION 2
Preview

Is violent behavior the primary characteristic of today's teenagers? In this article, you will learn how some researchers answer this question.

To Think About Before You Read

Before you read, think about your views on the topic of teenage violence by completing this graphic organizer, adding as many details as you can for each section.

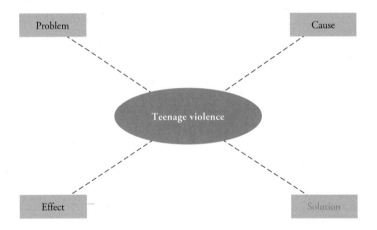

Terms to Know Before You Read

disproportionate (5) lack of proper relation; out of proportion

acute (10) critical

conventional (11) ordinary

synergistic (14) having the capacity to act in synergism: the interaction of separate conditions such that the total effect is greater than the sum of the individual effects

putative (15) commonly accepted

Wild in the Streets

■ By Barbara Kantrowitz*

1 Charles Conrad didn't have a chance. He was 55 years old, crippled by multiple sclerosis and needed a walker or wheelchair to get around. The boys who allegedly attacked him earlier this month were young—17, 15 and 14—and they were ruthless. Police say that when Conrad returned to his suburban Atlanta condominium while they were burgling it, the boys did what they had to do. They got rid of him. Permanently.

2 Over a period of many hours—stretching from dusk on July 17 until dawn of the next day—they stabbed him with a kitchen knife and a barbecue fork, strangled him with a rope, and hit him on the head with a hammer and the barrel of a shotgun, according to a statement one of the boys, 14-year-old Carlos Alexander Nevarez, reportedly gave to police. At one point they realized they were hungry. So they heated up the macaroni and cheese they found in Conrad's kitchen and washed it down with Dr Pepper.

3 Despite this torture, Conrad survived. According to the statement published by *The Atlanta Journal-Constitution,* a grievously wounded Conrad begged the boys to shoot him and put a swift end to his agony.

From *Newsweek,* 2 August 1993, 40–46.

But, Nevarez said, the boys were afraid people would hear the gunshots. So they allegedly beat him some more, and then poured salt into his wounds to see if he was still alive. When his body twitched in response to the pain, they threw household knickknacks at him. After he was struck in the back by a brass eagle, "he stopped breathing," Nevarez told police. The boys then took off in Conrad's wheelchair-equipped van with their hard-earned loot: a stereo, a VCR, a camcorder and a shotgun, according to an indictment handed down last week. Even law-enforcement officials were shocked when they arrested the boys the next day. The DeKalb County district attorney, J. Tom Morgan, calls it "the worst crime I've ever seen."

4 Conrad's death was particularly gory, but it was not an isolated incident. Each day seems to bring a new horror story of vicious crimes by boys—and a few girls. Near Ft. Lauderdale, Fla., on July 14, a group of teenagers allegedly beat and stabbed a friend to death; police have yet to come up with a motive. A few days earlier in New York, a Brooklyn mother made the front pages for the saddest of distinctions: losing all three of her young sons to street violence. Some victims, such as the mentally retarded girl sexually assaulted by high-

school football players in Glen Ridge, N.J., get whole forests of publicity. But most victims are mourned only by the people who loved them. In February, Margaret Ensley's 17-year-old son Michael caught a bullet in the hallway of his high school in Reseda, Calif. She says a teen shot her son because he thought Michael gave him a funny look. The shooter, she says, is now serving 10 years in a youth-authority camp. "But I have life imprisonment without the possibility of parole," says Ensley, "because I won't ever have my son back again . . . When they were filling his crypt, I said, 'Lord, let me crawl up there with him,' because the pain was so unbearable."

5   Law-enforcement and public-health officials describe a virtual "epidemic" of youth violence in the last five years, spreading from the inner cities to the suburbs. "We're talking about younger and younger kids committing more and more serious crimes," says Indianapolis Prosecuting Attorney Jeff Modisett. "Violence is becoming a way of life." Much of it, but by no means all, can be found in poor neighborhoods, where a disproportionate number of victims and victimizers live side by side. But what separates one group from another is complex: being neglected or abused by parents; witnessing violence at an early age on the street or in the house; living in a culture that glamorizes youth violence in decades of movies from "A Clockwork Orange" to "Menace II Society"; the continuing mystery of evil. To that list add the most dangerous ingredient: the widespread availability of guns to kids. In a Harvard

School of Public Health survey released last week, 59 percent of children in the sixth through the 12th grades said they "could get a handgun if they wanted one." More than a third of the students surveyed said they thought guns made it less likely that they would live to "a ripe old age." Cindy Rodriguez, a 14-year-old living in gang-riddled South-Central Los Angeles, is a testament to the ferocity of unrestrained firepower. Two and a half years ago, a gang bullet ripped through her body as she was talking to the mailman outside her house. Now she's paralyzed for life. And the bullets keep coming. "We hear gunshots every day," she says. "Sometimes I get scared. I'm in the shower and I hear it and I get all scared. But you have to live with the reality."

Violence is devastating this generation, 6 as surely as polio cut down young people 40 years ago. Attorney General Janet Reno says youth violence is "the greatest single crime problem in America today." Between 1987 and 1991, the last year for which statistics are available, the number of teenagers arrested for murder around the country increased by an astounding 85 percent, according to the Department of Justice. In 1991, 10- to 17-year-olds accounted for 17 percent of all violent-crime arrests; law-enforcement officials believe that figure is even higher now. Teenagers are not just the perpetrators; they're also the victims. According to the FBI, more than 2,200 murder victims in 1991 were under 18—an average of more than six young people killed every day. The Justice Department estimates that each year, nearly a million young people between 12 and 19 are raped, robbed, or assaulted, often by their peers.

UNMEASURED VIOLENCE

7 That's the official count. The true number of injuries from teen violence could be even higher. When emergency medical technicians in Boston recently addressed a class of fifth graders, they were astonished to find that nearly three quarters of the children knew someone who had been shot or stabbed. "A lot of violence goes unmeasured," says Dr. Deborah Prothrow-Stith, assistant dean of the Harvard School of Public Health and author of "Deadly Consequences," a book about teen violence. Paramedic Richard Serino, who is a supervisor in the emergency room at Boston City Hospital, estimates that doctors save seven or eight wounded teens for every one who dies. Many of the "lucky ones," Serino says, end up paralyzed or with colostomy bags.

8 The statistics are shocking—and so is the way some teenagers react when they're caught and accused of brutal crimes. "Hey, great! We've hit the big time," 17-year-old defendant Raul Omar Villareal allegedly boasted to another boy after hearing that they might be charged with murder. Villareal was one of six Houston teens arrested and charged last month in the brutal rape and strangulation of two young girls who made the fatal mistake of taking a shortcut through a wooded area where, police say, the boys were initiating two new members into their gang. In Dartmouth, Mass., this April, two 16-year-olds and one 15-year-old armed with clubs and knives barged into a high-school social-studies class and, police say, fatally stabbed a 16-year-old. One of the accused killers reportedly claimed that cult leader David Koresh was his idol and laughed about the killing afterward.

Dartmouth is a suburb of New Bedford, 9 the sort of place city dwellers flee to, thinking they'll find a respite from city crime. While the odds may be a bit better, a picket fence and a driveway is no guarantee. Indeed, even suburban police departments around the nation have taken to keeping watch on groups they worry may develop into youth gangs. Thus far, most of these kids seem like extras from "West Side Story," bunches of boys content to deface walls and fight with clubs and chains.

The casual attitude toward violence is 10 most acute in inner-city neighborhoods, where many youngsters have grown up to the sounds of sirens and gunshots in the night and the sight of blood-spattered sidewalks in the morning. After so many years in a war zone, trauma begins to seem normal. This is how Shaakara, a sweet-faced 6-year-old who lives in Uptown, one of Chicago's most dangerous areas, calmly describes one terrible scene she witnessed at a neighbor's apartment: "This lady, she got shot and her little baby had got cut. This man, he took the baby and cut her. He cut her on the throat. He killed the baby. All blood came out. This little boy, when he saw the baby, he called his grandmother and she came over. And you know, his

READING

grandmother got killed, but the little boy didn't get killed. He comes over to my house. That man, he took the grandmother and put her on the ground, and slammed her, and shut her in the door. Her whole body, shut in the door." After telling her tale, Shaakara smiles. "You know what I want to be when I grow up? A ballerina or a mermaid."

11   In this heightened atmosphere of violence, normal rules of behavior don't apply. As traditional social supports—home, school, community—have fallen away, new role models have taken their place. "It takes an entire village to raise a child, but the village isn't there for the children anymore," says Modisett, the Indianapolis prosecutor. "The only direction these kids receive is from their peers on the street, the local drug dealers and other role models who engage in criminal conduct." Katie Buckland, a Los Angeles prosecutor who volunteers in the city's schools, says the kids she sees have already given up the idea of conventional success and seize the opportunities available. "The kids that are selling crack when they're in the fifth grade are not the dumb kids," she says. "They're the smart kids. They're the ambitious kids . . . trying to climb up their own corporate ladder. And the only corporate ladder they see has to do with gangs and drugs."

12   With drugs the route to easy money, prison is the dominant institution shaping the culture, replacing church and school. In the last few years, more young black men have gone to jail than to college. Fathers, uncles, brothers, cousins have all done time. April Allen, a 15-year-old who lives in Boston's Roxbury section, has friends who think of jail as a kind of sleep-away camp. "The boys I know think it's fun to be in jail because other boys they know are in jail, too," she says. Prison is a way of looking: the dropped-waist, baggy-pants look is even called "jailing" in Miami. And prison is a way of acting. "In prison, the baddest, meanest guy runs the cell," says H. T. Smith, a lawyer and African-American activist who practices in Miami's Overtown ghetto. "Your neighborhood, your school—it's the same. You've got to show him you're crazy enough so he won't mess with you."

13   If prison provides the method of social interaction, guns provide the means. Alexis Vega, a 19-year-old New Yorker, explains the mentality on the streets where she grew up: "If a man threatens me, that's a threat to my life. So I go get a gun and make sure I shoot him first before he shoots me. Even though he might not mean it. Just by saying it, it may scare me so much that I'm going to get him first." Vega has seen run-of-the-mill arguments turn into tragedies. "A bullet doesn't have anybody's name on it," says Vega. "Somebody shoots, they're so nervous, they'll catch you even though you don't have anything to do with it."

14   One kid with a gun is a finite danger; a gang equipped with Uzis, AK-47s and sawed-off shotguns means carnage. Unlike adult criminals, who usually act alone, violent teens normally move in a pack. That's

typical teen behavior: hanging together. But these are well-equipped armies, not just a few kids milling outside a pizza parlor. There's a synergistic effect: one particularly aggressive kid can spur others to commit crimes they might not think of on their own. The victims are often chosen because they are perceived as weak or vulnerable, say social scientists who study children and aggression. As horrible as some of the crimes are, kids go along with the crowd rather than go it alone.

A DANGEROUS BREED

15 Some social scientists argue that teenage aggression is natural. In another era, they say, that aggression might have been channeled in a socially acceptable way—into the military, or hard physical labor—options that are still available to putative linebackers and soldiers. But other researchers who have studied today's violent teens say they are a new and dangerous breed. At a conference on teen-violence prevention in Washington, D.C., last week, psychologists and social workers discussed the causes of skyrocketing teen-crime rates. In one of the largest longitudinal studies of violent youth, scientists followed about 4,000 youngsters in Denver, Pittsburgh and Rochester, N.Y., for five years. By the age of 16, more than half admitted to some form of violent criminal behavior, says Terence P. Thornberry, the principal investigator in Rochester and a psychologist at the State University of New York in Albany. "Violence among teenagers is almost normative in our society," Thornberry told the conference. But not all violent teens were the same: the researchers found that 15 percent of the sample were responsible for 75 percent of the violent offenses.

"RISK FACTORS"

What made the bad kids so bad? Thornberry and his colleagues identified a number of "risk factors" in the youths' background. "Violence does not drop out of the sky at age 15," Thornberry says. "It is part of a long developmental process that begins in early childhood." Kids who grow up in families where there is child abuse and maltreatment, spouse abuse and a history of violent behavior learn early on to act out physically when they are frustrated or upset. Poverty exacerbates the situation. Parents who haven't finished high school, who are unemployed or on welfare, or who began their families while they themselves were teenagers are more likely to have delinquent children. In New York and other big cities, counselors who work with delinquent youths say they see families with a history of generations of violence. Angela D'Arpa-Calandra, a former probation officer who now directs the Juvenile Intensive Supervision Program, says she recently had such a case in Manhattan family court. When she walked into the courtroom, she saw a mother and a grandmother sitting with the 14-year-old offender. "I had the grandmother in criminal court in 1963," D'Arpa-Calandra says. "We didn't stop it there. The grandmother was 14

16

when she was arrested. The mother had this child when she was 14. It's like a cycle we must relive."

17 Problems in school also increase the likelihood that the youngster will turn to violence, the study found. People who work with young criminals report that many are barely literate. Learning disabilities are common among teens in the probation system, says Charntel Polite, a Brooklyn probation officer who supervises 30 youthful offenders. "I have 15- or 16-year-olds in ninth or 10th grade whose reading levels are second or third grade."

18 Thornberry says the most effective prevention efforts concentrate on eliminating risk factors. For example, students with learning problems could get extra tutoring. Parents who have trouble maintaining discipline at home could get counseling or therapy. "Prevention programs need to start very early," Thornberry says, maybe even before elementary school. "Waiting until the teenage years is too late."

19 After a while, life on the streets begins to feel like home to older teenagers. Joaquin Ramos, a 19-year-old member of the Latin Counts in Detroit, says he spends his time "chillin' and hanging" with the Counts when he's not in jail. He's spent two years behind bars, but that hasn't made him turn away from the gang. The oldest of seven children, he never met his father, but he has been told that he was a member of the Bagly Boys, a popular gang a generation ago. Ramos began carrying a gun when he was 9; he became a full-fledged Count at the age of 13. He has watched three good friends—Bootis, Shadow and Showtime— die in street wars.

20 Bootis was shot when he left a party. "I looked right into his eyes and it looked like he was trying to say something," Ramos recalls. "There was snow on the ground and the blood from the back of his head was spreading all over it. Another buddy tried to lift his head but the back of it was gone. He had a small hole right in the middle of his forehead. And then he was gone. He died. That was my buddy. We were real tight." He adds, "Would you say in the story that we love him and miss him and Shadow and Showtime, too?"

21 Some kids do manage to leave gang life, usually with the help of a supportive adult. William Jefferson, now 19, quit the Intervale gang in Boston's Roxbury section after he was shot. "My mom talked to me and told me I had to make a decision whether I wanted to do something with my life or stay on the street and possibly get killed." He started playing basketball and football at school; then he had to keep up his grades to stay on the teams. Last month he became the first of his mother's four children to graduate from high school. He plans to enter junior college this fall. Now, he says, he'll behave because "I have a lot to lose."

22 Two lives, two different choices. At the risk of sounding melodramatic, Joaquin Ramos and William Jefferson represent different paths for a generation at risk. The young men made their own decisions, but clearly they were influenced by those dear to them: for Ramos it was the gang, for Jefferson, his mother. Day by day, block by

block, these are the small judgments that will end up governing our streets. There is little reason to be very optimistic.

* With Debra Rosenberg, in Boston, Lucille Beachy in New York, Peter Annin in Houston, Shawn D. Lewis in Detroit, Jeanne Gordon in Los Angeles, Peter Katel in Miami and Melinda Liu in Washington.

Evaluation of the Article
Difficulty rating ☐ 1 ☐ 2 ☐ 3 ☐ 4 ☐ 5
(1 = easy; 5 = difficult)

What reading difficulties did you encounter?_____

_____

How did you handle these difficulties? _____

_____

Postreading Comprehension Development

Rewriting Sentences

To check your understanding of some of the key concepts of this essay, rewrite each of the following sentences in your own words, keeping the original idea. (See Chapter 1.)

1. Much of it, but by no means all, can be found in poor neighborhoods, where a disproportionate number of victims and victimizers live side by side. (5)

   _____

   _____

2. With drugs the route to easy money, prison is the dominant institution shaping the culture, replacing church and school. (12)

   _____

   _____

3. If prison provides the method of social interaction, guns provide the means. (13)

_____

_____

Author's Main Idea

1. The main idea of this article is that

    _____ a. we need to work together to end teenage violence.

    _____ b. violence is becoming a way of life among teens.

    _____ c. the solution to teenage violence is a supportive adult.

    _____ d. some teens are able to escape the cycle of violence.

2. What kind of information does the author give the reader to develop this main idea?

    _____

    _____

3. Of the paragraphs listed below, which one most clearly states the author's main point?

    ____ a. 1

    ____ b. 2

    ____ c. 3

    ____ d. 4

4. Create a new title for this selection that you think would help a reader predict its major focus.

    _____

5. What predictions do you believe a reader could make from your title?

    _____

    _____

Inferences, Metaphors, and Vocabulary in Context

1. The author's purpose for opening this article with a description of the attack on Conrad was to

    _____a. help the reader understand how difficult the police's job is.

    _____b. create sympathy for Conrad.

    _____c. help the reader understand household crimes.

    _____d. create a picture of teenage violence.

2. Check each statement with which you think the author would agree. Be prepared to justify your answers.

    _____a. If you move to the suburbs, you will escape teen violence.

    _____b. The church no longer keeps teens from turning violent.

    _____c. There are multiple causes for teen violence.

    _____d. Teen violence will continue to get worse.

    _____e. Researchers are not interested in studying teenage violence.

    _____f. A simple argument between teens can lead to death.

    _____g. Teen delinquency can extend for generations in a single family.

    _____h. Crime victims are usually people who had difficulties in school.

3. The author's tone throughout most of this article is

    _____a. persuasive.

    _____b. argumentative.

_____c. pessimistic.

_____d. resentful.

4. Which of the following does the author imply in paragraph 7? Be prepared to justify your answer.

_____a. Not all teen crimes are reported.

_____b. Children in elementary school have little familiarity with crime.

_____c. Emergency medical technicians should be doing their jobs, not going to schools to talk with kids.

_____d. Some neighborhoods are safer than others.

5. Which of the following does the author imply in paragraph 12? Be prepared to justify your answer.

_____a. Teens in prison become insane.

_____b. For some teens, jail represents hope.

_____c. Teens who are in prison would like to get out and lead a normal life.

_____d. Teens act violent out of fear of other teens.

6. Which of the following does the author imply in paragraph 15? Be prepared to justify your answer.

_____a. Today's teens do not have the same avenues to express violence as did those from earlier generations.

_____b. Today's teens are not aware of less violent ways to express their aggression.

_____c. Research studies on teenage violence should be conducted over a longer period of time.

_____d. Today's teens want more violent ways to express their aggression.

7. Using only the context, define each of the following words. Do not use a dictionary.

   a. gory (4) _____

   b. ferocity (5)_____

   c. devastating (6) _____

   d. respite (9) _____

   e. dominant (12) _____

   f. normative (15) _____

   g. exacerbates (16)_____

8. According to the author, does jail help violent teens turn their lives around? Explain your answer with evidence from the article.

   _____

   _____

   _____

9. In your own words, explain what the author means when she says, "Day by day, block by block, these are the small judgments that will end up governing our streets." (22)

   _____

   _____

   _____

Recalling Details

1. Indicate whether each item is a major (MAJ) or minor (MIN) detail of this article. Be prepared to justify your answers.

   _____a. Charles Conrad was crippled by multiple sclerosis and needed a walker or wheelchair to get around.

   _____b. The teens poured salt into Conrad's wounds.

_____ c. The boys took off in Conrad's wheelchair-equipped van, with their hard-earned loot.

_____ d. A Harvard School of Public Health survey reported that 59 percent of children in the sixth through twelfth grades said they "could get a handgun if they wanted one."

_____ e. The Justice Department estimates that each year, nearly a million young people between 12 and 19 are raped, robbed or assaulted, often by their peers.

_____ f. Emergency medical technicians in Boston recently addressed a class of fifth graders.

_____ g. Dartmouth is a suburb of New Bedford, the sort of place to which city dwellers flee, thinking they'll find a respite from city crime.

_____ h. Kay Buckland is a prosecutor in Los Angeles.

_____ i. April Allen has friends who think of jail as a kind of sleep-away camp.

_____ j. Unlike adult criminals, who usually act alone, violent teens normally move in a pack.

_____ k. Parents who haven't finished high school are more likely to have delinquent children.

_____ l. The most effective prevention efforts concentrate on eliminating risk factors.

2. Draw lines to match each part of this article with the paragraph number in which that part begins.

   a. Problem   1. (7)

   b. Cause   2. (19)

   c. Effect   3. (11)

   d. Solution   4. (5)

3. What information in this article is supported by the table that follows? Be specific in your response.

_____

_____

_____

_____

_____

_____

ASSOCIATION BETWEEN THREATENING OR DELINQUENT ACTIVITIES AND USE OF ALCOHOL OR OTHER DRUGS BY 6TH THROUGH 12TH GRADERS

Type of Substance Used	Percentage of Students Who			
	Carried a Gun to School	Participated in Gang Activities	Threatened to Harm Another	Got into Trouble with the Police
Liquor	76.4	68.4	51.7	65.3
Marijuana	71.1	59.7	36.7	54.2
Inhalants	38.2	26.9	13.8	18.1
Cocaine	37.2	19.4	7.8	12.8

Source: National Parents' Resource Institute for Drug Education, 1997. _PRIDE Questionnaire Report: 1996–97 National Summary Grades 6 through 12._ Atlanta, GA: National Parents' Resource Institute for Drug Education. Reprinted by permission from Robert W. Drowns and Karen M. Hess, _Juvenile Justice,_ Belmont, CA: Wadsworth, 2000), 256.

Critical Thinking: Reaction and Discussion

1. The author says, "Some social scientists argue that teenage aggression is natural." Do you agree? With your class, prepare a debate on this topic. Use references to provide support for your arguments.

2. The lyrics sung by some rap stars are criticized for being violent. In an essay of at least 250 words, discuss the lyrics of one song and explain why you agree or disagree with the criticism. If possible, attach a copy of the lyrics to your essay.

3. Review the contents of a daily newspaper for one day. How many articles about violent acts by teens are included? How many articles about other teen activities are included? What conclusions can you draw from your findings?

USING TECHNOLOGY FOR FURTHER UNDERSTANDING

Visit the Web site of the Office of Juvenile Justice and Delinquency Prevention of the U.S. Justice Department:

http://ojjdp.ncjrs.org/

Prepare a class presentation on one piece of information found at this site that interests and/or surprises you. Discuss how this information relates to what you have learned from the article you've read.

☙ SELECTION 3

Preview

Do you know anyone who seems to "march to a different drummer," someone whose habits and values appear to be very different from those of most people you know? This article, written by two anthropologists, describes such an experience one of them had when he was teaching in a foreign country. Read to learn how he tried to understand the differences between himself and his students.

To Think About Before You Read

In an essay of approximately 250 words, describe how your culture, as you understand it, influences your activities. Include information about such cultural features as clothing, food and meal times, romance, familial relationships, nonverbal communication, and occupations.

Terms to Know Before You Read

apathetic (12) unemotional; unresponsive

fatalistic (12) believes that all events are determined by fate

Social Time: The Heartbeat of Culture

■ By Robert Levine,
with Ellen Wolff

1 *If a man does not keep pace with his companions, perhaps it is because he hears a different drummer."* This thought by Thoreau strikes a chord in so many people that it has become part of our language. We use the phrase "the beat of a different drummer" to explain any pace of life unlike our own. Such colorful vagueness reveals how informal our rules of time really are. The world over, children simply "pick up" their society's time concepts as they mature. No dictionary clearly defines the meaning of "early" or "late" for them or for strangers who stumble over the maddening incongruities between the time sense they bring with them and the one they face in a new land.

2 I learned this firsthand, a few years ago, and the resulting culture shock led me halfway around the world to find answers. It seemed clear that time "talks." But what is it telling us?

3 My journey started shortly after I accepted an appointment as visiting professor of psychology at the federal university in Niteroi, Brazil, a midsized city across the bay from Rio de Janeiro. As I left home for my first day of class, I asked someone the time. It was 9:05 a.m., which allowed me time to relax and look around the campus before my 10 o'clock lecture. After what I judged to be half an hour, I glanced at a clock I was passing. It said 10:20! In panic, I broke for the classroom, followed by gentle calls of "Hola, professor" and "Tudo bem, professor?" from unhurried students, many of whom, I later realized, were my own. I arrived breathless to find an empty room.

4 Frantically, I asked a passerby the time. "Nine forty-five" was the answer. No, that couldn't be. I asked someone else. "Nine fifty-five." Another said: "Exactly 9:43." The clock in a nearby office read 3:15. I had learned my first lesson about Brazilians: Their timepieces are consistently inaccurate. And nobody minds.

5 My class was scheduled from 10 until noon. Many students came late, some very late. Several arrived after 10:30. A few showed up closer to 11. Two came after that. All of the latecomers wore the relaxed smiles that I came, later, to enjoy. Each one said hello, and although a few apologized briefly, none seemed terribly concerned about lateness. They assumed that I understood.

6 The idea of Brazilians arriving late was not a great shock. I had heard about

From *Psychology Today* (March 1985): 28–30+.

"mānha," the Portuguese equivalent of "mañana" in Spanish. This term, meaning "tomorrow" or "the morning," stereotypes the Brazilian who puts off the business of today until tomorrow. The real surprise came at noon that first day, when the end of class arrived.

7   Back home in California, I never need to look at a clock to know when the class hour is ending. The shuffling of books is accompanied by strained expressions that say plaintively, "I'm starving. . . . I've got to go to the bathroom. . . . I'm going to suffocate if you keep us one more second." (The pain usually becomes unbearable at two minutes to the hour in undergraduate classes and five minutes before the close of graduate classes.)

8   When noon arrived in my first Brazilian class, only a few students left immediately. Others slowly drifted out during the next 15 minutes, and some continued asking me questions long after that. When several remaining students kicked off their shoes at 12:30, I went into my own "starving/bathroom/suffocation" routine.

9   I could not, in all honesty, attribute their lingering to my superb teaching style. I had just spent two hours lecturing on statistics in halting Portuguese. Apparently, for many of my students, staying late was simply of no more importance than arriving late in the first place. As I observed this casual approach in infinite variations during the year, I learned that the "mānha" stereotype oversimplified the real Anglo/Brazilian differences in conceptions of time. Research revealed a more complex picture.

With the assist[...] West and Harry Re[...] sense of 91 male an[...] Niteroi with that of 10[...] California State Universi[...] universities are similar in a[...] and size, and the cities are b[...] metropolitan centers with po[...] about 350,000.

We asked students about their [...]tions of time in several situations, s[...] what they would consider late or earl[...] a hypothetical lunch appointment wit[...] friend. The average Brazilian student de[...]fined lateness for lunch as 33½ minutes after the scheduled time, compared to only 19 minutes for the Fresno students. But Brazilians also allowed an average of about 54 minutes before they'd consider someone early, while the Fresno students drew the line at 24.

Are Brazilians simply more flexible in 12 their concepts of time and punctuality? And how does this relate to the stereotype of the apathetic, fatalistic and irresponsible Latin temperament? When we asked students to give typical reasons for lateness, the Brazilians were less likely to attribute it to a lack of caring than the North Americans were. Instead, they pointed to unforeseen circumstances that the person couldn't control. Because they seemed less inclined to feel personally responsible for being late, they also expressed less regret for their own lateness and blamed others less when they were late.

We found similar differences in how stu- 13 dents from the two countries characterized e who were late for appointments. ke their North American counterparts, Brazilian students believed that a per- who is consistently late is probably re successful than one who is consis- ntly on time. They seemed to accept the dea that someone of status is expected to arrive late. Lack of punctuality is a badge of success.

4   Even within our own country, of course, ideas of time and punctuality vary considerably from place to place. Different regions and even cities have their own distinct rhythms and rules. Seemingly simple words like "now," snapped out by an impatient New Yorker, and "later," said by a relaxed Californian, suggest a world of difference. Despite our familiarity with these homegrown differences in tempo, problems with time present a major stumbling block to Americans abroad. Peace Corps volunteers told researchers James Spradley of Macalester College and Mark Phillips of the University of Washington that their greatest difficulties with other people, after language problems, were the general pace of life and the punctuality of others. Formal "clock time" may be a standard on which the world agrees, but "social time," the heartbeat of society, is something else again.

15   How a country paces its social life is a mystery to most outsiders, one that we're just beginning to unravel. Twenty-six years ago, anthropologist Edward Hall noted in *The Silent Language* that informal patterns of time "are seldom, if ever, made explicit. They exist in the air around us. They are ei-

ther familiar and comfortable, or unfamiliar and wrong." When we realize we are out of step, we often blame the people around us to make ourselves feel better.

Appreciating cultural differences in time 16 sense becomes increasingly important as modern communications put more and more people in daily contact. If we are to avoid misreading issues that involve time perceptions, we need to understand better our own cultural biases and those of others.

When people of different cultures inter- 17 act, the potential for misunderstanding exists on many levels. For example, members of Arab and Latin cultures usually stand much closer when they are speaking to people than we usually do in the United States, a fact we frequently misinterpret as aggression or disrespect. Similarly, we assign personality traits to groups with a pace of life that is markedly faster or slower than our own. We build ideas of national character, for example, around the traditional Swiss and German ability to "make the trains run on time." Westerners like ourselves define punctuality using precise measures of time: 5 minutes, 15 minutes, an hour. But according to Hall, in many Mediterranean Arab cultures there are only three sets of time: no time at all, now (which is of varying duration) and forever (too long). Because of this, Americans often find difficulty in getting Arabs to distinguish between waiting a long time and a very long time.

According to historian Will Durant, 18 "No man in a hurry is quite civilized." What do our time judgments say about our attitude toward life? How can a North American, coming from a land of digital precision, relate to a North African who may consider a clock "the devil's mill"?

19 Each language has a vocabulary of time that does not always survive translation. When we translated our questionnaires into Portuguese for my Brazilian students, we found that English distinctions of time were not readily articulated in their language. Several of our questions concerned how long the respondent would wait for someone to arrive, as compared with when they hoped for arrival or actually expected the person would come. In Portuguese, the verbs "to wait for," "to hope for" and "to expect" are all translated as "esperar." We had to add further words of explanation to make the distinction clear to the Brazilian students.

20 To avoid these language problems, my Fresno colleague Kathy Bartlett and I decided to clock the pace of life in other countries by using as little language as possible. We looked directly at three basic indicators of time: the accuracy of a country's bank clocks, the speed at which pedestrians walked and the average time it took a postal clerk to sell us a single stamp. In six countries on three continents, we made observations in both the nation's largest urban area and a medium-sized city: Japan (Tokyo and Sendai), Taiwan (Taipei and Tainan), Indonesia (Jakarta and Solo), Italy (Rome and Florence), England (London and Bristol) and the United States (New York City and Rochester).

21 What we wanted to know was: Can we speak of a unitary concept called "pace of life"? What we've learned suggests that we can. There appears to be a very strong relationship (see chart) between the accuracy of clock time, walking speed and postal efficiency across the countries we studied.

THE PACE OF LIFE IN SIX COUNTRIES

	Accuracy of Bank Clocks	Walking Speed	Post Office Speed
Japan	1	1	1
United States	2	3	2
England	4	2	3
Italy	5	4	6
Taiwan	3	5	4
Indonesia	6	6	5

Numbers (1 is the top value) indicate the comparative rankings of each country for each indicator of time sense.

22 We checked 15 clocks in each city, selecting them at random in downtown banks and comparing the time they showed with that reported by the local telephone company. In Japan, which leads the way in accuracy, the clocks averaged just over half a minute early or late. Indonesian clocks, the least accurate, were more than three minutes off the mark.

23 I will be interested to see how the digital-information age will affect our perceptions of time. In the United States today, we are reminded of the exact hour of the day more than ever, through little symphonies of beeps emanating from people's digital watches. As they become the norm, I fear our sense of precision may take an absurd twist. The other day, when I asked for the time, a student looked at his watch

and replied, "Three twelve and eighteen seconds."

24   *"Will you walk a little faster?' said a whiting to a snail. 'There's a porpoise close behind us, and he's treading on my tail.'"*

25   So goes the rhyme from *Alice in Wonderland,* which also gave us that famous symbol of haste, the White Rabbit. He came to mind often as we measured the walking speeds in our experimental cities. We clocked how long it took pedestrians to walk 100 feet along a main downtown street during business hours on clear days. To eliminate the effects of socializing, we observed only people walking alone, timing at least 100 in each city. We found, once again, that the Japanese led the way, averaging just 20.7 seconds to cover the distance. The English nosed out the Americans for second place—21.6 to 22.5 seconds—and the Indonesians again trailed the pack, sauntering along at 27.2 seconds. As you might guess, speed was greater in the larger city of each nation than in its smaller one.

26   Our final measurement, the average time it took postal clerks to sell one stamp, turned out to be less straightforward than we expected. In each city, including those in the United States, we presented clerks with a note in the native language requesting a common-priced stamp—a 20-center in the United States, for example. They were also handed paper money, the equivalent of a $5 bill. In Indonesia, this procedure led to more than we bargained for.

27   At the large central post office in Jakarta,

I asked for the line to buy stamps and was directed to a group of private vendors sitting outside. Each of them hustled for my business: "Hey, good stamps, mister!" "Best stamps here!" In the smaller city of Solo, I found a volleyball game in progress when I arrived at the main post office on Friday afternoon. Business hours, I was told, were over. When I finally did get there during business hours, the clerk was more interested in discussing relatives in America. Would I like to meet his uncle in Cincinnati? Which did I like better: California or the United States? Five people behind me in line waited patiently. Instead of complaining, they began paying attention to our conversation.

When it came to efficiency of service, 28 however, the Indonesians were not the slowest, although they did place far behind the Japanese postal clerks, who averaged 25 seconds. That distinction went to the Italians, whose infamous postal service took 47 seconds on the average.

"A man who wastes one hour of time has 29 *not discovered the meaning of life. . . ."*   30

That was Charles Darwin's belief, and many share it, perhaps at the cost of their health. My colleagues and I have recently begun studying the relationship between pace of life and well-being. Other researchers have demonstrated that a chronic sense of urgency is a basic component of the Type A, coronary-prone personality. We expect that future research will demonstrate that pace of life is related to rate of heart disease, hypertension, ulcers, suicide,

READING

alcoholism, divorce and other indicators of general psychological and physical well-being.

31   As you envision tomorrow's international society, do you wonder who will set the pace? Americans eye Japan carefully, because the Japanese are obviously "ahead of us" in measurable ways. In both countries, speed is frequently confused with progress. Perhaps looking carefully at the different paces of life around the world will help us distinguish more accurately between the two qualities. Clues are everywhere but sometimes hard to distinguish. You have to listen carefully to hear the beat of even your own drummer.

Evaluation of the Article
Difficulty rating ☐ 1 ☐ 2 ☐ 3 ☐ 4 ☐ 5
(1 = easy; 5 = difficult)

What reading difficulties did you encounter?_____
_____

How did you handle these difficulties?_____
_____

Postreading Comprehension Development

Rewriting Sentences

To check your understanding of some of the key concepts of this essay, rewrite each of the following sentences in your own words, keeping the original idea. (See Chapter 1.)

1. We use the phrase "the beat of a different drummer" to explain any pace of life unlike our own. (1)

    _____

    _____

2. When we asked students to give typical reasons for lateness, the Brazilians were less likely to attribute it to a lack of caring than the North Americans were. (12)

   _____

   _____

3. My colleagues and I have recently begun studying the relationship between pace of life and well-being. (30)

   _____

   _____

Authors' Main Idea

1. The authors seem to have written this article primarily to explain

   _____a. why Brazilian students do not compete very well against students from other cultures where time is more valued.

   _____b. how the concept of time varies from culture to culture.

   _____c. how some cultures do not value time.

   _____d. why it is difficult to teach in Brazilian classrooms.

2. How does paragraph 4 contribute to the main idea of this essay?

   _____a. It sets up the problem that the authors hoped to solve.

   _____b. It provides scientific evidence for the authors' point of view.

   _____c. It is an example of the Brazilian indifference to exact time.

   _____d. It persuades the reader to accept the authors' argument.

3. The authors develop their key point primarily through use of

   _____a. secondary sources.

   _____b. original sources.

   _____c. unreliable sources.

   _____d. eyewitness reports.

Inferences, Metaphors, and Vocabulary in Context

1. Refer to the author–title page of this essay. Why do two names appear in the author heading?

    _____a. The second author had the same experience as the first.

    _____b. The first author was the main author, and the second one worked on the article, but not as much.

    _____c. The two authors went to Brazil together.

    _____d. The second author was a graduate student who needed her name on an article in order to graduate.

2. The authors probably discussed the students in California in order to

    _____a. show how much more attentive they were than Brazilian students.

    _____b. show how anxious they were to leave class, unlike Brazilian students.

    _____c. contrast them to Brazilian students.

    _____d. define the Californian students' sense of time.

3. We can assume that the professor's decision to conduct the research study with his colleagues

    _____a. occurred after the professor started teaching in Brazil.

    _____b. was agreed to before the professor left for Brazil.

    _____c. was made while he was in California and was finalized when he reached Brazil.

    _____d. was begun once the professor returned home from Brazil.

4. Before the professor met with his first class, he seemed

    _____a. anxious to arrive on time.

    _____b. concerned that his lecture would not go well.

_____c. aware that he was passing his students on the street.

_____d. anxious to get back to his research.

5. The sentence in paragraph 9 that best states the Brazilian students' concept of time is

_____a. sentence 1.

_____b. sentence 2.

_____c. sentence 3.

_____d. sentence 4.

6. Using only the context, define each of the following words. Do not use a dictionary.

a. incongruities (1) _____

b. plaintively (7) _____

c. attribute (9) _____

d. lingering (9) _____

e. counterparts (13) _____

f. explicit (15) _____

g. articulated (19) _____

h. unitary (21) _____

7. We can conclude from paragraph 11 that a person scheduled for a 3:15 P.M. meeting who arrives at 2:45 P.M. would be considered

_____a. on time, in Brazil.

_____b. late, in Fresno.

_____c. late, in Brazil.

_____d. early, in Fresno.

8. We can also conclude from paragraph 11 that a person scheduled for an 11:30 A.M. lunch date who arrives at 12:15 P.M. would be considered

_____a. on time, in Fresno.

_____b. on time, in Brazil.

_____c. late, in Brazil.

_____d. early, in Fresno.

9. It appears that, in Brazil, people who arrive for their meetings at the scheduled time are considered

   _____a. rude.

   _____b. unsuccessful.

   _____c. to have successful careers.

   _____d. to be positive role models.

10. In your own words, explain the distinction the authors make between *clock time* and *social time*. _____

   _____

11. The authors probably refer to Hall's book to provide

   _____a. an example of the variation in people's attitudes towards time.

   _____b. support for the idea that it is hard to define *social time* in any culture.

   _____c. reasons why we blame others to make ourselves feel better.

   _____d. Hall's expertise as an anthropologist.

12. We can conclude from paragraphs 17 and 18 that

   _____a. the American concept of time is better than that of Arab nations.

   _____b. people in Germany would have difficulty communicating their time concepts to Americans.

_____c. we would have fewer conflicts with people of other cultures
        if we tried to understand their concepts of time.

_____d. the pace of life is strikingly similar through the world.

13. Write three conclusions you draw from the chart entitled "The Pace
     of Life in Six Countries." Be prepared to explain how you drew these
     conclusions.

a. _____

b. _____

c. _____

14. Which statement below *best* summarizes the author's attitude about pace
     of life?

_____a. Other nations have remained poor because their pace of life
        is too slow.

_____b. We are not going to be competitive worldwide unless we
        change our pace of life.

_____c. There is much to be learned from Japanese efficiency and
        speed.

_____d. The fastest is not necessarily the best.

15. The "two qualities" referred to in the last paragraph of this essay are

_____a. accuracy and speed.

_____b. carefulness and progress.

_____c. speed and progress.

_____d. differences and internationalism.

Recalling Details

1. The professor's reason for being in Brazil was to

_____a. learn about Brazilian culture.

_____b. conduct a study on pace of life among Brazilians.

_____c. to work with local anthropologists.

_____d. to teach psychology at a university.

2. The professor's initial attitude towards his Brazilian students was

_____a. anger.

_____b. humor.

_____c. surprise.

_____d. annoyance.

3. The primary language of the people of Brazil is

_____a. Spanish.

_____b. Portuguese.

_____c. English.

_____d. Brazilian.

4. The percentage of students who arrived "on time" for the professor's first day of class was

_____a. 10 percent.

_____b. 20 percent.

_____c. 30 percent.

_____d. not mentioned.

5. Which of the following does *not* describe the student population that the authors researched?

_____a. They were urban students.

_____b. Their cultures were varied.

_____c. They were all extremely bright.

_____d. They were all college students.

6. The pattern of organization used in paragraph 16 is a

    _____a. problem and solution.

    _____b. simple listing.

    _____c. comparison or contrast.

    _____d. thesis and proof.

7. The pattern of organization used in paragraph 17 is a

    _____a. problem and solution.

    _____b. simple listing.

    _____c. definition.

    _____d. comparison or contrast.

8. The number of statistical research studies conducted by the authors for which results were reported in this article is(are)

    _____a. one.

    _____b. two.

    _____c. three.

    _____d. four.

9. What is represented by the third column on the chart entitled "The Pace of Life in Six Countries"?

    _____a. The rankings of postal clerks around the world, based on how long it took them to sell one stamp

    _____b. How quickly the postal clerks told about their relatives

    _____c. How "on time" postal clerks were around the world, based on when they said they'd work and when they actually did

    _____d. The regularity with which post offices kept the posted business hours

Critical Thinking: Reaction and Discussion

1. Is beauty culturally defined? Create a drawing or make a collage from a magazine that represents what you believe to be a beautiful person. Compare your sense of beauty with that of other students in your class and then write a summary of your observations.

2. Discuss with a group: How does your sense of time compare with the Brazilian and the Californian students discussed in this article? Compare and contrast the "pace of life" as it is experienced by members of your group.

3. Either in an essay or with a group, consider how this article would have been different if it had been written by a researcher from another discipline, one other than anthropology. What dimensions of time might they have studied? What other aspects of the classroom might have been analyzed? Consider these questions for each of the following areas:
   a. Psychology
   b. History
   c. Education
   d. Science or technology

Using Technology for Further Understanding

Use the Internet to learn more about one aspect of Brazilian culture, such as sports, dating, or familial relationships. Be careful to distinguish between fact and opinion. Be prepared to share your findings with your class.

CHAPTER ELEVEN

Readings in Business and Business Technology

Most of the trouble with business . . . is not the product of evil intentions but of the enormous difficulty of carrying out the best intentions.

—*Sales Management,* 15 January 1969;
cited in James B. Simpson,
Simpson's Contemporary Quotations
(New York: HarperCollins, 1997), 195.

READING

Guidelines for Reading in Business and Business Technology

For many students, majoring in business provides the perfect opportunity to think about what they might do with the rest of their lives. Through business courses, they learn about many career options, including options if they work for others or if they start their own businesses. Reading in business fields, such as marketing or advertising, like reading in other fields, will be easier for you if you keep in mind some specific strategies.

Specific Strategies

* **Be certain you have the appropriate framework in mind when you first approach a business or business technology reading.** Business and business technology materials often have their basis in a number of other disciplines, including economics, psychology, sociology, law and ethics, and science. Portions of an accounting text, for example, are probably based on principles drawn from economics. On the other hand, theories or practices discussed in a marketing or management text might be rooted in psychology or sociology. Texts on business technology may be based in science, language, or one of the social sciences, depending on the purpose of the text. If you note the appropriate framework when you begin your reading assignment, you will be able to relate what you know from these broader areas to the text at hand.

* **Draw on your experiences in the real world, to increase your comprehension.** Many of your life experiences have already connected you to business and related technology. You have been a consumer for many years. Perhaps you also have been in a workplace where you have had responsibilities for finance or for using technology. Your recall of these experiences will contribute to the knowledge pool from which you can draw to make business and business technology readings more relevant and the comprehension of text easier.

* **Be aware that the language in these readings is often technical.** Today's businesses rely heavily on technology for a wide range of

their needs, including communication, product design, record keeping, conducting research, and increasing production. (Note that the technology reading in this chapter is of this type, not the type of highly specialized reading that students majoring in computer science would encounter.) When you read, look for special uses given to "everyday" words: in business, words such as *compound, discount,* and *futures;* in business technology, terms such as *groupware, network,* and *graphics;* in many subspecialties, such as the securities markets and investments, such terms as *margin, security,* and *market,* which take on new meaning.

❋ **Be familiar with visual aids.** Visual aids are often used to illustrate a wide variety of concepts and to provide statistical information. Knowing how to read charts, graphs, and tables is critical. These visual aids play an important role in reading business-related materials. They serve to explain complex ideas in a more concrete way, and they will help you visualize the relationships between abstract concepts. Data involving numbers or percentages are remembered more easily when their relationship to other data, such as the relationship between management style and profit margin, is shown in a graphic.

As you work with charts and graphs in your texts, you will need to draw conclusions from them. What do the data tell you? Often the conclusions you draw are the most important points being made in a section of the text you are reading. The author has included the graph to make these points more vivid.

Keep these suggestions in mind as you read the following articles from business or business technology.

What are some fields of business or business technology that interest you?

_____

_____

What additional suggestions can you make for reading in business or business technology?

_____

_____

_____

_____

_____

❧ SELECTION 4
Preview

Many people have decided to start their own businesses rather than work for someone else. This article explores some of the reasons for this decision, as well as the requirements and prospects for small-business owners.

To Think About Before You Read

Imagine you are planning to start a small business of your own. Based on your interests and what you already know about small-business ownership, answer the following questions:

1. What type of business would you start? _____

2. How many employees would you have? _____

3. What training would you have had to prepare you for this new business?

   _____

   _____

4. Which of your personality traits would help you have a successful business? _____

   _____

   _____

5. What would you expect your annual gross sales to be? _____

6. What would you expect your annual profit to be? _____

Small Business: A Profile

■ By William M. Pride, Robert J. Hughes, and Jack R. Kapoor

1 The Small Business Administration (SBA) defines a **small business** as "one which is independently owned and operated for profit and is not dominant in its field." How small must a firm be not to dominate its field? That depends on the particular industry it is in. The SBA has developed the following specific "smallness" guidelines for the various industries.

* *Manufacturing*—a maximum of 500 to 1,500 employees, depending on the products manufactured
* *Wholesaling*—a maximum of 100 employees
* *Retailing*—maximum yearly sales or receipts ranging from $5 million to $21 million, depending on the industry
* *General construction*—average annual receipts ranging from $13.5 million to $17 million, depending on the industry
* *Special trade construction*—annual sales ranging up to $7.5 million

From *Business*, 6th ed. (Boston: Houghton Mifflin, 1999), 115–20.

* *Agriculture*—maximum annual receipts of $0.5 million to $9 million
* *Services*—maximum annual receipts ranging from $2.5 million to $21.5 million, depending on the type of service

In 1996 the SBA revised and simplified its small-business size regulations.

2 Annual sales in the millions of dollars may not seem very small. However, for many firms, profit is only a small percentage of total sales. Thus, a firm may earn only $30,000 or $40,000 on yearly sales of $1 million—and that *is* small in comparison to the profits earned by most medium-sized and large firms. Moreover, most small firms have annual sales well below the maximum limits in the SBA guidelines.

THE SMALL-BUSINESS SECTOR

3 A surprising number of Americans take advantage of their freedom to start a business. There are, in fact, about 22.1 million businesses in this country. Only just over 14,000 of these employ more than 500 workers—enough to be considered large.

4 Interest in owning or starting a small business has never been greater than it is today. Since 1982, the number of small

businesses in the United States has increased 49 percent, and for the last few years, new business formation in the United States has broken successive records. During 1995, there were 819,000 new firms—a 1.5 percent increase over the record 807,000 in 1994. Furthermore, part-time entrepreneurs have increased fivefold in recent years; they now account for one-third of all small businesses.

5 Statistically, over 70 percent of new businesses can be expected to fail within their first five years. The primary reason for these failures is mismanagement resulting from a lack of business know-how. The makeup of the small-business sector is thus constantly changing. In spite of the high failure rate, many small businesses succeed modestly. Some, like Apple Computer, Inc., are extremely successful—to the point where they can no longer be considered small. Taken together, small businesses are also responsible for providing a high percentage of the jobs in the United States. According to some estimates, the figure is well over 50 percent.

INDUSTRIES THAT ATTRACT SMALL BUSINESSES

6 Some industries, such as auto manufacturing, require huge investments in machinery and equipment. Businesses in such industries are big from the day they are started—if an entrepreneur or group of entrepreneurs can gather the capital required to start one.

7 By contrast, a number of other industries require only a low initial investment and some special skills or knowledge. It is these industries that tend to attract new businesses. Growing industries, such as outpatient care facilities, are attractive because of their profit potential. However, knowledgeable entrepreneurs choose areas with which they are familiar, and these are most often the more established industries.

8 Small enterprise spans the gamut from corner newspaper vending to the development of optical fibers. The owners of small businesses sell gasoline, flowers, and coffee to go. They publish magazines, haul freight, teach languages, and program computers. They make wines, movies, and high-fashion clothes. They build new homes and restore old ones. They fix appliances, recycle metals, and sell used cars. They drive cabs and fly planes. They make us well when we are ill, and they sell us the products of corporate giants.

9 The various kinds of businesses generally fall into three broad categories of industry: distribution, service, and production. Within these categories, small businesses tend to cluster in services and retailing. The table shows the fifteen fastest growing types of small businesses.

FASTEST GROWING TYPES OF SMALL BUSINESSES, 1993–1994

Business	Employment Increase (thousands)	Employment Increase (%)
Boat building and repairing	9.4	20.2
Medical-equipment rental and leasing	5.8	16.9
Dairy-product stores	2.6	15.5
Carpentry and floor work	25.5	13.3
Masonry, stonework, tile setting, and plastering	51.0	12.9
Aluminum foundries	2.8	12.4
Equipment rental and leasing	16.5	11.4
Employment agencies	27.0	11.0
Nonferrous foundries	8.6	10.9
Painting and paperhanging	17.3	10.6
Automotive repair shops	24.5	10.4
Heavy construction equipment, rental and leasing	3.8	10.3
Child day care services	53.8	10.3
Heating equipment manufacture	2.0	10.0
Furniture stores	28.4	10.0
Total	279.0	11.4

Source: From *The State of Small Business: A Report of the President,* Washington, D.C., U.S. Government Printing Office, 1996, p. 59.

Distribution Industries

10   This category includes retailing, wholesaling, transportation, and communications—industries concerned with the movement of goods from producers to consumers. Distribution industries account for approximately 33 percent of all small businesses. Of these, almost three-quarters are involved in retailing, that is, the sale of goods directly to consumers. Clothing and jewelry stores, pet shops, bookstores, and grocery stores, for example, are all retailing firms. Slightly less than one-quarter of the small distribution firms are wholesalers. Wholesalers purchase products in quantity from manufacturers and then resell them to retailers.

Service Industries

11   This category accounts for over 48 percent of all small businesses. Of these, about three-quarters provide such nonfinancial services as medical and dental care; watch, shoe, and TV repairs; hair-cutting and styling; restaurant meals; and dry cleaning. About 8 percent of the small service firms offer financial services, such as accounting, insurance, real estate, and investment counseling. An increasing number of self-

employed Americans are running service businesses from home.

Production Industries

12 This last category includes the construction, mining, and manufacturing industries. Only about 19 percent of all small businesses are in this group, mainly because these industries require relatively large initial investments. Small firms that do venture into production generally make parts and subassemblies for larger manufacturing firms or supply special skills to larger construction firms.

THE PEOPLE IN SMALL BUSINESSES: THE ENTREPRENEURS

13 Small businesses are typically managed by the people who started and own them. Most of these people have held jobs with other firms and could still be so employed if they wanted. Yet owners of small businesses would rather take the risk of starting and operating their own firms, even if the money they make is less than the salaries they might otherwise earn.

14 Researchers have suggested a variety of personal factors as reasons why people go into business for themselves. One that is often cited is the "entrepreneurial spirit"— the desire to create a new business. Other factors, such as independence, the desire to determine one's own destiny, and the willingness to find and accept a challenge, certainly play a part. Background may exert an influence as well. In particular, researchers think that people whose families have been in business (successfully or not) are most apt to start and run their own businesses. Those who start their own businesses also tend to cluster around certain ages—more than 70 percent are between 24 and 44 years old.

15 Finally, there must be some motivation to start a business. A person may decide she has simply "had enough" of working and earning a profit for someone else. Another may lose his job for some reason and decide to start the business he has always wanted rather than seek another job. Still another person may have an idea for a new product or a new way to sell an existing product. Or the opportunity to go into business may arise suddenly, perhaps as a result of a hobby, as was the case with Cheryl Strand. Strand started baking and decorating cakes from her home while working full-time as a word processor at Clemson University. Her cakes became so popular that she soon found herself working through her lunch breaks and late into the night to meet customer demand.

16 After deciding in July 1989 to start her own business, Strand contacted the Clemson University Small Business Development Center. The center helped her prepare for the business start-up and develop a loan package—complete with a detailed business plan and financial statements for presentation at local banks. Strand obtained the $10,000 she needed. Since then, Cakes by Cheryl has doubled in size and increased sales by approximately 56 percent per year. It now offers fresh breads, deli sandwiches, a tempting line of baked goods, and catering and carry-out services.

17   Cheryl Strand is one of a growing number of women who are small business owners. According to a 1995 study by the National Foundation for Women Business Owners and Dun & Bradstreet, there are now 7.7 million women-owned firms providing jobs for 15.5 million people—more than are employed in the Fortune 500 companies. The latest data from the Department of Commerce on women- and African American-owned businesses for 1987 and 1992 reveal that these businesses fared well in the strong economy of the late 1980s. During this period, the number of women-owned small proprietorships and partnerships rose from 4.1 million to 5.9 million, an increase of about 43 percent. The total receipts of women-owned small proprietorships and partnerships nearly tripled over this same period, rising from $278.1 billion in 1987 to $642.5 billion in 1992. During the same period, the number of African American-owned businesses rose by 46 percent.

18   In some people, the motivation to start a business develops slowly, as they gain the knowledge and ability required for success as a business owner. Knowledge and ability—especially management ability—are probably the most important factors involved. A new firm is very much built around the entrepreneur. The owner must be able to manage the firm's finances, its personnel (if there are any employees), and its day-to-day operations. He or she must handle sales, advertising, purchasing, pricing, and a variety of other business functions. The knowledge and ability to do so are most often acquired through experience working for other firms in the same area of business.

WHY SMALL BUSINESSES FAIL

19   Small businesses are prone to failure. Capital, management, and planning are the key ingredients in the survival of a small business, and also the most common reasons for failure. Businesses can experience a number of money-related problems. It may take several years before a business begins to show a profit. Entrepreneurs need to have not only the capital to open a business but also the money to operate it in its possibly lengthy start-up phase. One cash-flow obstacle often leads to others. And a series of cash-flow predicaments usually ends in a business failure.

20   Many entrepreneurs lack the management skills required to run a business. Money, time, personnel, and inventory all need to be effectively managed if a small business is to succeed. Starting a small business requires much more than optimism and a good idea.

21   Success and expansion sometimes lead to problems. Frequently entrepreneurs with successful small businesses make the mistake of overexpansion. But fast growth often results in dramatic changes in a business. Thus, the entrepreneur must plan carefully and adjust competently to new and potentially disruptive situations.

22   Every day, and in every part of the country, people open new businesses. Though many will fail, others represent well-conceived ideas developed by entrepreneurs

who have the expertise, resources, and determination to make their businesses succeed. As these well-prepared entrepreneurs pursue their individual goals, our society benefits in many ways from their work and creativity. Such billion-dollar companies as Apple Computer, McDonald's Corporation, and Proctor & Gamble are all examples of small businesses that expanded into industry giants.

Evaluation of the Article
Difficulty rating ☐ 1 ☐ 2 ☐ 3 ☐ 4 ☐ 5
(1 = easy; 5 = difficult)

What reading difficulties did you encounter?_____

_____

How did you handle these difficulties?_____

_____

Postreading Comprehension Development

Rewriting Sentences

To check your understanding of some of the key concepts of this essay, rewrite each of the following sentences in your own words, keeping the original idea. (See Chapter 1.)

1. Furthermore, part-time entrepreneurs have increased fivefold in recent years; they now account for one-third of all small businesses. (4)

   _____

   _____

2. Wholesalers purchase products in quantity from manufacturers and then resell them to retailers. (10) _____

   _____

3. A new firm is very much built around the entrepreneur. (18) _____

_____

Authors' Main Idea

1. What is the topic of this article?

_____

2. How do the subtitles clarify the focus the authors will have on this topic?

_____

_____

3. Create a new title for this selection that you think would help a reader predict its major focus.

_____

4. What predictions do you believe a reader could make from your title?

_____

5. The authors develop their key point primarily through use of

_____a.   secondary sources.

_____b.   original sources.

_____c.   unreliable sources.

_____d.   eyewitness reports.

Inferences, Metaphors, and Vocabulary in Context

1. Which of the following conclusions can be drawn from this article? Check all that apply. Be prepared to justify your answers.

_____a. Someone who has been fired from a job would feel too defeated to start his or her own business.

_____b. It is possible for something that starts as a small business to expand into a huge conglomerate.

_____c. The global marketplace will use more small businesses than corporate giants.

_____d. SBA guidelines are intended to discourage small-business ownership.

_____e. The economy is dependent on the success of small businesses.

_____f. If you lack motivation, you should not try to open a small business.

_____g. People in the United States have become increasingly confident that they can be successful small-business owners.

2. The authors' tone throughout most of this essay is

_____a. critical.

_____b. informative.

_____c. persuasive.

_____d. argumentative.

3. Using only the context, define each of the following. Do not use a dictionary.

a. dominant (1) _____

b. gamut (8) _____

c. initial (12) _____

d. venture (12) _____

e. entrepreneurial (14) _____

f. exert (14) _____

g. fared (17) _____

h. proprietorships (18) _____

4. Which of the following do the authors imply in paragraph 16? Be prepared to justify your answer.

_____ a. Cheryl Strand had prepared well for the meetings with banks.

_____ b. Strand was not confident that she would be able to run a small business.

_____ c. Strand had little experience in working with people.

_____ d. Strand had parents who would support her if the banks did not come through.

5. One assumption we can make about Cheryl Strand is that

_____ a. her parents helped her start her business.

_____ b. she was a business major at Clemson University.

_____ c. she inherited her cake-decorating skills.

_____ d. she was a risk taker.

6. The authors say, "Starting a small business requires much more than optimism and a good idea." In your view, have they proved their point? Explain your answer on the lines below.

_____

_____

_____

_____

Recalling Details

1. Identify each of the following as either a distribution (D), service (S), or production (P) industry:

_____ a. Computer repair

_____ b. Grocery store

_____ c. Child-care center

_____d. Landscape business

_____e. Newspaper-printing business

_____ f. Pet-grooming shop

_____g. Travel agency

_____h. Hair salon

2. Which of the following are cited as reasons for small-business failures?

     _____a. Too many customers, owner's lack of motivation, owner's lack of business experience

     _____b. Online competition, mismanagement, owner's lack of motivation

     _____c. Lack of capital, mismanagement, owner's lack of motivation

     _____d. Online competition, too many customers, owner's lack of business experience

3. What purpose do the statistics serve in each of the following paragraphs?

Paragraph 11 _____

Paragraph 18 _____

4. The pattern of organization used in paragraph 8 is a

     _____a. comparison or contrast.

     _____b. problem and solution.

     _____c. definition or explanation.

     _____d. simple listing.

5. The pattern of organization used in paragraph 19 is a

     _____a. comparison or contrast.

     _____b. problem and solution.

     _____c. definition or explanation.

     _____d. simple listing.

6. Look at the accompanying graph and answer the following:
   a. What ideas from this article are supported by the graph?

   _____

   _____

   _____

   b. What additional information about small business does it provide?

   _____

   _____

   _____

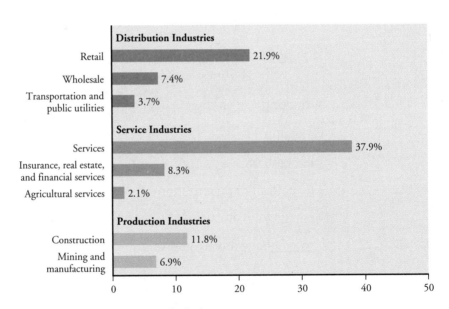

Percentages of Small Businesses by Industry

Source: Adapted from *The State of Small Business: A Report of the President* (Washington, DC: US Government Printing Office, 1993), 48–51.

Critical Thinking: Reaction and Discussion

1. Return to the section "To Think About Before You Read." Make any changes to your answers that you now feel are necessary, based on the information in this article.

2. With a partner, create a set of questions you might ask if you were to interview someone who owns a small business that you believe is successful. If possible, conduct the interview and report your findings to your class.

3. Would you like to own a small business? In an essay of at least 250 words, discuss your reasons for either wanting or not wanting to do this. Use information from the article as well as what you know about yourself and small businesses you have heard about or worked for or whose products or services you have used.

Using Technology for Further Understanding

Visit the Small Business Administration Web site:

http://www.sba.gov

How helpful would this site be to someone who is just starting a business? Explain your answer by referring to specific types of information you find at this site.

SELECTION 5
Preview

Technology has had an impact on every kind of business imaginable. In this article, you will read how it has influenced the farming industry.

To Think About Before You Read

What are some of the advantages and disadvantages of owning an online business as to owning a more traditional, offline one? Place your answers in the following contrast box. Think in terms of concerns that might be very important to a business owner.

OWNING AN ONLINE BUSINESS

Advantages	Disadvantages

Old MacDonald Has a Web Site

■ By Darnell Little

1 On his pig farm in Arena, Wis., Rick Lawinger is planning to sell some swine, namely 230 castrated male feeders being fattened for market. But instead of making his way to the nearest livestock auction, Lawinger heads to his computer. For this herd, the journey to the slaughterhouse begins online. Lawinger has gone hog-wild for the pig auctions held every Tuesday at Farms.com, an Internet farming and livestock exchange. When Lawinger first tried the Web site in late February, the 47-year-old farmer sold 300 pigs at $63 a head, even though he had estimated their value at only $56 a head. Now, Lawinger hopes to cybersell 10,000 pigs this year—his entire herd. "When local dealers come around looking to buy, I refer them to the Web site," he says.

2 Farming, one of the world's oldest industries, is learning some New Economy tricks. Hit by the lowest commodity prices in 13 years, farmers are increasingly looking to the Internet to hike sales and cut costs. The Web gives them a global marketplace to sell their products. Instead of driving to auctions and sales sometimes two or three states away—spending money on motels and restaurants and missing a day or two of field work—farmers can go online in mere minutes. And by cutting out middlemen such as dealers and distributors, sites such as DirectAg.com, XSAg.com, and Farmbid.com can offer savings of up to 30% on everything from seed and fertilizer to crop-protection chemicals. "With our profit margins so tight, those savings can mean a lot," says Alabama cotton farmer Larkin Martin.

3 The Internet and farming may seem like an odd couple, but in reality, they may be a perfect match. The farming industry is highly fragmented, with lots of buyers and sellers and a thick layer of intermediaries adding substantial markups at each level. That, say analysts, is fertile ground for a more efficient system, particularly online exchanges where buyers and sellers can haggle. "By cutting out all those extra layers, these farming exchanges are really putting downward pressure on prices," says Bruce A. Babcock, director of the Center for Agriculture & Rural Development at Iowa State University.

4 They're attracting customers, too. Already, an estimated two dozen agriculture e-commerce sites are up and running, with more in the works targeting the $826 billion industry. The sites appeal largely to the small and midsize independent farmer who doesn't buy in enough volume to demand

From *Business Week*, 15 May 2000, EB 83–88.

rebates or discounts from dealers. While the online market is still young and many cybersavvy farmers are trying these sites for the first time this year, major manufacturers of farm products, such as DuPont and Cargill Inc., are heading to the Net. Goldman, Sachs & Co. predicts that $35 billion worth of farming commerce will be conducted over the Internet this year. By 2004, sales will skyrocket to $124 billion, when agriculture's share of the entire business-to-business online economy will be over 8%, the fifth-highest industry sector. "We're suggesting to all of our 1,000 members that they develop an Internet strategy," says Paul E. Kindinger, president of the Agricultural Retailers Assn., a trade group for nutrient and seed sellers.

5   Investors aren't ready to bet the farm yet. While the majority of farming exchanges are still private ventures, the most notable exception, eMerge Interactive Inc., a Florida-based e-commerce company that owns Cyberstockyard.com, has been floundering. On Feb. 4, eMerge closed its first day of trading at more than $47 a share, but it is currently trading around its asking price of $15. Analysts say there's a perception that agriculture is a slow-moving industry populated by Luddites. "It's not even bricks and mortar. It's dirt," says Marshall Cooper, executive vice-president of Kennedy Information Research Group, a Fitzwilliam (N.H.) market researcher.

6   Farmers may be more cybersavvy than people think. The number of U.S. farms with Internet access has more than doubled in the past two years, according to a report by the National Agricultural Statistics Service. In 1999, 29% of all U.S. farms were online, and 52% of farms with sales above $250,000 had Net access. Some experts note that farmers have traditionally been willing to adopt new technologies in areas such as weather forecasting, satellite imaging, and biotechnology. Why not the Net? "Farmers will look at any new technology that makes their jobs easier," says Babcock.

7   That doesn't mean there has been a stampede to the Web. Ben Zaitz, a North Carolina cattleman and founder of Farms.com, says he was laughed at by fellow cattlemen five years ago when he started his online business. "They thought I was crazy." Zaitz had grown frustrated with shrinking profit margins as the dairy business struggled through the '90s. He saw promise in the Net, got out of the cattle business, and in 1995 created Cattle Offerings Worldwide (COW), an online database of classified listings of beef and dairy cattle. Zaitz eventually branched out into grain- and crop-protection chemicals and changed the name of the business from COW to Farms.com. Then he added live auctions. In addition to the weekly pig auctions, Farms.com holds live cattle auctions every two weeks. Zaitz moves 15,000 head of swine and 5,000 head of cattle per week. The site has 1,000 registered customers, and Zaitz believes that more will follow as farmers get comfortable with livestock auctions on the Internet. "We had a difficult time proving to the industry that this would work," he says.

8   Pig farmer Lawinger doesn't need more

proof. By reaching far beyond the Wisconsin area, Farms.com auctions have increased his hog prices an average of $5 a head—without spending extra thousands on advertising or traveling expenses to show the hogs outside the state. "This is a part of our business now," he says. "I couldn't be happier." Using Farms.com also gives Lawinger more quality control over the selling process. Pigs are highly susceptible to several diseases, and, by selling and shipping directly to buyers, Lawinger can keep his hogs away from potentially infectious animals in traditional auction pens.

9 Auctions on Farms.com work similarly to consumer auction sites such as eBay. The buyer and seller handle the transfer of funds and transportation of products, while the seller pays Farms.com a 2% transaction fee. Farms.com also generates revenue by selling classified listings and online advertising, but the real goal is to turn the site into an information-and-services portal, says CEO Robert Sparks, an agribusiness entrepreneur who was brought in to run the business in mid-March.

10 Livestock is just a small slice of the agriculture products being peddled online. Farmers spend $24 billion on animal feed annually and $7 billion more on seed, both of which can be bought in cyberspace. Launched in January, 1999, North Carolina–based XSAg.com sells seed and agriculture chemicals from manufacturers that include DuPont, AstraZeneca, and Bayer. Buyers can choose fixed-price products from an online catalog, participate in an auction, or name their own price for products, just as it's done on priceline.com. Buyers and sellers must register, providing banking information, regulatory-licensing data, and a shipping address. When a purchase is made, XSAg's bank, Bank of America Corp., automatically pulls the funds from the buyer's account and puts them in escrow. A freight company is dispatched to pick up and deliver the goods. The buyer has 48 hours to inspect the product. If there are no complaints, the money is transferred to the seller, minus a 2% transaction fee.

11 At XSAg, sellers have the option of remaining anonymous during the entire transaction. That way, a supplier that normally sells pesticide at $35 a gallon can unload excess inventory at $28 a gallon without angering his higher-paying customers. "Whenever you allow a seller to be truly anonymous, the savings can be outrageous," says Fulton Breen, founder and CEO of XSAg's parent company, XS Inc. Breen estimates that buyers can average more than 29% savings on products bought at XSAg. To date, the site has 50,000 registered users.

12 Texas cotton grower Jerry Brightbill started using XSAg.com in March, 1999, to buy herbicides and insecticides. He bought 15% of his chemicals through the site last year and saved $25,000. "It has been fantastic," he says. Brightbill plans to purchase nearly 40% of his chemicals online this year and hopes to save $50,000.

13 The low overhead needed to start an Internet e-marketplace allows many entrepreneurs to get rolling with little capital investment. Ted Farnsworth launched

Farmbid.com last July with personal funds and loans from family and friends totaling $500,000. To date, he has 90,000 registered users. Farnsworth has been able to expand his Fort Lauderdale (Fla.) company from a strictly farm-equipment auction site to an agriculture portal offering news, weather, and online-catalog sales. "We want to be the Amazon.com of the agriculture business," Farnsworth says.

14   He has a long way to go. So far, Farmbid's largest transaction was $60,000 for a tractor. The smallest? "Two dollars for cow tags," Farnsworth says. "I was shocked people would buy them online." Farnsworth plans to add more commodities and livestock in the near future. Farmbid auctions are similar to consumer–product auctions such as the ones on eBay. Sellers select a minimum bid and determine how long the auction will last—anywhere from 1 to 30 days. The buyer and seller handle the transfer of funds and shipping of the items, and the seller pays a 5% transaction fee. Farmbid's fixed-price online catalog contains some 1,300 items from 12 suppliers, who pay a sales commission of 5% to 15%. "Suppliers can sell globally, and buyers can avoid the usual 15% to 20% markup applied by the middlemen," Farnsworth says.

15   Farmbid offers everything from John Deere tractors to New Holland manure spreaders. Gary Pope, a farming equipment dealer in Eau Claire, Mich., began using Farmbid in February to sell tractors and other equipment to augment his usual sales channels of trade-magazine ads and equipment brokers. In less than three months,

Pope has sold $200,000 worth of goods online. He estimates that it would have taken nearly twice as long to do that through traditional channels. "I've increased sales at least twice as much," Pope says.

16   The real prize may be in ancillary services. Farnsworth's ultimate goal is to turn Farmbid into a virtual co-op, a buying club for farmers who can purchase agriculture goods in bulk and demand large rebates. He also wants to offer discount rates on insurance, banking, and travel to harried farmers. "Their scarcest commodity is time," he says. "There's a huge market out there for someone who can provide that convenience."

17   That may be the best way to rise above the growing online competition. With 15 suppliers and 20,000 registered users, Kip Pendleton, CEO of farming site DirectAg.com, is heading in that direction. In addition to selling machinery, seed, and animal-health products, DirectAg also offers financial services.

18   Otherwise, agricultural entrepreneurs such as Pendleton could get crushed. In March, agribusiness giant Cargill, chemicals manufacturer DuPont, and farming co-op Canex Harvest States announced that they are developing an e-commerce mall called Rooster.com. Scheduled to launch on May 1, Rooster will sell seed, pesticides, fertilizers, and farming equipment. Rooster signals a change in direction for DuPont. The company's subsidiary, Pioneer Hi-Bred International Inc., the nation's top seed supplier, previously balked at the idea of online sales, insisting that seed

was too complex. "E-commerce is here, it's real, it's not going away, and we need to figure out a strategy," says Tom Hanigan, chief information officer at Pioneer.

19 Although they're coming late to the game, the big guys have the edge. A successful online exchange needs volume, and major suppliers can attract the masses. The test will be whether sites such as Rooster can remain neutral, allowing equal access to a broad range of suppliers. "Farmers will get suspicious if they suspect an e-marketplace is in the pocket of a few large suppliers," says Forester Research Inc. analyst Bruce Temkin.

20 So far, farmers such as Lawinger are sold on Web exchanges. The Net saves time, and for farmers, "time is money" is gospel. "This is definitely where the market is going—putting the producer in direct contact with the buyer," says Lawinger. Improving efficiency and cutting farmers' costs may be enough to turn these Web exchanges from cow chips into blue chips.

Evaluation of the Article

Difficulty rating □ 1 □ 2 □ 3 □ 4 □ 5
(1 = easy; 5 = difficult)

What reading difficulties did you encounter?_____

_____

How did you handle these difficulties?_____

_____

Postreading Comprehension Development

Rewriting Sentences

To check your understanding of some of the key concepts of this essay, rewrite each of the following sentences in your own words, keeping the original idea. (See Chapter 1.)

1. Hit by the lowest commodity prices in 13 years, farmers are increasingly looking to the Internet to hike sales and cut costs. (2)

    _____

    _____

2. The low overhead needed to start an Internet e-marketplace allows many entrepreneurs to get rolling with little capital investment. (13)

    _____

    _____

3. Although they're coming late to the game, the big guys have the edge. (19)

    _____

    _____

Author's Main Idea

1. In the space provided, state the author's main idea.

    The author wants me to understand that _____

    _____

2. Which paragraph most clearly states the author's main point?

    _____a. 1

    _____b. 2

    _____c. 3

    _____d. 4

3. To develop this main idea, what kind of information does the author give the reader?

    _____

    _____

Inferences, Metaphors, and Vocabulary in Context

1. Which of the following does the author imply in paragraph 3? Be prepared to justify your answer.

    _____a. Farmers' profits will increase if they do their business on the Internet.

    _____b. Farmers will find it more complicated to conduct business on the Internet.

    _____c. The Internet will increase markups on agricultural products.

    _____d. Iowa State University is helping farmers develop Web sites.

2. Which of the following statements provide evidence of the success of the Internet for farmers? Check all that apply. Be prepared to justify your answers.

    _____a. Farming is a $826 billion industry.

    _____b. On February 4, eMerge closed its first day of trading at more than $47 a share, but it is currently trading around its asking price of $15.

    _____c. The number of U.S. farms with Internet access has more than doubled in the past two years.

    _____d. Zaitz moves 15,000 head of swine and 5,000 head of cattle per week.

    _____e. Auctions on Farms.com work similarly to consumer auction sites such as eBay.

    _____f. Brightbill plans to purchase nearly 40 percent of his chemicals online this year.

    _____g. In less than three months, Pope has sold $200,000 worth of goods online.

3. Using only the context, define each of the following words. Do not use a dictionary.

    a. haggle (3) _____

    b. floundering (5) _____

c. escrow (10) _____

d. portal (13) _____

e. ancillary (16) _____

f. balked (18) _____

4. Which of the following does the author imply in paragraph 7? Be prepared to justify your answer.

   _____a. Criticism of Zaitz's plans was justified.

   _____b. Zaitz is a clever businessman.

   _____c. Farmers should leave online business ownership in the hands of established businessowners.

   _____d. Zaitz made a bad decision when he changed the name of his business.

5. Lawinger's relationship to Farms.com is that he

   _____a. buys from the site.

   _____b. consults for them.

   _____c. sells through the site.

   _____d. owns the site.

6. In your own words, explain what Farnsworth means when he says, "We want to be the Amazon.com of the agriculture business." (13)

   _____

   _____

7. xsAg.com is discussed because it

   _____a. allows buyers to remain anonymous.

   _____b. represents large manufacturers.

   _____c. shows a huge profit.

   _____d. sells something other than livestock.

8. The author's tone throughout most of this article is

_____a. critical.

_____b. humorous.

_____c. argumentative.

_____d. informative.

9. One conclusion that can be drawn from this article is that

_____a. e-commerce for agriculture does not have a bright future.

_____b. the federal government, out of concern for quality control, will put a stop to auctions taking place at e-commerce sites.

_____c. large companies threaten to put small agriculture sites out of business.

_____d. farmers might accept e-commerce, but they will have little interest in other advances in technology.

10. Discuss the expression "You can't teach an old dog new tricks" as it pertains to this article.

_____

_____

Recalling Details

1. Which of the following are factual statements in this article? Which are opinions? Use (F) or (O) for your response. For those you label opinion, write any support for the opinion that is given in this article.

_____a. Already an estimated two dozen agriculture e-commerce sites are up and running.

_____b. Buyers and sellers must register, providing banking information, regulatory-licensing data, and a shipping address.

_____c. Whenever you allow a seller to be truly anonymous, the savings can be outrageous.

_____d. Farmbid offers everything from John Deere tractors to New Holland manure spreaders.

_____e. There's a huge market out there for someone who can provide that convenience.

_____f. Rooster signals a change in direction for DuPont.

_____g. Although they're coming late to the game, the big guys have the edge.

_____h. Farmers will get suspicious if they suspect an e-marketplace is in the pocket of a few large suppliers.

2. Using a problem-and-solution pattern, create an outline for paragraph 2 on the lines below.

_____

_____

_____

_____

_____

_____

_____

_____

_____

_____

_____

3. Which sentence in paragraph 3 describes how the traditional agriculture business operates?

_____a. 1

_____b. 2

_____c. 3

_____d. 4

4. The primary pattern of organization used in paragraph 3 is

_____a. opinion and reason.

_____b. problem and solution.

_____c. cause and effect.

_____d. definition or explanation.

5. Indicate whether each item below is a major (MAJ) or minor (MIN) detail of this article. Be prepared to justify your answers.

_____a. Now, Lawinger hopes to cybersell 10,000 pigs this year—his entire herd.

_____b. On February 4, eMerge closed its first day of trading at more than $47 a share.

_____c. The number of U.S. farms with Internet access has more than doubled in the past two years.

_____d. Farmers may be more cybersavvy than people think.

_____e. In addition to the weekly pig auctions, Farms.com holds live cattle auctions every two weeks.

_____f. Farms.com also generates revenue by selling classified listings and online advertising.

_____g. Texas cotton grower Jerry Brightbill started using XSAg.com in March 1999 to buy herbicides and insecticides.

6. List three reasons why farmers are using the Internet to conduct business:

a. _____

b. _____

c. _____

Critical Thinking: Reaction and Discussion

1. Return to the box you filled-in at the beginning of this article. What additional advantages or disadvantages can you add? Compare your responses with a group or a partner. Do the advantages outweigh the disadvantages? Would you want to own an online business?

2. Imagine that you did own an online business. What would it be? Then either

    a. design (on paper) what your Web site home page might look like or

    b. create an ad for your online business that might appear in a magazine or newspaper.

    Using information from this article, include features your business would need to have to attract customers.

3. Review the business offerings at your college. Is there a business department, or are different business courses offered by different departments? For example, accounting might be offered by the mathematics department. What are some business areas in which students can specialize? What business courses can you find that introduce students to using technology for business purposes? Which of these, if any, sound particularly interesting to you? What else would you want to know about programs in business before you decided on it as a major?

Using Technology for Further Understanding

Look at some of the agricultural Web sites mentioned in this article. Do they still exist? Have their offerings changed at all from those mentioned in the article? What additional information have you gained about agriculture online by looking at these sites? What other sites are they linked to, if any? What conclusions can you draw from these links?

CHAPTER TWELVE

Readings in Health Science and the Helping Professions

How many goodly creatures are there here!
How beauteous mankind is! O brave new world,
That has such people in't.

—William Shakespeare;
The Tempest (1611), act 5, scene 1, line 182;
quoted in *The Oxford Dictionary of Quotations,* 5th ed.,
ed. Elizabeth Knowles
(New York: Oxford University Press, 1999), 699.

Guidelines for Reading Health Science and the Helping Professions

Many college students choose to major in one of the helping professions, such as nursing, dental technology, education, fire science, criminal justice (or police science), and social work. Practical application of skills based on scientific or technical knowledge is a primary goal of studies in these fields. In addition, each field has a theoretical foundation. For instance, if you are studying fire science, you would need to understand scientific principles of heat combustion, as well as how to participate effectively as a team member. Social workers might need to know about drug interactions and their effects on children of different ages, as well as how to communicate with parents whose culture is different from your own.

Thus, reading materials in these fields usually requires a combination of strategies, some that are drawn from the social sciences and some drawn from the sciences. Chapter 10 has already provided you with guidelines for reading social sciences; here you learn those appropriate for reading science and other technical material. You will want to use both sets of guidelines to get the most from your reading in this chapter.

Specific Strategies

* **Read slowly.** Technical material tends to be very detailed. It requires one, or even several, slow readings. How fast you read something should be determined partly by your purpose for reading. If you are reading material for pleasure, you can go rapidly and skip parts that don't interest you. If, however, your intention is to learn the material and to read for study purposes, you must slow down. Your familiarity with the subject will also influence your reading rate. If you bring a great deal of knowledge to a particular reading assignment, you can read at a faster pace than if you bring little or no background information.

* **Preview the material before you begin to read for details.** This strategy is important for all types of reading. You should always become acquainted with the general outline of the topic before

you begin to read in depth. Try to learn from your preview what aspects of a particular topic are going to be discussed in the chapter or article. As part of the preview, you should at least think about the following:

1. The title
2. Major subheadings
3. Introductory and concluding paragraphs
4. Question at the end of the chapter
5. Charts or diagrams within the chapter or article and the explanations accompanying them.

When you have finished previewing, you should be able to identify the concepts that the author will discuss.

* **Learn the specialized terminology.** Every field has a specialized vocabulary, and some words take on different meanings in different fields. For instance, if you are learning strategies for building your vocabulary, the word *root* has one meaning; this meaning is totally different if you are studying dental technology. A number of new terms often appear within a single article or chapter. You need to understand and memorize them. To help you with this terminology, do some of the following:

1. Check the context (the sentences surrounding the new term) to see whether the meaning has been supplied for you directly within the text.
2. If you are working with a textbook, check its glossary for a precise definition if one is not supplied in the context.
3. Try to use the word in class to verify your understanding.
4. Notice how your professor uses the term.

To help with memorization of new terminology, do the following:

1. *Learn word parts.* Often, a particular field of study will have a large number of words that use the same root or prefix. In education, for instance, the words *phonics, phonemics,* and *phonetics* all have a common root and are related, but each has a different, specific meaning. Learning the meanings of the common word parts will help you determine the meanings of new words of similar origin.

2. *Create flash cards.* On the front of your card, put the word. On the back, write the meaning and use the word in a sentence. Refer to these cards frequently for review.

❋ **Study visual aids carefully.** Diagrams, graphs, and charts are frequently included in technical writing. They help clarify the text material. Be sure you understand the relationship of each part of the visual aid to each other part and that you are clear about what each set of numbers or each label on the visual aid represents. Try re-creating the diagram on your own paper.

❋ **Mentally visualize what you recall.** This strategy is especially helpful if you are reading about a process—for example, how food is digested. The picture you create in your mind will assist you with recall at a later date.

❋ **Create some of your own charts, graphs, and diagrams to show relationships discussed in the material.** This strategy encourages you to think about the connections between the different ideas. Again, the concrete visual aid will be easier to recall than the words in the text.

❋ **Look for writing patterns while you read.** Technical material is frequently organized according to one of four different pattern types:

1. *Classification* (showing groups and subgroups)
2. *Process* (how something occurs)
3. *Experimental* (steps taken to test something)
4. *Problem and solution* (usually a statement of some problem, its causes and effects, and solutions to the problem)

❋ **Use outside sources if some ideas are still unclear to you.** Specialized encyclopedias and journals, as well as young adult books, often explain complicated ideas in an easier way than that used in college textbooks. Although using outside resources takes additional study time, it may be time well spent if the assigned reading material is especially difficult for you.

❋ **Make personal connections with what you read.** Think about how you may have already observed some topic or theory you are reading about, even though you did not completely understand it at the time. Or consider how this information might affect your life.

❋ **Restate in your own words as many of the main points as you can.** Repeating in your own words what you have read verifies your understanding. This practice points out areas that you are not sure of and that you will need to reread. Practice making restatements by writing out your ideas or by discussing with a friend what you have read.

Keep these suggestions in mind as you read the following articles from health science and the helping professions.

What are some fields of health science or the helping professions that interest you?

_____

_____

What additional suggestions can you make for reading in health science or the helping professions? _____

_____

_____

_____

_____

_____

☙ SELECTION 6
Preview

Why is social work considered a *helping profession?* What are some of the qualities of successful social workers? In this article, the answers to these and other questions are provided about this important profession.

To Think About Before You Read

The director of a social service agency for the homeless, you are conducting interviews for the position of social worker at your agency. During the interview, what five questions would you ask each candidate that would let you know that person's effectiveness?

1. _____

   _____

2. _____

   _____

3. _____

   _____

4. _____

   _____

5. _____

   _____

Terms to Know Before You Read

precludes (6) rules out in advance; makes impossible

versatile [subtitle above (12) and in (13)] embracing a variety of subject fields

auspices [table, p. 464] protection or support

Central Themes of Social Work

■ BY ARMANDO T. MORALES AND
BRADFORD W. SHEAFOR

1   In simplest terms, social workers help people strengthen their inter-action with various aspects of their world—their children, parents, spouse or other loved one, family, friends, cowork-ers, or even organizations and whole com-munities. Social work is also committed to changing factors in the society that di-minish the quality of life for all people, but especially for those persons who are most vulnerable to social problems.

2   Social work's mission of serving both people and the social environment is ambi-tious. To fulfill that mission, social workers must possess a broad range of knowledge about the functioning of people and social institutions, as well as have a variety of skills for facilitating change in how individ-uals, organizations, and other social struc-tures operate. This comprehensive mission has made social work an often misunder-stood profession. Like the fable of the blind men examining the elephant with each be-lieving that the whole elephant is like the leg, trunk, ear, and so on that he examined, too often people observe one example of social work and conclude that it represents the whole of professional activity. To appre-ciate the full scope of this profession, it is useful to examine its most fundamental characteristics—the themes that character-ize social work.

THE CENTRAL THEMES UNDERPINNING SOCIAL WORK

Five themes can be identified that reflect 3 the character of social work. No one theme is unique to this profession, but in combi-nation they provide a foundation on which to build one's understanding of social workers and their practice.

A Commitment to Social Betterment

Belief in the fundamental importance of 4 improving the quality of social interaction for all people, that is, *social betterment,* is a central value of the social worker. The social work profession has taken the position that all people should have the opportunity for assistance in meeting their social needs. The source of that assistance might be family, friends, or more formal social programs.

Social work has maintained an idealism 5 about the ability and responsibility of this society to provide opportunities and re-sources that allow each person to lead a full and rewarding life. It has been particu-larly concerned with the underdog—the most vulnerable people in the society. This

From *Social Work: A Profession of Many Faces* (Needham Heights: MA: Allyn and Bacon, 1998), 28–32.

idealism must not be confused with naivete. Social workers are often the most knowledgeable people in the community about the plight of the poor, the abused, the lonely, and others who for a variety of reasons are out of the mainstream of society or experiencing social problems. When social workers express their desire for changes that contribute to the social betterment of people, it is often viewed as a threat by those to want to protect the status quo. At times criticized as "bleeding heart do-gooders," social workers would contend that if this label implies that they care for and advance the cause of the less successful members of society, they wear that label proudly.

A Goal to Enhance Social Functioning

6 The commitment to social betterment precludes a narrow focus on specific social problems. In fact, social work takes the position that social betterment involves more than addressing problems—it also involves assisting those who want to improve some aspect of their lives, even though it may not be considered as problematic. Social work, then, is concerned with helping people enhance their *social functioning,* that is, the manner in which they interact with people and social institutions.

7   Social workers help people and social institutions change in relation to a rapidly changing world. The technology explosion, information explosion, population explosion, and even the threat of nuclear explosion dramatically impact people's lives. Those who can readily adapt to these changes—and are not limited by discrimination due to race, cultural background, gender, age, or physical, emotional, or intellectual abilities—seldom use the services of social workers. Others who have become victims of this too rapidly changing world and its unstable social institutions, however, are likely to require professional help in dealing with this change.

An Action Orientation

Social work is a profession of doers. So- 8 cial workers are not satisfied just to examine social issues. Rather, they take action to prevent problems from developing, attack problematic situations that can be changed, and help people deal with troublesome situations that cannot be changed. To do this, social workers provide services that include such activities as individual counseling, family and group therapy, linking people to the network of services in a community, fund-raising, and even social action.

Indeed, social work is an applied science. 9 Social workers must possess considerable knowledge about people and various social groups and institutions, but the development of such knowledge is not the primary focus of their work. They borrow much of their basic knowledge from other disciplines, such as cultural anthropology, economics, political science, psychology, human physiology, and sociology. Selecting carefully from the important work of these and other disciplines, social workers merge that knowledge with their own understanding and translate it into services to people and social institutions.

An Appreciation for Human Diversity

10 To deal effectively with the wide range of individual and institutional change to which social work is committed, it has become a profession characterized by *diversity*—diversity of clientele, diversity of knowledge and skills, and diversity of services provided. In addition, social workers themselves come in all shapes, colors, ages, and descriptions.

11 Social workers view diversity as positive. They consider human difference desirable and appreciate the richness that can be offered a society through the culture, language, and traditions of various ethnic, racial, and cultural groups. They value the unique perspectives of persons of different gender, sexual orientation, or age groups, and they recognize and develop the strengths of persons who have been disadvantaged. What's more, social workers view their own diversity as an enriching quality that has created a dynamic profession that can respond to human needs in an ever-changing world.

A Versatile Practice Perspective

12 The wide range of human problems with which social workers deal, the variety of settings in which they are employed, the extensive scope of services they provide, and the diverse populations they serve make it unrealistic to expect that a single practice approach could adequately support social work practice. Rather, the social worker must have a comprehensive repertoire of knowledge and techniques that can be used to meet the unique needs of individual clients and client groups.

13 The versatile social worker, then, must have a solid foundation of knowledge about the behavior of people and social institutions in order to understand the situations their clients bring to them. He or she also needs to understand that differing beliefs may affect the way people will interpret and react to those situations. And, finally, the social worker must have mastered a number of helping techniques from which he or she can imaginatively select and skillfully use to help individuals, families, groups, organizations, and communities improve their social functioning.

14 How do these themes affect social work practice? The following case example* is just one of many situations where a social worker might help a client:

15 Karoline Truesdale, a school social worker, interviewed Kathy and Jim Swan in anticipation of the Swans' oldest son, Danny, beginning school in the fall. The Swans responded to Ms. Truesdale's invitation to the parents of all prospective kindergartners to talk over any concerns they might have about their children's schooling. When making the appointment, Kathy Swan indicated that her son, Danny, was near the cut-off age for entering school and may not be ready yet for kindergarten. When questioned further, Kathy expressed considerable ambivalence indicating that having him in a school would help to relieve other

*Sonia Nornes and Bradford W. Sheafor originally developed this case material for the Fort Collins (Colorado) Family Support Alliance.

READING

burdens at home, but may be too much for Danny.

16 Karoline's notes from the interview contained the following information:

17 Kathy Swan is 20 years old and about to deliver her third child. She indicates that they certainly did not need another mouth to feed at this time, but "accidents happen" and she will attempt to cope with this additional child when it is born (although she already appears physically and emotionally depleted). Jim is 21 years old and holds a temporary job earning minimum wage. He moved the family to the city because "money in agriculture has gone to hell" and a maintenance job was available at a manufacturing plant here. However, he was laid off after three months when the plant's workforce was reduced. Jim is angry that he moved the family for this job, yet the company felt no obligation to keep him on. He stated that "people in the country don't treat others like that." He is also worried that his temporary job will last only a few more weeks and commented that Kathy "spends money on those kids like it was going out of style." Jim said in no uncertain terms that he did not want and they could not afford another baby, but Kathy had refused to even consider an abortion.

18 The children are quite active and Danny pays little attention to Kathy's constant requests that he calm down. When Jim attempts to control Danny, Kathy accuses him of being too physical in his discipline. When questioned about this, Jim reported that his Dad "beat me plenty and that sure got results." Kathy complains that Jim does not appreciate the difficulty of being home with the children all of the time, and she objects to the increasing amount of time he is away in the evenings. Jim replied rather pointedly that "it is not much fun being at home anymore." Tension between Kathy and Jim was evident.

19 When questioned about their social contacts since moving to the city, both Kathy and Jim reported that it had been hard to make friends. They knew "everyone in town" before they moved, but it is different now. With his changing employment, Jim has not made any real friends at work, and Kathy feels isolated at home since Jim takes the car to work each day and the bus is her only means of transportation. She did indicate that one neighbor has been friendly, and they have met two couples they liked at church.

20 When asked specifically about Danny, Kathy reported that he has been ill frequently with colds and chronic ear infections. She hesitantly described his behavior as troublesome and hoped the school's structure would help him. Kathy described a Sunday school teacher who called him hyperactive and suggested that she not take him to Sunday school anymore. Kathy wondered if there was some kind of treatment that would help Danny and allowed that she was "about at the end of her rope with that child."

21   It was clear to Karoline that both Kathy and Jim wanted Danny to begin school. But was Danny ready for school—and would the school be ready for Danny? Would Danny's entering school be best for him? Would it resolve the family's problems? Are there other things that could be done to help this family and, perhaps, prevent other problems from emerging?

22   Within the strict definition of her job, Ms. Truesdale could assist the Swans in reaching a decision about school attendance and complete her service to this family. With her "social betterment" concern, however, resolution of only the question about Danny entering school would not be sufficient. As a social worker, Karoline would hope to help the Swan family address some of the more basic issues they face in order to improve the overall quality of their lives.

23   Social workers are not experts on all problems clients may experience. Ms. Truesdale's experience, for example, would not prepare her to make judgments about Danny's health and the possible relationship between his chronic colds and ear infections and his behavior problems. She might refer the Swans to a low-cost medical clinic where a diagnosis of Danny's health problems can be made. She is, however, an expert in *social functioning* and can help Jim and Kathy Swan work on their parenting skills, strengthen the quality of their communication, assist them in developing social relationships in the community, and

perhaps, help Jim obtain job training and stable employment. Karoline's "action orientation" would not allow her to procrastinate. She would be anxious to engage this family in assessing the issues it faces and would support Kathy and Jim as they take action to resolve them.

24   The Swan family represents at least one form of "human diversity." They are a rural family attempting to adapt to an urban environment. Ms. Truesdale knows that it will take time and probably some help to make this adjustment. She will explore strengths that may have been derived from their rural background. Perhaps Jim's skills in gardening and machinery repair would prove to be an asset in some lines of employment. Also, their rural friendliness may prove beneficial in establishing new social relationships, and they might be helped to build friendships through their church or neighborhood, or to use other resources where they can find informal sources of support (i.e., natural helping).

25   Service to the Swan family will require considerable practice "versatility." Ms. Truesdale will need to assist the family in problem solving around whether or not to send Danny to school. She will hopefully engage them in more in-depth family counseling. She might invite them to join a parents' group she leads to discuss child-rearing practices, link them with medical and psychological testing services for Danny, and help Mr. Swan obtain job training. If Danny does attend school next year, Karoline might work closely with his teacher and Mrs. Swan to monitor Danny's

progress and address any problems in his social functioning that may arise. If he does not attend school, an alternative program might be found where he can develop the socialization skills required in the classroom. Clearly, a wide range of practice activities would be needed and Karoline must be versatile in her practice to apply them.

Evaluation of the Article

Difficulty rating □ 1 □ 2 □ 3 □ 4 □ 5
(1 = easy; 5 = difficult)

What reading difficulties did you encounter? _____

_____

How did you handle these difficulties? _____

_____

Postreading Comprehension Development

Rewriting Sentences

To check your understanding of some of the key concepts of this essay, rewrite each of the following sentences in your own words, keeping the original idea. (See Chapter 1.)

1. This comprehensive mission has made social work an often misunderstood profession. (2)

   _____

   _____

2. When social workers express their desire for changes that contribute to the social betterment of people, it is often viewed as a threat by those who want to protect the status quo. (5)

   _____

   _____

3. Within the strict definition of her job, Ms. Truesdale could assist the Swans in reaching a decision about school attendance and complete her service to this family. (22)

_____

_____

Authors' Main Idea

1. The main idea expressed in this article is that

    _____a. social workers are not paid enough for the work they do.

    _____b. the work of social workers demonstrates their commitment to improving society.

    _____c. social workers are in a profession that puts them in a variety of settings where they must make difficult decisions.

    _____d. the themes underlying the practice of social work show that social workers must know their communities and the people and institutions in them.

2. What kind of information do the authors give the reader to develop this main idea?

_____

_____

Inferences, Metaphors, and Vocabulary in Context

1. Check each statement with which you think the authors would agree. Be prepared to justify your answers.

    _____a. Social workers believe family members have responsibilities to each other.

    _____b. Social workers usually help wealthy people.

_____c. Social workers would like to see better conditions for homeless individuals.

_____d. Social workers do not deal with job training and unemployment issues.

_____e. Social workers formulate theories about helping people that others can put into action.

_____f. Social workers typically work with only one type of population—for example, the homeless or abused children.

2. The authors describe Truesdale's visit to Kathy and Jim in order to

_____a. give the reader an inside view of a social worker's job.

_____b. show how difficult life can be for families with few resources.

_____c. explain the complex issues of when to send children to school.

_____d. suggest that couples use some form of birth control.

3. Which of the following can be inferred from paragraph 15? Be prepared to justify your answer.

_____a. Kathy wasn't sure the school would accept Danny at such a young age.

_____b. Administrators at Danny's school feel some parents are anxious when their children start kindergarten.

_____c. Truesdale felt that visiting this family was going to be a waste of her time.

_____d. Danny was looking forward to starting school.

4. Which of the following can be inferred from paragraph 17? Be prepared to justify your answer.

_____a. Kathy wanted the new baby a great deal.

_____b. Jim thought having this new baby would help his marriage.

     _____c. Danny was looking forward to having a baby in the house.

     _____d. Neither Jim nor Kathy really wanted the new baby.

5. Why do you think the author uses the term *ambitious* when referring to the social worker's mission?

    _____

    _____

6. The purpose of paragraph 22 is apparently to

     _____a. show how Truesdale arrived at the decision that Danny should go to school.

     _____b. discuss the factors that Truesdale had to consider before suggesting a resolution to the issue of Danny's school entrance.

     _____c. explain how Truesdale would work within the strict definition of her job.

     _____d. show the complexity of Truesdale's job.

7. The authors' tone in paragraph 24 is

     _____a. factual.

     _____b. optimistic.

     _____c. curious.

     _____d. argumentative.

8. Using only the context, define each of the following words. Do not use a dictionary.

    a. diminish (1)_____

    b. comprehensive (2) _____

    c. contend (5) _____

    d. dynamic (11) _____

    e. prospective (15) _____

f. ambivalence (15) _____

g. depleted (17) _____

Recalling Details

1. In your own words, explain how each trait contributes to being an effective social worker.

   a. A commitment to social betterment

   _____

   _____

   b. A goal to enhance social functioning

   _____

   _____

   c. An action orientation

   _____

   _____

   d. An appreciation for human diversity

   _____

   _____

   e. A versatile practice perspective

   _____

   _____

2. What are some new ideas about being a social worker that you have learned from this article? _____

   _____

3. What are five conclusions that you can draw from the information in the table on page 464? List each and be prepared to provide evidence for them.

a. _____

b. _____

c. _____

d. _____

e. _____

Critical Thinking: Reaction and Discussion

1. Return to the interview questions you created before you read this article. Which questions would you keep? What others would you add?

2. Look at a newspaper's classified ads for social workers. What qualifications are required? In what ways do these reflect the job requirements evident in this article? In what types of settings are social workers being employed?

3. Discuss the quotation below, especially with reference to the activities of social workers as you understand them from the description of Truesdale's experience.

There can be hope only for a society which acts as one big family, and not as many separate ones.

—Anwar al-Sadat, *In Search of Identity: An Autobiography* (New York: Harper and Row, 1978).

Using Technology for Further Understanding

Think about the five themes of social work that were presented in this article. Then find a piece of music, either a song or instrumental, that you believe reflects one of the themes. Be prepared to explain your choice to others.

CHARACTERISTICS OF BACCALAUREATE-, MASTER'S-, AND DOCTORAL-LEVEL SOCIAL WORKERS

Social Worker Characteristic	BSW	MSW	DSW
Gender: Female	89.7%	78.5%	58.5%
Minority Group Member	13.7	11.3	13.6
Annual Income from Full-Time Employment			
Less than $15,000	10.0	1.4	1.0
$1500 to $19,999	20.1	2.6	0.4
$20,000 to $29,999	46.4	26.6	8.3
$30,000 to $39,999	16.6	38.0	25.5
$40,000 or more	6.8	31.5	64.7
Primary Employment Setting			
Social services agency	33.7	20.5	10.1
Health/mental health facility (hospital and outpatient)	26.6	38.9	20.0
Residential care facility	21.1	6.4	2.2
School (preschool through grade 12)	3.8	7.1	3.2
Private practice	3.1	20.2	24.1
Courts/justice system	2.6	3.9	0.6
College/university	2.6	2.6	37.2
Other	6.3	3.0	2.5
Primary Auspices of Employment			
Federal/state/local government	41.6	33.0	41.0
Private (nonprofit) agency	40.4	38.6	31.6
Private (for-profit) agency	18.1	28.3	27.5
Primary Practice Area			
Children-families	29.2	24.9	19.6
Mental health	18.3	39.6	40.7
Medical health	17.0	13.2	7.7
Aging	16.7	4.2	3.7
Schools	2.6	5.4	4.1
Criminal justice	2.5	1.1	1.1
Other	13.2	10.8	22.2
Primary Job Function			
Clinical/direct service	65.5	71.1	40.4
Administration/management	10.6	15.7	16.7
Teaching/training	5.9	2.8	32.1
Supervision	4.6	5.7	2.3
Other	13.5	4.2	8.4

Source: Margaret Gibelman and Philip H. Schervish, *Who We Are: A Second Look* (Washington, D.C.: NASW Press, 1997), pp. 54, 59, 71, 86, 103, 114, and 134. Taken from Morales and Sheafor, p. 45.

⚱ SELECTION 7
Preview

This article introduces you to the discovery and development of one of the most important medical procedures of modern medicine. While you read it, think about how your life or the lives of others you know might have been affected if X-ray procedures were not available.

To Think About Before You Read

Think about a technology-based product that you use and that has undergone changes since you began using it, such as the television, computer, telephone, or radio. How has this product changed? How have the changes affected you or aspects of your life? Write your response in an essay of five to seven paragraphs.

Term to Know Before You Read

conduction (1) transmission through or by means of a conductor; the transfer of heat through matter by communication of kinetic energy from particle to particle, with no net displacement of the particles

X-Rays: Their Discovery and Development

■ BY STEWART C. BUSHONG

DISCOVERY OF X-RAYS

1 X-rays were not developed; they were discovered, quite by accident. During the 1870s and 1880s many university physics laboratories were involved in the investigation of the conduction of cathode rays, or electrons, through a large, partially evacuated glass tube known as a Crookes tube. Sir William Crookes was an Englishman from a rather humble background who was a self-taught genius. The tube that bears his name was the forerunner of modern fluorescent lamps and neon sign–type lamps. There were many different types of Crookes tubes; the majority of them were capable of producing x-rays.

2 On November 8, 1895, Roentgen was working in his laboratory at Würzburg University in Germany. He had darkened his laboratory and completely enclosed his Crookes tube with black photographic paper so that he could better visualize the effects of the cathode rays in the tube. A plate coated with barium platinocyanide, a fluorescent material, happened to be lying on a bench top several feet from the Crookes tube. No visible light escaped from the Crookes tube because of the black paper enclosing it. But Roentgen noted that the barium platinocyanide fluoresced regardless of its distance from the Crookes tube. The intensity of fluorescence increased as the plate was brought closer to the tube; consequently, there was little doubt about the origin of the stimulus for fluorescence. Roentgen's immediate approach to investigating this "X-light," as he called it, was to interpose various materials—wood, aluminum, his hand—between the Crookes tube and the fluorescing plate. He feverishly continued these investigations for several weeks.

3 There are several amazing features about the discovery of x-rays that cause it to rank high in the events of human history. First, the discovery was quite by accident. Second, probably no fewer than a dozen contemporaries of Roentgen had previously observed x-radiation, but none of these other physicists had recognized its significance or investigated it. Third, Roentgen followed his discovery with such scientific vigor that within little more than a month he had ascribed to x-radiation nearly all the properties recognized today. His initial investigation was extremely thorough, and he was able to report his experimental results to the scientific community before the end of 1895. For this work he received in 1901 the first Nobel prize in physics. Finally,

From *Radiologic Science for Technologists: Physics, Biology, and Protection*, 5th ed. (St. Louis: Mosby, 1993), 7–11.

Roentgen recognized the value of his discovery to medicine. He produced and published the first medical x-ray, one of his wife's hand.

DEVELOPMENT OF MODERN RADIOLOGY

4 There are two general types of x-ray procedures: radiographic examinations and fluoroscopic examinations. Radiographic examinations employ x-ray film and usually an x-ray tube mounted from the ceiling on a track that allows the tube to be moved in any direction. Such examinations provide the radiologist with fixed photographic images. Fluoroscopic procedures are usually conducted with an x-ray tube located under the examining table. The radiologist is provided with moving, or dynamic, images portrayed on a fluoroscopic screen or television monitor. There are many variations of these two basic types of examinations, but in general the x-ray equipment is similar. Although the x-ray equipment used today is quite sophisticated, there have not been many basic changes since Roentgen's time.

5 To produce a satisfactory x-ray, one must supply the x-ray tube with a high voltage and a sufficient electric current. X-ray voltages are measured in kilovolts peak (kVp). One kilovolt (kV) is equal to 1000 V of electric potential. X-ray currents are measured in milliamperes (mA), where the ampere (A) is a measure of electric current. Normal household current is a few amperes. The prefix kilo stands for 1000; the prefix milli, for 1/1000, or 0.001. Today,

voltage and current are supplied to an x-ray tube through rather complicated electric circuits, but in Roentgen's time simple static generators were all that were available. These units could only provide currents of a few milliamperes and voltages to perhaps 50 kVp.

Radiographic procedures employing 6 equipment with these limitations of electric current and potential often required exposure times of 30 or more minutes for a satisfactory examination. One development that helped reduce this exposure time was the use of a fluorescent intensifying screen in conjunction with the glass photographic plates. Michael Pupin is said to have demonstrated the technique in 1896, but only several years later did it receive adequate recognition and use. Radiographs during Roentgen's time were made by exposing a glass plate with a layer of photographic emulsion coated on one side. Charles L. Leonard found that by exposing two glass x-ray plates with the emulsion surfaces together, exposure time was reduced and the image was considerably enhanced. This demonstration of double emulsion radiography was conducted in 1904, but double-emulsion film did not become commercially available until 1918.

During World War I, radiologists began 7 to make use of film rather than glass plates. Much of the high-quality glass used in radiography came from Belgium and other European countries. This supply was interrupted during World War I. The demands of the army for increased radiologic services made a substitute for the glass plate necessary. The substitute base for the photographic emulsion was cellulose nitrate. It quickly became apparent that the substitute was better than the original.

8 The fluoroscope was developed in 1898 by the American inventor Thomas A. Edison. Edison's original fluorescent material was barium platinocyanide, a widely used laboratory material. He investigated the fluorescent properties of over 1800 other materials, including zinc cadmium sulfide and calcium tungstate, two materials in use today. There is no telling what further inventions Edison might have developed had he continued his x-ray research, but he abandoned it when his assistant and longtime friend, Clarence Dally, suffered a severe x-ray burn that eventually required amputation of both arms. Dally died in 1904 and is counted as the first x-ray fatality in the United States.

9 Two devices designed to reduce the exposure of patients to x-rays and thereby minimize the possibility of x-ray burn were introduced before the turn of the century by a Boston dentist, Dr. William Rollins. Dr. Rollins used x-rays to visualize teeth and found that restricting the x-ray beam with a sheet of lead having a hole in the center, a diaphragm, and inserting a leather or aluminum filter improved the diagnostic quality of his radiographs. This first application of collimation and filtration was followed very slowly by general adoption of these techniques. It was later recognized that these devices reduce the hazard that is associated with the application of x-rays.

10 Two developments that occurred at approximately the same time transformed the use of x-rays from a novelty in the hands of a few physicians and physicists into a valuable, large-scale medical specialty. In 1907 H. C. Snook introduced a substitute high-voltage power supply, an interrupterless transformer, for the static machines and induction coils then in use. Although the Snook transformer was far superior to these other devices, its capability greatly exceeded the capacity of the Crookes tube. It was not until the introduction of the Coolidge tube that the Snook transformer was widely adopted.

11 The type of Crookes tube that Roentgen used in 1895 had existed for a number of years. Although some modifications were made by x-ray workers, it remained essentially unchanged into the second decade of the twentieth century. After considerable clinical testing, William D. Coolidge unveiled his hot-cathode x-ray tube to the medical community in 1913. It was immediately recognized as far superior to the Crookes tube. It was a vacuum tube and allowed x-ray intensity and energy to be selected separately and with great accuracy. This had not been possible with gas-filled tubes, which made standards for techniques difficult to obtain. X-ray tubes in use today are refinements of the Coolidge tube.

12 The era of modern radiography is dated from the matching of the Coolidge tube with the Snook transformer; only then did acceptable levels of kVp and mA become possible. Few developments since that time

have had such a major influence on diagnostic radiology. In 1921 the Potter-Bucky grid, which greatly increased image contrast, was developed. In 1946 the light amplifier tube was demonstrated at the Bell Telephone Laboratories. This device was adapted for fluoroscopy by 1950. Today, image-intensified fluoroscopy is commonplace. Each recent decade has seen remarkable improvement in diagnostic imaging: diagnostic ultrasound appeared in the 1960s; positron emission tomography (PET) and x-ray combined tomography (CT) were developed in the 1970s; and magnetic resonance imaging (MRI) became an accepted modality in the 1980s.

REPORTS OF RADIATION INJURY

13 The first x-ray fatality in the United States occurred in 1904. Unfortunately, radiation injuries occurred fairly frequently in the early years. These injuries usually took the form of skin damage (sometimes severe), loss of hair, and anemia. Physicians and, more commonly, patients were afflicted, primarily because of the long exposure time required for an acceptable radiograph and the low energy of radiation that was available at the time.

14 By about 1910 these acute injuries began to be controlled as the biologic effects of x-radiation were scientifically investigated and reported. With the introduction of the Coolidge tube and the Snook transformer, the frequency of reports of injuries to superficial tissues decreased. Years later it was discovered that radiologists were developing blood disorders such as aplastic ane-

mia and leukemia at a much higher rate than other physicians. Because of these observations, protective devices and apparel, such as lead gloves and aprons, were developed for use by radiologists. X-ray workers were routinely observed for any effects of their occupational exposure and were provided with personnel radiation-monitoring devices. This attention to radiation safety in radiology has resulted in the disappearance of reports of any type of radiation effect on x-ray workers. Radiology is now considered a completely safe occupation.

15 Today the emphasis on radiation control in diagnostic radiology has shifted back to protection of the patient. Current studies suggest that even the low doses of x-radiation employed in routine diagnostic procedures may result in a small incidence of latent harmful effects. It is also well established that the human fetus is highly sensitive to x-radiation early in pregnancy. This sensitivity decreases as the age of the fetus increases. There is also concern that even low levels of radiation exposure may produce harmful genetic results.

16 It is hoped that this introduction has emphasized the importance of providing adequate protection for both radiologic technologist and patient. As you progress through your training in radiologic technology, you will quickly learn how to operate your x-ray equipment safely, with minimal radiation exposure, by adhering to certain standard techniques and procedures. One caution is in order early in your training: after having worked with x-ray machines for a period of time, you will

become so familiar with your work environment that you may become complacent about radiation control. Do not allow yourself to develop this attitude, because it can lead to an accidental overexposure.

Evaluation of the Article

Difficulty rating ☐ 1 ☐ 2 ☐ 3 ☐ 4 ☐ 5
(1 = easy; 5 = difficult)

What reading difficulties did you encounter? _____ _____ _____

_____

How did you handle these difficulties?_____

_____

Postreading Comprehension Development

Rewriting Sentences

To check your understanding of some of the key concepts of this essay, rewrite each of the following sentences in your own words, keeping the original idea. (See Chapter 1.)

1. The tube that bears his name was the forerunner of modern fluorescent lamps and neon sign–type lamps. (1)

   _____

   _____

2. Radiographic procedures employing equipment with these limitations of electric current and potential often required exposure times of 30 or more minutes for a satisfactory examination. (6)

   _____

   _____

3. Two devices designed to reduce the exposure of patients to x-rays and thereby minimize the possibility of x-ray burn were introduced before the turn of the century by a Boston dentist, Dr. William Rollins. (9)

_____

_____

Author's Main Idea

1. What is the topic of this article?

_____

2. What is the author's focus on this topic?

_____

3. In the space provided, state the author's main idea.
   The author wants me to understand that _____

   _____

   _____

   _____

4. What kind of information does the author give the reader to develop this main idea?

   _____

   _____

5. How does the author's organization of information help accomplish his purpose for writing this article?

   _____

   _____

Inferences, Metaphors, and Vocabulary in Context

1. Which of the following does the author imply in paragraph 1? Be prepared to justify your answer.

    _____a. Sir William Crookes worked in a university physics lab.

    _____b. Few Crookes tubes would have caused the same result for Roentgen.

    _____c. Wilhelm Roentgen worked in a university physics lab.

    _____d. Crookes and Roentgen worked together.

2. What are two inferences about Roentgen's personality that you can draw from this article? For each, cite supporting evidence.

    a. Inference:_____

       Evidence: _____

    b. Inference:_____

       Evidence: _____

3. Using only the context, define each of the following words. Do not use a dictionary.

    a. forerunner (1) _____

    b. interpose (2) _____

    c. contemporaries (3) _____

    d. emulsion (6) _____

    e. enhanced (6) _____

    f. novelty (10) _____

    g. commonplace (12) _____

    h. modality (12) _____

    i. latent (15) _____

4. Which of the following does the author imply in paragraph 11? Be prepared to justify your answer.

_____a. The medical community is reluctant to make changes in how things are done.

_____b. Prior to 1913, x-ray equipment was not very precise.

_____c. William Coolidge was a secretive person.

_____d. William Coolidge was in a rush to get his findings out to the medical community.

5. What conclusion can you draw about the adequacy of Roentgen's original x-ray equipment design? Cite evidence for your conclusion.

Conclusion: _____

_____

Evidence: _____

_____

6. Write a paragraph (five to seven sentences) in which you agree or disagree with the following statement. Use information from this article to support your ideas.

Scientists use a combination of logic and imagination in their work.

Recalling Details

1. Why does the author refer to Roentgen's discovery of x-rays as an "accident"?

_____

_____

_____

2. List three improvements made to radiographic procedures since Roentgen's original discovery. Note the value of each discovery in the space provided.

   a. Improvement: _____

      Value: _____

   b. Improvement: _____

      Value: _____

   c. Improvement: _____

      Value: _____

3. What details from this article would you use to convince someone that radiology is a safe occupation? Indicate the paragraph number where you find each detail.

_____

_____

_____

_____

_____

4. On your own or with a group, create a timeline of events that you believe are important in this article. Be prepared to explain why you believe that each event you include is significant. You should include at least ten items on your timeline.

5. Reread paragraph 3. What paragraph patterns are used? For each that you find, list the pattern and the signal words for it in the space provided below.

Pattern   Signal Words Found

_____

_____

6. Reread paragraph 7. What paragraph patterns are used? For each that you find, list the pattern and the signal words for it in the space provided below.

Pattern   Signal Words Found

_____

_____

7. Each sentence below is a detail sentence from this article. Decide whether the sentence has major (MAJ) or minor (MIN) importance in this article. Put your answer in the space provided next to each sentence.

    _____a. The first x-ray fatality in the United States occurred in 1904.

    _____b. Sir William Crookes was an Englishman from a rather humble background who was a self-taught genius.

    _____c. A plate coated with barium platinocyanide, a fluorescent material, happened to be lying on a bench top several feet from the Crookes tube.

    _____d. Although the x-ray equipment used today is quite sophisticated, there have been many basic changes since Roentgen's time.

    _____e. To produce a satisfactory x-ray, one must supply the x-ray tube with a high voltage and a sufficient electric current.

_____ f.   Dr. Rollins used x-rays to visualize teeth and found that restricting the x-ray beam with a sheet of lead having a hole in the center, a diaphragm, and inserting a leather or aluminum filter improved the diagnostic quality of his radiographs.

_____ g.   The era of modern radiography is dated from the matching of the Coolidge tube with the Snook transformer; only then did acceptable levels of kVp and mA become possible.

Critical Thinking: Reaction and Discussion

1. With a partner or a small group, identify the variety of ways in which x-rays are used today. Think of as many different occupations and activities as you can. List each and explain what the effects might be if x-rays were not available for this use.

2. Explore the career path of x-ray technicians. What specialized courses do they take? Where are these offered? What career advancement opportunities exist? Use college and local libraries as well as the Internet for information.

3. Look at an issue of the *New York Times* science section (appears on Tuesdays) or use the science section of another newspaper or weekly magazine. Find an article about a recent scientific discovery that is of interest to you. Be prepared to discuss what makes it interesting and why you think the discovery is (or is not) beneficial to humanity.

Using Technology for Further Understanding

Look at the timeline you made earlier for this reading selection. Using tools and graphics available on a computer, such as drawing tools and clip art, make your timeline more elaborate. Add any details not on your original timeline that you feel will enhance your visual.

SELECTION 8

Preview

In the last few years, gun control has been discussed by nearly everyone, and Congress has passed a number of bills addressing this subject. In this article, we get one person's view that may be somewhat different from others you have heard.

To Think About Before You Read

Consider the question raised in the title of this essay. What do you think? Write your ideas in an essay of at least 250 words.

Term to Know Before You Read

empirical (17) experimental; hypothetical; something to be researched

Will More Guns Mean Less Crime?

■ BY JOHN R. LOTT JR.

1   American culture is a gun culture—not merely in the sense that 75 to 86 million people own a total of about 200 to 240 million guns, but in the broader sense that guns pervade our debates on crime and are constantly present in movies and the news. How many times have we read about shootings, or how many times have we heard about tragic accidental gun deaths—bad guys shooting innocent victims, bad guys shooting each other in drug wars, shots fired in self-defense, police shootings of criminals, let alone shooting in wars? We are inundated by images through the television and the press. Our kids are fascinated by computer war games and toy guns.

2   So we're obsessed with guns. But the big question is: What do we really know? How many times have most of us actually used a gun or seen a gun being used? How many of us have ever seen somebody in real life threatening somebody else with a gun, witnessed a shooting, or seen people defend themselves by displaying or firing guns?

3   The truth is that most of us have very little firsthand experience with using guns as weapons. Even the vast majority of police officers have never exchanged shots with a suspect. Most of us receive our images of guns and their use through television, film, and newspapers.

4   Unfortunately, the images from the screen and the newspapers are often unrepresentative or biased because of the sensationalism and exaggeration typically employed to sell news and entertainment. While news stories sometimes chronicle the defensive uses of guns, such discussions are rare compared to those depicting violent crime committed with guns. Since in many defensive cases a handgun is simply brandished, and no one is harmed, many defensive uses are never even reported to the police. I believe that this underreporting of defensive gun use is large, and this belief has been confirmed by the many stories I received from people across the country after the publicity broke on my original study in the *Journal of Legal Studies*.

5   If national surveys are correct, 98% of the time that people use guns defensively, they merely have to brandish a weapon to break off an attack. Such stories are not hard to find: pizza deliverymen defend themselves against robbers, carjackings are thwarted, robberies at automatic teller machines are prevented, and numerous armed robberies on the streets and in stores are foiled, though these do not receive the na-

From *Consumer's Research* (December 1998): 18–22.

tional coverage of other gun crimes. Yet the cases covered by the news media are hardly typical; most of the encounters reported involve a shooting that ends in a fatality. Indeed, some conventional wisdom claims that the best approach is not to resist attack. According to a recent *Los Angeles Times* article, "'active compliance' is the surest way to survive a robbery. Victims who engage in active resistance . . . have the best odds of hanging on to their property. Unfortunately, they also have much better odds of winding up dead."

6   While resistance is generally associated with higher probabilities of serious injury to the victim, not all types of resistance are equally risky. By examining the data provided from 1979 to 1987 by the Department of Justice's National Crime Victimization Survey, Lawrence Southwick of SUNY, Buffalo found that the probability of serious injury from an attack is 2.5 times greater for women offering no resistance than for women resisting with a gun. In contrast, the probability of women being seriously injured was almost four times greater when resisting without a gun than when resisting with a gun. In other words, the best advice is to resist with a gun, but if no gun is available, it is better to offer no resistance than to fight.

7   Men also fare better with guns, but the benefits are significantly smaller. Behaving passively is 1.4 times more likely to result in serious injury than resisting with a gun. Male victims, like females, also run the greatest risk when they resist without a gun, yet the difference is again much

smaller: resistance without a gun is only 1.5 times as likely to result in serious injury than resistance with a gun. The much smaller difference for men reflects the fact that a gun produces a smaller change in a man's ability to defend himself than it does for a woman.

8   Although usually skewed toward the dramatic, news stories do shed light on how criminals think. Anecdotes about criminals who choose victims whom they perceive as weak are the most typical. While "weak" victims are frequently women and the elderly, this is not always the case. For example, in a taped conversation with police investigators reported in *The Cincinnati Enquirer,* Darnall "Bubba" Lowery described how he and Walter "Fatman" Raglin robbed and murdered musician Michael Bany on December 29, 1995:

> 9   Mr. Lowery said on tape that he and Walter "Fatman" aglin, who is also charged with aggravated robbery and aggravated murder and is on trial in another courtroom, had planned to rob a cab driver or a "dope boy."
>
> 10   He said he gave his gun and bullets to Mr. Raglin. They decided against robbing a cab driver or drug dealer because both sometimes carried guns, he said.
>
> 11   Instead, they saw a man walking across the parking lot with some kind of musical instrument. He said as he looked out for police, Mr. Raglin approached the man and asked for money.
>
> 12   After getting the money, Mr. Raglin asked if the man's car was a stick or an

automatic shift. Then Mr. Raglin shot the man.

13 Criminals are motivated by self-preservation, and handguns can therefore be a deterrent. The potential defensive nature of guns is further evidenced by the different rates of so-called "hot burglaries," where a resident is at home when a criminal strikes. In Canada and Britain, both with tough gun-control laws, almost half of all burglaries are "hot burglaries." In contrast, the United States, with fewer restrictions, has a "hot burglary" rate of only 13%. Criminals are not just behaving differently by accident. Convicted American felons reveal in surveys that they are much more worried about armed victims than about running into the police. The fear of potentially armed victims causes American burglars to spend more time than their foreign counterparts "casing" a house to ensure that nobody is home. Felons frequently comment in these interviews that they avoid late-night burglaries because "that's the way to get shot."

14 To an economist such as myself, the notion of deterrence—which causes criminals to avoid cab drivers, "dope boys," or homes where the residents are in—is not too surprising. We see the same basic relationships in all other areas of life: when the price of apples rises relative to that of oranges, people buy fewer apples and more oranges. To the non-economist, it may appear cold to make this comparison, but just as grocery shoppers switch to cheaper types of produce, criminals switch to attacking more vulnerable prey. Economists call this, appropriately enough, "the substitution effect."

15 Deterrence matters not only to those who actively take defensive actions. People who defend themselves may indirectly benefit other citizens. Cab drivers and drug dealers who carry guns produce a benefit for cab drivers and drug dealers without guns. In the example involving "hot burglaries," homeowners who defend themselves make burglars generally wary of breaking into homes. These spillover effects are frequently referred to as "third-party effects" or "external benefits." In both cases criminals cannot know in advance who is armed.

16 The case for allowing concealed handguns—as opposed to openly carried handguns—relies on this argument. When guns are concealed, criminals are unable to tell whether the victim is armed before striking, which raises the risk to criminals of committing many types of crimes. On the other hand, with "open-carry" handgun laws, a potential victim's defense ability is readily identified, which makes it easier for criminals to choose the more vulnerable prey. In interviews with felony prisoners in 10 state correctional systems, 56% claimed that they would not attack a potential victim who was known to be armed. Indeed, the criminals in states with high civilian gun ownership were the most worried about encountering armed victims.

17 Substitutability means that the most obvious explanations may not always be correct. For example, when the February 23,

1997, shooting at the Empire State Building left one person dead and six injured, it was not New York's gun laws but Florida's—where the gun was sold—that came under attack. New York City Mayor Rudolph W. Giuliani immediately called for national gun-licensing laws. While it is possible that even stricter gun-sale regulations in Florida might have prevented this and other shootings, we might ask: Why did the gunman travel to New York and not simply remain in Florida to do the shooting? It is important to study whether states that adopt concealed-handgun laws similar to those in Israel experience the same virtual elimination of mass public shootings. Such states may also run the risk that would-be attackers will substitute bombings for shootings, though there is the same potential downside to successfully banning guns. The question still boils down to an empirical one: Which policy will save the largest number of lives?

THE NUMBERS DEBATE AND CRIME

18 Unfortunately, the debate over crime involves many commonly accepted "facts" that simply are not true. For example, take the claim that individuals are frequently killed by people they know. According to the FBI's Uniform Crime Reports, 58% of the country's murders were committed either by family members (18%) or by those who "knew" the victim (40%). Although the victims' relationship to their attackers could not be determined in 30% of the cases, 13% of all murders were committed by complete strangers.

19 Surely the impression created by these numbers has been that most victims are murdered by close acquaintances. Yet this is far from the truth. In interpreting the numbers, one must understand how these classifications are made. In this case, "murderers who know their victims" is a very broad category. A huge but not clearly determined portion of this category includes rival gang members who know each other. In larger urban areas, where most murders occur, the majority of murders are due to gang-related turf wars over drugs.

20 The Chicago Police Department, which keeps unusually detailed numbers on these crimes, finds that just 5% of all murders in the city from 1990 to 1995 were committed by nonfamily friends, neighbors, or roommates. This is clearly important in understanding crime. The list of nonfriend acquaintance murders is filled with cases in which the relationships would not be regarded by most people as particularly close: for example, relationships between drug pushers and buyers, gang members, prostitutes and their clients, bar customers, gamblers, and cabdrivers killed by their customers.

21 Claims of the large number of murders committed against acquaintances also create a misleading fear of those we know. To put it bluntly, criminals are not typical citizens. As is well known, young males from their mid-teens to mid-thirties commit a disproportionate share of crime, but even this categorization can be substantially narrowed. We know that criminals tend to have low IQs as well as atypical personalities.

For example, delinquents generally tend to be more "assertive, unafraid, aggressive, unconventional, extroverted, and poorly socialized," while nondelinquents are "self-controlled, concerned about their relations with others, willing to be guided by social standards, and rich in internal feelings like insecurity, helplessness, love (or its lack), and anxiety," as criminologists James Q. Wilson and Richard Herstein have reported. Other evidence indicates that criminals tend to be more impulsive and put relatively little weight on future events.

22   The news media also play an important role in shaping what we perceive as the greatest threats to our safety. Because we live in such a national news market, we learn very quickly about tragedies in other parts of the country. As a result, some events appear to be much more common than they actually are. For instance, children are much less likely to be accidentally killed by guns (particularly handguns) than most people think. Consider the following numbers: in 1995 there were a total of 1,400 accidental firearm deaths in the entire country. A relatively small portion of these involved children: 30 deaths involved children up to four years of age and 170 more deaths involved five- to 14-year-olds. In comparison, 2,900 children died in motor-vehicle crashes, 950 children lost their lives from drowning, and over 1,000 children were killed by fire and burns. More children die in bicycle accidents each year than die from all types of firearm accidents.

Of course, any child's death is tragic, and 23 it offers little consolation to point out that common fixtures in life from pools to heaters result in even more deaths. Yet the very rules that seek to save lives can result in more deaths. For example, banning swimming pools would help prevent drowning, and banning bicycles would eliminate bicycling accidents, but if fewer people exercise, life spans will be shortened. Heaters may start fires, but they also keep people from getting sick and from freezing to death. So, whether we want to allow pools or space heaters depends not only on whether some people may be harmed by them, but also on whether more people are helped than hurt.

Similar trade-offs exist for gun-control 24 issues, such as gun locks. As President Clinton has argued many times, "We protect aspirin bottles in this country better than we protect guns from accidents by children." Yet gun locks require that guns be unloaded, and a locked, unloaded gun does not offer ready protection from intruders. The debate is not simply over whether one wants to save lives or not; it involves the question of how many of these 200 accidental gun deaths would have been avoided under different rules versus the extent to which such rules would reduce people's ability to defend themselves. Without looking at data, one can only guess the net effects. Unfortunately, despite the best intentions, evidence indicates that child-resistant bottle caps actually have resulted in "3,500 additional poisonings of children under age five annually from [aspirin-related drugs] . . . [as] consumers have been lulled into a less-safety-conscious mode of behavior by the existence of safety caps," according to research by Kip Viscusi, of Harvard University. If President Clinton were aware of such research, he surely wouldn't refer to aspirin bottles when telling us how to deal with guns.

25 Another common argument made in favor of banning guns involves the number of people who die from guns each year: there were 17,790 homicides and 18,169 suicides in 1992 alone. Yet just because a law is passed to ban guns, it does not automatically follow that the total number of deaths will decline. Given the large stock of guns in the country, and given the difficulties the government faces in preventing other illegal items, such as drugs, from entering the country, it is not clear how successful the government would be in eliminating most guns. This raises the important question of whether the law would primarily reduce the number of guns held by law-abiding citizens. How would such a law alter the relative balance of power between criminals and law-abiding citizens?

26 Our primary questions therefore should be the following: Will allowing citizens to carry concealed handguns mean that otherwise law-abiding people will harm each other? Will the threat of self-defense by citizens armed with guns primarily deter criminals? Without a doubt, both "bad" and "good" uses of guns occur. The question isn't really whether both occur; it is, rather, Which is more important? In general, do concealed handguns save or cost lives? Even a devoted believer in deterrence cannot answer this question without examining the data, because these two different effects clearly exist, and they work in opposite directions.

27 To some, however, the logic is fairly straightforward. Philip Cook, an economist at Duke University, argues that "if you introduce a gun into a violent encounter, it increases the chance that someone will die." A large number of murders may arise from unintentional fits of rage that are quickly regretted, and simply keeping guns out of people's reach would prevent deaths. Others point to the horrible public shootings that occur not just in the United States but around the world, from Tasmania, Australia, to Dunblane, Scotland.

28 The survey evidence of defensive gun use weighs importantly in this debate. At the lowest end of these estimates, again according to Philip Cook, the U.S. Department of Justice's National Crime Victimization Survey reports that each year there are "only" 108,000 defensive uses of guns during assaults, robberies, and household burglaries. Other national polls weight regions by population and thus have the advantage, unlike the National Crime Victimization Survey, of not relying too heavily on data from urban areas. These national polls should also produce more honest answers, since a law-enforcement agency is not asking the questions. They imply much higher defensive use rates. Fifteen national polls, including those by organizations such as the *Los Angeles Times,* Gallup, and Peter Hart Research Associates, imply that there are 760,000 to

3.6 million defensive uses of guns per year. Yet even if these estimates are wrong by a very large factor, they still suggest that defensive gun use is extremely common.

29   During state legislative hearings on concealed-handgun laws, the most commonly raised concerns involved fears that armed citizens would attack each other in the heat of the moment following car accidents or accidentally shoot a police officer. The evidence shows that such fears are unfounded: although 31 states have so-called nondiscretionary concealed-handgun laws, some of them decades old, there exists only one recorded incident of a permitted, concealed handgun being used in a shooting following a traffic accident, and that involved self-defense. No permit holder has ever shot a police officer, and there have been cases where permit holders have used their guns to save officers' lives.

30   Let us return to the fundamental issue of self-protection. For many people, the ultimate concern boils down to protection from violence. Unfortunately, our legal system cannot provide people with all the protection that they desire, and yet individuals are often prevented from defending themselves. As a Chicago cabdriver recently told me: "What good is a police officer going to do me if you pulled a knife or a gun on me right now?" Nor are rural, low-crime areas immune from these concerns. Illinois State Representative Terry Deering (Democrat) noted that "we live in areas where if we have a state trooper on duty at any given time in a whole county, we feel very fortu-

nate." Some counties in downstate rural Illinois don't even have 24-hour police protection. The police cannot feasibly protect everybody all the time, and perhaps because of this, police officers are typically sympathetic to law-abiding citizens who own guns.

31   Although people with concealed handgun permits must generally view the police as offering insufficient protection, it is difficult to discern any pattern of political orientation among celebrities who have concealed-handgun permits: Bill Cosby, Cybill Shepherd, U.S. Senator Dianne Feinstein (D–Calif.), Howard Stern, Donald Trump, William F. Buckley, Arthur O. Sulzberger (chairman of *The New York Times*), union bosses, Laurence Rockefeller, Tom Selleck, Robert De Niro, and Erika Schwarz (the first runner-up in the 1997 Miss America Pageant). The reasons these people gave on their applications for permits were quite similar. Laurence Rockefeller's reason was that he carries "large sums of money"; Arthur Sulzberger wrote that he carries "large sums of money, securities, etc."; and William Buckley listed "protection of personal property when traveling in and about the city" as his reason. Some made their decision to carry a gun after being victims of crime. Erika Schwarz said that after a carjacking she had been afraid to drive at night.

32   And when *The Denver Post* asked Sen. Ben Nighthorse Campbell (R–Colo.) "how it looks for a senator to be packing heat," he responded: "You'd be surprised how

many senators have guns." Campbell said that "he needed the gun back in the days when he exhibited his Native American jewelry and traveled long distances between craft shows."

Evaluation of the Article
Difficulty rating □ 1 □ 2 □ 3 □ 4 □ 5
(1 = easy; 5 = difficult)

What reading difficulties did you encounter? _____

_____

How did you handle these difficulties?_____

_____

Postreading Comprehension Development

Rewriting Sentences

To check your understanding of some of the key concepts of this essay, rewrite each of the following sentences in your own words, keeping the original idea. (See Chapter 1.)

1. While resistance is generally associated with higher probabilities of serious injury to the victim, not all types of resistance are equally risky. (6)

   _____

   _____

2. Deterrence matters not only to those who actively take defensive actions. (15)

   _____

   _____

3. Other national polls weight regions by population and thus have the advantage, unlike the National Crime Victimization Survey, of not relying too heavily on data from urban areas. (28)

_____

_____

Author's Main Idea

1. What answer does the author give to the question raised by the title?

_____

2. What kind of information does the author give the reader to develop this main idea?

_____

3. Which paragraph most clearly states the author's main point?

   _____a. 3

   _____b. 4

   _____c. 5

   _____d. 6

Inferences, Metaphors, and Vocabulary in Context

1. Which of the following does the author imply in paragraph 6? Be prepared to justify your answer.

   _____a. Women should avoid working in unsafe environments.

   _____b. Women who work in unsafe environments should carry guns.

   _____c. Unsafe environments should be patrolled more often by local police.

_____d. There are too many unsafe environments where women work.

2. What conclusions can you draw from paragraphs 6 and 7?

_____a. Male criminals are less likely to feel threatened by men with guns than by women with guns.

_____b. Male criminals avoid confronting males who look as though they would fight back.

_____c. Male criminals are more intimidated by gun-carrying men than by gun-carrying women.

_____d. Male criminals are not intimidated by anyone, even if an intended victim has a gun.

3. How do you think the author wants the reader to feel after reading this selection? What are the reasons for your beliefs?

_____

_____

4. Using only the context, define each of the following words. Do not use a dictionary.

a. pervade (1) _____

b. inundated (1) _____

c. chronicle (4) _____

d. brandished (4)_____

e. deterrent (13) _____

f. vulnerable (14 and 16) _____

g. atypical (21) _____

h. consolation (23) _____

i. unfounded (29) _____

5. Which of the following does the author imply in paragraph 13? Be prepared to justify your answer.

   _____a. There are few burglaries in the United States as compared with other countries.

   _____b. There are fewer burglaries committed in the evening than during the day.

   _____c. Burglaries in the home happen only when the criminals know a door is unlocked.

   _____d. Burglars like to commit their crimes in the evening when they cannot be seen by passersby.

6. In paragraph 16 the author argues in favor of

   _____a. "open-carry" handgun laws.

   _____b. victims' rights.

   _____c. criminals choosing the more vulnerable prey.

   _____d. concealed handguns.

7. The author's tone throughout most of this essay is

   _____a. informative.

   _____b. persuasive.

   _____c. depressed.

   _____d. optimistic.

8. What does the phrase "conventional wisdom" (5) mean as it is used in this selection?

   _____

   _____

9. What does the phrase "hot burglary" (13) mean as it is used in this selection?

   _____

   _____

10. What does the phrase "the substitution effect" (14) mean as it is used in this selection?

    _____

    _____

Recalling Details

1. Which of the following are factual statements in this article? Which are opinions? Use (F) or (O) for your response. For those you label opinion, write any support for the opinion that is given in this article.

   _____a. We are inundated by images through the television and the press.

   _____b. So we're obsessed with guns.

   _____c. Behaving passively is 1.4 times more likely to result in serious injury than resisting with a gun.

   _____d. Criminals are motivated by self-preservation, and handguns can therefore be a deterrent.

   _____e. People who defend themselves may indirectly benefit other citizens.

   _____f. When the February 23, 1997, shooting at the Empire State Building left one person dead and six more injured, it was not New York's gun laws but Florida's—where the gun was sold—that came under attack.

   _____g. Claims of the large number of murders committed against acquaintances also create a misleading fear of those we know.

_____h. No permit holder has ever shot a police officer, and there have been cases where permit holders have used their guns to save officers' lives.

2. Indicate whether each of the following is true (T) or false (F), based on the selection. Be prepared to cite evidence for your answers.

_____a. Fewer gas station attendants would be robbed if criminals thought more of them had handguns.

_____b. Criminals like the challenge of robbing people who might have guns.

_____c. Guns are not effective as defensive weapons.

_____d. Most crime victims are murdered by close acquaintances.

_____e. The media affects our ideas about how safe we are.

_____f. We overestimate how many children are killed by guns.

_____g. The author is an economist.

3. What purpose do the statistics serve in each of the following paragraphs?

Paragraph 18 _____

Paragraph 28 _____

4. The pattern of organization used in paragraph 6 is a

_____a. simple listing and spatial.

_____b. contrast.

_____c. problem and solution.

_____d. opinion and reason.

5. The pattern of organization used in paragraph 15 is a

_____a. simple listing and spatial.

_____b. contrast.

_____c.   problem and solution.

_____d.   opinion and reason.

Critical Thinking: Reaction and Discussion

1. How has this article affected your views on gun control? Modify the essay you wrote before you read this selection, using the new information you have from reading.

2. With a group, discuss the topic of gun control. Develop three gun control laws that your group would like to see enacted in order to reduce crime. Be prepared to discuss why you think that these laws would be helpful and how they could be enforced. Note that some of the following measures that have been proposed (and, in some states, are law):

    a. A national system for registering guns and ammunition
    b. Instant background checks on people attempting to buy guns or ammunition
    c. Stiffer sentences for gun crimes
    d. Gun education
    e. General education
    f. Hand-grip ID tagging ("registering" guns to one person's palm prints)

3. With your class, prepare a debate on the following statement:

    Guns are more of a danger than a means of security.

Using Technology for Further Understanding

Use the Internet to find the legislature for your state. See if you can identify any gun control legislation that has recently been enacted or is under consideration by either your state assembly or state senate. How do you feel about the new or proposed laws?

CHAPTER THIRTEEN

Readings in the Arts

No artist is ahead of his time.
He is his time; it is just that others
are behind the time.

—Martha Graham (choreographer);
recalled on Graham's death, 1 April 1991,
in James B. Simpson,
Simpson's Contemporary Quotations
(New York: HarperCollins, 1997), 498.

Guidelines for Reading in the Arts

The products created by such artists as musicians, actors, poets, and painters are deeply personal. Each piece primarily results from the imagination and feelings of the individual artist. We often appreciate the work of art in a way that is different from how we appreciate a well-written article in a scientific journal.

Similarly, the materials that you read that are related to the arts are often the result of a writer's personal response to an art form or particular artist, rather than the more objective writing, such as data analyses, that we find in other fields. This is true whether you are reading a review of a new recording artist's CD, a critic's response to a play, or a review of an art opening at a local gallery.

The approach you take when you read material from the arts must account for these differences.

Specific Strategies

* **Keep in mind that most of what you will read will reflect the writer's personal taste.** Whether it is a critique of a play, a review of a film, or a response to a new musical composition or performer, while you read, ask yourself: What is the writer's preference? What comments are made that have given me insight into the writer's taste? While you do this, consider how the author's background has influenced his or her point of view. You may know the writer's cultural, social, or political perspective. If you do, think about how this perspective might have been different if the writer had lived during a different time or had been of a different cultural background.

* **Determine the author's perspective.** Some writing about the arts is intended to provide guidance to others. There are many "how-to" books for young actors, photographers, writers, sculptors, and singers. Each book offers suggestions for improving the art form. What is sometimes left unsaid is that each reflects a particular bias, such as a particular school of acting (the method school, for instance, or the Saint-Denis model). The introduction or preface to the book often lets you know the author's point of

view or bias about particular techniques or schools of thought. This information should guide you while you read. Find materials that also reflect different points of view so that, if necessary, you can decide the approach that would work best for you.

✳ **Make the connection between a work of art and the time or place of its creation.** Reading about the arts can help you understand a piece that seems odd to you or that you do not appreciate. Any art product that does not make sense to you—whether it's a dance, a piece of music, poetry or a play—may actually reflect the period or the culture within which it was created. It may make a social or political statement. Although some works done in the past may seem pretty conservative to you, they may have been radical for their times. For instance, an oil painting done by an American artist in 1785 that depicts a female physician might have been viewed as extremist by critics in the late 1700s, given the very small number of female physicians in the United States at that time. Some works may have cultural elements unknown to you. If you are reading about the life of a Russian composer, for instance, it would be important to know the cultural context in which the compositions were written. Those who write about the arts can help you recognize the economic, political, and other forces of a society that are important for a more complete appreciation of an artist's work. Your awareness of the period when the work of art was created will help you view, read, or listen to the work in a more informed way.

✳ **Know the criteria by which a work of art is often judged.** These long-lasting and widely held criteria have to do with composition, expression, form, image, style, and symbolism and how the artist has developed each. While you read, look for mention of these criteria and notice how they are applied to the particular area you are studying (such as painting, music, dance, theater, or film). These criteria will appear repeatedly in class discussions, and you may be asked to apply them to your own artworks. For instance, in an arts appreciation class, you will learn how to analyze, interpret, and evaluate artwork by using these criteria. Or in an art or music history class, you may study how the content of and the criteria for judging each of these elements have changed over time. You then may be asked to write a critique of a work of art and to use the same analytical framework. In a performance class, your performance may be judged according to these criteria.

❋ **Read with an open mind.** You will naturally have your personal preferences in any of the arts. You bring to your reading your own extensive experience as a critic. You know what kinds of movies you prefer; you probably have a favorite radio station that plays a particular kind of music; you might enjoy going to one kind of art museum, but not to another. When you read in the arts, you need to set your personal preferences aside for a while and to open your mind to the possibility that your own tastes will change as you learn more about different aspects of the arts and those who create them.

❋ **Be attentive to yourself and to your world.** If you are a reflective observer of your own life and the events around you, you are more likely to make connections to artistic statements made by others and to create themes of your own. As you read literature, view a painting, or listen to a musical score, it is important that you respond imaginatively to it and look for personal meaning. As you become more sensitive to your own environment and to those things in it to which you respond, you are better able to enter the artist's world and to understand the artist's point of view.

Keep these suggestions in mind as you read the following articles from social science.

What are some arts-related fields that interest you?

_____

_____

What additional suggestions can you make for reading in the arts?

_____

_____

_____

_____

☙ SELECTION 9
Preview

Are you a Ricky Martin fan? Why is he so popular right now? What has caused changes in the type of music that appeals to today's American youth? These questions are explored by the authors of this article.

To Think About Before You Read

What kind of music do you like to hear? Use the lines below to list the features of music that you feel contribute the most to your enjoyment. Under your list, write a few sentences that explain how your preferred kind of music reflects who you are.

_____

_____

_____

_____

_____

_____

_____

_____

_____

Terms to Know Before You Read

ultimatum (11) a demand

affable (26) friendly

Latin Music Pops

■ BY CHRISTOPHER JOHN FARLEY*

1
2 RIIIIICKYYYYYYYYYY!"
Outside a Tower Records store in
Manhattan, a chorus of screams is
going up. Mostly sopranos, a few altos, no
tenors and certainly no basses. "*Riiiiiick-
yyyyyyyyyyyyy!* I love you!" The crowd of
5,000, mainly young women between the
ages of *Dawson's Creek* and *Felicity* (with a
few *Rugrats* and *Ally McBeals* mixed in),
have gathered to catch a glimpse of the latest heartthrob, their *corazón.* The fans at
the front of the line enter the store and
stumble out with a signature scrawled
across a CD or on a poster or even on their
skin. Some leave crying tears of joy. At a
multiplex across the street, Fox is holding
one of the first screenings of *The Phantom
Menace.* You can see a flicker of hesitation
on the faces of a few *Phantom* ticket holders. I thought *I* was in the red-hot center,
the flicker seems to say. What's going on
over there?

3 Ricky Martin is what's going on. The
hip-shaking Latin pop star has the No. 1
song in America, *Livin' la Vida Loca.* His
self-titled new CD is setting sales records at
stores across the U.S. And Martin is at the
center of something bigger than himself. A

host of other Hispanic performers, including vocalist Marc Anthony and actress
turned pop diva Jennifer Lopez, are poised
to release highly anticipated Latin-tinged
CDs soon. Martin, in an interview with
TIME, was so euphoric over his success he
bordered on being Roberto Benigni-esque.
"What? are you kidding me?" says Martin.
"I'm flying, I'm flying!"

Ricky Martin is a fresh face, but he is not 4
an entirely new one. For 15 years now the
27-year-old singer has enjoyed a kind of
second-tier, ESPN2 level of fame: he was a
member of the teen group Menudo, he
once co-starred in *Les Misérables* on Broadway, has appeared on the ABC soap *General
Hospital.* The cultural wave Martin is riding—Latin pop—we must admit, is also
not an entirely new phenomenon. Salsa,
rumba, mambo and other Latin musical
forms have made inroads on American pop
music—Celia Cruz, Rubén Blades, Gloria
Estefan, Ritchie Valens, Los Lobos, Anto-
nio Carlos Jobim, Machito, Willie Colón,
Tito Puente and many, many others have,
for decades now, scored hits, excited
crowds and pioneered new sounds. TIME's
"discovering" Latin pop would be a bit like
Columbus discovering Puerto Rico.

What *is* new is this: As the century turns 5
to double zero, a new generation of Latin

From *Time,* 24 May 1999, 75–79.
*With reporting by David E. Thigpen and Autumn de Leon.

artists, nurtured by Spanish radio, schooled in mainstream pop, are lifting their voices in English. Of this group, Martin is the hottest; Lopez, 28, the most alluring; Anthony, 29, the most artistic. With Hispanics poised to become America's largest minority group within the next few years, this music could be the sound of your future. Latin-tinged pop is blowing up because it fits the musical times: it has a bit of the street edge of hip-hop (Lopez worked with rapper Sean ["Puffy"] Combs on one track on her CD), some of the bouncy joy of dance-pop (Martin is hunkier than all the Backstreet Boys put together) and the fizzy fresh feel of that ever sought-for thing in modern pop, the Next Big Thing.

6   "None of this could have happened 15 years ago," says producer Emilio Estefan, husband and manager of crossover trailblazer Gloria Estefan. "Gloria and I went through the hardest part. A dozen years ago, a label threw me out when I tried to use congas on a recording. They said, 'Get rid of that, and take out the horns and the timbales too.' Now people are buying records by Arturo Sandoval and Buena Vista Social Club. The younger generation is now reacting to Latin music."

7   Because Latin pop draws from different cultures, it also has the power to bring people together. "Latino people have a golden key in their hands, a common treasure," says Colombian-born pop-rocker Shakira, 22, who is working with Gloria Estefan to adapt her acclaimed 1998 Spanish-language CD *Dónde Están los Ladrones?* into English. "That treasure is fusion. The fu-

sion of rhythms, the fusion of ideas. We Latinos are a race of fusion, and that is the music we make. And so at the dawn of a new millennium, when everything is said and done, what could possibly happen besides a fusion?"

8   Puerto Rico is where it starts. It is an island inhabited by the descendants of black slaves and Spanish conquistadors; here cultures collided, rhythms intermingled, and salsa emerged, inspired by Africa and Europe and by New York City. Marc Anthony's parents hail from the island, and Jennifer Lopez, though born and raised in the Bronx, also has roots there. As for Ricky Martin, he was born in Puerto Rico, the only child of Enrique Martin, a psychologist, and Nereida Morales, an accountant (Martin's parents separated when he was two).

9   Look at Martin today, and you can tell he was a child star—he wears the spotlight like ordinary folks wear house slippers. Indeed, Martin got started early: at 12 he auditioned to join Menudo, a Latin singing group comprised of boys ages 12 to 16 whose roster rotated when members grew too old. Martin was rejected on his first try because he was too small and too young-looking. Martin tried out again. Rejected again. On the third try, he made it. It was an early sign: what Martin lacked in talent he made up for in pure doggedness. "He was small, not a big singer, and his voice was not so good then," recalls the group's manager, Edgardo Díaz. "But we thought he could learn a lot by being with the group."

10   Martin was immediately caught up in Menudo's *vida loca*. He visited Italy, Japan, Guam and Spain before he was old enough to shave. During one stretch, he and his young bandmates played for a month in Brazil (singing in Portuguese), then flew to the Philippines (singing in English) before returning to Latin America for a series of shows in Spanish. Life became a blur.

11   Not surprisingly, perhaps, Martin's home-life suffered—both his parents wanted to see more of him, and his father asked him to choose between him and his mother. Hurt and angered by the ultimatum, Martin stopped talking to his father for almost a decade. A few years ago, they reconciled.

12   Over the years reports have surfaced that the social and emotional lives of the kids in Menudo were poorly supervised, even neglected. Díaz will admit only that the group did have "problems," though he denies he was the root cause. Says Díaz: "I think a lot of problems come from the house, from the family, some of the parents the kids have." Martin, Díaz says, actually fared better than most. "Ricky had that special personality, like a charm," says Díaz. "He could handle himself."

13   In fact, Martin dreamed of breaking out of the group's constraints and setting off on his own. Producer-performer Robi Rosa recalls talking to Martin about his ambitions when they were both in Menudo: "Mainly our conversations were about life and being true and making it and doing something great."

14   After finally leaving the group at age 17, Martin embarked on a commercially successful Spanish-language solo career. He was signed by Sony, which early on saw a future in Latin pop (Anthony, Lopez and Shakira are all on various Sony labels). Says Sony Music CEO Tommy Mottola: "The heart and soul of the music will be able to break down barriers easily. It's undeniable."

15   And Martin has plenty of both. His performance of the soccer anthem *La Copa de la Vida* at the 1998 World Cup confirmed his superstar status internationally; his pelvic-swiveling rendition of the song at the Grammys earlier this year proved a breakthrough as well. He had done the impossible: he had sung about soccer in Spanish and got Americans to care. What could be harder? A French-language ode to cricket? At the Grammys, Beck stood and clapped. Madonna signed on for a duet. Martin's stateside career was launched. Several publishers, including HarperCollins and St. Martin's, are already rushing out books on him.

16   "A lot of people say, 'Well, why English, why do you want to do it in the States?'" says Martin. "It's all about communicating. The last album [*Vuelve*] did really good, to be quite honest—I want to be humble about this—all over the world. One of the songs was No. 1 in 22 countries. And it was in Spanish. So I didn't *have* to go to English to make it."

17   But his timing—and we're trying to be humble about this too—was perfect. Spanish-language radio is booming, and it has proven to be a terrific launching pad for Latin crossover artists. Today Spanish-

language FM stations are top rated in New York City and Los Angeles. "Music has a stronger connection with Hispanics than with other groups," says Cary Davis, general manager for New York City's La Mega 97.9. "In a sense you have a double hit with Hispanics: it's good music, but it also takes you back to your culture."

18 Spanish-language radio hasn't always received its due from advertisers. Early this year, a study sponsored by the Federal Communications Commission found that advertisers who spend $1 per listener for general-market stations pay only 78¢ on comparably rated minority-formatted stations. Report author Kofi Ofori says he also found that 91% of minority-radio broadcasters had run into advertisers who had instructions not to buy time on urban or Spanish-language stations. A sales manager for a Spanish-language station is quoted in the report as saying that an account supervisor for a major car manufacturer told him, "We're wasting our time here . . . You know Hispanics don't buy or lease cars."

19 But record labels, eager for a hot new sound have started to court Latin pop stars. The death of Tejano star Selena in 1995 and the sales boom in her music that followed got many label suits thinking: If Selena can sell millions of CDs posthumously, how much money could we make with a Latin pop star who can still tour? Says Maria Zenoz, CEO of Caliente Entertainment, a New York City–based record company: "The untimely death of Selena caused the mainstream labels to take a look."

20 It's perhaps appropriate that the Latin female singer who is best positioned to grab hold of a Selena-proportioned success is the woman who portrayed her on film. Gregory Nava, director of the 1997 biopic *Selena,* cast Jennifer Lopez in the lead. The finished film used Selena's real voice for the musical sequences, but, Nava says, Lopez would sing through her scenes during the filming. The experience inspired Lopez to launch a singing career. "I did a demo in Spanish after *Selena* and submitted it to the Work label," says Lopez. "They said, 'We like it, but we want you to do it in English.'" So she did. Her album, *On the 6,* is due out June 1.

21 Enrique Iglesias, who was rejected by several major labels at the start of his career but who has since sold more than 3 million CDs worldwide, recently got a call at home from actor Will Smith, asking him to contribute a song to Smith's upcoming film *Wild Wild West.* Iglesias' English-language song *Bailamos* will be on the *Wild* sound track, and he is now considering recording a CD in English. But he says he will never leave Spanish behind. "I gotta remember something—what got me here was Spanish," says the 24-year-old Iglesias, son of crooner Julio Iglesias. "If it wasn't for my Spanish record sales, I wouldn't have these record companies after me."

22 Still, some longtime aficionados fear that the new pop Latin wave could wash away important cultural connections. Esmerelda Santiago, author of the memoir *When I Was Puerto Rican,* says the current crop of singers being pushed by the major labels

could use some skin-tone diversity. She feels the artists who are being promoted to superstardom mostly look Anglo, leaving the darker performers behind. "It's fascinating to me, and a little upsetting, that this is still the white face of the Caribbean," says Santiago. "I'm sure that there are equally talented and gifted artists out there whose facial features don't conform as much to the European ideal."

23   In a studio in Manhattan, Marc Anthony is working on his new English-language album. He is dressed simply in jeans and a white T-shirt, and his voice is ringing out, pure and direct. Sony chief Mottola sits in the control booth, listening, looking, betting on a hit. These are good days for Anthony: he recently completed work on a featured role in Martin Scorsese's film *Bringing Out the Dead,* co-starring Nicolas Cage. In a few weeks he'll begin recording a duet with neo-soul singer Maxwell. And Anthony's duet with Lopez, *No Me Ames,* is already a hit on Spanish-language radio.

24   Yet he is unsatisfied. Although Anthony knows Martin well and is good friends with Lopez, he is wary of media stories lumping them into a single group. "I don't know what they're talking about with this Latino crossover thing," he says. "I could see it if I was doing a salsa album in English. But you know what? We're not doing Latin music on our English stuff. Latin-tinged, yes."

25   Anthony says there are still many stereotypes in the media about Latin performers. The other day, he recalls, he was watching *25 Lame* (an MTV show about bad videos),

and one of the hosts kept putting on a sombrero when a video by a Latin artist came on. Anthony also feels there's not enough effort put into promoting more traditional forms of Latin music.

Anthony's own English-language album,[26] judging from an early listen, sounds extremely promising. What makes him great is his commitment to make vocal art, not simply trendy entertainment. Martin, of course, succeeds by doing the opposite. His new CD is not high art, but it is the kind of relentlessly affable confection that transcends radio formats, crosses generations and sells like crazy. Lopez, too, is well positioned. Her voice is slight, but then again, so is Madonna's. Lopez's talent lies in its diversity—she sings, she can act, and, as a former *In Living Color* "Fly Girl," she can dance. VH1 is already panting over her first video.

Trends come and go, stars wink and fade[27] out. How long will this new crop hold out? "It's impossible to predict who will be a pop star forever," says Wayne Isaak, executive vice president of music and talent for VH1. "But [Martin, Anthony and Lopez] could have a longer career than most. Even if their pop following wanes a bit, they will always have this Latin fan base that can keep them playing Madison Square Garden and working with the best producers of the day."

And no doubt Latin music will continue[28] to thrive as well. The Argentine writer Jorge Luis Borges once wrote a story about an empire so obsessed with maps that its cartographers constructed a map as large as the empire itself. Indeed, one by one,

Spanish-language stars are being mapped, represented in another form. This new map will no doubt prove useful for Anglo listeners unfamiliar with the territory. But true music lovers would be well advised to check out CDs like Anthony's *Contra la Corriente* or Elvis Crespo's *Pintame* or Shakira's *Dónde Están los Ladrones?* in addition to any Latin-tinged pop CDs they might buy. There is real ground beneath the map.

Evaluation of the Article

Difficulty rating ☐ 1 ☐ 2 ☐ 3 ☐ 4 ☐ 5
(1 = easy; 5 = difficult)

What reading difficulties did you encounter? _____

_____

How did you handle these difficulties? _____

_____

Postreading Comprehension Development

Rewriting Sentences

To check your understanding of some of the key concepts of this essay, rewrite each of the following sentences in your own words, keeping the original idea. (See Chapter 1.)

1. Ricky Martin is a fresh face, but he is not an entirely new one. (4)

   _____

   _____

2. But record labels, eager for a hot new sound, have started to court Latin pop stars. (19)

   _____

   _____

3. Still, some longtime aficionados fear that the new pop Latin wave could wash away important cultural connections. (22)

_____

_____

Author's Main Idea

1. In the space provided, state the author's main idea.
    The author wants me to understand that _____

    _____

2. What kind of information does the author give the reader to develop this main idea?

    _____

3. Which paragraph most clearly states the author's main point?

    _____a. 4

    _____b. 5

    _____c. 6

    _____d. 7

4. The author discusses Ricky Martin because he

    _____a. is a popular Latin music performer who sings in English.

    _____b. is the author's favorite singer.

    _____c. succeeded in the music industry despite tough times.

    _____d. began his career as part of Menudo.

Inferences, Metaphors, and Vocabulary in Context

1. Ricky Martin's story supports the idea that

    _____a. opportunity knocks once.

    _____b. luck, in part, is being in the right place at the right time.

    _____c. love is better the second time around.

    _____d. look before you leap.

2. The importance of Emilio Estefan's remarks in paragraph 6 is that the reader

    _____a. learns the roots of Latin music.

    _____b. is asked to sympathize with Estefan.

    _____c. realizes that Estefan expects others to be grateful to him.

    _____d. learns how attitudes toward Latin influence on music have changed.

3. In your own words, explain what is meant by *fusion* as it is discussed in paragraph 7.

    _____

    _____

4. Why is Gloria Estefan referred to as a "crossover trailblazer?" (6)

    _____

    _____

5. One similarity between Esmerelda Santiago and Marc Anthony is that

    _____a. both are concerned about the Anglicizing of Latin music.

    _____b. both refuse to sing in English.

    _____c. neither will perform with non-Latin-looking singers.

    _____d. neither approves of Ricky Martin.

6. The purpose of the statistics in paragraph 18 is to _____

   _____

7. Using only the context, define each of the following words. Do not use a dictionary.

   a. *corazón* (2) _____

   b. euphoric (3) _____

   c. nurtured (5)_____

   d. doggedness (9) _____

   e. constraints (13) _____

   f. rendition (15) _____

   g. posthumously (19) _____

   h. transcends (26) _____

8. We can conclude from the author's final paragraphs that

   _____a. he believes there is value in Spanish-only CDs.

   _____b. he believes Ricky Martin is rated too highly.

   _____c. he thinks Ricky Martin will appeal to Anglo listeners.

   _____d. true music listeners do not like Ricky Martin.

9. It is reasonable to conclude from this selection that

   _____a. Latin music will continue to be popular.

   _____b. Ricky Martin will leave singing and devote himself to acting full time.

   _____c. eventually, Latin singers will tire of singing in English and will return to Spanish.

   _____d. the music industry exploits its youngest stars.

Recalling Details

1. What evidence in this selection confirms the comments Motolla makes in paragraph 14?

   _____

   _____

2. The major pattern of organization used in paragraph 2 is

   _____a. problem and solution.

   _____b. effect.

   _____c. simple listing.

   _____d. comparison and contrast.

3. The major pattern of organization used in paragraph 4 is

   _____a. problem and solution.

   _____b. effect.

   _____c. simple listing.

   _____d. comparison and contrast.

4. What new information about Latin pop music did you gain from reading this selection?

   _____

   _____

   _____

   _____

5. What are some questions about music in America that might occur to members of other cultural groups in the United States after they read this article?

_____

_____

Critical Thinking: Reaction and Discussion

1. Conduct research on the recording industry to find out how radio stations determine which songs to play, especially songs by new artists. Report your findings to your class.

2. Listen to music from different eras or different cultures. Then write an essay of at least 250 words in which you describe some of the differences you find. They may be differences in content, form of expression, instruments used, and so on.

3. In some situations, as in the following example, music can provoke pretty strong reactions. Read the newspaper editorial that follows. Then, with a group, try to answer the author's question.

What Would You Do?

Here's a little real life morality play about suburban life and manners in sedate northern Westchester.

You pull into a gas station with your 9-year-old daughter in the back seat. At the pump across from you is a black Toyota playing the tape deck so loud it could make a car shake in Bergen County. It's typical boom box fare, thunderous, throbbing rap—not your kind of music, but it's a free country, more or less, and it takes all kinds.

But as you get out of the car to fill your tank, you realize that almost every word you can decipher is one that can't be used in this newspaper. (Indeed, it strikes you in passing as sort of an intriguing linguistic riddle—how can the artiste, whoever he may be, spew out so many verboten words in such profusion and still end up with something approximating a real sentence?)

You are not, you like to think, a totally clueless, hopeless, addled, over-the-hill, geezer fossil, but this does seem like thoroughly offensive and even provocative behavior. You wouldn't allow that music anywhere near your kids anyplace you had control of. You wouldn't consider imposing it on someone else. Should you sit quietly and live with it on a sunny Sunday at the gas station in Millwood or should you politely tell the other driver you wish he'd keep his music to himself?

Let's add a complication: the driver is black—a large black man with his shirt mostly unbuttoned in the midafternoon heat and a badge identifying him as a prison guard. You are white, and the casual encounter is taking place in a part of Westchester that will never win any awards as the diversity capital of America.

You could argue that the problem with your suburban life is that there's not enough of this—that it's a big, messy, diverse, often foul world out there and there are worse things than having your kid encounter a minor, harmless sliver of it amid the comfortable monochrome of suburbia. If the guy was implicitly or explicitly (well, let's make that explicitly) sending a signal you didn't want to hear, maybe he was onto something. You could argue that you'll be there for five minutes at the most, so it's no big deal. It's not likely a polite request will produce an instant cessation of the annoyance anyway. And what could be messier than an ugly clash at the gas pump? What good could come out of it?

Not one for confrontation, you fill up and drive on. Still, you wonder. What if the driver were white, some snotty rich kid in his dad's Land Rover? Would it be appropriate then to tell him he's welcome to his own choice of profanity but he doesn't have to share it with you? If appropriate then, why not with the Toyota? What if it were a working-class white kid, spewing forth either profane or racist garbage? What if you were black but just as offended by the X-rated rap? Would it be appropriate to speak up?

It's pretty safe to assume that in most cases, certainly in the ones focused on race, a sense of suburban politesse trumps everything else. Most people would keep their qualms to themselves and figure their daughter won't be irreparably harmed—if she's even tuning in—by a few minutes of syncopated filth. Some people, you assume, would take a welcome-to-the-real world view of the whole thing or provide standard liberal nostrums about the real obscenity being the violence all across the media, not a stream of offensive words thundering out of some prison guard's car.

You don't really think—or would not even want to think—that living in a green corner of Westchester gives you and your kids a free pass from the messiness hovering just down the road, up the alley, back in the city. Still, the moment with its wisp of race and anger stays with you like an intrusive thought that hovers in your brain.

Race, as this newspaper has been reminding us of late, remains the great divide. But it can seem an invisible one in many corners of the suburbs. It's there, of course, percolating just beneath the surface as close, it turns out, as the car at the next gas pump and the millions of questions that a brief encounter can produce.

So, dear reader, over to you. Is there a real dilemma here or just white-bread squeamishness? What would you do? Why would you do or not do it? You can reach me at Jersey@nytimes.com.

Source: *New York Times,* 23 July 2000, sect. 14, 1.

Using Technology for Further Understanding

1. Watch a video of Ricky Martin or another Latin singer. Does the video seem to suggest the Latin culture in any way? How does the video add to or detract from the music?

2. See if you can find a Web site that tells you more about Latin pop music. What else do you learn at this site about the music or those who sing it?

SELECTION 10
Preview

For performers, the audition is often the first step to employment. In this article, you learn about what needs to be considered if you hold an audition and how these preparations can affect the final outcome for both performer and director.

To Think About Before You Read

Imagine that you are a director who is planning to hold auditions for a community theater production. There are parts for several leads, male and female, as well as a number of smaller parts. Before you hold your auditions, you realize you will need to answer the following questions. Consider each and write your responses in the space provided.

1. How or where would you announce the auditions?

2. What would you do to make your actors feel comfortable during the audition?

3. How many people would read for parts at the same time?

4. What criteria would you use for selecting the actors?

5. What qualities would performers be looking for in you, to know if they want to be in your production?

_____

_____

6. How would you inform people of the outcome of their audition?

_____

_____

Terms to Know Before You Read

harried (2) disturbing; distressing

enervating (10) destroying energy or vitality

plausible (24) likely; credible

Auditions

■ BY LOUIS E. CATRON

1   Auditions are theatre's mass employment hall, bringing performers and director together under carefully designed conditions that allow performers to show their abilities and the director to evaluate whether their artistic and personal qualities will contribute to the planned production. For performers auditions are uncertain times at best, and the necessary ego involvement creates complex psychological reactions that require directors to exercise great sensitivity; a friendly and sincerely supportive attitude helps performers demonstrate their true abilities. Charged with the responsibility of conducting auditions in a manner that is both artistically effective for the production and visibly fair from the performer's view, directors may find auditions even more difficult than performers do, and their vision of the production will often seem at risk until auditions have produced a satisfactory cast.

2   Casting, which is based on directorial insights obtained during unfortunately brief and often regrettably harried auditions, determines much of the production's ultimate quality. Auditions have long-range impact

From Louis E. Catron, *The Director's Vision* (Mountain View, CA: Mayfield, 1989), 154–63.

on the tone of rehearsals, the attitudes of performers toward the director and the playscript, the interpretation of the script and production, and the director's ability to weave all portions of production into a single and cohesive whole.

3   Performers who are cast will have a number of conscious and subconscious conclusions about the director's professional abilities and interest in the cast, based on how they feel auditions are conducted. The management of auditions may even affect actor's responses to one another; poorly conducted auditions may create images of favoritism, special favors, or disregard of talent that can be burrs in actors' minds during rehearsals.

4   Auditions may also lead performers who were not cast to speak of the director or production in a way that positively or negatively influences public perception of the play. Those comments can affect ticket sales, audience expectations, and other performers' willingness to participate in future auditions conducted by that director or theatrical organization.

5   Because of the importance of auditions, all members of the theatrical staff—designers, technicians, assistants, and secretarial and office staff—must help the director make the process run as smoothly as

possible. The staff should minimize distractions; nothing should be permitted to interfere with smooth-running auditions, because the director must be free to concentrate fully on the performers, searching for those who will bring the desired personal and artistic qualities to the roles.

6   In well-rounded amateur theatres, auditions encourage those interested in technical theatre to meet with appropriate backstage personnel. This practice helps the theatre find badly needed recruits for properties, carpentry, scene painting, lighting, costumes, box office, and publicity. Educational and community theatres interested in building a core of support workers will encourage this aspect of auditions by having the technical staff present to answer questions and to show, by their presence and attitude, interest in volunteer workers. The theatre with too few volunteer workers is generally one that fails to recruit people at auditions and conveys an attitude that inexperienced volunteers are not worthy of attention.

AUDITION SYSTEMS

7 Not surprisingly there are several different audition systems. No one procedure is best for all needs. The director should select the variation that most suits the situation. As they gain experience, directors will create new methods by combining pieces from these standard systems.

General, Open

8 The general, open audition accepts all interested performers without restriction (hence "general") and takes place in an auditorium or comparably large room where all performers listen to others while waiting their turn (hence "open"). There are no reservations. The performers are called to read at least once and often repeatedly. This particular technique is popular in educational and community theatres.

Advantages.   The system allows detailed 9 communication, director to performers: If all are present at the beginning of the audition period, the director can make announcements to the assembled group, clarifying what will happen during auditions and describing essential elements of the play and characters. Open auditions allow performers to observe auditions of others, which may lead them to understand your final selection of a cast as well as allowing them insight into acting techniques. Good readings often inspire other performers to higher achievements. The open audition helps build a new stock of performers for the college or community theatre because it encourages inexperienced actors, bolstered by friends and the presence of so many others, to try out spontaneously.

Disadvantages.   The general, open system 10 is inefficient if many performers show up, and long delays can be enervating. The presence of a crowd can be distracting, and often this system creates an impersonal "cattle call" atmosphere. Good readings may produce either carbon copies or deliberate efforts to avoid imitation; neither alternative is especially desirable.

General, Closed

11 The general, closed audition system accepts all who are interested, but instead of having all performers in the room listening to others audition, the closed audition brings small groups of performers into the audition room while others wait outside in the lobby. Usually directors limit the groups to two to five actors at a time.

12 *Advantages.* The general, closed procedure has fewer distractions because the director deals with only a few performers at a time. The cattle call atmosphere is lessened, at least in the audition room itself. Further, performers' auditions are their own, not influenced by others who auditioned earlier.

13 *Disadvantages.* The general, closed audition technique is inefficient because of the time it takes each group of performers to leave and the next group to enter. Further, because directors do not see the size of the waiting crowd, they may tend to work with each group to the point that those waiting outside grow impatient and simply leave without auditioning. The closed audition does not allow performers to hear and see each other, lessening its educational value for actors. Finally the closed audition may convey a star-chamber image, which bothers some performers.

By Appointment

14 Auditions by appointment require performers to make reservations. This system is usually worked in conjunction with one or more other audition techniques. For example, to use the appointment concept with the open and closed audition methods a director might set up an appointment for ten or twelve actors per hour.

15 *Advantages.* Appointments are an efficient use of both the performers' and the director's time. The director controls the amount of time to work with performers. Because all will be in the audition hall, announcements can be made that all will hear. The method encourages performers to plan ahead and to prepare audition pieces carefully.

16 *Disadvantages.* With back-to-back appointments, it is easy for a director to get off schedule; once off, the effect accumulates unless the director has anticipated the problem and allowed several "cushion" periods with no appointments. The appointment system also discourages the spontaneous, spur-of-the-moment audition. Most seriously, if the appointment system is for individuals instead of groups, the performer's solo reading does not allow a director to evaluate how well the actor responds to others.

Interview

17 The interview audition consists of a private meeting, often in the director's office, between performer and director. This system gives both an opportunity to get to know each other and to pursue questions about the play, production, character interpretation, and working conditions.

18 *Advantages.* The interview system is favored by directors and performers who believe that the large cattle call audition

techniques do not encourage individualism. Interviews permit actors and director to exchange ideas. A basic premise underlying this system is that the performer is a known quantity—the interview system is seldom found in the amateur theatre—and that the director already has an idea of the performer's ability.

19 *Disadvantages.*   Interviews can be wearing for the director. Only a few performers can be seen per day. The interview provides few opportunities for the performer to show acting abilities.

Seasonal

20 The seasonal audition seeks to cast a full season's shows, not just one production. Performers audition for the theatre's annual or summer season, often a matter of four or more productions involving a like number of different directors.

21 *Advantages.*   The seasonal audition system is convenient for organizations drawing from a fixed company to produce a limited number of shows in a set period of time, such as a summer or an academic year. It is useful in repertory theatres. Because the system allows carefully planned assignment of performers for their artistic growth and for the theatre's advantage in selecting plays, it is used in some universities with specialized acting programs, such as those that lead to MFA performance degrees, and in summer theatre programs, such as Shakespeare festivals.

Disadvantages.   The seasonal audition sys- 22 tem is not popular in many educational or community theatres because if a given performer is cast in, say, three of the four shows of the season—hypothetically numbers 1, 3, and 4—the later productions may distract the actor from full concentration on the earlier show, especially if the director of show 4 begins work while the performer is still rehearsing show 1 or 3. More significantly, if an entire season is cast, performers who move into town or enroll in classes after seasonal auditions will have no chance to participate, thereby making the theatre appear to be a closed shop. Finally, if the full season is cast but several performers must leave a production for some reason, will the director wish to reopen auditions for all roles in order to rebalance the production? If so, morale problems loom on the horizon.

Readings from Script and Improvisations

Readings from the script to be produced al- 23 low the director to hear the performer read from the play to be cast; improvisational auditions without script give insight into performer abilities not likely to be visible from merely reading the script. The former method shows the actors' interpretive ability for characters they may play; the latter eliminates an overlay of interpretation that may be incorrect.

Drawbacks.   Readings from the script can 24 become monotonous, especially if a large number of people are auditioning and only a few passages from the script have been selected. The improvisational approach is often time-consuming, especially if the performers involved are relatively inexperienced and need instructions and situational setups; improvisations also require the director to know how to create plausible situations.

Prepared Pieces or Cold Readings

25 The director can choose between asking performers to bring prepared pieces to auditions or to read "cold," or unprepared. Each has advantages and disadvantages.

26 *Prepared pieces* may be from the play being cast or from other plays. The former is preferred because the latter gives little to use in judging the performer. The prepared piece from another play is typically a scene the actor has already performed, full of interpretations and blocking perhaps correct for the circumstances of that production but awkward without all of those trappings. At best a prepared piece from another production shows only what the performer did in collaboration with another director and other performers. In musical auditions, however, a selection from a previous production is acceptable because it shows the performer's technique, dancing or singing range, and polished best efforts.

27 Prepared pieces from the play being cast gives the director insight into a performer's ability to create the particular roles being considered. Here directors must exercise a great deal of insight to see past the performer's interpretations of the play; the actor's vision of the character is less significant than his or her ability to bring

the character to life. The prepared piece has the advantage of letting the performer be seen with the rough edges sanded down a bit.

28 The "cold" piece shows the performer's ability to sight-read the play and interpret lines out of context. The cold reading has two advantages: It opens auditions to a number of performers who have not been able to find the script to prepare; and it serves as a preliminary screen to put performers into the "acceptable" or "not acceptable" category, with further decisions to be made at a subsequent audition.

The Callback

29 The callback is an essential ingredient of all audition systems. After all performers have auditioned, a list of the top contenders is put together. The director asks them to return for callbacks, which will determine final casting. For both director and performer, callbacks are the final audition. It is in the production's interest for each performer to do the best audition possible, and therefore the director should be as supportive and helpful as possible during callbacks.

30 Callbacks allow the director to consider the ensemble. The group, not solo performers, is being cast, and directors need to look at combinations ("marriages") of the top candidates. For example, if there are three candidates for Juliet and two for Romeo, the decision-making process involves not only which is the "best" Juliet and which the "best" Romeo but also which pair will work together most effectively.

Evaluation of the Article

Difficulty rating ☐ 1 ☐ 2 ☐ 3 ☐ 4 ☐ 5
(1 = easy; 5=difficult)

What reading difficulties did you encounter? _____

_____

How did you handle these difficulties? _____

_____

Postreading Comprehension Development

Rewriting Sentences

To check your understanding of some of the key concepts of this essay, rewrite each of the following sentences in your own words, keeping the original idea. (See Chapter 1.)

1. Charged with the responsibility of conducting auditions in a manner that is both artistically effective for the production and visibly fair from the performer's view, directors may find auditions even more difficult than performers do. (1)

   _____

   _____

   _____

2. Good readings may produce either carbon copies or deliberate efforts to avoid imitation; neither alternative is especially desirable. (10)

   _____

   _____

   _____

3. Finally, if the full season is cast but several performers must leave a production for some reason, will the director wish to reopen auditions for all roles in order to rebalance the production? (22)

_____

_____

_____

Author's Main Idea

1. The author develops the main idea primarily through

   _____a. providing definitions of stage terms.

   _____b. discussing the most common production problems and offering solutions.

   _____c. explaining different types of auditions and the advantages and drawbacks of each.

   _____d. illustrating, through examples, how popular directors address directorial problems, especially casting problems.

2. The paragraph in which the author's main point is most clearly stated is

   _____a. 1

   _____b. 3

   _____c. 5

   _____d. 6

3. Create a title for this selection that you think would help a reader predict the major focus of this selection. Write it on the line below.

   _____

4. What predictions about the content of the article do you believe a reader could make from your title?

_____

_____

Inferences, Metaphors, and Vocabulary in Context

1. What is the audience for whom this article is written?

_____a. People studying playwriting

_____b. People studying acting

_____c. People studying to be theater stagehands

_____d. People studying theater directing

2. Which of the following does the author imply in paragraph 6? Be prepared to justify your answer.

_____a. Auditions help technical crews work more efficiently.

_____b. Inexperienced volunteers cannot find work in theater.

_____c. Educational and community theatres are dependent on volunteer technical assistance.

_____d. Most theatre technical crews dislike having volunteers working on such things as costumes and scene painting.

3. Where would the information in this article most likely appear?

_____a. In an ad for a casting call

_____b. In a textbook on directing

_____c. In a magazine for aspiring actors

_____d. In a technical research journal on theater production

4. The type of audition that would allow director and actor to learn the most about each other, in addition to performing ability and directing style, is probably the

    _____a. general open.

    _____b. interview.

    _____c. general closed.

    _____d. seasonal.

5. The type of audition that would enable actors to learn the most about a production is probably the

    _____a. general open.

    _____b. interview.

    _____c. general closed.

    _____d. seasonal.

6. One conclusion we can draw from this article is that

    _____a. actors who have not experienced an audition should not participate in them.

    _____b. directors would be well advised to study directing in England before they consider producing in the United States.

    _____c. auditions vary little in how they are arranged and most yield the same feelings and information for actors.

    _____d. an audition's poor atmosphere will result in a poor production.

7. The author's tone is primarily

    _____a. informative.

    _____b. sarcastic.

    _____c. humorous.

    _____d. lively.

8. Using only the context, define each of the following words. Do not use a dictionary.

    a. cohesive (2) _____

    b. perception (4) _____

    c. clarifying (9) _____

    d. bolstered (9) _____

    e. wearing (19) _____

    f. improvisational (24) _____

    g. polished (26) _____

9. Is the metaphor "cattle call" in paragraph 10 used appropriately? In the space below, give reasons for your opinion.

_____

_____

10. In your own words, explain what the author means by the expression "closed shop" in paragraph 22.

_____

_____

11. Read the statement below and decide whether the author of this article would agree or disagree with it. Use information from the article to help you make your decision. Then write your response in the space provided beneath the sentence.

Directors have less to worry about during auditions than the actors who are auditioning.

_____

_____

_____

Recalling Details

1. Which of the following are factual statements in this article? Which are opinions? Use (F) or (O) for your response. For those you label opinion, write any support for the opinion that is given in this article.

_____a. Auditions may also lead performers who were not cast to speak of the director or producer in a way that positively or negatively influences public perception of the play.

_____b. The general, closed audition system accepts all who are interested.

_____c. The general, closed audition technique is inefficient.

_____d. Auditions by appointment require performers to make reservations.

_____e. The interview audition consists of a private meeting, often in the director's office.

_____f. Interviews can be wearing for the director.

2. The pattern of organization used in paragraph 6 is

_____a. definition.

_____b. opinion and reason.

_____c. comparison and contrast.

_____d. simple listing.

3. The pattern of organization used in paragraph 17 is

_____a. definition.

_____b. opinion and reason.

_____c. comparison and contrast.

_____d. simple listing.

4. The pattern of organization used in paragraph 26 is

    _____a. definition.

    _____b. opinion and reason.

    _____c. comparison and contrast.

    _____d. simple listing.

5. The word *former* in paragraph 26 refers to

    _____a. prepared pieces.

    _____b. cold readings.

    _____c. the play you are casting.

    _____d. other plays.

6. Which of the following was not mentioned as a consideration for deciding the type of audition to hold?

    _____a. Time

    _____b. Cost

    _____c. Space

    _____d. Psychological impact

7. What information in this selection about auditions surprised you? Use the space below to write your response.

    _____

    _____

    _____

    _____

    _____

8. Use the information in this selection to create a comparison and contrast box for two different types of auditions.

Critical Thinking: Reaction and Discussion

1. Review your responses in the Before You Read section for this article. Make any changes to your answers that have resulted from your reading of this selection. Now compare your responses with those of another student.

2. There are some similarities between auditioning for a stage performance and having a traditional job interview. With a group, discuss the similarities and your job interview or audition experiences, as well as which of these experiences you would prefer.

3. Write an essay of at least 250 words in which you describe how you, if you were a director, would try to ensure that auditions for your productions would be fair. What are some guidelines you would follow to be sure you are being impartial and that all who audition have an equal opportunity to exhibit their abilities? What will you do so that you will minimize bruising the egos of the actors you don't choose for your production?

4. Discuss the following questions with a partner:
   a. Should all undergraduates, regardless of major, be required to take a course in the performing arts?
   b. Is there any reason why a performing arts student should take courses in such subjects as history, science, literature? Explain your response.
   c. After your discussion with your partner, review your college's catalog (or another college's if yours does not have a major in one of the performing arts), such as theater, music, and/or dance. Decide how your responses match what is actually required of performing arts majors. Be prepared to share your findings with the class.

Using Technology for Further Understanding

What kind of information about auditions can you find on the internet? Make a list of the types of information that are available on the lines below. How useful would this information be to college students who were interested in one of the performing arts? How useful would a theater director find this information? Share your findings with a group.

1. _____

2. _____

3. _____

4. _____

5. _____

CHAPTER FOURTEEN

Readings about Contemporary Society

We are not victims of the world we see.
We are victims of the way we see the world.

—Shirley MacLaine, *Dancing in the Light;*
 cited in James B. Simpson,
 Simpson's Contemporary Quotations
 (New York: HarperCollins, 1997), 378.

Guidelines for Reading about Contemporary Society

When we are reading about contemporary society, we are usually reading about how things have changed from previous generations, especially with regard to the following:

* Lifestyles (including how people use their money and their leisure time)

* Social relations (including race relations, crime, emergence of new social groups—for example, "techies," "baby boomers")

* Social attitudes (including attitudes about dating and premarital sex; attitudes toward those of different races or sexual orientations)

* Forms of personal expression (including trends in fashion, music, and art)

Thus, when you read material about contemporary society, you need to be aware that the concept of *change* is central to whatever else is being discussed.

Specific Strategies

* **Identify the group being discussed.** Every generation puts its own "spin" on things, resulting in what is often referred to as a *generation gap.* This gap can be found in many aspects of life, including dress styles, courtship/dating patterns, attitudes toward work and leisure, music, and political and religious views. Teens and their parents often say that this gap causes communication difficulties in families. Magazines, radio stations, and TV programs that want to reach the younger generation reflect these changes, which are often not understood by those who were teens during different times. Much research about contemporary society focuses on young peoples' attitudes and preferences and how these contrast to those of their parents' generation.

   Media are developed for and researchers study contemporary life of other groups as well, including senior citizens, working families, various ethnic groups, and women.

❋ **Relate your personal experience to your reading.** If you are reading about today's twentysomethings or trends among seniors, ask yourself whether you can relate to what is said by thinking about people you know or experiences you have had, even if your experiences are not the same. The author's ideas may enable you to think about a group of people a little differently or to better understand some of your experiences and acquaintances. Making such personal connections can help you comprehend the text.

❋ **Identify limitations of the research.** Determine whether the information the author provides, whether it is academic research or anecdotal examples, is limited to one gender, age, ethnicity, or geographic location. Even if the author does not point these limitations out to you, you need to identify them and to be aware that the findings or examples might not be applicable to other groups. You want to avoid generalizing what you read about one population to all populations.

❋ **Ask about the author's perspective and bias.** Who is the audience, and what is the author's purpose for writing? Periodicals tend to attract different audiences; some are more conservative; some have special-interest audiences, such as working mothers or senior citizens. The author might have a specific agenda that has determined the type of research that has been done. For instance, if the author wants to convince readers that today's youth are more willing to contribute service to their communities, young people who are interviewed might be attending schools where community service is required, or they might live in communities where students can get free merchandise in return for such service or in towns where incomes are high enough that teenagers do not typically have part-time jobs.

❋ **Consider what other opinions might be held on this topic.** If an author can be biased about events or changes in contemporary society, then there must be other points of view. The critical reader tries to identify what these might be in order to obtain a balanced perspective and develop a well-informed personal opinion.

Keep these suggestions in mind as you read the following articles about contemporary society.

What are topics related to changes in contemporary society that interest you?

_____

_____

What additional suggestions can you make for reading about contemporary society? _____

_____

_____

_____

_____

_____

⟿ SELECTION 11

Preview

How is your generation different from your parents' with regard to its attitudes toward love, sex, and marriage? In this article, you learn about some trends of today's 18- to 24-year-olds, sometimes referred to as Generation Y, as compared to the generation that preceded them, Generation X.

To Think About Before You Read

Use the Venn diagram to note the differences as well as the similarities you have observed between Generation Y and Generation X, with regard to attitudes toward love, sex, and marriage.

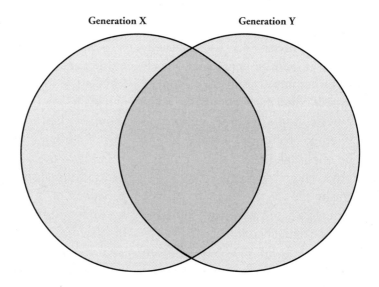

Generation X   Generation Y

Terms to Know Before You Read

jaded (15) exhausted; dulled by experience

tongue-in-cheek (24) with insincerity, irony, or whimsical exaggeration

retro (39) return to the past

Y Not Love?

■ BY HELENE STAPINSKI

1 Ryan K. has searched all his life for his soul mate, and when he finally finds her, he will romantically propose marriage, rather than living together. He will have sex with his bride for the first time on their wedding night. He has no respect for women who sleep around. But that doesn't stop him from wearing Between the Sheets cologne.

2 On a recent date with a potential mate, Ryan (cologne liberally applied) wore a suit and took Bachelorette No. 1 on a traditional night out—dinner and a play. He almost bought her flowers, but then thought twice about it, figuring it would be awkward for her to lug a bouquet around all night. When he's feeling a bit more adventurous, he might take a date to play miniature golf or even go bowling.

3 Though he fits the profile of the classic male of the 1950s, Ryan is not from the Ozzie-and-Harriet generation.

4 He is a 19-year-old snowboarder from Vail, Colorado, a college freshman majoring in business at Georgetown University who is looking for love in all the right places. And in many ways, he's more idealistic than his baby boomer parents ever were, at least when it comes to matters of the heart—and

more conservative, too. Picture Eisenhower, but with a pierced eyebrow.

5 "The soul mate thing is so huge," Ryan says. "I still believe there's one person out there that you're meant for. It sounds naive. But this generation kind of has a trust in fate. When I talked to my mom about it, she told me she could have married seven or eight different people, that my father was the best choice at the time. Not 'He was my true love.' I was like, 'Oh, thanks.'"

6 With Ryan and his cohorts in mind, market analysts are predicting a values shift for Gen Y lovers—whose dating, mating, and child-rearing habits may be more like those of their grandparents than like the cast of *Melrose Place*.

7 "One of the macro-trends we're seeing is neotraditionalism," says Kirsty Doig, vice president of Youth Intelligence, a market research and trend forecasting group based in New York City. "These kids are fed up with the superficialities of life. They have not had a lot of stability in their lives. It's a backlash, a return to tradition and ritual. And that includes marriage. It's all about finding the right one—as opposed to sleeping around."

8 Though census data has yet to reflect the trend—marriage and childbearing have continued to occur at later ages, and living

From *American Demographics* (February 1999): 63–68.

together is still on the rise—the pundits all agree: We're headed for a second coming of family values. And with it, boosted sales of white wedding gowns, subscriptions to bridal magazines, and perhaps a future surge in sales of Pampers.

9   "This generation is very much into the spirituality of love," says Doig. "They're much more optimistic than Generation X . . . They know they'll find their soul mate."

10   Last year, when asked if they would get married if they found the right person, 80.5 percent of 18-to-24-year-olds answered a resounding "Yes!" Only 69 percent of Gen X—the 25-to-31-year-olds—held the same romantic view, according to the General Social Survey of the University of Chicago.

11   Rather than base their lives on people like Sylvester Stallone—whose daughter was nine months old when he and mom, Jennifer Flavin, wed in 1997—Generation Ys are more likely to follow the example set by young Macaulay Culkin, the *Home Alone* star raised in a turbulent, common-law marriage, who tied the knot with his 17-year-old girlfriend last year.

12   People like Culkin—and even snowboarding business majors like Ryan—are what marketing consultant Liz Nickles of Chicago-based Nickles & Ashcraft calls the early adopters: opinion and style leaders who set the trends. "They don't show up on the government charts," she admits, "but the rest of the population follows them."

13   Nickles, who's been conducting surveys with partner Laurie Ashcraft for the past 18

years, predicts a surge in teen marriage and a trend toward bigger families, whether because of the threat of AIDS or simply as a rebellion against what their free-lovin', baby boomer parents did in the '60s. Or perhaps more importantly, what Mom and Dad did in the '80s.

14   "[Gen Y's] role models were mothers focused on their careers," says Nickles. "But today you can have a career and your first priority can still be your home. For these young women, their heart is in the home."

15   In their latest survey, "The New Millennium Woman," Nickles and Ashcraft found that 82 percent of 29-to-24-year-olds thought motherhood was the most important job in the world, compared to 72 percent in the more jaded 25-to-34-year-old Gen X category.

16   Sociologist Linda Waite, codirector of the Alfred P. Sloan Center on Parents, Children and Work at the University of Chicago, says that because children usually rebel against their parents, it makes sense that Generation Y may get hitched earlier. "Part of the women's movement," she explains, "was involved in trying to make sure women weren't trapped in bad marriages. Certainly some marriages are bad but marriage has its advantages, too."

17   Perhaps the younger set knows instinctually what Waite has spent years researching—that married people are much more healthy psychologically and physically than those who are just living together. For women, according to Waite's forthcoming book, *The Case for Marriage* (Harvard University Press), the state of matrimony

improves their access to health insurance, provides safer places to live, and even boosts their endocrine and immune systems. Men reap the benefits as well, with improved careers and extended life spans.

18   It's not only in the outside world that Waite sees changes. "My 20-year-old daughter won't live with her boyfriend," says Waite, laughing. "She's talking about marrying him."

19   Young women who return to more traditional ways in the new millennium will do so on their own terms, however. Millie Martini Bratten, editor-in-chief of *Bride's*, says there's been a definite swing toward traditional weddings: young women are buying beautiful long gowns, exchanging time-honored vows, and gathering family and friends to break bread. Eighty percent of brides are tossing their garters, 78 percent are walked down the aisle by Daddy, and almost all brides expect to be carried across the threshold, Bratten reports.

20   "What has changed, though, is who's paying for the wedding," she adds. "Nearly 30 percent of couples pay for their own wedding. And many couples plan it together, rather than just the bride and her mother. As a result, we're seeing more personalized weddings, couples making it different and unique, whether that's adding a few lines to the traditional vows or taking 30 of your closest friends and family members to Tuscany for the ceremony."

21   That idea—taking tradition and running with it—will spill over into child-rearing as well, experts say. "For these young women, it's not so much doing it

all," says Nickles "but rather selecting certain elements and crafting your lifestyle. This generation leaves behind words like 'juggling.' For instance, they'll have that career, but they'll work from home instead."

22   Because of the trend toward early coupling, whether married or living together, companies like Maytag and Black and Decker need to pay heed, market researchers say.

23   "The makers of major appliances are ignoring that generation," according to David Morrison, president of TwentySomething Inc., a strategy planning and market research firm that works with such Fortune 500 companies as General Motors, Coca-Cola, and AT&T. "They have to stop thinking of X and Y as IKEA patrons and more as Whirlpool customers."

24   Advertisers, however, would be wise to stay away from old-fashioned pitches, Morrison warns. Even though they believe in marriage and having babies, Gen Yers won't respond to ads featuring "the husband, wife, two kids, and the white picket fence," says Morrison. "You do that and you're going to hit barriers. Unless you're doing it tongue-in-cheek."

25   Though they're arriving at the same conclusions their grandparents did—find a life partner and stick with them—Gen Y is savvier and, in some ways, much more tolerant than the generations that came before it, experts say. Marriage can apply to men with men, and women with women. Cross-cultural and interracial unions are not taboo, but in fashion. In other words, the kids may like tradition, but they are hardly traditional.

26   The perfect prototype for the new generation, says Morrison, is the Volkswagen commercial—what he calls the "Da da da" ad—in which the heroes, a young black man and a young white man are driving down the street in their VW. They stop to pick up a discarded chair, place it in the back seat and then, without exchanging a bit of dialog, realize the chair has a terrible odor and/or bad vibe, and dump it back on the street. It's all backed up with a suitably enigmatic soundtrack. "Da da da," sung by a band called Trio.

27   "Are these guys gay? Are they straight?" asks Morrison. "No one really cares. The commercial works."

28   Young people may be more mature and careful about their life choices, whether they're looking for a sofa or shopping for a partner, but not because they're under pressure from their parents, says Morrison; they're under pressure from the world at large. "These young people are still sexually active but they're terrified of having multiple partners," Morrison says. "They have more of the fear of God in them. Having a lasting partner," he says, "guarantees some safety."

29   According to the General Social Survey, young people's attitudes toward sex have certainly become more conservative over the past two decades, especially compared to their elders' views. In 1972, a mere 10.4 percent of the 18-to-24-year-olds surveyed said it was "always wrong" to have sex before marriage. Over the years, those numbers have shifted slowly but surely. Last year, they more than doubled: 23.3 percent of 18-to-24-year-olds believed sex was almost always wrong before marriage.

30   These days it's Mom and Dad who say sex before marriage isn't so evil. Back in 1972, only 19.1 percent of 45-to-54-year-olds believed it was okay to have sex before marriage. But last year, the number grew to a whopping 48.5 percent. Then again, who listens to Mom and Dad?

31   In 1988, 83.9 percent of 18-to-24-year-olds said they had been sexually active. By 1998, that number had dropped to 76.6 percent. Of those involved romantically, 31.7 percent of 18-to-24-year-olds lived together in 1996. In just two years, that number dropped over 10 percentage points, to 21.6 percent.

32   Numbers don't speak as loudly as real voices, though. Stacey H., a 22-year-old legal assistant/writer/actress living in New York City, says she will never live with a boyfriend—based simply on the examples set by her peers.

33   "I've decided I would never live out of wedlock," says Stacey. "I've seen too many instances where the relationship's soured. Living together takes the specialness out of it. My friends who live together go through all the problems of a marriage, but they don't have the joy of being married. One of my friends just told me straight, 'Don't do it.' And I won't. For sure. I would not live with a guy."

34   Like other women her age, Stacey says she plans on getting married only once. But singling out that perfect man has not been easy. Ah, for the good old days of cotillions, socials, and fancy-dress balls.

35   "I pity our times," says Stacey, who despises meeting guys in bars. "We don't have big balls to go to with big dresses. You can't be classy about meeting someone these days."

36   Some of Stacey's friends have resorted to nontraditional means, like frequenting a bar called Drip—a matchmaking establishment on Manhattan's Upper West Side, where patrons fill out forms, can read each other's "stats," and are matched up by the bartender on request. On a recent Friday night outside Drip, a young twentysomething could be overheard making small talk with her supposed match: "Let's see. I'll try and summarize my whole life in a few sentences," she said, tongue firmly planted in cheek.

37   Morrison says coffee bars are the latest trend in dating safety. "A coffee bar allows you to hear the other person without an 80-decibel band blaring behind you," he says. "You may get a caffeine rush, but because there's no alcohol, you're not becoming impaired." The coffee rendezvous also allows daters to cut short the date if it's not going well, or continue on to the more traditional dinner and a movie if things are looking up.

38   Because of the growing popularity of the coffee bar dating trend, many of them have even morphed back into restaurants, serving food and playing light music in the background, says Morrison. Some even serve liquor. "You can get a Guinness in some coffee bars, which brings us right back to the old-fashioned pub," he says, laughing.

39   Another retro trend in dating is traveling in groups of four, six or ten friends. "People are doing things like swing dancing or ballroom dancing," says Morrison.

40   More and more common are Blockbuster nights, involving several friends "hooking up" in front of the television set.

41   In some cases, employers are picking up on dating desperation and are arranging employee nights for some of their harder workers—those who work 20-hour days and can't get out to meet that perfect someone.

42   "Employers even encourage you to bring a friend," says Morrison. "There's cross-pollinating, if you will, with other employees out there."

43   Doig suggests that some young people are meeting each other in church—how's that for tradition? "This is a very spiritual group, remember," she says.

44   Then, of course, there is finding love online, a phenomenon that continues to grow, particularly for Gen Y. "As hokey as they are, those chat rooms are real places, filled with real people," says Morrison. "It's a place to share your passions. It would take you 1,000 bars—if you're lucky—to find that person you can find online."

45   In 1996, America Online handled a few hundred personal ads on Love@AOL for Valentine's Day. Today they have more than 125,000 ads year round. Of those, 23,000 came from people between the ages of 21 to 25. The 18-to-20-year-olds come in at a close second, with about 20,000.

46   "The younger generation is very comfortable with computers," says AOL's Bill

Schreiner, who calls himself the CEO of Love and was hired to develop and oversee Love@AOL two years ago. "They've been on mom and dad's computer since they were 10 years old." Schreiner compares online chatting with the long telephone conversations of the early 1960s teenager.

47 "To my parents, the phone was a thing on which you called somebody briefly for a meeting or to exchange quick information," he says. "But for the younger generation, it was a means of communication. We stayed on the phone for hours. Well, that's the same thing for these kids—the computer is a living form of communication."

48 Unlike the Tom Hanks/Meg Ryan romance in *You've Got Mail,* Gen Y singles may meet someone through a personal ad, but then they connect in a chat room. Schreiner says that experienced chatters know within the first five minutes whether the other person qualifies as potential soul mate material. "The greatest pursuit of all time is the pursuit of the love of your life," explains Schreiner. "Imagine the number of people you can contact online in three or four hours?"

49 Once onliners hook up through e-mail love letters and online chats, they generally "go to voice." Translation: they resort to old-fashioned methods and have a telephone conversation. Then, if all goes well, the meeting takes place. In chat room speak, that's F2F—or Face to Face. Hopefully, the online courtship will culminate in the Cyber Vows chat room, where people "get married" online by a "love doctor." People invite 20 of their closest friends and, after the hour-long "ceremony," open the chat room to their guests. It's a reception for the new millennium.

50 Schreiner says it certainly won't replace more traditional weddings. "But some people use it as a dress rehearsal for the real thing, or as an addendum to the real wedding."

51 College professor Richard Booth, author of *Romancing the Net,* a book about finding love online, says the trend will continue to grow, but controls need to be stricter for online searchers to be more successful—and safer. The biggest problem online is misrepresentation: sending fake photos or telling lies, he says.

52 "We're not that far away from chat sessions where you will be able to see the person," says Booth. "It will change the nature of online dating, but it will make it more useful in the long run."

53 And it will help the younger generation do what the generation before them and the generation before that may have found impossible: finding that one true love through accelerated—yet fairly safe—trial and error.

54 "In the '70s, people were like bees, wanting to get a little nectar from every flower in the garden. But this generation seems more concerned with finding the one man, one woman," says Schreiner. "And, you know, I gotta say, it's kind of cool."

Evaluation of the Article

Difficulty rating □ 1 □ 2 □ 3 □ 4 □ 5
(1 = easy; 5 = difficult)

What reading difficulties did you encounter? _____

_____

How did you handle these difficulties?_____

_____

Postreading Comprehension Development

Rewriting Sentences

To check your understanding of some of the key concepts of this essay, rewrite each of the following sentences in your own words, keeping the original idea. (See Chapter 1)

1. Though he fits the profile of the classic male of the 1950s, Ryan is not from the Ozzie-and-Harriet generation. (3)_____

_____

2. Young women who return to more traditional ways in the new millennium will do so on their own terms, however. (19)_____

_____

3. Numbers don't speak as loudly as real voices, though. (32) _____

_____

Author's Main Idea

1. What is the topic of this article? _____

_____

2. What is the author's focus on this topic? _____

   _____

3. In the space provided, state the author's main idea.
   The author wants me to understand that _____

   _____

   _____

4. How does the description of Ryan in the opening paragraphs help clarify the author's main idea? _____

   _____

5. The author develops the main idea primarily through

   _____a. unsupported opinions.

   _____b. expert opinions.

   _____c. informed opinions.

   _____d. facts and statistics.

6. Create a new title for this selection that you think would help a reader
   predict its major focus._____

   _____

7. What predictions do you believe a reader could make from your title?

   _____

   _____

Inferences, Metaphors, and Vocabulary in Context

1. Which of the following does the author imply in paragraph 5? Be prepared to justify your answer.

   _____a. Ryan thought he was an adopted son.

   _____b. Ryan accepted that some children are born out of wedlock.

_____c.   Ryan had little use for his mother's opinions.

_____d.   Ryan wanted his dad to be his mom's true love.

2.   The author's attitude toward Generation Y is

_____a.   positive.

_____b.   negative.

_____c.   critical but accepting.

_____d.   neutral.

3.   In your own words, explain what Nickles means when she says, "They don't show up on the government charts." (12) _____

_____

_____

4.   One conclusion that can be drawn from this article is that

_____a.   the generation that follows Generation Y will be more like Generation X.

_____b.   generations to come will be more conservative than Generation X.

_____c.   people between ages 18 to 24 are always more conservative than those who are older.

_____d.   Generation Y will eventually hold the same values as Generation X.

5.   Another conclusion that can be drawn from this article is that

_____a.   market researchers sometimes use false data.

_____b.   the results of Census 2000 will be useful to product developers.

_____c.   little is known about Generation Y's attitudes toward love, sex, and marriage.

_____ d. little relationship occurs between what a person buys and that person's values.

6. What does the metaphor about bees in paragraph 54 mean as it is used in this selection?

_____

_____

7. What information in the article is confirmed by the accompanying graph? Write your response on the lines beneath the graph.

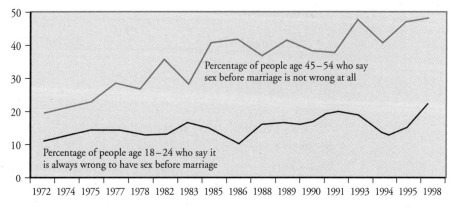

Sex before Marriage

Source: General Social Survey, 1999.

_____

_____

_____

_____

_____

_____

8. Using only the context, define each of the following words. Do not use a dictionary.

a. potential (2)_____

b. cohorts (6) _____

c. backlash (7) _____

d. surge (8) _____

e. heed (22) _____

f. prototype (26) _____

g. culminate (49)_____

h. addendum (50) _____

Recalling Details

1. Which of the following statements describe Generation X, and which describe Generation Y? Put your response (X or Y) on the line next to each characteristic. Be prepared to cite evidence for your answers.

_____a. Women are less likely to buy white bridal gowns.

_____b. Unmarried couples are more likely to live together.

_____c. Men are more likely to send flowers to women.

_____d. Parents are more likely to say sex before marriage is okay.

_____e. A mate is more likely to be sought in a chat room.

_____f. Men are less concerned with finding true love than with finding sexual partners.

_____g. Women of this generation are more likely to work at home.

2. Which of the following are cited or implied as some of the reasons for Generation Y's traits? Check all that apply. Be prepared to cite evidence for your answers.

_____a.   High divorce rate

_____b.   AIDS

_____c.   Low salaries for women

_____d.   Experiences of older friends

_____e.   Familiarity with technology

_____f.   Parental attitudes

_____g.   High cost of housing

_____h.   Smaller number of singles

Critical Thinking: Reaction and Discussion

1. Review the Venn diagram you created in the section "To Think About Before You Read." Make any changes that are appropriate, based on what you have learned from reading this article.

2. Discuss the article with someone from Generation X and someone from an older generation. How do their perceptions of Generation Y agree with those suggested in this article? If there are differences of opinion, how do you account for these? Write your findings in an essay of at least 250 words.

3. With a group, discuss the following paragraph and prepare to present your responses with the class:

   Much has been made of seeking romance on the Internet. If your child were to engage in this behavior, how would you respond? Is this a suitable way to find a mate? What advice would you give your child about seeking a partner?

Using Technology for Further Understanding

Look at a popular movie from the 1950s that included teenagers. How are they portrayed? What values about sex, love, and marriage are evident? Is anything about the behavior of teens in this movie similar to teens of today whom you know? Prepare to discuss your findings with your class.

SELECTION 12
Preview

Modern medical knowledge has made it possible to make our bodies bigger, stronger, and faster by using steroids. Is it worth it? Who uses them and what are the consequences?

To Think About Before You Read

This essay is divided into four basic parts, as diagrammed in the following Structured Overview. These divisions are the statement of the problem, the causes of the problem, some of the effects of the problem, and several solutions to the problem. All these parts are connected to the main topic, teenagers using steroids. Think about these parts. Before you read the essay, write in any details that you expect to be mentioned in each part of the essay. Use what you already know about this subject to help you. When you finish reading the selection, you will complete this Structured Overview by revising your original details and adding others so that the final overview corresponds to the content of the essay.

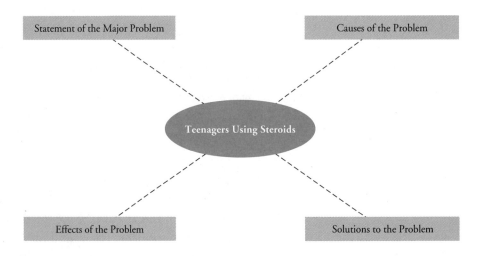

Statement of the Major Problem

Causes of the Problem

Teenagers Using Steroids

Effects of the Problem

Solutions to the Problem

Terms to Know Before You Read

rationalize (10) to make excuses

invincibility (15) indestructibility; mightiness

Pumped Up

■ BY JOANNIE M. SCHROF

1   It's a dangerous combination of culture and chemistry. Inspired by cinematic images of the Terminator and Rambo and the pumped-up paychecks of athletic heroes with stunning physiques and awesome strength, teenagers across America are pursuing dreams of brawn through a pharmacopeia of pills, powders, oils and serums that are readily available—but often damaging. Despite the warnings of such fallen stars as Lyle Alzado, the former football player who died two weeks ago of a rare brain cancer he attributed to steroid use, a *U.S. News* investigation has found a vast teenage subculture driven by an obsession with size and bodybuilding drugs. Consider:

2   ❋   An estimated 1 million Americans, half of them adolescents, use black-market steroids. Countless others are choosing from among more than 100 other substances, legal and illegal, touted as physique boosters and performance enhancers.

3   ❋   Over half the teens who use steroids start before age 16, sometimes with the encouragement of their parents. In one study, 7 percent said they first took "juice" by age 10.

From *U.S. News & World Report,* 1 June 1992, 55–63.

❋   Many of the 6 to 12 percent of boys 4 who use steroids want to be sports champions, but over one third aren't even on a high-school team. The typical user is middle-class and white.

❋   Fifty-seven percent of teen users say 5 they were influenced by the dozen or so muscle magazines that today reach a readership of at least 7 million; 42 percent said they were swayed by famous athletes who they were convinced took steroids.

❋   The black-market network for per- 6 formance enhancers is enormous, topping $400 million in the sale of steroids alone, according to the U.S. Drug Enforcement Administration. Government officials estimate that there are some 10,000 outlets for the drugs—mostly contacts made at local gyms—and mail-order forms from Europe, Canada and Mexico can be found anywhere teenagers hang out.

❋   The nation's steroid experts signaled 7 the state of alarm when they convened in April in Kansas City to plan the first nationwide education effort.

8 ❋ Even Arnold Schwarzenegger, who has previously been reluctant to comment on his own early steroid use, has been prompted to speak out vigorously about the problem. The bodybuilder and movie star is the chairman of the President's Council on Physical Fitness and Sports.

9 Performance drugs have an ancient history. Greek Olympians used strychnine and hallucinogenic mushrooms to psyche up for an event. In 1886, a French cyclist was the first athlete known to die from performance drugs—a mixture of cocaine and heroin called "speedballs." In the 1920s, physicians inserted slices of monkey testicles into male athletes to boost vitality, and in the '30s, Hitler allegedly administered the hormone testosterone to himself and his troops to increase aggressiveness.

10 The use of anabolic steroids by weight lifters in the Eastern bloc dates back at least to the 1950s, and the practice has been spreading ever since among the world's elite athletes. But recent sensations in the sports world—Ben Johnson's record-shattering sprints at the Seoul Olympics and the signing of Brian Bosworth to the largest National Football League rookie contract even *after* he tested positive for steroids—have attracted both young adults and kids to performance enhancers like never before, say leading steroid experts. These synthetic heroes are revered rather than disparaged in amateur gyms around the country, where wannabe Schwarzeneggers rationalize away health risks associated with performance-enhancing drugs.

WEIGHING IN

11 The risks are considerable. Steroids are derivatives of the male hormone testosterone, and although they have legitimate medical uses—treatment of some cancers, for example—young bodybuilders who use them to promote tissue growth and endure arduous workouts routinely flood their bodies with 100 times the testosterone they produce naturally. The massive doses, medical experts say, affect not only the muscles but also the sex organs and nervous systems, including the brain. "Even a brief period of abuse could have lasting effects on a child whose body and brain chemistry are still developing," warns Neil Carolan, who directs chemical dependency programs at BryLin Hospitals in Buffalo and has counseled over 200 steroid users.

12 Male users—by far the majority—can suffer severe acne, early balding, yellowing of the skin and eyes, development of female-type breasts and shrinking of the testicles. (In young boys, steroids can have the opposite effect of painfully enlarging the sex organs.) In females, the voice deepens permanently, breasts shrink, periods become irregular, the clitoris swells and hair is lost from the head but grows on the face and body. Teen users also risk stunting their growth, since steroids can cause bone growth plates to seal. One 13-year-old who had taken steroids for two years stopped growing at 5 feet. "I get side effects," says another teen who has used steroids for

three years. "But I don't mind; it lets me know the stuff is working."

13   In addition to its physical dangers, steroid use can lead to a vicious cycle of dependency. Users commonly take the drugs in "cycles" that last from four to 18 weeks, followed by a lengthy break. But during "off" time, users typically shrink up, a phenomenon so abhorrent to those obsessed with size that many panic, turning back to the drugs in even larger doses. Most users "stack" the drugs, taking a combination of three to five pills and injectables at once; some report taking as many as 14 drugs simultaneously. Among the most commonly used are Dianabol ("D-Ball"), Anavar and Winstrol-V, the same type of steroid Ben Johnson tested positive for in 1988. "You wouldn't believe how much some guys go nuts on the stuff," says one teen bodybuilder from the Northeast. "They turn into walking, talking pharmacies."

14   Despite massive weight gains and sharply chiseled muscles, many steroid users are never quite happy with their physiques—a condition some researchers have labeled "reverse anorexia." "I've seen a kid gain 100 pounds in 14 months and still not be satisfied with himself," reports Carolan. If users try to stop, they can fall into deep depressions, and they commonly turn to recreational drugs to lift their spirits. Even during a steroid cycle, many users report frequent use of alcohol and marijuana to mellow out. "I tend to get really depressed when I go off a cycle," says one Maryland teen, just out of high school.

"On a bad day, I think, 'Gee, if I were on the stuff this wouldn't be happening.'"

15   "Juicers" often enjoy a feeling of invincibility and euphoria. But along with the "pump" can come irritability and a sudden urge to fight. So common are these uncontrolled bursts of anger that they have a name in the steroid culture: "roid rages." The aggression can grow to pathological proportions; in a study by Harvard researchers, one eighth of steroid users suffered from "bodybuilder's psychosis," displaying such signs of mental illness as delusions and paranoia. So many steroid abusers are ending up behind bars for violent vandalism, assault and even murder that defense attorneys in several states now call on steroid experts to testify about the drugs' effects.

16   What steroids do in the long run is still unknown, largely because not one federal dollar has been spent on long-term studies. Although Lyle Alzado was convinced that steroids caused his brain cancer, for example, there is no medical evidence to prove or disprove the link. But physicians are concerned about occasional reports of users falling ill with liver and kidney problems or dropping dead at a young age from heart attacks or strokes. Douglas McKeag, a sports physician at Michigan State University, is compiling a registry of steroid-related illnesses and deaths to fill the gaping hole in medical knowledge. McKeag sees preliminary evidence that steroid use might cause problems with blood-cell function that could lead to embolisms in the heart or lungs. "If that turns out to be true," he

says, "then bingo—we'll have something deadly to warn kids about."

DIANABOL DESPERADOES

17 Unfortunately, even that sort of documented health threat is unlikely to sway committed members of the steroid subculture. One widely shared value among users is a profound distrust of the medical community. Their suspicion is not totally unjustified. When steroid use was first becoming popular in the late 1950s, the medical community's response was to claim that they didn't enhance athletic ability—a claim that bulked-up users knew to be false. When that failed to deter users, physicians turned to scare tactics, branding steroids "killer drugs," again without hard evidence to back up the claim. As a result, self-styled "anabolic outlaws" and "Dianabol desperadoes" have sought guidance not from doctors but from the "Underground Steroid Handbook," a widely distributed paperback with detailed instructions for the use of more than 80 performance enhancers. "I know that proper steroid therapy can enhance your health; it has enhanced mine," writes author Daniel Duchaine. "Do you believe someone just because he has an M.D. or Ph.D. stuck onto the end of his name?" Or kids simply make up their own guidelines. "If you take more kinds at once, you get a bigger effect, and it's less dangerous because you're taking less of each kind," reasons one 18-year-old football player who has been taking steroids for over two years.

18 Although even the steroid handbook mentions health risks particular to children and adolescents, in the end most young users seem unfazed by the hazards. In one poll, 82 percent said they didn't believe that steroids were harming them much, and, even more striking, 40 percent said they wouldn't stop in any case. Their motto: "Die young, die strong, Dianabol."

19 The main drawback to steroids, users complain, is that many brands must be administered with huge syringes. The deeper the needle penetrates the muscle, the less juice squandered just under the skin. Inserting the 1½-inch needles into their buttocks or thighs leaves many teens squeamish, and they often rely on trusted friends to do the job. "The first time I tried to inject myself, I almost fainted, and one of my friends did faint," remembers a 19-year-old from Arizona. "Sometimes one of the guys will inject in one side of his butt one day and the other the next. Then, we all laugh at him because he can barely sit down for the next three days."

20 Local "hard core" gyms, patronized by serious weight lifters, are the social centers of the steroid culture. Teenagers caught up in the bodybuilding craze—typically white, middle-class suburbanites—commonly spend at least three hours a day almost every day of the week there, sometimes working out in the morning before school and again after school is out. Here they often meet 20-to-30-year-old men using steroids to bulk up for power lifting and bodybuilding shows or members of what steroid experts call the "fighting elite"—firefighters, bouncers, even

policemen—synthetically boosting the physical strength they need to do their jobs. "Our role model is this older guy, the biggest guy at the gym," says one 17-year-old. "He's not a nice guy, but he weighs 290 pounds without an ounce of fat . . . that's our goal."

21   The older steroid veterans not only inspire kids to try the drugs but often act as the youngsters' main source for the chemicals. Sometimes, it's the gym owner who leads kids to a stash of steroids hidden in a back room; sometimes, it's a lifter who keeps the drugs in a dresser drawer at home and slips kids his phone number. Once in a while, it's a doctor or veterinarian who writes out endless prescriptions for the boys or for an unscrupulous coach. And too often, it's overzealous parents who push the drugs on their children. "My stepdad says he's going to start me up on steroids as soon as I'm done growing," says one freshman who wants to play pro football, "But I think he's just joking." Greg Gaa, director of a Peoria, Ill., sports-medicine clinic, says he has gotten calls from up to a dozen parents a year who want him to supply illegal performance enhancers to their children.

22   A vast black market across America guarantees kids ready access to steroids in big cities and small towns alike. Typically, the drugs are shipped via private couriers from sources in other countries. Two order forms obtained by *U.S. News* require a minimum order of $75, offer 14 different steroids (ranging from $15 to $120 per bottle) and promise 48-hour delivery for an extra $20. Though the order forms, sent out six months apart, are identical and obviously

the work of the same operation, the company name and address have been changed, apparently to outsmart investigators. In the earlier mailing, it's Mass Machine, located in Toronto. In the later form, it's Gym Tek Training, located in New Brunswick, Canada. Jack Hook, with the U.S. Drug Enforcement Administration in San Diego, describes a sting operation in which undercover agents from the DEA and the California Bureau of Narcotics posing as bodybuilders met up with a European gym owner and ordered $312,000 worth of steroids; the seller was nabbed in February when the shipment arrived via Federal Express.

23   Sometimes, kids themselves get into the act. Twenty-five percent say they sell the drugs to support their expensive habit. One Virginia 12th grader tells of fellow students who stole steroids from a drugstore where they worked and made "a killing" selling them around school. "Everybody knows you just go to this one guy's locker, and he'll fix you up," says the teen. A typical 100-tablet bottle of steroids—a month's supply—usually runs from $80 to $100 on the black market, but naive high schoolers often pay three times that amount.

24   "The challenges of getting ahold of the stuff is half the fun," admits one 17-year-old from Iowa, who tells of meeting dealers in parking lots and taste-testing drugs that look like fakes. Drug-enforcement agents estimate that 30 to 50 percent of the illegal muscle builders teens buy are phony. One Chicago-area youth spent $3,000 on what turned out to be a saline solution. Inves-

tigators have seized pills that turned out to be penicillin—deadly to some—and phony oils that were poorly packaged and rampant with bacteria. In April, two Los Angeles dealers were convicted of selling a counterfeit steroid that caused stomach pain, vomiting and a drop in blood pressure; the substance was a European veterinary drug used in show animals.

SUBBING DANGERS

25 Since February 1991, when nonmedical steroid distribution became a federal offense punishable by five years in prison, several drugs touted as steroid alternatives have also flourished underground. The top seller this year is a compound called clenbuterol, which is used by veterinarians in other countries but is not approved for any use in the United States. The drug recently led to problems in Spain, where 135 people who ingested it fell ill with headaches, chills, muscle tremors and nausea.

26   Human growth hormone, the steroid alternative Lyle Alzado used during his failed efforts at an NFL comeback, is medically used to treat dwarfism by stimulating growth. Its price, up to $1,500 for a two-week supply, is formidable, yet 5 percent of suburban Chicago 10th-grade boys surveyed in March by Vaughn Rickert of the University of Arkansas for Medical Sciences claim to have used the hormone. Although the body produces the substance naturally, too much can cause acromegaly, or "Frankenstein's syndrome," which leads to distortion of the face, hands and feet and eventually kills its victims.

27 Gamma-hydroxybutyrate (GHB) is a dangerous substance now popular among size seekers because it stimulates the release of human growth hormone. It also leads to comas. One Midwestern teen drank a GHB formula before going out to his high-school prom. He never made it. Within 20 minutes, he fell comatose and was rushed to the hospital to be revived. The Centers for Disease Control reports 80 recent hospitalizations from GHB use.

28 Many of the steroid alternatives that kids turn to come from an unlikely source: the local health-food store. For years, well-meaning coaches have persuaded kids to stay off steroids by opting for legal (and presumably safe) performance aids advertised ad nauseam in muscle magazines and sold in every shopping mall. Kids, happy to find a legal boost, empty their pockets on colorful packages that can cost up to $200 for a month's supply. But chemicals marketed as dietary supplements—essentially as food—undergo far less scrutiny than those marketed as drugs. "We have virtually no idea what's inside some of these products," warns Food and Drug Administration supplement specialist Don Leggett. "Just the other day someone asked about three new chemical compounds, and we couldn't even identify them. The substances aren't even on the books yet." Not long ago, he points out, clenbuterol and GHB were available in some health stores. Leggett is part of a task force now trying to assess the safety of a dozen common ingredients found in the bulking-up formulas, including chromium, boron and plant sterols.

READING

CRACKING THE CULTURE

29 Meanwhile, the ambiance of gyms and health-food stores serves to cloak the use of performance-enhancing drugs in the veneer of a healthy lifestyle. Since all of the trappings of their world have to do with hard work, fitness and vitality, kids who use the substances see them as just another training aid, not much different from Gatorade or a big steak dinner. "We're not freaks or addicts," asserts one teen. "We're using modern science to help us reach our goals."

30   Educators agree that users tend to be mainstream kids. "These kids aren't your typical drug abuser," says Dick Stickle, director of Target, the high-school sports association that hosted a meeting in April of 65 experts who worked to plot a strategy for educating teens about the drugs' risks. "They have goals, they have pride; we've got to play on that pride." The group plans to send a book of guidelines for combating the use of steroids and other performance enhancers to every secondary school, 37,000 in all, early this fall. But reaching secondary schools may not be enough: A Peoria, Ill., teacher was recently taken aback by a fourth grader who said he'd like to try the steroids his sixth-grade brother uses. Previous education efforts have at times backfired; in Oregon, students who learned about the dangers of steroids were more likely to use them than those who didn't. Testing all high-school football players alone would cost $100 million and be nearly useless, since most teens know how to beat the tests with the use of "masking" drugs available underground.

31   At the forefront of education efforts are Charles Yesalis, professor of health policy at Pennsylvania State University and the nation's premiere steroid expert, and Steve Courson, a former NFL star who used steroids. Both say that curbing steroid use requires nothing less than a revamping of American values. "We don't allow our kids to play games for fun anymore," says Yesalis. "We preach that God really does care who wins on Friday night, when we should be teaching our children to be satisfied to finish 27th, if that's their personal best."

32   Courson, in his recent book, "False Glory," tells of being introduced to steroids at age 18 by a college trainer, using steroids throughout his college and pro career and developing an accelerated heartbeat during his heaviest cycle. He is currently awaiting a heart transplant. "In the NFL, I was nothing more than a highly paid, highly manipulated gladiator. I was spiritually bankrupt," says Courson, now a Pennsylvania high-school football coach. "I want kids to know they can be greater than gladiators, that they can use a sport to learn lessons about life and not let the sport use them."

33   Ultimately, to reach children, educators will have to crack the secretive steroid subculture. So inviting is the underground world that, according to one study, 1 in 10 users takes steroids primarily out of desire to belong to the tightknit group. Those who opt out are quickly ostracized. Bill, a 17-year-old junior from New England, says he was a wallflower with only a couple of

friends before he got into steroids. Two and a half years and 16 cycles of steroid use made him part of the fellowship. But Bill vividly remembers one day last winter: It's the day his parents found a needle he forgot to discard. Since then, he hasn't seen much of his friends. "I had to switch gyms because they were all teasing me about shrinking up and pressuring me to use the stuff," he says. "I never see them now—we don't have anything to talk about anymore—but they're all betting I'll go back on it. Right now, the only way I know I'll stay off steroids is if I can find a guarantee that I'll reach 220 pounds without them. No, make that 230."

Evaluation of the Article

Difficulty rating □ 1 □ 2 □ 3 □ 4 □ 5
(1 = easy; 5 = difficult)

What reading difficulties did you encounter? _____

_____

How did you handle these difficulties?_____

_____

Postreading Comprehension Development

Rewriting Sentences

To check your understanding of some of the key concepts of this essay, rewrite each of the following sentences in your own words, keeping the original idea. (See Chapter 1)

1. Despite massive weight gains and sharply chiseled muscles, many steroid users are never quite happy with their physiques—a condition some researchers have labeled "reverse anorexia." (14)

_____

_____

2. Unfortunately, even that sort of documented health threat is unlikely to sway committed members of the steroid subculture. (17)

_____

_____

3. Meanwhile, the ambiance of gyms and health-food stores serves to cloak the use of performance-enhancing drugs in the veneer of a healthy lifestyle. (29) _____

_____

_____

Author's Main Idea

1. Another title that would convey the main idea of this selection is

   _____a. "Steroids: A Teen Addiction That We Must End."

   _____b. "Steroids: How They Affect Teen Growth."

   _____c. "Teens Speak Out on Why They Use Steroids."

   _____d. "Steroid Therapy."

2. In the space provided, state the author's main idea.
   The author wants me to understand that _____

   _____

   _____

3. What kind of information does the author give the reader to develop this main idea? _____

   _____

   _____

Inferences, Metaphors, and Vocabulary in Context

1. Which of the following does the author imply in paragraph 16? Be prepared to justify your answer.

    _____ a. Lyle Alzado got brain cancer from using steroids.

    _____ b. Douglas McKeag wants to prove a link between steroids and illnesses and death.

    _____ c. The federal government is extremely concerned about steroid use.

    _____ d. Too much research has already been done on steroid use, and it isn't helping keep teenagers from using the drugs.

2. Which of the following does the author imply in paragraph 21? Be prepared to justify your answer.

    _____ a. Parents do not want their teenagers taking steroids.

    _____ b. Teenagers know better than to listen to coaches who suggest they use steroids.

    _____ c. Adults can influence teens to use steroids.

    _____ d. Teenagers need parental permission to use steroids.

3. How do you think the author wants the reader to feel after reading this selection? Be prepared to state the reasons for your beliefs.

    _____ a. Angry with teenagers for using steroids

    _____ b. Critical of the medical community for not conducting more research

    _____ c. Satisfied with what is being done about the steroid problem

    _____ d. Very concerned about use of steroids among teenagers

4. For whom does the author seem to be writing?

    _____ a. Teens

    _____ b. Parents

_____c. The general public

_____d. High school educators

5. Using only the context, define each of the following words. Do not use a dictionary.

a. revered (10) _____

b. disparaged (10) _____

c. arduous (11) _____

d. stunting (12) _____

e. abhorrent (13) _____

f. deter (17) _____

g. patronized (20) _____

h. unscrupulous (21) _____

i. ambiance (29) _____

j. veneer (29) _____

6. What does the term *subculture* mean as it is used in this selection?

    _____

7. Bill, the 17-year-old junior from New England, was cited in this article (33) because _____

    _____

    _____

Recalling Details

1. Which groups are mentioned as encouraging teenagers to use steroids? Check all that apply.

    _____a. Parents

_____b.   Coaches

_____c.   Peer groups

_____d.   Doctors

_____e.   Gym trainers

_____f.   Science teachers

_____g.   Clothing designers

_____h.   Movie stars

_____i.   Sports stars

2.   Which of the following are factual statements in this article? Which are opinions? Use (F) or (O) for your response. For those you label opinions, write any support for the opinion that is given in this article.

_____a.   "The challenge of getting ahold of the stuff is half the fun," admits one 17-year-old from Iowa, who tells of meeting dealers in parking lots and taste-testing drugs that look like fakes.

_____b.   The Centers for Disease Control reports 80 percent hospitalizations from GHB use.

_____c.   The deeper the needle penetrates the muscle, the less juice squandered just under the skin.

_____d.   A vast black market across America guarantees kids ready access to steroids in big cities and small towns alike.

_____e.   Since all of the trappings of their world have to do with hard work, fitness and vitality, kids who use the substance see them as just another training aid, not much different from Gatorade or a big steak dinner.

_____f.   Ultimately, to reach children, educators will have to crack the secretive steroid subculture.

3. Indicate whether each of the following is true (T) or false (F), based on the selection. Be prepared to cite evidence for your answers.

    _____a. Children usually start to use steroids in their late teens.

    _____b. Steroid alternatives are safe.

    _____c. The teen group using steroids the most are from ethnic minority groups.

    _____d. Long-term studies have provided much information about steroid use.

    _____e. Teenagers are not convinced that steroids are harmful.

    _____f. Female teenagers are now using steroids as much as males.

    _____g. Educators have been trying to solve this problem for many years.

    _____h. The "Underground Steroid Handbook" cautioned teens about using steroids.

    _____i. There is a long history of athletes using performance enhancers.

4. The pattern of organization used in paragraph 9 is

    _____a. problem.

    _____b. effect.

    _____c. simple listing.

    _____d. thesis and proof.

5. The pattern of organization used in paragraph 12 is

    _____a. problem.

    _____b. effect.

    _____c. simple listing.

    _____d. thesis and proof.

6. Return to the structured overview you created at the beginning of this selection. Add to it any information you now know from reading the article.

Critical Thinking: Reaction and Discussion

1. Imagine that you are the parent of a teenager who uses steroids. Write a letter to your child, expressing your point of view about this.

2. Investigate this problem further. What is available in local health-food stores? Through mail order? Discuss this problem with sports coaches and students at your college. What conclusions can you draw about the prevalence and accessibility of performance enhancers in your community? Discuss your findings in an essay of approximately 250 words.

3. With a group, discuss the strategies that are mentioned in the article for solving this problem. How effective are they? What else can be done? Then, as a group, decide on three additional steps that could be taken and discuss why you believe these would be more effective. Share your suggestions with your class.

Using Technology for Further Understanding

Visit the Office of National Drug Control Policy's site and read its overview on steroids:

http://www.nida.nih.gov/ResearchReports/Steroids/anabolicsteroids3.html#health

After reading the overview, click on one of the research articles linked to the overview and read the material on steroids that you find at this linked site.

1. Following your reading, make a list of new information you have learned about steroid use and abuse that you think would be valuable to teenagers and parents.

2. Beneath your list, explain why you think this information is from a reliable source.

SELECTION 13

Preview

In this article, you learn about one author's exploration of the topic of sexual identity and some complex related issues.

To Think About Before You Read

Some words people use to describe themselves provoke strong reactions from others, both positive and negative. The following list contains adjectives that a person might use in a self-description. Using a scale that ranges from (1) "no reaction" to (4) "strong reaction," rate the response each word evokes in you. "Strong" is for either a positive or negative reaction.

DESCRIPTOR	RATING (CIRCLE ONE)			
hardworking	1	2	3	4
handsome	1	2	3	4
quiet	1	2	3	4
gay	1	2	3	4
Republican	1	2	3	4
depressed	1	2	3	4
intelligent	1	2	3	4
bisexual	1	2	3	4
creative	1	2	3	4
confident	1	2	3	4
hyperactive	1	2	3	4
wealthy	1	2	3	4

Terms to Know Before You Read

premise (6) basis for an argument

dichotomous (13) divided into two parts

provocative (19) exciting, stimulating

defies (22) challenges

The Sexual Blur

■ BY TED GIDEONSE

1 With straights falling for gays, lesbians dating men, and gay men in love with women, is anybody anything anymore? Just how important is *sexual* identity?

2 When Anne Heche sat down next to her girlfriend, Ellen DeGeneres, on *The Oprah Winfrey Show* and said, "I was not gay before I met her," many in Oprah Winfrey's audience—and Winfrey herself—were a bit bewildered. "That confuses me," Winfrey said. One woman in the audience asked Heche to explain what she meant, because "we're led to believe that people who are gay tend to know from birth, and you kind of disputed that." The only thing Heche could say in response was, "I didn't all of a sudden feel, I'm gay—I just all of a sudden felt, Oh, I love." That wasn't a good enough answer for Winfrey, who decided to do a second show on "how someone becomes gay." Five days later Winfrey pitted scientists, psychologists, and journalists against each other in a debate over the nature of same-sex desire. Despite the sometimes belligerent, occasionally loud discussion about genetics, cultural anxiety, and the differences between men's and women's sexuality, not much was concluded, and vastly more questions were raised than answered.

From *The Advocate*, 24 June 1997, 28.

3 The problem wasn't the idea that homosexuality is a biological, innate trait. That seems to be a well-accepted concept nowadays. Instead, what many people had a lot of trouble understanding and accepting is the sort of sexuality that Anne Heche represented to Winfrey's audience: fluid sexuality. This is changing sexuality, the sexuality that doesn't fit in a box, the sexuality that might reject labels, the sexuality that causes all sorts of political problems in a gay movement in which some spokespeople have for years been insisting, "We're born this way, we can't change, and—damn it!—if we could, don't you think we would have?"

4 The fact is that many people do change—or to be exact, they don't stay the same. "Gay," "lesbian," "bisexual," and "straight" are just labels, but the way people behave is a different issue entirely. "Whether you are homosexual, heterosexual, or bisexual is not really important," says psychologist Adria Schwartz, author of the forthcoming book *Sexual Subjects: Lesbians, Gender, and Psychoanalysis.* "It might be appropriate to the way an individual experiences their sexuality but not appropriate for the way human sexuality works."

5 No one really knows how it works, but people such as Alfred Kinsey, the famed

sexologist of the 1940s and '50s, tried to categorize it. While crude and simplistic, the Kinsey Scale is somewhat helpful in looking at the spectrum of human sexual behavior. On the scale a 0 represents exclusive heterosexuality, and a 6 exclusive homosexuality. The people who exhibit bisexual behavior fall somewhere between those two poles, making them, for example, 2s or 4s. There seems to be some agreement that among women such sexual variability is as common if not more common than strict homosexuality, but the numbers for men are in dispute. Some argue there are just as many men; others say that male bisexuality is extremely rare. Nevertheless, few disagree that human sexuality manifests itself in very different ways and that it can even change at various points in a person's life. Ron Fox, a psychotherapist and researcher in San Francisco, says, "Some people have the same orientation all their life with the same kind of sexual fantasies, and other people don't."

6   Once you have settled into an identity and built a life around it, anything that doesn't fit can be disconcerting and upsetting. This is true not only for heterosexuals who come to the realization at some point in their lives that they are attracted to people of the same sex but also for people who have long identified as homosexual and who develop or begin to notice attractions for the opposite sex. Schwartz says that many of her clients, most of whom are lesbians, report sexual dreams and fantasies about both men and women. "They come in worrying that they may really be straight," Schwartz says. "There's a false premise that if you are something, then that's all you are." That's easier said than practiced. What you call yourself has all sorts of meanings, both political and cultural, and once you call yourself something—"lesbian," for example—you're expected to act a certain way. Few places is this a more contentious issue than in some (but not all) lesbian communities when a member of that group enters a relationship with a man.

Filmmaker Elaine Holliman likens it to   7 being treated like Marilyn Munster, the Marilyn Monroe look-alike on the TV show *The Munsters* who looked nothing like her more beastly relatives. "They were so disappointed by her," Holliman says, laughing.

When Holliman was nominated for an   8 Oscar in 1994 for her documentary about same-sex marriage, *Chicks in White Satin,* she had been openly lesbian for years but had just started dating a man. "I wasn't prepared for being in the limelight with someone hairy on my arm," she says. Holliman, who is working on the documentary series *Gone Straight . . . to Hell!* which concerns this issue, said she had to hide her relationship while riding the success of *Chicks in White Satin.* "There were all these rumors going around that I was straight," she says.

While Holliman seems to be amused by   9 the reactions to her bisexual behavior, JoAnn Loulan isn't. When Loulan, a longtime lesbian activist and the author of *Lesbian Sex,* became involved with a man and decided to talk about it, she subsequently received a great deal of criticism from other lesbians. (On *Oprah* she jokingly called her relationship "deviant behavior.") She rejects the term bisexual because she fell for this particular man, not men in general. But that's hard to get across. "I understand they're upset and don't want me to have the privileges of being a lesbian and having heterosexual privileges at the same time," Loulan says. "But I'm proud of myself for telling the truth."

10 Not everyone who has crossed these borders is so open, and they're not all women. Filmmaker Gregg Araki—who, like Loulan, has a commercial identity closely connected to homosexuality—is now romantically linked to Kathleen Robertson (of *Beverly Hills, 90210* fame), who appears in his new film, *Nowhere*. Past films such as *The Living End* and *Totally F***ed Up* dealt with gay life and built Araki a strong gay audience.

11 Loulan, a therapist, says she has turned down speaking engagements and may have lost referrals because of her disclosure, but it remains to be seen how Araki's gay following will react. He doesn't talk about the relationship and through his producer turned down an interview with *The Advocate*. Says Holliman: "He turned Sundance [film festival] on its ear when he showed up with a girl on his arm."

12 The truth can be hard. Lesbians who have come out about being involved with a man have to deal with possible rejection from gays as well as questions about their cultural and political identity. "We all had that sinking-ship feeling when we came out

[the first time]," Holliman says. Maria Maggenti, the director of *The Incredibly True Adventure of Two Girls in Love,* echoed that sentiment in an interview with *The Advocate* in 1995: "It's pretty strange that 12 years [after I came out as a lesbian] I would fall in love with a man, be totally traumatized by it, and have to come out again."

13 When a JoAnn Loulan or a Maria Maggenti comes out about her opposite-sex love, the uneasiness among some lesbians isn't surprising. The bisexual behavior of a friend or a role model throws into question your own sexuality and identity. "The discomfort is very understandable in our culture, which is dominated by dichotomous thinking and polarization," says Beth Firestein, a psychologist and editor of *Bisexuality: The Psychology and Politics of an Invisible Minority.* "People get nervous about it because we're taught it can't happen," says Loraine Hutchins, a bisexual activist and coeditor of the anthology *Bi Any Other Name: Bisexual People Speak Out.* "We're taught that we have to choose sides, that we can't not choose sides."

14 Sociologist Paula Rust has found that up to 90% of women who identify themselves as lesbians have had sex with men and that nearly 65% say that they're at least somewhat attracted to men. "In terms of behavior and attraction then, many lesbians could be called bisexual," says Rust, who teaches at Hamilton College in Clinton, N.Y. "Yet they call themselves lesbians. . . . [They do this] not only because of attraction and behavior but also for political reasons."

15   Because many of these women think bisexuality doesn't exist, Rust says, they don't see it as an option in describing their identities. Rust looks to the origins of the gay movement for explanations. In the early days of gay liberation and feminism, the goal was to break down the distinctions between the genders as well as between gay and straight. However, during the 1970s as the movement solidified, it also "ethnicized," Rust says. It took on the political methods of the civil rights movement, which had been successful by exposing the ways people of different races were treated. In other words, homosexuality was treated as an ethnicity. "In order to use ethnic politics, they had to pretend as if there was a clear boundary between gay and straight," she says. While it was probably a good strategy, it didn't leave room for anyone who was neither gay nor straight. "When someone comes along and says, 'I'm bisexual,'" Rust says, "it makes the line between gay and straight ambiguous again and throws into question our ethnic form of political movement."

16   Deeply ingrained in this mode of political argument is the "Biology is destiny" mantra, the idea of having no choice. The political inclusion of bisexuals as well as transgendered people in the larger gay and lesbian movement complicates this explanation. It's not that bisexuality isn't also a result of some biological process but rather that it becomes difficult to say "We had no choice" when, to a certain extent, bisexuals do. Kate Bornstein, the performance artist and transgender activist, says that for many of the transgendered, transgressing the laws of gender is a moral and ethical decision, not a genetic predisposition.

17   Some feel that on its face the biology-and-genetics argument is useless, if not offensive. "I don't need to think I was born that way to accept my gay feelings. I'm just fine about those gay feelings," says Jonathan Ned Katz, author of *The Invention of Heterosexuality.* "A lot of people have adopted the idea that it's all right to be gay if you're born that way. If you say your experience is different, it upsets those people who have justified their feelings with that type of explanation, and it upsets straight people that the line between straight and gay isn't so clear."

18   Amy Agigian, who teaches "queer theory" at Brandeis University, agrees. "I've never found the 'I can't help it' argument very persuasive or very helpful in the politics of sexuality," she says. "As a feminist, for me it's about being able to follow your heart and being able to love who you love and desire who you desire." Agigian says there needs to be room for the people who don't necessarily have a fixed sexual orientation.

19   This is the central issue of one of the year's most provocative films, *Chasing Amy.* The Kevin Smith comedy is about a comic-book artist named Holden (played by Ben Affleck) who falls in love with another comic-book artist named Alyssa (Joey Lauren Adams). Alyssa is a lesbian, and to Holden's surprise she falls in love with him.

However, though Alyssa calls herself a lesbian and lets Holden think that it is just him—not men in general—she's attracted to, her past behavior turns out to have been actively bisexual, and the relationship falls apart. Holden can't handle Alyssa's "wild sexuality" nor the fact that she's had more experiences than he's had. While he likes thinking of himself as someone totally unique and special in her sexual life, once he realizes he is only part of something bigger, he falls apart. For Alyssa, on the other hand, it's about having the right to love whomever she falls in love with. Being able to choose empowers her.

20   "Why is everybody freaking out about it being a choice? It's a great choice," Loulan says. "I don't know why the genetics argument is going to help us. It didn't help blacks. I think it is a pathetic argument to say 'I can't help it.' I don't think it exists for everybody, and I don't think it matters."

21   Katz, along with Loulan, was a guest on the "origins of homosexuality" Oprah show. After they finished taping the show, Katz says that the discussion continued for about 40 minutes, during which "Oprah said that she had a revelation that, 'Oh, it's OK to be gay even if you're not born that way.'"

22   Clearly, these are confusing issues. Fluid and variable sexuality is something that cannot easily be pinned onto an identity, much like multiethnicity, which defies simple racial categories like black, white, or Asian. As identities become more ambiguous, identity politics will falter, Bornstein says, adding that "people pinned their hopes on identity and not on values, and now they are terrified as they feel their identities falling around their ankles." Identities are fragile and constructed, according to Bornstein. "There are no pure identities," she says. "In any system of identity politics, someone is going to be left out because their identity isn't 'pure enough.' Value politics, on the other hand, takes some thinking. It means everyone who is involved with a value-based politic needs to make the decision of 'Yes, I agree with that value.' It's not a matter of 'I'm a ____, so I automatically should follow the politics of that ____ identity.'"

23   So what is Heche's identity? Is she lesbian? Bisexual? Straight? From what we know of her through the media (Heche turned down an interview with *The Advocate*), that isn't the issue. Certainly a case could be made that since Heche's father was gay, her same-sex attraction has a genetic basis. However, because her father lived in the closet and died of AIDS complications, she says that she will live her life only truthfully and that it was these morals—or ethics or values—that led her to accept her love for DeGeneres and be so open about it. What's the problem then? As a movement are we concerned more about genes or about truth?

Evaluation of the Article

Difficulty rating ☐ 1 ☐ 2 ☐ 3 ☐ 4 ☐ 5
(1 = easy; 5 = difficult)

What reading difficulties did you encounter? _____

_____

How did you handle these difficulties?_____

_____

Postreading Comprehension Development

Rewriting Sentences

To check your understanding of some of the key concepts of this essay, rewrite each of the following sentences in your own words, keeping the original idea. (See Chapter 1)

1. Nevertheless, few disagree that human sexuality manifests itself in very different ways and that it can even change at various points in a person's life. (5)_____

    _____

    _____

2. Not everyone who has crossed these borders is so open, and they're not all women. (10)_____

    _____

    _____

3. Because many of these women think bisexuality doesn't exist, Rust says, they don't see it as an option in describing their identities. (15)

_____

_____

Author's Main Idea

1. What is the topic of this article? _____

_____

2. What is the author's focus on this topic? _____

_____

3. How appropriate is the title of this article? Give reasons for your opinion._____

_____

_____

4. Create another title for this selection that you think would help a reader predict its major focus. _____

_____

Inferences, Metaphors, and Vocabulary in Context

1. The last sentence in the opening paragraph asks a question. In which paragraph is it answered?

_____a. 4

_____b. 5

_____c. 6

_____d. 7

2. Check each statement with which you think the author would agree. Be prepared to justify your answers.

    _____a. Sexual orientation is not a good subject for television.

    _____b. Sexual orientation can change over a person's lifetime.

    _____c. Oprah Winfrey discusses controversial subjects on her show.

    _____d. People should love whomever they want.

    _____e. Bisexuals can easily explain their behavior to others.

    _____f. Society is not tolerant of differences.

    _____g. Men are more open about their bisexuality than women.

    _____h. A person's career can be affected by a disclosure of bisexuality.

3. Which of the following does the author imply in paragraph 5? Be prepared to justify your answer.

    _____a. Men are less honest about bisexuality than women.

    _____b. Sexual fantasies are the best indicator of sexual orientation.

    _____c. An individual's sexual orientation stays fixed for life.

    _____d. Researchers have known about bisexuality for a number of decades.

4. Which of the following does the author imply in paragraph 15? Be prepared to justify your answer.

    _____a. Using strategies from the civil rights movement helped gay rights activists.

    _____b. Homosexuality is usually limited to certain ethnic groups.

    _____c. The movements of the 1970s would not be successful if they occurred today.

    _____d. Gays and straights were not supportive of each other during the civil rights movement.

5. In your own words, explain what the term *identity* means as it is used in this selection. _____

_____

_____

6. How does Bornstein's comment, "There are no pure identities" (22), relate to the main idea of this selection? _____

_____

_____

7. We can infer from Winfrey's comment (21) that she

_____a. is narrow-minded.

_____b. finds it annoying when the audience participates in her interviews.

_____c. stays away from controversial topics.

_____d. learns things from the guests she has on her show.

8. The author's tone throughout most of this essay is

_____a. humorous.

_____b. informative.

_____c. cautionary.

_____d. scornful.

9. Using only the context, define each of the following words. Do not use a dictionary.

a. contentious (6) _____

b. subsequently (9) _____

c. polarization (13) _____

d. distinctions (15) _____

e. solidified (15) _____

f. ambiguous (15) _____

g. predisposition (16) _____

h. pathetic (20) _____

Recalling Details

1. Which of the following are factual statements in this article? Which are opinions? Use (F) or (O) for your response. For those you label opinion, write any support for the opinion that is given in this article.

_____ a. On the scale a 0 represents exclusive heterosexuality, and a 6 exclusive homosexuality.

_____ b. Once you have settled into an identity and built a life around it, anything that doesn't fit can be disconcerting.

_____ c. Few places is this a more contentious issue than in some (but not all) lesbian communities when a member of that group enters a relationship with a man.

_____ d. Past films such as *The Living End* and *Totally F***ed Up* dealt with gay life and built Araki a strong gay audience.

_____ e. Sociologist Paula Rust has found that up to 90% of women who identify themselves as lesbians have had sex with men and that nearly 65% say that they're at least somewhat attracted to men.

_____ f. Because many of these women think bisexuality doesn't exist, Rust says, they don't see it as an option in describing their identities.

_____ g. Alyssa is a lesbian, and to Holden's surprise she falls in love with him.

_____ h. I think it is a pathetic argument.

2. In which paragraph does the author state the central problem?

_____a. 1

_____b. 2

_____c. 3

_____d. 4

3. In which paragraph does the author state a cause of the problem?

_____a. 3

_____b. 4

_____c. 5

_____d. 6

4. Indicate whether each item below is a major (MAJ) or minor (MIN) detail of this article. Be prepared to justify your answers.

_____a. Marilyn Munster of the TV show *The Munsters* looked nothing like her more beastly relatives.

_____b. While Holliman seems to be amused by the reactions to her bisexual behavior, JoAnn Loulan isn't.

_____c. Not everyone who has crossed these borders is so open, and they're not all women.

_____d. Loulan, a therapist, has turned down speaking engagements and may have lost referrals because of her disclosure.

_____e. Maria Maggenti directed *The Incredibly True Adventure of Two Girls in Love.*

_____f. We're taught that we have to choose sides, that we can't not choose sides.

_____g. Some feel that on its face the biology-and-genetics argument is useless, if not offensive.

_____h. Holden can't handle Alyssa's "wild sexuality" nor the fact that she's had more experiences than he's had.

_____ i. Katz, along with Loulan, was a guest on the "origins of homosexuality" Oprah show.

5. Using information from this article, write your responses on how openness about bisexuality complicates each of the following.

   a. gay rights movement _____

   _____

   _____

   b. biological destiny argument_____

   _____

   _____

   c. concept of personal identity_____

   _____

   _____

6. What information in the article is confirmed by the graphs and charts that follow? Write your answers on the lines below.

   _____

   _____

   _____

   _____

   _____

   _____

   _____

Is it generally a good thing for our society or a bad thing for our society or doesn't it make much difference that more gay and lesbian couples are raising children?

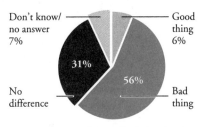

*Figures do not include replies indicating both causes, no cause or no opinion.

Do you personally believe homosexual behavior is morally wrong or is not morally wrong?

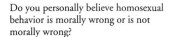

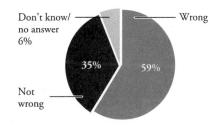

In your view, is homosexuality something a person is born with or is homosexuality due to other factors such as upbringing or environment?

In general, do you think homosexuals should or should not have equal rights in terms of job opportunities?

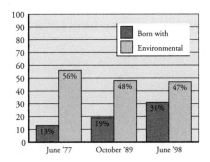

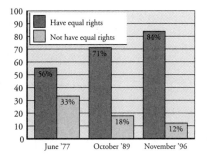

Polls on Gay Rights

Source: Adapted from the *New York Times*, 2 August 1998.

Critical Thinking: Reaction and Discussion

1. With your classmates, prepare a debate on the following statement:

   Sexual identity is the most important element of personal identity.

2. When Ellen DeGeneres first "came out of the closet" on her television show, considerable controversy arose among viewers about

whether weekly sit-coms and other programs should depict gay relationships. In an essay of at least 250 words, express your views on this subject.

3. Return to the section "To Think About Before You Read." Which descriptors provoked strong reactions in you? Using prior knowledge as well as information contained in this article, analyze your reasons for these reactions. Share your findings with a group.

Using Technology for Further Understanding

Use the Internet to see what you can find out about opinion polling.

1. What kinds of polls are taken online?
2. What are some of the other kinds of polls that are taken offline but then reported on the Internet?
3. Who might make use of the information that seems to be available from polls?

APPENDIX

*Readability Levels for Essays**

Social Science

Why We Need Miss America   9.5†

Wild in the Streets   8.5

Social Time: Heartbeat of a Culture   10.00

Business and Business Technology

Small Business: A Profile   11.0

Old MacDonald Has a Web Site   9.9

Health Sciences and Helping Professions

Central Themes of Social Work   11

X-Rays: Their Discovery and Development   13

Will More Guns Mean Less Crime?   11.7

The Arts

Latin Music Pops   8.5

Auditions   13

Contemporary Issues

Y Not Love?   9.4

Pumped Up   12.0

The Sexual Blur   11.0

---

* In addition to those readability factors taken into account by the formulas, others that affect difficulty were considered for determining text placement.

† Based on Fry Readablity and Flesch–Kincaid Formulas.

CREDITS

p. 4 and p. 5: Reprinted with permission from Jill Lewis, "The Effects of a Precollege Reading Course on the Academic Self-Esteem of Underprepared College Students," *Inquiries in Literacy Learning and Instruction,* College Reading Association Yearbook (Fall 1993): 43-55. **p. 30, p. 91, p. 101:** Leon Megginson et al., *Business.* Copyright © 1985 by D.C. Heath and Company. Reprinted by permission of Houghton Mifflin Company. **p. 45, p. 193, p. 254:** Excerpt from *Power and Society: An Introduction to the Social Sciences,* Sixth Edition by Thomas R. Dye, copyright © 1993 by Harcourt, Inc., reprinted by permission of the publisher. **p. 66:** Copyright © 2000 by Houghton Mifflin Company. Reproduced by permission from *The American Heritage Dictionary of the English Language,* Fourth Edition. **p. 77:** Paul D. Leedy, *A Key to Better Reading.* Copyright © 1968 by The McGraw-Hill Companies. Reprinted by permission of The McGraw-Hill Companies. **p. 105:** R. Black, "Taking the Fear Out of Choosing a Childcare Provider," *Newsweek,* September 28, 1998. Copyright © 1998 Newsweek, Inc. All rights reserved. Reprinted by permission. **p. 108, p. 195, p. 308:** Douglas A. Bernstein, *Psychology,* Fourth Edition. Copyright © 1997 by Houghton Mifflin Company. Reprinted with permission. **p. 108–109, p. 195:** Douglas A. Bernstein, *Psychology,* Fourth Edition. Copyright © 1997 by Houghton Mifflin Company. Reprinted with permission. **p. 126:** From *Newsweek,* November 29, 1999. Copyright © 1999 Newsweek, Inc. All rights reserved. Reprinted by permission. **p. 132:** Howe, "Were You Born That Way," *Life Magazine.* Copyright © Time Inc. Reprinted with permission. **p. 133:** "Batty About Flying Foxes."

From "Batty About Flying Foxes," *Smithsonian,* vol. 31, issue #2, May 2000, pg. 100. **p. 137:** Voss, "Sacred Qualities." Reprinted by permission of the author from Parabola, vol. 24, issue 3, Fall 1999, pg. 32. **p. 137 and p. 138:** From Lewis Andrews and Marvin Karlins, *Psychology: What's In It For Us?* 2/e, © 1975 Random House, pp. 115, 147. **p. 142 and p. 143:** *Next Time She'll Be Dead* by Ann Jones. Copyright © 1994 by Ann Jones. Reprinted by permission of Beacon Press, Boston. **p. 143 and p. 144:** From *The Facts on File Encyclopedia of Word and Phrase Origins,* Revised and Expanded Edition by Robert Hendrickson. Copyright © 1997 by Robert Hendrickson. Reprinted by permission of Facts on File, Inc. * **p. 145, p. 180, p. 181:** Mary Beth Norton et al., *A People and a Nation,* Brief Edition, Fourth Edition. Copyright © 1996 by Houghton Mifflin Company. Reprinted with permission. **p. 157, 162:** Reprinted with permission from Ed Ezor and Jill Lewis, *From Paragraph to Essay: A Process Approach for Beginning College Writing.* Copyright © 1984 The McGraw-Hill Companies. **p. 182, p. 183, p. 184:** From *Lasers: The New Technology of Light* by Charlene W. Billings. Copyright © 1992 by Charlene W. Billings. Reprinted by permission of Facts on File, Inc. **p. 186:** Joinson & Case, "Suburbs vs. Cities." From Carla Joinson and Laurie Case, "Suburbs vs. Cities," *HR Magazine,* 44(c) 1999. Reprinted with the permission of *HR Magazine,* published by the Society for Human Resource Management, Alexandria, Va. **p. 187, p. 292:** David Northrup, ed., *The Atlantic Slave Trade.* Copyright © 1994 D.C. Heath and Company. Reprinted by permission of Houghton Mifflin Company. **p. 193, p. 194:** Excerpt from *Why Glass Breaks,*

Rubber Bends, and Glue Sticks, copyright © 1977 by Malcolm E. Weiss, reprinted by permission of Harcourt, Inc. **p. 197:** "HIV: Where We Are Today, What Tomorrow May Bring," *Current Health 2,* 26, no.6 (February, 2000). Copyright © 2000 by Weekly Reader Corporation. All rights reserved. **p. 198:** Used with permission from *Family Guide to Natural Medicine,* copyright © 1993 by The Reader's Digest Association, Inc., Pleasantville, New York, 10570, www.readersdigest.com. **p. 236:** Brennan, "Roof Safety." Tom Brennan, "Roof Safety," from *Fire Engineering,* 153(4). Copyright © 2000. **p. 238:** Aalborg, "The View From the Big Road." From *Newsweek,* December 20, 1993. Copyright © 1993 Newsweek, Inc. All rights reserved. Reprinted by permission. **p. 248:** As appeared in the *Daily Southtown,* June 17, 2000. **p. 263 and p. 264:** Copyright © 1998, *The Washington Post.* Reprinted with permission. **p. 266 and p. 267:** Reprinted with permission. **p. 269:** Republished by permission of Dow Jones, Inc. via Copyright Clearance Center, Inc. © 1998 Dow Jones and Company, Inc. All rights reserved worldwide. **p. 271:** From *The Encyclopedic Dictionary of Sociology,* Fourth Edition, edited by Richard Lachmann, copyright © 1991 by The Dushkin Publishing Group, Inc. Reprinted by permission of McGraw-Hill/Dushkin, a division of The McGraw-Hill Companies, Guilford, CT 06437. **p. 272:** Reprinted with permission from *The World Almanac and Book of Facts 1993.* Copyright © 1992 Wold Almanac Education Group. All rights reserved. **p. 273:** From Philip G. Zimbardo and Ann L. Weber, *Psychology,* Second Edition. Copyright © 1997 Allyn & Bacon. Reprinted by permission. **p. 274:** from Sylvia Mader,

INDEX